Regulatory Insights on Artificial Intelligence

Regulatory Insights on Artificial Intelligence
Research for Policy

Edited by

Mark Findlay

Professorial Research Fellow and Director, Centre for Artificial Intelligence and Data Governance, Singapore Management University, Singapore

Jolyon Ford

Professor and Associate Dean, ANU College of Law, Australian National University, Australia

Josephine Seah

Doctoral Candidate, University of Cambridge, Affiliate, CAIDG, Singapore Management University, Singapore

Dilan Thampapillai

Associate Professor and Education Director, Centre for Social Impact, University of New South Wales, Australia

 Edward Elgar
PUBLISHING

Cheltenham, UK • Northampton, MA, USA

Cover artwork painted by Mark Findlay

Published by
Edward Elgar Publishing Limited
The Lypiatts
15 Lansdown Road
Cheltenham
Glos GL50 2JA
UK

Edward Elgar Publishing, Inc.
William Pratt House
9 Dewey Court
Northampton
Massachusetts 01060
USA

A catalogue record for this book
is available from the British Library

Library of Congress Control Number: 2022932890

This book is available electronically in the **Elgar**online
Law subject collection
http://dx.doi.org/10.4337/9781800880788

ISBN 978 1 80088 077 1 (cased)
ISBN 978 1 80088 078 8 (eBook)
Printed and bound by CPI Group (UK) Ltd, Croydon, CR0 4YY

Contents

List of contributors   vii

Preface   xi

1   Regulatory insights on artificial intelligence: research for policy   1
    Mark Findlay and Jolyon Ford

2   Editors' reflections   16
    Mark Findlay and Jolyon Ford

3   Artificial intelligence and sensitive inferences: new
    challenges for data protection laws   19
    Damian Clifford, Megan Richardson and Normann Witzleb

4   Revaluing labour? Secondary data imperialism in platform
    economies   46
    Mark Findlay and Josephine Seah

5   Gauging the acceptance of contact-tracing technology: an
    empirical study of Singapore residents' concerns and trust
    in information sharing   71
    Ong Ee Ing and Loo Wee Ling

6   Regulating personal data usage in COVID-19 control conditions   102
    Mark Findlay and Nydia Remolina

7   Editors' reflections   129
    Mark Findlay and Jolyon Ford

8   Coding legal norms: an exploratory essay   133
    Will Bateman

9   Artificial intelligence and the unconscionability principle   151
    Dilan Thampapillai

10 The possibilities of IF-THEN-WHEN   163
    Sally Wheeler

11   Doing it online: is mediation ready for the AI age?   188
      Nadja M Alexander

12   Editors' reflections   215
      Mark Findlay and Jolyon Ford

13   Ethical AI frameworks: the missing governance piece   219
      Jolyon Ford

14   The accountability of algorithms on social media platforms   240
      Philippa Ryan

15   Models and data trade regulation and the road to an agreement 262
      Henry Gao

Index   277

Contributors

Nadja M Alexander is a Professor of Law (Practice) at the Yong Pung How School of Law at the Singapore Management University and is the Director of the Singapore International Dispute Resolution Academy (SIDRA). She is also a Senior Fellow at the Dispute Resolution Institute in the Mitchell Hamline Law School and an Honorary Professor at the University of Queensland. In addition, she holds numerous appointments in several organisations, for instance serving as the Director and Board Member of the Singapore International Mediation Institute and the Vice Chair of the Mediation Committee of the International Bar Association. She is also a member of the Standards Commission of the International Mediation Institute in The Hague.

Will Bateman is an Associate Professor and the Associate Dean (Research) at the ANU College of Law at the Australian National University. His research entails the legal aspects of finance, technology and public administration. He heads several research projects, especially concerning the regulation of artificial intelligence, for instance in the formulation of model legal frameworks to govern artificial intelligence in the public sector or in designing ethical and lawful algorithmic decision systems. He also heads projects that deal with the legal regulation of public and private finance, with a special focus on central banking, sovereign debt markets, national budget formulation and sustainable investing. He received his PhD and LLM from the University of Cambridge.

Damian Clifford is a Senior Lecturer at the College of Law at the Australian National University. He is also an Associate Researcher at the Information Law and Policy Centre at the Institute of Advanced Legal Studies (University of London). His research interests include data protection and privacy, as well as EU law and consumer protection law. He was previously a Postdoctoral Research Fellow at the ANU College of Law and a Visiting Lecturer at the Dickson Poon School of Law at King's College London. He undertook his PhD at the KU Leuven Centre for IT & IP Law (CiTiP).

Mark Findlay is a Professorial Research Fellow at the Yong Pung How School of Law and the Director of the Centre for AI and Data Governance in the Singapore Management University. His research interests also include regulation and governance, international and comparative criminal justice, law's regulatory relevance in global crises, legal theory, public international law and cultural criminology. He also serves as an Honorary Professor at the Faculty of Law of the University of New South Wales and at the College of Law at the Australian National University. He holds fellowships at the Law School, University of Edinburgh and the British Institute for International and Comparative Law. Before joining SMU, he was previously at the University of Sydney as the Chair in Criminal Justice, the Director of the Institute of Criminology and the Head of School and Pro-Dean.

Jolyon Ford is a Professor and the Associate Dean (International) at the College of Law at the Australian National University. He has numerous research interests, including the regulation of corporate responsibility, emerging regulatory frameworks on business and human rights, public policy on promoting conflict-sensitive business practices, the regulation of responsible AI and governance of responsible innovation, human rights and the rule of law, as well as transnational tort actions (corporations and human rights). He was previously an Associate Fellow of the Royal Institute for International Affairs at Chatham House and a Research Associate of the Global Economic Governance programme at the University of Oxford's Blavatnik School of Government.

Henry Gao is Associate Professor of Law at the Yong Pung How School of Law at the Singapore Management University and Senior Fellow at the Centre for International Governance Innovation (CIGI). He sits on the Advisory Board of the WTO Chairs Programme of the WTO Secretariat, as well as the editorial boards of the *Journal of International Economic Law* and *Journal of Financial Regulation*. He also serves as an advisor in the Asia-Pacific Research and Training Network (ARTNeT) under the UN Economic and Social Commission for Asia and the Pacific (UNESCAP). He's currently working on issues relating to digital trade, TPP, and the Belt and Road Initiative.

Ong Ee Ing is a Senior Lecturer of Law at the Yong Pung How School of Law at the Singapore Management University. Her research centres around legal writing and legal pedagogy, as well as consumer rights and ethics (including the intersection of AI and ethics). Before joining SMU, she was a Senior Associate at Milbank Tweed Hadley & McCloy LLP, specialising in international finance and merger and acquisition transactions. Ee Ing attained a Juris Doctor (cum laude) degree from the George Mason University School of Law.

Loo Wee Ling is an Associate Professor of Law (Education) at the Yong Pung How School of Law at the Singapore Management University. Her research interests include contract and commercial law, credit and security law, consumer law, and data ethics. Before her current role, she was previously an Associate Professor of Law (Practice) at SMU. Prior to joining SMU, she was an Assistant Professor of Law at Nanyang Technological University. She received her LLM from the University of Sydney.

Nydia Remolina is an Assistant Professor of Law in the Yong Pung How School of Law at the Singapore Management University. Her research interests include the capital markets, banking law, financial regulation, Fintech, digital ethics, AI governance, and the intersection of law and technology. She is also a member of the Swiss FinTech Innovation Lab at the University of Zurich, where she is enrolled in a PhD. Before her current role, she was a Research Associate at the Centre for AI and Data Governance in SMU. Nydia has been an instructor of the Global Certificate Program jointly organized by Harvard Law School and the International Organization of Securities Commissions and has been invited to speak about Fintech at the International Monetary Fund, the Securities and Exchange Commission of the United States and the Monetary Authority of Singapore. Nydia received her JSM from Stanford University.

Megan Richardson is a Professor of Law at the Melbourne Law School at the University of Melbourne. She is also currently a Chief Investigator at the ADM+S Centre's University of Melbourne Node for the ARC Centre of Excellence for Automated Decision-Making and Society. Her research interests include intellectual property, privacy and personality rights, law reform and legal theory. She has previously served on numerous advisory panels and committees, including the New South Wales Law Reform Commission's invasion of privacy review and the Australian Law Reform Commission's reference on Serious Invasions of Privacy in the Digital Era.

Philippa Ryan is a barrister, an Associate Professor at the ANU College of Law, and the Director of the ANU LLM program at the Australian National University. Her research interests include trust and distrust in digital economies and autonomous systems, including smart contracts enabled by blockchain technology, as well as the accountability of algorithms. She has numerous appointments, including her position as a Non-Executive Director on the board of Lander & Rogers, and is the Chair of the Standards Australia Blockchain Technical Committee Smart Contracts Working Group; she is also on the Editorial Board of the *Stanford Journal of Blockchain Law & Policy*.

Josephine Seah was a Research Associate at the Centre for AI and Data Governance in the Yong Pung How School of Law at the Singapore Management University. She is currently researching her PhD at the University of Cambridge. Her research interests included ethical and responsible AI, sociotechnical systems, smart cities and critical data/algorithm studies. She contributed to several major projects during her time at CAIDG, including, the 'AI Ethics Hub' project that promotes dialogues around ethics and principled design in AI development and big data use.

Dilan Thampapillai is an Associate Professor and the Director of Education at the Centre for Social Impact at the University of New South Wales. His research interests include artificial intelligence, contracts, inequality, and intellectual property, and he has written several pieces on the relationship between AI and copyright law. Before joining UNSW, he was a Senior Lecturer at the Centre for Commercial Law in the ANU College of Law at the Australian National University and a Senior Lecturer at Deakin University prior to that. He received his PhD from the University of Melbourne.

Sally Wheeler is the Deputy Vice-Chancellor (International Strategy) and the Dean of the ANU College of Law at the Australian National University. Her research interests include socio-legal studies, corporate law, contract law, and law and technology. She is also a Visiting Full Professor at the UC Sutherland School of Law at the University College Dublin and an Adjunct Professor at the University of Waikato. She was previously a Professor and Pro Vice-Chancellor for Research and Enterprise at Queen's University Belfast. In 2017, she received an OBE for services to higher education in Northern Ireland and in 2018 became a Fellow of the Australian Academy of Law.

Normann Witzleb is an Associate Professor at the Faculty of Law at the Chinese University of Hong Kong. His research interests include privacy and data protection law, the law of torts and remedies, and comparative law. He was previously an Associate Professor at the Faculty of Law and the Convenor of the Privacy and Access to Information Group in the Castan Centre for Human Rights Law at Monash University, where he is also currently an Adjunct Associate Professor, conducting an LLM course on privacy and surveillance in the age of AI. He received his PhD from the European University Viadrina Frankfurt (Oder).

Preface

As with every research enterprise this collection has its own story. It commences long before the meeting between Australian National University and Singapore Management University when scholars sat around a table in Singapore and interrogated each other with exciting thinking about the regulation and governance of new technologies and big data. Some of the participants in that meeting had scholarly connections with each other which well pre-date that event, and extend into legal and social science fields before our interest in AI. Since that meeting the world has been riven by COVID-19 and many human, social, economic, political and existential foundations have cracked open and demand reconceptualising. The development of this collection – from its original intentions as a showcase of discrete research, into an exploration of 'doing research' and now as an interwoven consideration of many of the challenges that are driven by data in the modern world, and the governance of the human/AI interface – is a story of interdisciplinary reflection, in which the relevance of law is constantly in issue.

This collection is about law and change in times of global crises. If there is a meta theme binding the contributions, it is the need to come at the governance of AI and big data from any intellectual angle that provides a pathway for fresh thinking. The contributors are primarily legal academics from two distinctly different jurisdictions, working in remarkably different cities and university contexts. Their backgrounds and professional histories are assorted. Their approaches to research are varied and their comfort zones are widely divergent. Even so, a common concern prevails – that AI and big data should achieve social good, be regulated and governed not ignoring that motivation, and will benefit from as many legal influences as can be creatively activated in the regulatory sphere.

Returning to stories and storytelling, the contributions to the collection each have a message about the relationship between law and AI governance, and questions about law's regulatory relevance. These are stories to make law stronger as a regulatory agent and the place of AI in communities more orderly, respectful and sensitive of social need.

An example might clarify the importance of stories and storytelling in research. Currently the Centre for AI and Data Governance (CAIDG) is exploring the need and potentials available for regulating AI and mass data sharing in smart cities. As part of that research, we have been drawn back into a neighbourhood concept deeply embedded in the evolution of Singapore: the Kampong spirit. In its simplest and most applied rendition, Kampong spirit is the oral history dynamics of village life in the Straits territories. What has this to do with AI and smart cities? The answer is storytelling.

How can a practical research agenda emerge from such eclectic observations? Because CAIDG's essential research and policy precinct is regulation and governance, which have no dominant disciplinary location. There is nothing, except the tyranny of time, to stop its work from progressing into any sources connected with AI and data once there is a clear idea determined about what drives the need to read, research and reflect. The attraction of storytelling grew from a contemporary interest in neighbourhoods which, through COVID control restrictions, have become a more important locus of the social (actual and virtual). Recalling the Kampong spirit theme, this research uses neighbourhoods as a place to examine and understand the dynamic relationships inherent in AI in community, where the pathways for social bonding can be stories. This thinking moved out to smart cities and why 'smart' was a technological rather than a social determinant. Smart cities seem much more focused in a policy sense on material infrastructure rather than building and sustaining social networks. If AI can be used to help govern tech and data for public benefit, then the social good out of storytelling in this case is neighbourhood sustainability. AI-assisted information tech can provide pathways for stories to flourish through accessible methods of communication, curation and conservation.

Any and all of our contributors are storytellers. Their research charts stories along different intellectual connections. The collection overall is intended to offer the reader a range of stimulating, multi-disciplinary engagements with the regulation and governance of AI in vital social contexts that can suggest how law will lead to change, and how the regulatory enterprise changes law as it operates within information economies and tech-driven societies.

The editors would like to acknowledge the financial support of the ANU College of Law at the Australian National University, the funding of the preparatory meeting by the Yong Pung How School of Law, Singapore Management University, and the ongoing assistance of both institutions with the many resources required to bring a collection like this to completion. For their very constructive assistance in marshalling and managing the referencing and layout of the text, the editors wish to thank Dominic Nguyen and Aman Singh Kler. The contributors from Singapore Management University acknowledge that their research is supported by the National Research Foundation, Singapore under its Emerging Areas Research Projects (EARP) Funding Initiative. Any opinions, findings and conclusions or recommendations expressed in this material are those of the author(s) and do not reflect the views of National Research Foundation, Singapore.

1. Regulatory insights on artificial intelligence: research for policy

Mark Findlay and Jolyon Ford[1]

1. ISSUES AND CHALLENGES

The bundle of technologies referred to as artificial intelligence (AI), impacting on all aspects of human life, is an under-regulated phenomenon. Many communities are confused by its complexity and technicality, while simultaneously perceiving that AI is increasingly pervasive and represents risk to their social world. Such anxiety feeds off uncertainty as to whom AI will most benefit, and what will be lost or displaced or amplified as its applications reach out into fields of life, like wage labour, where citizens and communities are otherwise vulnerable. Corporate and government promoters of AI move their justifications for the technology from inevitability to blind faith, with ill-informed trust at its core. In the context of negative or ignorant community consciousness, the prevailing reassurance and legitimisation approach from state administrations, intergovernmental organisations and Big Tech firms – as agents for AI – has been to roll out a 'new' vocabulary of ethics and responsibility. This approach relies on broadly-framed ethics frameworks intended to moralise market dynamics top-down, to elicit socially responsible corporate behaviour among developers and users of AI platforms and tools. However, as historic 20th-century campaigns for corporate environmental responsibility have shown, the public is right to be concerned where industry-driven ethics strategies are advanced as the main or sole regulatory formula for risk and trust.

Prevailing ethical frameworks, codes and advisory boards are intended to engender trust across communities, yet all too often are failing to engage with the pressing perceptions and realities of AI anxiety. A cynical reaction to the push to transfer human values into machine technology is that it deflects

[1] This research is supported by the National Research Foundation, Singapore under its Emerging Areas Research Projects (EARP) Funding Initiative. Any opinions, findings and conclusions or recommendations expressed in this material are those of the author(s) and do not reflect the views of National Research Foundation, Singapore.

responsibility for risk or data appropriation from creators, commercialisers and regulators, by generating a smokescreen of broadly unobjectionable and agreeable but fundamentally fuzzy principles that travel no further down the value chain than the boardroom or the ministry.

Within AI and big data ecosystems there is a need for regulation to have relevance at all levels of innovation and eventual use. The current concentration on ethical attribution at the management sector is important but cannot substitute for distribution of principled design responsibilities across all important decision sites in the data-use chain. A contextual challenge for the regulator is working in two AI 'worlds': the science/commerce domain, and the social/communal realm. Bridging these different contexts are economic and political motivations meeting in the material well-being of sustainable markets. From within the scientific/commercial world, profitability is an important consideration, just as risk aversion or minimisation are for the social/communal world. In the context of slowing and shifting global economic growth patterns, and a relentless devaluing of labour, AI is being expected to remedy financial ills while at the same time not exacerbating employment insecurity. For economies where the demographic is aging and the workforce is partly foreign, AI is sometimes held out as panacea for eventual social dysfunction. Climate change, global economic inequality and resultant mass social unrest are creating atmospheres of anxiety in which AI technologies – as complex yet ubiquitous, influential yet amorphous – may be viewed among some in society as an ever-present and expanding contributor.

The prevailing ethics-based preference for self-regulation does not necessarily envisage a principal role for law as a regulatory vector. This is so even while that ethical discourse is couched in terms that imply and indeed heavily implicate law and legal regulatory techniques and institutions. 'Transparency', 'accountability', 'explainability', 'non-discrimination', 'remedy' and, above all else, 'fairness', resonate with the fundamental normative principles expected from the Rule of Law. At the same time, the governance challenge in relation to AI is one that cannot be reduced merely to a set of legal compliance factors in the relatively narrow sense that law is sometimes conceived. Instead, AI simultaneously requires a broad strategic view of *how we wish to live together* (and what role technology plays and does not play in that big scheme) and a swathe of practical, particular interventions intended to meet societal goals such as to mitigate social harm and maximise social benefit.

Traditional regulatory policy, particularly in its law-based dimensions, is designed to influence human decision-making and resultant behaviours. It commonly depends on leveraging shared values and common experiences. Regulatory research and policy is inevitably primarily human-centric even where it concentrates on institutional and market frames, frameworks and models. Therefore, translating conventional regulatory technology across to an

AI/big data universe is a fraught and perhaps fruitless endeavour. In the same way, some wholesale transplantation of human virtues resonating with legal normative principles into a machine-driven consciousness may do little more than offer a gloss over much deeper regulatory challenges. Despite all this, the prevailing 'turn to ethics' and corresponding aversion to state-sponsored legal regulation in terms of rights and responsibilities require critical examination, particularly when human dignity (especially through automated decision-making and the errant use of personal data) is at stake. Recent attempts to open up the data practices of the financial sector, and to govern productive and responsible data sharing may present important opportunities for regulatory graduation to law enforcement, where 'compliance' based around goodwill and self-regulation prove insufficient. A blunt 'rights-based approach' is not necessarily the option in trying to ground ethical values in legal frameworks. It is not obvious what effects such an approach – even if one could envisage it gaining traction – might have on legitimate concerns such as market access for innovation.

2. LAW'S REGULATORY REVERSION

We live in an age where law's regulatory relevance is constantly questioned.[2] Big data has shifted and strained conventional models of personal data protection and privacy rights. Platform economies are disrupting established employment relationships. Visual recognition intrudes into many aspects of our personal lives and surreptitiously commodifies human dignity through marketing secondary data. Whether these developments are best interpreted as the undeniable consequences of a surveillance culture, or are to be confronted as questionable qualifications of civil rights, their surreptitious operational realities make legal regulatory interventions both problematic and largely post-fact to the existing pre-intervention embeddedness of the technologies. An example is consent requirements intended to empower the data originator by providing an 'opt-out' alternative when secondary use is intended. Many major social media providers offer the consent option but link any withdrawal to a denial of services. In any conventional context, it is hard to see how anyone might argue that this comprises 'consent' in any recognisable legal sense. This realisation concerning the compromised reality of the consent 'barrier' is a perfect topic for critical legal regulatory research and commentary. Additionally, privacy codes broadcast by the big platforms are written in a language and format that encourage most users to scroll to the bottom and tick without reading. There is

[2]   M Findlay, *Law's Regulatory Relevance? Property, Power and Market Economies* (Edward Elgar, 2017).

also the complicity of data creators in social media realms who are so cavalier with the information they share and the audiences that they engage with, that strict interpretations of data protection and privacy become incompatible with convenient streaming. Another important regulatory question is the place of law in digital societies where privacy and surveillance are so contested.

Law as a tool for positive social engineering in digital contexts must better meet the stimulus and adoption of AI, rather than playing clumsy catch-up after the risks and violations produce harm and damage. For instance, if the state sees AI as an answer to the negative futures of unsustainable socio-demographics, or rigid and unresponsive labour markets, then under-regulated AI reliance could make any of the following risks into realities:

- widespread employment displacement in sectors where up-skilling, labour mobility and re-deployment are problematic;
- physical safety and professional indemnity, even if the dangers are more perceived than empirical;
- urban and community reconfiguration with limited human engagement;
- military robotics and their incompatibility with the conventions of armed conflict; and
- automated service delivery and the depersonalisation of welfare and consumer protection.

The facts of law's regulatory engagement with AI and big data reveal reversion to protection models designed in the days before these new technologies and the associated data explosion. Otherwise, law offers the guarantee of fragile market relationships (such as employer/employee) which the new platform operators deride as inapplicable to their customer/service-provider connection model.

The definition of 'regulation' for our purposes is a very broad one, and not confined to a legal lens. It draws on Black's description of intentional behavioural change which can be measured and which is undertaken by reference to some known standards and/or is accountable to a given external social purpose.[3] In such a sense, regulation as conceived here is not necessarily confined as a province of the state. Private sector and community stakeholders are included as potential participants (albeit empowered and informed in varying ways) in the regulatory frame. The idea of evaluating accountability suggests the inextricable relationship between regulation and research as we view them. The essential place of research in measuring regulatory relevance rests in Black's definitional essential that if regulation is about behavioural change

---

[3]   J Black, 'Critical Reflections on Regulation' (2002) 27 *Australian Journal of Legal Philosophy* 1.

then the evaluation of this dynamic can only satisfactorily be evidenced-based, requiring critical research.

3.   REGULATORY CHASM

There are those that say the regulatory terrain in which AI is developing is robust and expansive. Such assertions are usually supported by maps or charts of pluralistic global regulatory activity, in the form of sporadic and disconnected legislation and rules regarding data protection and privacy rights, along with the promulgation of ethics charters and codes of conduct. However, simply to identify the spread of national, transnational or corporate AI policies or frameworks says little or nothing about the effectiveness of regulatory coverage. There is precious little associated research testing the mapping method for establishing regulation and development synergies, and not much that interrogates the slippage and void between AI roll-out and regulatory recognition. Even the narrow question of uptake (cf. promulgation) of voluntaristic corporate-internal or national normative frameworks appears under-researched. It is partly in this context that this collection attempts to meet a need for more people-centred qualitative and other research on what is being traded-off in a policy and regulatory approach premised on productivity and efficiency.[4]

If anything, AI technologies are fast subsuming fundamental activities that could be said to make up a good proportion of those activities that shape and affect the human condition. These activities would, in any other scientific and technological context, be rigorously protected at the design and development stages by strong standard-setting ring-fences. The prevalence and diversity of AI technologies appear to lend an air of inevitability and ubiquity that itself militates against conceiving of any regulatory approach to these creations and processes. Visual perception, speech recognition, language translation, threat analysis, probability evaluation and professional analytics now present themselves in automated, computer-assisted variations. Besides their invasive and pervasive functional understandings, different styles of AI offer subsets like machine learning, big data applications, and natural language processing that are extensively applied to a variety of crucial human welfare situations with little regard for regulating to deal with even the most obvious risk reverberations. We know of the bias inevitabilities in using algorithms to make

---

[4]   YK Dwivedi et al, 'Artificial Intelligence (AI): Multidisciplinary Perspectives on Emerging Challenges, Opportunities, and Agenda for Research, Practice and Policy' (2021) 57 *International Journal of Information Management* 19 ('Artificial Intelligence').

employment decisions, or to investigate crime. Yet AI applications are hardly suspended until the bias factor is addressed and neutralised. Why is this so? What is the regulatory posture of policymakers? The co-existence of identified problems with the roll-out of further applications contributes to the sense of an inevitable and irresistible phenomenon. This inevitability and corresponding passivity is contrary to all our post-modern insights into the constructed nature of things (and the consequent entry points for deliberate regulatory interventions).

Progressing from more contained forms of cognitive mirroring, the future of AI suggests further radical decision-making possibilities, while any attendant regulatory debate is absent. Whatever might be the present and the future of this information revolution, the demand for innovative regulation matching and even preceding technological advance is both necessary and pressing. However, some basic issues arise for consideration and determination before an appropriate regulatory posture and direction can be set, or appropriate models and techniques advanced. As noted, these basic questions are fundamental ones about ways of living with technology (technology-enhanced living), about who or what AI is meant to benefit: is it to unlock declining economic growth bringing wealth to some, or is the priority to explore how technology can improve the lives of many, reducing inequality, maximising inclusivity, and delivering justice?

Policymaking and regulatory design in this domain face twin but potentially conflicting impulses. On the one hand, there is the push to 'get on with it' and design effective schemes to address the governance gap around new technologies. On the other hand, there is the intuition that it makes little sense to descend to such detail without, including on a societal level, a much clearer overarching and ideally shared sense of *how to live* or more precisely *how technology can aid in achieving the 'good life'*. Such questions are prerequisite to setline on broad design choices for governance. Such broad perspectives necessarily inform particular policy and regulatory design choices, parameters and calibrations. Meanwhile, research and policy debate around the proper governance of AI technologies are conducted in the particular context of a digital/data economy disproportionately dominated by a handful of very large Big Tech firms. Such actors are hardly passive in debate about how responsibly to govern AI. How and with what effects these actors shape the very narrative of possible regulatory options, postures and products are surely among the most important questions for researching AI governance.

Another troubling, if under-considered, policy priority is the issue of constituency: who is policy to benefit? General claims for 'social good' do not recognise the complexity of this question. Take, as an example, the advance of 'smart cities'. Such urban enhancement policies rely on sharing massive data-sets, in which the citizen is viewed as a data object, an entity to be managed, manoeuvred and controlled for universal efficiencies, something to be surveilled at best for paternal communal benefits. If human flourishing and dignity was at the heart of smart city urbanisation, then regulatory policy governing urban design would find a meaning and message for regulation different in nature, intent and outcome than technologising city space for efficiency or cost motivations.

There remains a view that time is on our side for settling who should regulate the advance of AI, for whom, and how. Yet even a brief reflection on the extent to which algorithms and predictive or pattern logics (based on data-sets) *already* manage our lives ought to give pause for thought. From that perspective, are we satisfied to be told no more than that algorithms should (by reference to an ethics-based framework) be explainable, accountable and responsibly applied? How can we reconcile the trade secrets hidden in algorithms with an assurance that they will be transparently used? Are we not more concerned to know the accountable outcomes of a decision made or assisted by algorithm technology, than be trained in the maths behind their operation? Equally, how can we be satisfied with the regulatory relevance of a singular virtue ethics approach demanding explainability in a technological reality where only the knowledgeable few have keys to the algorithmic 'black-box'?

The regulatory challenge to produce responsible AI should not be underestimated. In a world of AI, facilitated by the internet of things, secured by blockchains, and powered by 5G, regulators familiar with simpler debates about privacy and data protection will be required to move from their comfort zones. As Palka reminds us:

> ...there is always a political decision to be taken. Regardless of whether it occurs explicitly through legislation; or implicitly by leaving the decisions to the market and allowing corporations to write their own rules, some decision occurs. We know what the rules written by corporations are. Hence it is up to us to decide. Will the substance of data management law result from our political action, or our failure to act?[5]

---

[5]   P Palka, 'Data Management Law for the 2020s: The Lost Origins and the New Needs' (2020) 68(2) *Buffalo Law Review* 559, 640.

4.   CALL TO ARMS – RESEARCH-DRIVEN REGULATION

Any inclusive regulatory *call to arms* comes on the back of Palka's case for three normative shifts in addressing data management, involving repositioning past approaches:

- First, there is a shift from privacy rights contestation towards considering the social costs of data management conceptualised as mitigating the negative effects of corporate data usage.
- Next is the need to go beyond individual interests, to account for collective concerns, and to replace a legal-instrumental reliance on contracts with pre-emptive regulation as a means of creating norms governing data management.
- Finally is the recognition that decisions about the application and prioritisation of these norms are deeply political and as such, political means need to be employed in place of technological solutions, and at the very least acknowledged.[6]

Essential to achieving these transformations is a research agenda that recognises the need for new thinking, and embraces inter-disciplinary methodologies capable of future-gazing. As AI has become integral to the business model of many firms and a key element of many government activities, research seeking a more holistic understanding of the range of impacts and implications of these technologies has grown (relative to the earlier AI research focusing on the performance implications of AI).[7] Research calculated to help policymakers develop adequate policies, regulations, guidance and a legal framework is now at a premium.[8] Law and regulation scholars may need to 'adapt the research toolkit' in search of more relevant questions or enlightening answers.[9]

Echoing Palka's contextual realisation, this book manifests a collaborative project intended to open up new regulatory pathways with realist understandings of their social importance and future relevance. The teams of legal scholars came together across two key Asia-Pacific jurisdictions in search of research synergies that would tackle some crucial concerns about the place of

---

[6]   Ibid.

[7]   Dwivedi et al, 'Artificial Intelligence' (n 4) 7.

[8]   Y Duan, J Edwards and YK Dwivedi, 'Artificial Intelligence for Decision-making in the Era of Big Data: Evolution, Challenges and Research Agenda' (2019) 48 *International Journal of Information Management* 63.

[9]   Dwivedi et al, 'Artificial Intelligence' (n 4) 21, promoting the multidisciplinary Culture-Based Development 'toolkit' combining moral philosophy, consumer behaviour, behavioural economics and area/political economy studies.

AI beyond market profit or economic advantage, important as these issues may be. In this endeavour we conceded that regulatory scholarship and policymaking were lagging behind technological enhancement, and that the language of AI was at risk of only being understood by a technocratic audience.

Initially, a motivation for our research conversation was to explore different contextual situations in which AI and big data applications present regulatory challenges. As the project developed, this contextual interest was recognised not as jurisdictional, politico-social, cultural or even market located, no matter how important each of these may be for the contributions to follow. Rather, context became a research concern in terms of particular regulatory challenges within specific institutional and process frames.

One of the earliest priorities for the teams was to rehabilitate AI understandings within more pluralist social locations. What about human rights, for example, and their place as a regulatory discourse, framework or platform when measuring responsible applications of AI? How do we address the exacerbation of human discriminatory bias once machines are introduced into the mix? Can automated decision-making provide a facility for greater access to justice in mundane dispute resolution? Are smart contracts smart enough to think beyond the functional certainty of terms and countenance when decisions not to enforce, or to interpret meaning beyond the literal, make sense as just outcomes above strict adherence to legal obligations? The answer to any and all of these fundamental questions will never be satisfactorily agreed between the technician and the lawyer until the lawyer better informs the technician of the conceptual richness of legal discretions, and the technician makes clear to the lawyer the constraints required in binary thinking. Research-for-policy in relation to AI governance involves an inherently cross-disciplinary perspective, if only to inform different expert communities of relevant boundaries. For technical experts, the normative and value constraints and logics and the space for discretion (for instance); for regulatory designers, knowing not only what AI is capable of, but also importantly what AI is not (or not yet) capable of.

5. REGULATORY ENHANCEMENT

To reiterate, AI (and big data) currently and potentially offer advantages world-wide, particularly when seen in the context of economic growth. At the same time, negative consequences (both real and perceived) are creating an atmosphere of anxiety around AI innovation, especially where it is seen as substituting for human occupation, welfare and contextual awareness.

Against this background, policymakers and regulators have a mission to:

• humanely promote the economic and market benefits of AI and big data;

- prevent, control or mitigate negative consequences of AI innovation and big data informatics;
- realistically identify and analyse risks posed by AI, as well as by a reluctance to employ AI or AI-assisted solutions;
- listen to community and industry concerns (conscious of the very different scales and influence of actors classified together as 'private sector' or 'industry') and understand the generation of anxiety around AI;
- communicate AI benefits, and the dynamics of regulatory strategies to minimise negative outcomes;
- encourage the adoption of responsible and ethical commitments from the AI development stage, through all the phases of its application; and
- evaluate the transparency, accountability and explainability of AI applications, not so much in terms of the technology itself, but rather its use in assisted-decision outcomes.

In keeping with a realist approach to the regulator's task, the developments and strategies researched in this collection focus on the process and outcomes of AI-assisted decision-making, rather than requiring algorithmic exposure and the knowledge ownership issues that would arise. In addition, when approaching ethics and responsibility, as our authors see it, the regulatory exercise should not be about providing market boundaries or minimum compliance standards, nor will it or should it focus alone on damage control. Adopting the regulatory rationale that AI applications must primarily achieve social good, values-infusion becomes as much integral to AI innovation and application as is algorithm design. We do not conceive of ethics as some regulatory overlay, or a seal of approval for algorithm design. Ethics and responsibility represent a grass-roots language and measure of social good in AI application. However, the contributions are premised on what is required to properly govern or regulate ethical and responsible behaviours, seen through the disciplinary lens of law.

A further theme on ethics which recurs throughout the collection is its contextual specificity. While universal principles governing such powerful and pervasive technologies are inescapable, the manner in which the human machine interface is to be viewed will depend on cultural attitudes to technologies as a whole, as well as to key concepts such as trust, duty, obligation, authority, responsibility, deference, remediation and communal location.

This collection breaks new ground by expressly situating the analysis of selected legal and regulatory dimensions of AI in the context of explicit critical reflections on the nature of the research challenge (and its public policy impact). Interrogating regulatory and policy insights in this fast-changing, complex and diverse field demands a self-conscious critique of policy research against the market and social expectations of the AI and big data revolution.

There is little existing literature on the nature of the research challenge in particular from a legal perspective, beyond general calls for the creation by governments of enabling conditions for research and researchers to flourish.[10] Yet technological research into AI systems must be accompanied by inputs from the humanities, law and social sciences if expectations of responsible and trustworthy AI products and systems are to be realised. In this collection, the reader will be assisted by important research outcomes focused on the regulation of AI at the interface with human agency. The authors reveal the particular research encounters and challenges behind these outcomes so as to guide those who wish to venture along similar or analogous analytical paths.

As the variety of contextual situations in which AI and big data are presenting regulatory challenges identify, regulation is not confined as a province of the state. Private sector and community stakeholders are informed subjects and participants in the regulatory frame. The necessity for evaluating behavioural change through the accountability of any regulatory object, mentioned earlier in our discussion of the regulation/research synergy, cannot in our view be quarantined either in the public or the private sectors, when these are so enmeshed in the AI and big data use project.

The research endeavour, when it is turned in no small part to demystifying the relationship between technological advances and community confidence, needs to talk to a wider audience than scholars with mutual interests. The topics chosen and the language employed in this collection are imbued with a commitment to identify contemporary regulatory challenges, thrown up by aspects of AI and big data in crisis, and discuss their ramifications for a readership concerned about their futures with AI. This thinking requires constant reflection about how we ensure transparency and public availability of insights on AI law and regulation. How do universities and other trusted knowledge centres enable integration and conversations across scientific/technical (on the one hand) and humanities/cognitive studies/law and governance fields (on the other)?[11] In addition:

- How do universities preserve a degree of openness towards AI resources, knowledge and collaboration (with commercial and state institutions) in the face of pressure to close off this space amid commercial and geo-political competition?[12]

---

[10] See for example Future of Life Institute, *AI Policy Challenges and Recommendations* <https://futureoflife.org/ai-policy-challenges-and-recommendations/>.

[11] M Jordan, 'Artificial Intelligence – The Revolution Hasn't Happened Yet', *Artificial Intelligence* (Blog Post, 18 April 2018) <https://perma.cc/4JM9-E4HC>.

[12] U Gasser, 'The Ethics and Governance of AI: On the Role of Universities', *Berkman Klein Center* (Blog Post, 22 January 2017) <https://medium.com/

- What role do university researchers play in bringing better understandings of AI to the public, including by translating AI issues for non-technical audiences, and how do researchers interested in this area navigate the issues without a strong technical background?[13]
- How do law, regulation and policy scholars navigate the multi-disciplinary nature of this field,[14] the increasing volume of scholarship,[15] and the lack of common understanding in different fields of some of the most basic terminologies (understood differently by researchers, industry professionals, educators and journalists),[16] even before they can address the wider social engagement (research translation) challenge?
- How do we bridge academic thinking and corporate or policymaker 'practitioner' thinking on issues such as AI ethics?[17] Who are academic researchers consulting with – or not – in developing their research on governance frameworks?[18]

Offering a general editorial-style introduction about the project and its aspirations, this framing chapter has explored the research challenge that underpins the exercise of making regulatory insights on AI. In keeping with a fresh eye slant to the regulatory task, one intention here has been to showcase research challenges, processes and outcomes when dealing with contemporary issues in regulating the AI/human intersection with an eye to informing and influencing policymaking and regulatory design. Consequently, the chapters are more than analysis and findings, although there is enough of such to give them value on this measure. The editors have also sought to classify the material into important regulatory realms. Through their commentaries on chapters 'bundled' by

---

berkman-klein-center/the-ethics-and-governance-of-ai-on-the-role-of-universities -6c31393fe602>.

[13] Ibid.

[14] See generally Dwivedi et al, 'Artificial Intelligence' (n 4).

[15] 'Artificial Intelligence: How knowledge is created, transferred, and used' (Report) <https://www.elsevier.com/__data/assets/pdf_file/0011/906779/ACAD-RL -AS-RE-ai-report-WEB.pdf>; see also on getting 'up to speed' on this area for researchers new to it, A Dafoe, 'AI Governance: A Research Agenda', *Future of Humanity Institute, University of Oxford* (Report, 27 August 2018) <https://www.fhi .ox.ac.uk/wp-content/uploads/GovAIAgenda.pdf>.

[16] ORBIT, '"An air of urgency" – why we need ethical governance of AI', *Elsevier Connect* (Blog Post, 15 January 2019) <https://www.elsevier.com/connect/an-air-of -urgency-why-we-need-ethical-governance-of-ai>.

[17] J Metcalf, E Moss and D Boyd, 'Owning Ethics: Corporate Logics, Silicon Valley, and the Institutionalization of Ethics' (2019) 86(2) *Social Research: An International Quarterly* 449.

[18] A Daly et al, 'Artificial Intelligence Governance and Ethics: Global Perspectives' (Report, 28 June 2019) <https://arxiv.org/pdf/1907.03848.pdf>.

topic or theme, the editors have sought some standardisation of reflection on the challenges faced in this sort of research for those who might follow any similar research direction.

6.   THE RESEARCH OBJECT

Rather than anywhere attempting to exhaustingly define AI and big data, the analytical approach exhibited in the collection is to interrogate real-life applications. The idea of locating AI and big data within specific situations recognises that both AI and big data are concepts very much 'in the eye of the beholder', and as such are constantly dynamic and changing. Indeed, in their application, AI (through deep learning) and big data (through the cross-fertilisation of data sets) are themselves grown and transformed via the application process. In this metamorphosis sits one of the major challenges for regulation: to be sufficiently elastic to be relevant in a transformational environment while not losing clear and apparent regulatory intentions.

Adopting an 'application' research mode is useful to policy framers in that they are concerned daily with the way features of the market and the social interact for good or ill. There is little point in regulating a static 'thing' when behavioural change is intended. As such, the need is to regulate arrangements, relationships, processes and interfaces.

The other methodological preference in the collection is to focus the discussion of regulation on specific regulatory challenges presented by AI and big data, and their introduction and sustainability in specified (and hardly exhaustive) contextual settings. These challenges will be understood either as crises for the present or possible crises if left uncontrolled. Crises may be real or perceived but nonetheless anxiety forming for communities coming to terms with a society partially or increasingly governed by or through AI applications. Through unpacking examples of AI applications, the policymaker or regulator can better see where regulation is necessary, and if it is absent, too limited or not interconnected across stakeholders, can see more particular ways in which negative externalities can be addressed by interventions calculated to elicit more positive societal outcomes.

However, taking an 'application' approach to policy invitation and formulation might fail the equally important test of practical universal relevance. Questions about the application of what, how, when, why, and 'so what' outcomes need to be addressed by some further specification. Recognising this tension between context and commonality, many of the chapters review the AI/big data question in terms of decision-making theory. Some of the most profound perceived anxieties about AI relate to the idea of taking people out of the decision loop, or deeming non-human decisions to have the authority of the human officials who deploy them. With that understanding, our authors target the need to regulate those occasions where, and manner in which, automation, technology, algorithmic determination and informatics data reliance sit within crucial decision sites, and how the human/machine interface in decision-making can promote rather than retard justice and the social good.

An example may be useful at this point. If automated data management is to reduce the opportunity for trainee lawyers to gain experience in the requirements of mundane document discovery, then the consequence for the eco-system of the law firm might be short-term profit positive but medium-term skills advancement negative. Law firm partners might be seduced by cost savings and the illusion that their own time will be freed up for more interesting work. With the regulatory intervention of law schools, law societies, legal practice licensers and client and worker representatives, a more holistic and sustainable balance might be achieved for the augmentation of data-driven analytics in legal services information analysis.

Continuing the theme of critical, realist relevance, there is an actual and present danger of the AI ethical discourse becoming universally spoken but rarely activated in an operational agenda. We can all talk about 'accountability', but to whom? Through what particular mechanisms that tie this oft-repeated value or principle into particular systems and processes? What if, initially, transparency brings about more anxiety than it solves? Too often now, AI proponents go to ethicists to draft minimum compliance standards, or certification for algorithms, or worse still, to offer damage limitation. More than ethical articulation or adoption, in a best-practice mode many of our contributors 'test-drive' AI ethics applications in specific operational, market settings which determine the potency and limits of ethics as a regulatory language or set of logics.

At the forefront of our interest in the research object, AI and big data, is the understanding that research which is insufficiently rigorous, critical and socially engaged will lead to bad policy outcomes and may further muddy already murky waters. The obligation rests with the editors to work for crystal clarity in such a fast-moving evolutionary space that sees the mystification of technology and the irresponsibility of financial gain as not only bi-products of AI but even necessary features and imperatives for its meteoric advance.

BIBLIOGRAPHY

Black, J, 'Critical Reflections on Regulation' (2002) 27 *Australian Journal of Legal Philosophy* 1

Duan, Y, J Edwards and YK Dwivedi, 'Artificial Intelligence for Decision-making in the Era of Big Data: Evolution, Challenges and Research Agenda' (2019) 48 *International Journal of Information Management* 63

Dwivedi, YK et al, 'Artificial Intelligence (AI): Multidisciplinary Perspectives on Emerging Challenges, Opportunities, and Agenda for Research, Practice and Policy' (2021) 57 *International Journal of Information Management* 19

Findlay, M, *Law's Regulatory Relevance? Property, Power and Market Economies* (Edward Elgar, 2017)

Metcalf, J, E Moss and D Boyd, 'Owning Ethics: Corporate Logics, Silicon Valley, and the Institutionalization of Ethics' (2019) 86(2) *Social Research: An International Quarterly* 449

Palka, P, 'Data Management Law for the 2020s: The Lost Origins and the New Needs' (2020) 68(2) *Buffalo Law Review* 559

2.   Editors' reflections

Mark Findlay and Jolyon Ford

- Artificial intelligence and sensitive inferences: new challenges for data protection laws (Damian Clifford, Megan Richardson and Normann Witzleb)
- Revaluing labour? Secondary data imperialism in platform economies (Mark Findlay and Josephine Seah)
- Gauging the acceptance of contact-tracing technology: an empirical study of Singapore residents' concerns with sharing their information and willingness to trust (Ong Ee Ing and Loo Wee Ling)
- Regulating personal data usage in COVID-19 control conditions (Mark Findlay and Nydia Remolina)

Data protection regimes primarily reliant on legal form are becoming untenable in a world increasingly reliant on AI and big data. For the past decade now, scholars have been calling attention to the need to re-think key concepts like data protection and privacy, and for enhanced citizen-engagement and participatory methods to be included in regulation and governance agendas. These reformulations and their goals – to both enhance trust in our institutions and prevent individual and social harms – run through the following four chapters.

Clifford, Richardson and Witzleb's chapter brings us up to speed with just how advancements in AI and machine learning (ML) have prompted scholars to grapple with delicate and unresolved tensions around data protection and data processing, and in particular the unmistakable trend across different jurisdictions to subject certain types of data to stricter legal protections. This binary between 'ordinary' and 'sensitive' (or 'special') data, the authors note, is an evolving debate but one that is nonetheless being freshly challenged by ML-enabled *inferred* data.

Ong and Loo's chapter explores another traditional binary being upended by recent practices of mass data sharing. Here, where the previous chapter explored the axis between 'ordinary' and 'sensitive' data, their chapter looks at attitudes towards *who* is collecting data – public or private agencies – and data subjects' willingness to share their data. Looking at the collection of data that underpin pandemic contact-tracing applications, their chapter suggests that even in countries like Singapore where trust in public governance has always been notably high, data subjects see limits to the collection of personal data and its use by the state and the private sector. Trust, their work reminds us, not simply of the technology itself, but of the institutions that adopt emerging technologies for various ends, and is a relationship that can never be assumed or taken for granted. Instead, it is what emerges from a constant negotiation between public bodies, industries and civil society. On the other hand, this distinction between data collection for public and private purposes, as their chapter distinguishes, is increasingly a mirage in an age of smart cities where public-private partnerships are the hallmark drivers of urban solutions. The reality, then, that 'processes of algorithmic definition and construction escape our control' (Barassi 2019) calls for greater attention to emerging, thornier questions around agency, autonomy and digital self-determination. The authors turn to surveying public opinion over issues fraught with misconception and misunderstanding. The challenges in researching dynamic trust relationships mean that empirical engagement also requires qualitative reflection to delve under the surface of data subject concerns and appreciate how socio-demographics play out in the formulation of critical voices.

As some have argued, there is a need to shift our discussions about the governance of AI-assisted public services away from its present paternalism and create more room for openly contestable systems. Findlay and Remolina's chapter offers multiple exploratory routes here. By grounding their discussion in normative principles and applying them towards data regulation, they suggest that more-informed citizen-participatory initiatives can be institutionalised in ongoing regulatory discussions; and, that these are not only possible but *necessary* in societies that have become accustomed to COVID-enhanced surveillance infrastructures. The chapter is an exercise in evidence-based policy projection. It endeavours, through the identification of thematic challenges to personal data integrity and civil liberties, to model a universalist frame for COVID control regulation unburdened by jurisdictional particularity.

Extending on this, Findlay and Seah's chapter uses the context of the pandemic and its re-categorisation of gig workers as essential workers to prompt a reformulation of platform regulation. The authors argue that existing arrangements for gig workers are potentially at their tipping point. In recognition of key information deficits and market power asymmetries that have come into being through platform economies, their chapter proposes a model of participatory self-regulation that might function as a precursor to enhanced regulatory responsibilities. In so doing the analysis draws on rich interdisciplinary theorising on the path to speculating how AI-assisted information technologies can be both part of the problem and the solution for balancing the current market divide in secondary data commodification.

These chapters, without veering too heavily into proscriptive policy proposals, speak directly to the ongoing cross-jurisdictional regulatory challenges of reformulating institutions to create pathways for both harm-alleviation and meaningful citizen engagement in an era of intense (and sometimes invasive) data harvesting. Implicit in each is the importance of trust not only in smoothing the way for control efficacy and market sustainability, but in genuinely recognising and remedying the power differentials in mass data use.

While these chapters speak thematically to each other, we might also stand to gain from their methodological differences. The four chapters sit on a methodological spectrum between traditional legal research and those more closely associated within the disciplines of social science. In doing so, the chapters touch on how legal research is itself adapting to questions posed by the increasing ubiquity of artificial intelligence and 'black boxes' in society. Clifford, Richardson and Witzleb's chapter along with Findlay and Remolina's chapter on data protection laws may be the most familiar ground here for legal and regulation scholars. Theoretical and conceptual while purposeful and direct in their policy recommendations, their process of inductive reasoning is situated most closely with the historical trajectory of legal research. Findlay and Seah's chapter on data imperialism straddles this ground and that of social science research, situating itself more firmly in the domain of social science legal studies to ask how the legal system itself has interacted with technological chances to give rise to challenges of information enclosures and labour disempowerment. Finally, Ong and Loo's chapter joins an increasingly populated – but far from unfamiliar – group of scholars going outside the typical limits of legal research to engage in empirical research and primary data collection often recognised as social science research methods.

What these chapters do, then, is to remind us that each time a field of potentially new research emerges it invites us to revisit traditional forms of inquiry to ask straightforward but pressing questions of what might be missing from existing theoretical, conceptual and empirical work. As the four chapters remind us, legal research and social science methodologies are very much complimentary and, as the chapters suggest, permutations of these may be increasingly *necessary* if we are to understand the challenges of autonomy, agency, fairness and justice that lie ahead.

3. Artificial intelligence and sensitive inferences: new challenges for data protection laws

Damian Clifford, Megan Richardson and Normann Witzleb[1]

1. INTRODUCTION

Data protection regulation is widely considered to be a key legal response to the use of personal information by proliferating information and communications technologies including now artificial intelligence. The catchall acronym of 'artificial intelligence' (or 'AI') refers to a range of technological developments largely underpinned by machine learning which allows for the prediction and classification of phenomena by training models through labelled data from the real world.[2] There has been significant attention on the capacity of data privacy legislation to effectively regulate the machine learning applications that make use of personal information. One concern has been the deployment of AI to generate sensitive inferences from seemingly anodyne personal data, including metadata. How such inferences should be treated under data protection laws is indeed a great challenge these regimes face in the twenty-first century.

Of course, concerns related to the processing of data are far from new. As elegantly surveyed by Cornelia Vismann,[3] fears about data processing were shaped by bureaucratic filing systems even before the advent of computerised technologies. Data protection (or 'data privacy') standards proliferated from the 1970s onwards. And, from the beginning, many of the legislative regimes gave enhanced protection to certain types of 'sensitive' (or 'special') data.

---

[1]   With thanks to Karin Clark for invaluable advice.
[2]   R Binns, 'Fairness in Machine Learning: Lessons from Political Philosophy' (2018) 81 *Proceedings of Machine Learning Research* 1, 1.
[3]   C Vismann, *Files: Law and Media Technology*, tr Geoffrey Winthrop-Young (Stanford University Press 2008).

The 'sensitive data' concept was developed under European regimes,[4] but has over the years garnered increasing following around the world. It continues to exercise strong appeal, as is evident from the reliance on sensitive data categories in the emerging data protection laws in California,[5] India[6] and Pakistan.[7] Despite the wide-spread acceptance, significant disparities in the regulatory choices remain with respect to 'sensitive' data, or 'special categories' data as it is termed in the EU General Data Protection Regulation 2016 ('GDPR').[8] Building on the work of other scholars,[9] we consider in this chapter why some data are protected as 'sensitive', or 'special', and why protection continues to vary while still being the same in certain core respects.

In particular, we consider the new challenges posed by intensive data processing underpinned by machine learning developments which are capable of producing sensitive inferences out of data that are not 'sensitive' on their face. We ask whether these significant technological developments threaten the utility of providing special protections to certain categories of personal data – or whether they are merely the latest in a long line of socio-technological transformations that have both expanded the understanding of how data may be 'sensitive' and blurred the lines between 'ordinary' and 'sensitive' personal data, while not destroying the validity of line-drawing as such. One thing at least is clear at this stage. Serious and realistic anxieties about how personal data may be used to harm certain individuals and groups in a world marked by

---

[4]   See Council of Europe, Convention for the Protection of Individuals with regard to Automatic Processing of Personal Data 1981, CETS No 108 ('CoE108'); Directive 95/46/EC of the European Parliament and of the Council of 24 October 1995 on the protection of individuals with regard to the processing of personal data and on the free movement of such data, OJ 1995 L281/31 ('Directive 95/46/EC').

[5]   California Privacy Rights Act 2020 (as adopted by Proposition 24 of the November 2020 ballot).

[6]   Data Protection Bill 2021 (as reported by Lok Sabha [Parliament of India], Joint Committee on the Personal Data Protection Bill, 2019, Report of the Joint Committee on the Personal Data Protection Bill, 2019, (December 2021), Annexure, cl 3(41).

[7]   Personal Data Protection Bill 2021 (Consultation Draft: V.25.08.21), cl 2(t).

[8]   Regulation (EU) 2016/679 of the European Parliament and of the Council of 27 April 2016 on the protection of natural persons with regard to the processing of personal data and on the free movement of such data ('GDPR'), OJ 2016 L119/1, art 9.

[9]   For instance, K McCullagh, 'Data Sensitivity: Proposals for Resolving the Conundrum' (2007) 2 *Journal of International Commercial Law and Technology* 190; P Ohm, 'Sensitive Information' (2014) 88 *Southern California Law Review* 1125; M Wang and Z Jiang, 'The Defining Approaches and Practical Paradox of Sensitive Data: An Investigation of Data Protection Laws in 92 Countries and Regions and 200 Data Breaches in the World' (2017) 11 *International Journal of Communication* 3286; BW YongQuan, 'Protection of Sensitive Personal Data' [2018] PDP Digest 19; P Quinn and G Malgieri, 'The Difficulty of Defining Sensitive Data – the Concept of Sensitive Data in the EU Data Protection Framework' (2021) 22 *German Law Journal* 1583.

power imbalances, economic inequalities and now a major pandemic[10] make it crucial for policymakers to understand and respond to the question of how to treat sensitive data under existing and emerging data protection frameworks.

This chapter aims to assist policymakers called on to address a major socio-technological challenge to the regulatory status quo. Its focus encompasses especially the GDPR, the California Consumer Privacy Act 2018 (CCPA) and the forthcoming California Privacy Rights Act 2020 in the US,[11] with some cross-references to other jurisdictions and regimes such as the Australian Privacy Act 1988 (Cth). The EU and US instruments have been selected based on their significance, their historically divergent approaches to sensitive data, and their influence on reform in other jurisdictions. The laws in other common law jurisdictions are provided to demonstrate the influence of the European approach. For instance, the Australian Privacy Act, which is currently undergoing a process of modernisation,[12] is instructive as an example of a common law regime which has sought to find a middle-way between the EU and US approaches. We begin with an historical review of the different approaches before moving on to consider the current developing position towards closer harmonisation, finishing up with some insights into the sensitive data category-based approach as an exercise in harm-alleviation that can usefully be drawn on to deal with the problem of inferred sensitive data in the era of AI.

2.　EUROPEAN DATA PROTECTION RULES AND THE EMERGENCE OF SENSITIVE DATA CATEGORIES

The European approach to treating certain types of sensitive data as necessitating special protection was already apparent in the Council of Europe Convention 108 ('CoE108') concluded in 1981. Article 6 identified certain 'special categories' of personal data as requiring additional protection,

---

[10]　See, for instance, European Data Protection Board, *Guidelines 04/2020 on the Use of Location Data and Contact Tracing Tools in the Context of the COVID-19 Outbreak* (21 April 2020) <https://edpb.europa.eu/sites/edpb/files/files/file1/edpb _guidelines_20200420_contact_tracing_covid_with_annex_en.pdf> [33]–[34].

[11]　California Consumer Privacy Act of 2018 (California Civil Code §§ 1798.100–1798.199) ('CCPA').

[12]　The Australian Government seeks to implement a number of reforms proposed in Australian Competition and Consumer Commission (ACCC), *Digital Platforms Inquiry*, Final Report, Canberra (June 2019); Australian Human Rights Commission (AHRC), *Human Rights and Technology*, Final Report, Canberra (2021); Attorney-General's Department, *Privacy Act Review*, Discussion Paper, Canberra (October 2021) ('Discussion Paper').

meaning that such data may be processed only where specific safeguards are observed. These categories comprised '[p]ersonal data revealing racial origin, political opinions or religious or other beliefs, as well as personal data concerning health or sexual life' and furthermore 'personal data relating to criminal convictions'. The premise of art 6 was that 'there are exceptional cases where the processing of certain categories of data is as such likely to lead to encroachments on individual rights and interests'.[13] As a consequence, the processing of such data was generally allowed only for specific purposes under special conditions. In its *Explanatory Report*, the Council of Europe stated that the listed categories of data were considered 'in all member States ... to be especially sensitive'.[14] However, the report acknowledged that this list is 'not exhaustive' and that Member States can identify other categories that should be subject to specific prescriptions or limitations. It continued:[15]

> The degree of sensitivity of categories of data depends on the legal and sociological context of the country concerned. Information on trade union membership for example may be considered to entail as such a privacy risk in one country, whereas in other countries it is considered sensitive only in so far as it is closely connected with political or religious views.

The reference to the 'legal and sociological context' recognises that the treatment of data may include a cultural dimension. Nevertheless, the associated 'privacy risk', such as the threat of discrimination or harm to identity, if such data are not properly handled references a range of tangible, economic and psychological harms that may be suffered by data subjects. CoE108 allowed Member States also to make reservations and declarations pursuant to art 3(2) in order to limit the scope of application of CoE108 in relation to particular types of personal data. Where these have been made, they also seem to reflect a mix of concerns – for instance they often concern data processed purely for personal use and personal data processed in the context of state secrets. The fact that CoE108 is of European origin and that the Council of Europe is specifically mandated with the protection of human rights may have helped with arriving at a common understanding as to what categories of data should be regarded as sensitive. In light of the protective purpose of attributing more stringent protections to categories of data that entail serious risks to data

---

[13]   See Council of Europe, Explanatory Report to the Council of Europe, *Convention for the Protection of Individuals with regard to Automatic Processing of Personal Data*, Strasbourg (1981) [43].

[14]   Ibid.

[15]   Ibid [48].

subjects if not properly handled, it is also unsurprising that the categories of sensitive data were not closed and could be expanded as new threats emerged.

The Member States of the Council of Europe and the other parties to the Convention agreed on a revised definition of 'sensitive information' during the modernisation of CoE108, as spelt out in the Explanatory Report to the Protocol Amending the Convention.[16] At the same time, art 3(2) has also been changed to make a general exemption for personal use. The special categories in art 6 of the modernised 'Convention 108+'[17] now comprise:

> genetic data; personal data relating to offences, criminal proceedings and convictions, and related security measures; biometric data uniquely identifying a person; personal data for the information they reveal relating to racial or ethnic origin, political opinions, trade-union membership, religious or other beliefs, health or sexual life.

Here again, the addition of genetic and biometric data, the protection of trade union membership as well as the inclusion of information relating to the criminal process demonstrate a judgment that the processing of these types of personal information can entail 'particular risk[s]' to the individual.[18] In relation to genetic and biometric data, for example, new technological developments have increased the risks of identification without explicit consent, of being singled out for unjustified discriminatory treatment, and of identity theft as a major practical concern based on deployment of a unique identifier.[19]

Taking inspiration from CoE108, the former Directive 95/46/EC and now the GDPR also impose more stringent protections for certain categories of data. Clearly, at the time the Directive was developed, the European Commission identified the differences between EU Member States to be an obstacle to the implementation of the Single Market. Consequently, the EU Data Protection Framework started off with an approach directed at harmonising the data protection rules across Member States. In a catalogue that largely coincides with the original CoE108 list,[20] the special categories of data in art 8(1) of

---

[16]   See Council of Europe, *Explanatory Report to the Protocol Amending the Convention for the Protection of Individuals with regard to Automatic Processing of Personal Data*, Strasbourg (2018) [55]–[61] ('CoE Report 2018').

[17]   Council of Europe, *Modernised Convention for the Protection of Individuals with Regard to the Processing of Personal Data*, CETS No 223, Strasbourg (2018) ('Convention 108+').

[18]   CoE Report 2018 (n 16) [57].

[19]   Cf Biometric Information Privacy Act 2008 (BIPA) 740 ILCS 14/15, s 5; see further MB Kugler, 'From Identification to Identity Theft: Public Perceptions of Biometric Privacy Harms' (2019) 10 *UC Irvine Law Review* 107.

[20]   For a discussion of the European developments from the Convention 108 to the adoption of the Directive, including the different approaches on sensitive data

Directive 95/46/EC were: personal data revealing racial or ethnic origin, political opinions, religious or philosophical beliefs, trade union membership, and the processing of data concerning health or sex life. Under the Directive, the processing of such personal data was prohibited unless there was a specific legal ground to process such data (and at the same time the Directive also identified the circumstances in which such data can be processed in art 8(2): the processing required the consent of the individual concerned or a specific exception). Member States were able to limit the processing further. Thus, art 8(3) also allowed Member States to create further exemptions for processing such data with suitable safeguards. This suggests that art 8 proceeded on the basis that the listed categories of data are particularly sensitive in all Member States, but contemplated that Member States might wish to declare additional data to be subject to special restrictions due to their sensitivity in that state. In addition, art 8(3) provided Member States with scope to modify the restrictions according to their policy preferences. Making use of this flexibility, Member States added further categories of special data, or required certain data to be treated with particular care. The most significant additions included personal data in employment matters, on debts, financial standing, the payment of social security as well as criminal convictions.[21] Scope for adaptations was also provided in art 8(7), where Member States retained the power to determine the conditions under which a national identification number or any other identifier of general application could be handled. Given that not all Member States used national identifiers and differed in their use of such identification systems (a variation that continues to this day), the exception was important and appropriate.

Directive 95/46/EC required implementation by the Member States, which allowed Member States to adopt measures in line with their preferences, provided that the standards contained in the Directives were transposed correctly. In contrast, the GDPR has aimed not only to create more uniformity in the substantive rules of data protection, but also to strengthen these standards, as well as enhancing and harmonising the enforcement of these rules.[22] As to

---

that existed between Member States prior to the Directive, see S Simitis, 'Revisiting Sensitive Data' (1999) <https://rm.coe.int/CoERMPublicCommonSearchServices/DisplayDCTMContent?documentId=09000016806845af>.

[21] D Korff, *Report on the findings of the study, EC Study on Implementation of Data Protection Directive* (Study Contract ETD/2001/B5-3001/A/49), Annex 3 (July–December 2002) ch 7.

[22] European Commission, *Communication from the Commission to the European Parliament and the Council, Data protection as a pillar of citizens' empowerment and the EU's approach to the digital transition – two years of application of the General Data Protection Regulation*, COM(2020) 264 final, Brussels (24.06.2020) 1.

sensitive data, the GDPR adopts an approach to creating special safeguards for the processing of 'special' data that is largely similar to the former Directive. However, in line with its aim to modernise the EU data protection laws, the further categories of 'genetic data', 'biometric data for the purpose of uniquely identifying a natural person' and data concerning a person's sexual orientation have been added. Article 9 GDPR currently defines sensitive personal data to cover:

> personal data revealing racial or ethnic origin, political opinions, religious or philosophical beliefs, or trade union membership, and the processing of genetic data, biometric data for the purpose of uniquely identifying a natural person, data concerning health or data concerning a natural person's sex life or sexual orientation ...

The terms 'genetic data', 'health data' and 'biometric data' are further defined in art 4 GDPR. Under art 9(2), the individual must give explicit consent to the processing for specific purposes unless another ground for an exception applies, on the rationale that '[p]ersonal data which are, by their nature, particularly sensitive in relation to fundamental rights and freedoms merit specific protection as the context of their processing could create significant risks to the fundamental rights and freedoms'.[23] Under art 9(4), Member States are allowed to maintain or introduce further conditions, including limitations, with regard to the processing of genetic data, biometric data or data concerning health. Recall that Convention 108+ now includes personal data relating to offences, criminal proceedings and convictions, and related security measures in the list of special categories of personal data. In contrast, the GDPR does not refer to such data in art 9, but it deals with them separately in art 10, which stipulates that such data may only be processed 'under the control of official authority or when the processing is authorised by Union or Member State law providing for appropriate safeguards for the rights and freedoms of data subjects'. Data protection standards of European origin, including the current GDPR and Convention 108+, thus quite clearly subject a long list of categories of data to more stringent regulation.[24]

---

[23]   GDPR (n 8) recital 51.

[24]   An interesting cross-reference here can be made to the 1990 UN Guidelines for the Regulation of Computerized Personal Data Files, adopted by General Assembly resolution 45/95 of 14 December 1990, Principle 5. This Principle of Non-Discrimination provides that personal information that is likely to give rise to unlawful or arbitrary discrimination should not be compiled unless an exception (which is likewise tied to human rights standards) applies. The indicative list refers to 'information on racial or ethnic origin, colour, sex life, political opinions, religious, philosophical and other beliefs as well as membership of an association or trade union'.

Moreover, these instruments are intended to operate across jurisdictional boundaries, such as the GDPR (with its adequacy requirement for the transfer of data to third countries), or provide models for internationally harmonised laws, such as Convention 108+. Indeed, the GDPR states this purpose explicitly in art 1(2) and is designed to facilitate the free flow of personal data across the EU Member States by providing common regulatory standards respecting the rights and freedoms in the Charter of Fundamental Rights of the EU,[25] and, in particular, the right to the protection of personal data in art 8.[26] In turn, CoE108 has been conceived as an open convention, which means that countries around the world can accede, not only member countries of the Council of Europe. Since 2010, CoE108 has been openly promoted as a global privacy standard and a number of countries outside Europe have acceded or made requests to accede.[27] As a result of these shifts, the 'European approach' of recognising categories of sensitive data is finding increasing international acceptance, although the GDPR rather than the Convention is now viewed as the predominant influential standard.[28]

3.   INFLUENCE OF THE CATEGORY-BASED APPROACH IN COMMON LAW JURISDICTIONS

Yet the category-based approach has not been adopted uniformly across the common law world (with the exception of the United Kingdom and Ireland, which progressively mirrored the European approach).[29] For instance,

---

[25]   Charter of Fundamental Rights of the European Union, OJ 2010 C83/389. The Charter gained binding force on 1 December 2009 with the adoption of the Lisbon Treaty.

[26]   Ibid art 8 (protection of personal data), supplementing art 7 (respect for private and family life).

[27]   G Greenleaf, 'The UN Should Adopt Data Protection Convention 108 as a Global Treaty: Submission on "The Right to Privacy in the Digital Age" to the UN High Commissioner for Human Rights', 8 April 2018, <https://www.ohchr.org/Documents/Issues/DigitalAge/ReportPrivacyinDigitalAge/GrahamGreenleafAMProfessorLawUNSWAustralia.pdf>.

[28]   See, for instance, PM Schwartz, 'Global Data Privacy Law – the EU Way' (2019) 94 *New York University Law Review* 771.

[29]   See, for instance, Data Protection Act 1984 (UK), c 35, s 2(3), which referenced CoE108 in singling out personal data consisting of information as to: (a) the racial origin of the data subject; (b) his political opinions or religious or other beliefs; (c) his physical or mental health or his sexual life; or (d) his criminal convictions as potentially warranting additional protection by order of the Secretary of State. The Data Protection Act 1998 (UK), designed to give effect to Directive 95/46/EC, also closely followed its approach to sensitive data (and further added categories of offences and alleged offences to the list): Data Protection Act 1998, c 29, s 2 and passim. The UK

Australia, as many common law countries, initially based its data protection law on the OECD Guidelines on the Protection of Privacy and Transborder Flows of Personal Data 1980.[30] The OECD Guidelines recognise the issue of sensitive data without, however, adopting that concept.[31] Instead, they contain the clarification that they should not be 'interpreted as preventing the application, to different categories of personal data, of different protective measures depending upon their nature and the context in which they are collected, stored, processed or disseminated'.[32] The updated Guidelines published in 2013 maintain this stance.[33] Following the same model, the APEC Privacy Framework also does not single out specific categories of personal data as having a 'sensitive' quality which merits extra legal protection.[34]

The Australian Privacy Act has progressively been expanded from its initial coverage of the Australian public sector to a regime also covering the private sector (albeit with some significant exceptions).[35] The Privacy Act also largely mirrors the EU's special data categories,[36] although the additional protections

---

General Data Protection Regulation, which took effect on 31 January 2020 following the UK Brexit from the EU, mirrors the approach of the GDPR (n 8). Furthermore, the Data Protection Act 2018, c 12, s 11(2) adds alleged offences by the data subject and proceedings for offences to the special categories.

[30] Organisation for Economic Co-operation and Development (OECD), *OECD Guidelines on the Protection of Privacy and Transborder Flows of Personal Data*, accompanied by an Explanatory Memorandum, Paris (1980).

[31] Ibid [1]. The Expert Group preparing the Guidelines was unable to reconcile the differences in approaches to protecting sensitive data that had developed between Europe and the US.

[32] Ibid [3(a)].

[33] Organisation for Economic Co-operation and Development, *OECD Privacy Framework*, Paris (2013) [7] and [3(a)].

[34] Asia-Pacific Economic Cooperation (APEC), *Privacy Framework* (2015). The 2005 version of the Framework was modelled upon the 1980 OECD Guidelines (1980), whereas the updated Framework (2015) also draws upon concepts introduced into the OECD Guidelines (2013).

[35] See Privacy Amendment (Private Sector) Act 2000 (Cth).

[36] See Privacy Act 1988 (Cth) s 6, as amended by the Privacy Amendment (Private Sector) Act 2000 (Cth) and Privacy Amendment (Enhancing Privacy Protection) Act 2012 (Cth), in force 12 March 2014. Specifically, the Act, as amended in 2000 and 2012, identifies 'sensitive information' in s 6 as comprising:

    (a)   information or an opinion about an individual's:
        (i) racial or ethnic origin; or
        (ii) political opinions; or
        (iii) membership of a political association; or
        (iv) religious beliefs or affiliations; or
        (v) philosophical beliefs; or
        (vi) membership of a professional or trade association; or
        (vii) membership of a trade union; or

available to such data are quite restricted.[37] We can expect – as on previous occasions – this process of partial harmonisation with EU standards to continue in Australia: The Australian Competition and Consumer Commission's Digital Platforms Report recommended a range of reforms to bring Australia's data protection regime more closely into alignment with the EU standards,[38] and the Australian government is currently considering these and other proposals for reform in its review of the Privacy Act.[39] The proposed data protection laws in India and Pakistan[40] also adopt the concept of sensitive data in their draft legislation and subject such data to more stringent protection standards.

At the other end of the spectrum, Canada, New Zealand and Singapore still formally follow the OECD model.[41] In Canada, the drafters of the Personal Information Protection and Electronic Documents Act 2000 (PIPEDA) eschewed the differentiation between sensitive and other data because they perceived difficulties 'to determine *a priori* what is sensitive information, for people tend to have different views on what they consider most sensitive, and the matter can vary from one context to another'.[42] Building on this, the data protection principles in Schedule 1 to PIPEDA state that 'any information can be sensitive depending on the context' and that 'some information (for example, medical records and income records) is almost always considered to be sensitive'.[43] Express consent is generally needed for the processing of

---

      (viii)   sexual orientation or practices; or
      (ix) criminal record;
that is also personal information; or
    (b)   health information about an individual; or
    (c)   genetic information about an individual that is not otherwise health information; or
    (d)   biometric information that is to be used for the purpose of automated biometric verification or biometric identification; or
    (e)   biometric templates.

[37] For relevant Australian Privacy Principles (where additional protection applies), see APP 3 on collection, APP 6 on use and disclosure and APP 7 on direct marketing.

[38] ACCC Digital Platforms Report (n 12).

[39] See n 12.

[40] See nn 6–7.

[41] See Privacy Act, RSC 1985, c p-21 (Can); Personal Information Protection and Electronic Documents Act, SC 2000, c 5 (Can); Privacy Act 2020 (NZ); Personal Data Protection Act 2012 (Singapore).

[42] S Perrin et al, *The Personal Information Protection and Electronic Documents Act: An Annotated Guide* (Irwin Law, 2001) 23 (as cited in Office of the Privacy Commissioner of Canada, *Consent and privacy: A discussion paper exploring potential enhancements to consent under the Personal Information Protection and Electronic Documents Act*, Gatineau (2016) 2).

[43] PIPEDA, Sch 1, cl 4.3.4 Principle 3 – Consent. The contextual approach, which also includes consideration of the data subject's reasonable expectations, is explained and applied in *Royal Bank of Canada v Trang* [2016] 2 SCR 412 [34]–[36].

sensitive information, whereas implied consent may suffice where information is less sensitive.[44] In New Zealand, the notifiable data breach regime likewise refers to the sensitivity of personal information as a factor relevant to assessing the likely seriousness of the harm caused by the data breach.[45] Similarly, Singaporean courts in recent cases have acknowledged that some types of data warrant greater care and are adopting an incremental approach to developing the list of sensitive data types.[46]

This necessarily brief overview demonstrates that, despite the absence of a uniform approach to dealing with sensitive data, there is a general trend emerging towards treating sensitive data as special. The European-style category-based approach, which applies in the UK, Ireland and Australia, is likely to be emulated by India and Pakistan. Canada, New Zealand and Singapore, on the other hand, do not have statutorily defined categories of sensitive data, but nonetheless recognise in practice that certain types of data have a greater propensity to cause privacy harm if mishandled and therefore impose stricter standards on their processing.

4. US EXCEPTIONALISM REGARDING SENSITIVE DATA CATEGORIES (OR NOT SO EXCEPTIONAL?)

The US has developed its own traditions regarding data protection. To date, its approach has been largely sectoral. Important statutes include the Privacy Act 1974 (governing practices of federal government agencies),[47] the Video Privacy Protection Act of 1988 (VPPA),[48] the Children's Online Privacy Protection Act of 1998 (COPPA),[49] the Health Insurance Portability and Accountability Act of 1996 (HIPAA),[50] the Genetic Information Nondiscrimination Act of 2008 (GINA),[51] and various state-based legislation, such as the Illinois Biometric

---

[44] Ibid. The proposed Consumer Privacy Protection Act (contained in Bill C-11 for a Digital Charter Implementation Act 2020) maintains the position of not defining 'sensitive information' in the abstract, but referring to the sensitivity of personal information as a relevant factor in defining the requirements of appropriate data processing.

[45] Privacy Act 2020 (NZ) s 113.

[46] See *Re Aviva Ltd* [2018] PDP Digest 245 and *Re Galaxy Credit & Investments Pte Ltd* [2019] PDP Digest 288, and YongQuan (n 9).

[47] Privacy Act 1974 (as amended) 5 USC § 552a.

[48] Video Privacy Protection Act 1988 (VPPA) 18 USC § 2710.

[49] Children's Online Privacy Protection Act of 1998 (COPPA) 15 USC §§ 6501.

[50] Health Insurance Portability and Accountability Act of 1996 (HIPPA) (codified as amended in scattered sections of 18, 26, 29, and 42 USC).

[51] Genetic Information Nondiscrimination Act of 2008 (GINA) 42 USC 2000.

Information Privacy Act of 2008 (BIPA).[52] In addition, § 5 of the Federal Trade Commission Act (FTCA), proscribing unfair or deceptive acts or practices in trade or commerce,[53] offers a measure of 'consumer data privacy' protection vis-à-vis business actors under the auspices of the Federal Trade Commission (FTC).[54] An important further development is the California Consumer Privacy Act (CCPA), which enacts evolving consumer data privacy standards for the state of California, and is regarded as offering the greatest hope of a more uniform US approach.[55]

It can be argued that the existence of some of the US statutes is evidence that the personal information to which the protections apply is regarded as sensitive. In a valuable article published in 2014,[56] Paul Ohm undertook a comprehensive review aimed at identifying the criteria which determined when personal information is sensitive under US law, compared to the EU, and at exploring potential gaps and inconsistencies in the law. In his analysis, data relating to health, sex and sexuality, financial information, information relating to personal safety (such as personal address information), criminal records, educational information, information relating to children, political opinion and personal information submitted to public records is regarded as particularly sensitive in the US. It should be noted, however, that although there are valuable insights provided by such comparisons, the starting points of the US and EU approaches are fundamentally different. For instance, Ohm relies inter alia on the existence of a purpose-specific legislative framework to denote the sensitivity of certain types of information in US law. But in the EU legislative framework, such matters may be dealt with (at least in part) through the embedding of specific safeguards in the legislative protections. An example here is financial information, which Ohm considers a category of sensitive information due to its special treatment under the US Financial Modernization Act of 1999 (the Gramm-Leach-Bliley Act).[57] This is not listed per se as sensitive personal data in art 9(1) of the GDPR, but the processing of which may reveal information falling within a sensitive data category (e.g. political opinions revealed through contributions to political causes or donations to a political party). Interestingly, Ohm does not consider consumer information as sensitive. Perhaps it might be argued that rather than consumer

---

[52]   Biometric Information Privacy Act 2008 (BIPA) 740 ILCS 14/15.

[53]   15 US Code § 45.

[54]   CJ Hoofnagle, *Federal Trade Commission Privacy Law and Policy* (Cambridge University Press, 2016).

[55]   See, for instance, A Chander, ME Kaminski and W McGeveran, 'Catalyzing Privacy Law' (2021) 105 *Minnesota Law Review* 1733.

[56]   Ohm (n 9).

[57]   Ibid 1155; and, generally, Gramm-Leach-Bliley Act of 1999, 12 USC § 1831u.

information being 'special', it is consumers who are a category of people who, practically speaking, enjoy special protection in the US due to the perceived power asymmetries vis-à-vis the trading entities they deal with.[58] (And the same might be said of children, awarded special protection under COPPA.[59])

The position continues under the CCPA and is reflected in its title of California Consumer Privacy Act. The CCPA, as stated in § 1798.175 Civil Code, is 'intended to further the constitutional right of privacy and to supplement existing laws relating to consumers' personal information'. In pursuit of this objective, the CCPA adopts a fairly broad definition of personal consumer information in § 1798.140(o) that includes 'inferences drawn from any of the information identified in this subdivision to create a profile about a consumer reflecting the consumer's preferences, characteristics, psychological trends, predispositions, behavior, attitudes, intelligence, abilities, and aptitudes'.[60] Obviously, the CCPA's framers were here, and with the Act as a whole, responding to the 2018 Cambridge Analytica scandal. Nevertheless, while generally all consumer information is subject to the same regulatory standards under the CCPA, there is some de minimis referencing to special types of information. § 1798.150 creates particular remedies, including class action rights, for data breaches relating to 'nonencrypted and nonredacted personal information, as defined in subparagraph (A) of paragraph (1) of subdivision (d) of Section 1798.81.5' of the California Civil Code (the California Data Safeguard Law). There, 'personal information' is defined as follows:

(A) An individual's first name or first initial and the individual's last name in combination with any one or more of the following data elements, when either the name or the data elements are not encrypted or redacted:

   (i) Social security number.
   (ii) Driver's license number, California identification card number, tax identification number, passport number, military identification number,

---

[58] See further Hoofnagle (n 54) ch 6 (deceptive and unfair practices considered harmful). Cf Competition and Consumer Act 2010 (Cth) Sch 2 ('Australian Consumer Law') s 18; see further D Clifford and J Paterson, 'Consumer Privacy and Consent: Reform in the Light of Contract and Consumer Protection Law' (2020) 94(10) *Australian Law Journal* 741.

[59] Note that §6502 of COPPA states specifically that its concern is the 'regulation of unfair and deceptive acts and practices in connection with collection and use of personal information from and about children on the Internet' (by prescribing inter alia standards for parental consent). Cf GDPR (n 8) recital 38 recalls that children 'merit specific attention' with regard to their personal data 'as they may be less aware of the risks, consequences and safeguards concerned and their rights in relation to the processing of personal data'.

[60] CCPA § 1798.140(o)(1)(K).

or other unique identification number issued on a government document commonly used to verify the identity of a specific individual.

(iii)   Account number or credit or debit card number, in combination with any required security code, access code, or password that would permit access to an individual's financial account.

(iv)   Medical information.

(v)   Health insurance information.

(vi)   Unique biometric data generated from measurements or technical analysis of human body characteristics, such as a fingerprint, retina, or iris image, used to authenticate a specific individual. Unique biometric data does not include a physical or digital photograph, unless used or stored for facial recognition purposes.

(B)   A username or email address in combination with a password or security question and answer that would permit access to an online account.

This provision suggests some acceptance of the idea that certain sensitive data warrants additional protection under the CCPA at least in one respect, namely the right for data subjects to bring an action in court and to obtain a remedy. While data subjects have rights to bring actions in court under the GDPR (with this not being limited to when specific types of sensitive data are misused), in California, this right could make a significant difference to the array of available claims, given the history and culture of mass-class actions as a way of activating rights.[61]

Further, a reform of the CCPA, the California Privacy Rights Act of 2020 (CPRA), will create additional protections for sensitive personal information collected from 1 January 2022.[62] Passed as Proposition 24 of the November 2020 ballot,[63] the reforms will introduce a definition of sensitive information that builds on the internationally familiar categories, such as a consumer's racial or ethnic origin, religious or philosophical beliefs, union membership;

---

[61]   Indeed, there was already at least one high profile class action proceeding against the video-conferencing platform Zoom, objecting to its processing of sensitive personal data including under stay-at-home pandemic circumstances, giving the example of transfers of data to Facebook, and citing the CCPA (along with the constitutional right to privacy and various common law and statutory privacy torts). The action settled against a payment by Zoom of $85 million and an undertaking to improve privacy practices, however, without admission of liability: *In re: Zoom Video Communications Inc Privacy Litigation*, U.S. District Court, Northern District of California, No. 20-02155.

[62]   California Privacy Rights Act 2020 (CPRA), full text available at <https://leginfo .legislature.ca.gov/faces/billTextClient.xhtml?bill_id=202120220AB1490>. The Act will take effect on 1 January 2023.

[63]   See M Kelly, 'California Poised to Establish a New Privacy Regulator with Ballot Measure Win – And Tougher Privacy Rules', *The Verge* (4 November 2020) <https://www.theverge.com/2020/11/4/21549514/california-prop-24-data-privacy -2020-election-andrew-yang>.

genetic data; biometric information; health, sex life or sexual orientation, as well as information that reveals a consumer's social security, driver's license, state identification card, or passport number; a consumer's financial account log-in information; a consumer's precise geolocation; as well as the contents of a consumer's mail, email, or text messages, unless the business is the intended recipient of the communication.[64] Other reforms proposed in the CPRA include additional requirements with regard to consumer notices, and limitations on the collection, use and retention of personal information, including sensitive personal information, and a new Privacy Regulator to provide oversight.[65] Therefore, while the US remains divided at the federal level over the issue of privacy protection, California is forging ahead with its influential standard for improved consumer privacy that has the potential to form a benchmark for further legislative reform in other states and possibly ultimately at the federal level.

5. HIERARCHY OF HARMS IN SENSITIVE DATA CATEGORIES

Despite their differences in detail, category-based approaches to sensitive data coincide in the acknowledgement that data processing in some contexts calls for more stringent restrictions than in others. For those prepared to move beyond a mechanical 'black-letter' treatment of the categories, there is a wide consensus that the sensitivity of certain categories of data derives from the increased potential of harm that may result if such data are mishandled. As Ohm puts it: 'The first, and perhaps only necessary, factor is a connection

---

[64] CPRA, § 14, inserting a new § 1798.140 (ae) Civil Code:
'Sensitive personal Information' means: (1) personal Information that reveals (A) a consumer's social security, driver's license, state Identification card, or passport number; (B) a consumer's account log-in, financial account, debit card, or credit card number in combination with any required security or access code, password, or credentials allowing access to an account; (C) a consumer's precise geolocation; (D) a consumer's racial or ethnic origin, religious or philosophical beliefs, or union membership; (E) the contents of a consumer's mail, email and text messages, unless the business is the intended recipient of the communication; (F) a consumer's genetic data; and (2)(A) the processing of biometric information for the purpose of uniquely identifying a consumer; (B) personal Information collected and analyzed concerning a consumer's health; or (C) personal Information collected and analyzed concerning a consumer's sex life or sexual orientation. Sensitive personal Information that is 'publicly available' pursuant to paragraph (2) of subdivision (v) of Section 1798.140 shall not be considered sensitive personal Information or personal information.

[65] The California Privacy Protection Agency will become the regulator responsible for implementing and enforcing both the CCPA and CPRA.

between the category of information and harm. Information is deemed sensitive if adversaries (to use the computer scientific term) can use it to cause harm to data subjects or related people'.[66] It can certainly be acknowledged that misuse of all types of personal data has a propensity to cause harm, affecting the autonomy, dignity and personality of persons and groups (often with downstream effects for society). The harms include the potential for surveillance,[67] manipulating their decision-making for commercial or other ends,[68] or treating them 'as an object accessible to an inventory'.[69] Yet, the rationale for singling out categories of sensitive data is that in these cases the harms resulting from misuse are likely to be more serious and pointed than in other contexts.[70]

We can also try to correlate common categories of sensitive data with the types of harm that are likely to be suffered. While accepting that a data subject's ability to exercise control over personal data is generally closely imbricated with human identity and flourishing, we can acknowledge that there can be a spectrum of harms suffered when data are misused. For instance, for some types of data the harms are especially liable to impact a data subject's *physical or economic* well-being – for instance, increasing the risk of physical attack, reducing employment options, affecting insurance premiums, or increasing the prospects of identity theft. Belonging in this group might be health and genetic information, as well as now biometric data offering the prospect of misuse of a person's unique identifiers.[71] However, for other types of sensitive data, concerning for instance sexuality, philosophical and religious beliefs or values,

---

[66]   Ohm (n 9) 1161.

[67]   See D Lyon, *The Culture of Surveillance: Watching as a Way of Life* (Polity, 2018).

[68]   See S Zuboff, *The Age of Surveillance Capitalism: The Fight for a Human Future at the New Frontier of Power* (PublicAffairs, 2019).

[69]   See G Hornung and C Schnabel, 'Data Protection in Germany I: The Population Census Decision and the Right to Informational Self-determination' (2009) 25 *Computer Law & Security Review* 84, 87, citing Federal Constitutional Court of Germany, BVerfGE 27, 1, 6 ('Mikrozensus').

[70]   See GDPR (n 8) recital 51: sensitive data pose 'significant risks' to 'fundamental rights and freedoms'; TZ Zarsky, 'Incompatible: The GDPR in the Age of Big Data' (2017) 47 *Seton Hall Law Review* 995, 1012; *GC, AF, BH, and ED v Commission Nationale de l'Informatique et de Libertes (CNIL), Premier ministre, and Google LLC*, ECLI:EU:C:2019:773 [44] (stating that search engines cannot enjoy a general derogation as that would undermine the purpose of the GDPR provisions, 'to ensure enhanced protection as regards such processing, which, because of the particular sensitivity of the data, is liable to constitute… a particularly serious interference with the fundamental rights to privacy and the protection of personal data, guaranteed by Articles 7 and 8 of the [EU] Charter'.

[71]   See, for instance (regarding BIPA), *Rosenbach v Six Flags Entertainment Corp*, 2019 IL 123186 (25 January 2019).

the harms from misuse are liable to be of a more *spiritual* character, going to the core of a person's identity (and, some might argue, reflecting most closely an ideal of sensitive data as quintessentially private data).[72] This is not to say that physical or economic harms may not also be suffered in cases of misuse of these types of data, but the predominant concern is 'intangible injury'.[73] Likewise, these data might give rise to harms that have a distinctly social or political aspect, i.e. are still concerned with a person's identity but may be experienced in more societal settings, for example by impacting on the ability to engage in deliberation and debate.[74]

Other types of sensitive data are probably even more likely to correlate with this category of intellectual, social and identity harm, such as information relating to racial or ethnic origin, and political opinions. And, of course, again, we should not rule out that misuse of these types of information may simultaneously impede physical welfare and/or employment prospects, for example providing the basis for unlawful discrimination. Acknowledging that there is often likely to be significant cross-over between harms, Figure 3.1 sets out the different dimensions of harm that can result from misuse of sensitive data. Any attempt at categorisation needs to bear in mind the general point, however, that the prospects of harms flowing from misuse cannot just be attributed to the content and qualities of the data but also depend on the socio-technological contexts in which they are collected, used or otherwise processed.

There are still some serious questions to be addressed in a further program of research on the treatment of sensitive, or special, personal data. For example, it would be helpful for terminological stability if a more common understand-

---

[72] See R Wacks, *Personal Information: Privacy and the Law* (Oxford University Press, 1989), arguing that the connections between 'sensitive' and 'private' data should be more explicit and rigorous.

[73] See Judge V Chhabria in the Cambridge Analytica consolidated class action, *In re Facebook, Inc*, 402 F Supp 3d 767, 784 (ND Cal 2019): 'the first alleged injury – that the plaintiffs' sensitive information was disseminated to third parties in violation of their privacy – is sufficient to confer standing', and 'courts have often held that this particular type of intangible injury – disclosure of sensitive private information, even without further consequence – gives rise to Article III standing' (rejecting Facebook's argument that 'bare' privacy violation, without 'credible risk of real-world harm' such as identity theft or other economic consequences, cannot reach the level of Article III injury).

[74] See N Richards, *Intellectual Privacy: Rethinking Civil Liberties in the Digital Age* (Oxford University Press, 2015); M Oostveen and K Irion, 'The Golden Age of Personal Data: How to Regulate an Enabling Fundamental Right?' in M Bakhoum et al (eds), *Personal Data in Competition, Consumer Protection and IP Law – Towards a Holistic Approach?* (Springer, 2017) 7.

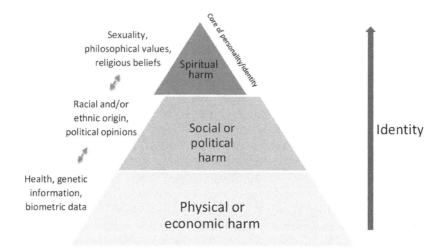

Figure 3.1   Sensitive data harms hierarchy

ing developed around the meaning of 'sensitive information'.[75] Further, it is evident that the existing categories do not represent the final word as to what is 'sensitive' or 'special' information. New technological or societal developments will lead to further shifts or expansion of our understanding of sensitivity. Here, Ohm proposes that building threat models to identify privacy harms might help provide a more rigorous assessment of the actual propensities for harm associated with an adversary's misuse of certain types of data – identifying geo-locational data, web browsing history, and remote biometric data as possible candidates for special protection in the current socio-technological environment. Some of the specific points have been overtaken by events – for instance, biometric data are now widely protected under the regimes surveyed in this article. However, the general proposal that a threat analysis be adopted to determine when fears about the misuse of particular types of data will be rational strikes us as a useful method to identify new categories of sensitive information. Likewise, public attitudes might provide a useful measure of current threats as perceived within a society, and certainly, such methods seem

---

[75]   Including outside the context of legislative definitions: see, for instance, Judge V Chhabria in *In re Facebook, Inc*, 402 F Supp 3d 767, 784 (ND Cal 2019), which considers the position before the CCPA. See also *Cullen v Zoom* (ND Cal, filed 30 March 2020) [69]: 'Defendant owed duties to Plaintiff and Class members arising from the sensitivity of Plaintiff's and Class members' information and privacy rights' – although of course the ability to bring the action based on the CCPA relies on more specific satisfaction of California Civil Code § 1798.81.5, para (1) of subdivision (d).

preferable to inclusion – or exclusion – of certain categories at the behest of and largely for the benefit of certain elites.[76]

Finally, a challenging question currently is how inferred data that falls within a sensitive personal data category should be treated, especially in the face of AI technologies and practices geared to generating and using such data. In the next section of this chapter, we suggest that a harm-based perspective offers a potentially helpful way to deal with this question.

6.   ALLEVIATING HARM AND SENSITIVE INFERENCES

There is still considerable uncertainty about how sensitive inferences should be treated under regimes that adopt a category-based approach and what this may mean for future legislative reforms. For instance, in Australia, the terms of reference of the government's current review note that new technologies such as AI result in 'more personal information about individuals ... being captured and processed'.[77] The government's Discussion Paper proposes to amend the definition of 'collection' to clarify that it includes inferred personal information, which would ensure that profiling that results in inferred sensitive information requires consent.[78]

The CCPA is the most recent regime under consideration here, and the one which most explicitly takes account of AI technologies and methods.[79] It defines 'personal information' specifically to include:

> Inferences drawn from any of the information identified in this subdivision to create a profile about a consumer reflecting the consumer's preferences, characteristics, psychological trends, predispositions, behavior, attitudes, intelligence, abilities, and aptitudes.[80]

Presumably this extended definition of inferred personal data as a category of personal data could be applied equally to inferred sensitive data for pur-

---

[76]   See McCullagh (n 9); and further, K McCullagh, *The Social, Cultural, Epistemological and Technical Basis of the Concept of 'Private Data'* (PhD Thesis, University of Manchester, 2011) ch 7.

[77]   See Attorney-General's Department, Privacy Act Review, Terms of Reference <https://www.ag.gov.au/integrity/consultations/review-privacy-act-1988>.

[78]   Australian Government, 'Discussion Paper' (n 12) proposal 2.4 and 134–135. Cf ACCC, *Digital Platforms Inquiry* (n 12) recs 16, 17.

[79]   But see also the Indian Personal Data Protection Bill 21 (n 6), which expressly 'include(s) any inference drawn from such data for the purpose of profiling' in its definition of 'personal data' (cl 3(33)).

[80]   California Civil Code § 1798.140 (definition of 'personal information').

poses of the CCPA remedies provision – and likewise to inferred sensitive data for purposes of the proposed rights attaching to sensitive data under the CPRA. However, note that for the CPRA's right for consumers to limit use and disclosure of sensitive personal information, as spelt out in § 1798.121 of the Civil Code, 'sensitive personal information that is collected or processed without the purpose of inferring characteristics about a consumer'[81] is specifically excluded – suggesting a potentially constraining qualification to the regime's prospective regulation of sensitive data. Viewed from a harm-based perspective it may be questioned whether this exclusion is justified – and we would certainly hope that it will not be stringently applied to limit regulation of sensitive inferences.

Inferred personal data also come within the GDPR's definition of 'special categories' data, although this is not explicitly stated in the statutory definition. Here, the Guidelines of the Article 29 Working Party, the former EU data protection advisory body, explain authoritatively that '[p]rofiling can create special category data by inference from data which is not special category data in its own right but becomes so when combined with other data'.[82] The UK Information Commissioner's Office (ICO) also points out that 'special category data includes not only personal data that specifies relevant details, but also personal data *revealing* or *concerning* these details'.[83] This guidance picks up on the language of art 9 of the GDPR, which states that data 'revealing' an individual's racial or ethnic origin, political opinions, religious or philosophical beliefs, or trade union membership, or 'concerning' health or a natural person's sex life or sexual orientation fall into the special categories. This definition appears wide enough to apply to data which are processed to reveal information on the protected attributes.

The ICO takes into account the degree of certainty regarding the inference and the intention of the data processor when deciding whether and at what point inferred data are to be treated as special category data.[84] *First*, it takes the position that *intentional* inferences of a sensitive nature may place the data into the special categories.[85] This approach imposes higher standards (in

---

[81]   CPRA, § 10 inserting a new § 1798.121 in the Civil Code.

[82]   Article 29 Working Party, *Guidelines on Automated individual decision-making and Profiling for the purposes of Regulation 2016/679* (wp251rev.01) (February 2018) 15. The Article 29 Working Party was the predecessor of the European Data Protection Board.

[83]   Information Commissioner's Office, Guide to the General Data Protection Regulation (GDPR), Special Category Data <https://ico.org.uk/for-organisations/guide-to-data-protection/guide-to-the-general-data-protection-regulation-gdpr/special-category-data/what-is-special-category-data/#scd7> (emphasis in original).

[84]   Ibid.

[85]   Ibid.

line with the classification of sensitive data) for deliberate efforts to engage in processing of data to reveal protected attributes (even before such attributes have been generated).[86] Some may doubt whether intent, by itself, should matter if harm-alleviation is the goal.[87] However, an intention to infer sensitive attributes from personal data is an indicator of the objectives pursued by those responsible for the processing and therefore (once that intention is manifested) provides a justification for imposing higher protection standards. In particular, intention can serve as a proxy for a need for protection where it is uncertain whether and what sensitive data may be generated through the processing activity. As the ICO puts it, 'if it is just a possible inference or an "educated guess", it is not special category data (unless you are specifically processing to treat someone differently on the basis of that inference)'.[88] Nevertheless, clearly intention to generate sensitive data cannot be a sole criterion. Experience shows that sensitive data may result from processing ordinary data even in the absence of an intention. Further, many harms resulting from big data analytics, including discriminatory treatments, are quite unintended, and sometimes unpredictable, effects of data processing.[89] Indeed, a key concern related to the design and deployment of machine learning is the potential for discriminatory and harmful effects, leading to an explosion in 'discrimination-aware data mining' or 'fair machine learning' research that aims to counteract the negative impact of machine learning.[90] Thus, a focus on purpose in carrying out processing cannot be sufficient if alleviation of harm is a guiding principle for applying the sensitive data categories.[91]

Secondly, the ICO proposes that information is to be categorised as special category data where the inference regarding the protected attribute has a manifested *reasonable degree of certainty*. As the ICO Guidance provides: 'If you

---

[86] A purpose-based approach was also advocated by Council of Europe, Consultative Committee on the Convention for the Protection of Individuals with regard to Automatic Processing of Personal Data (T-PD), *Report on the Application of Data Protection Principles to the Worldwide Telecommunication Networks*, T-PD (2004) 04 final <https://rm.coe.int/168068416a> 43.

[87] See, for instance, S Wachter, 'Data Protection in the Age of Big Data' (2019) 2 *Nature Electronics* 6, 7.

[88] Information Commissioner's Office (n 83). For a useful discussion, see Quinn and Malgieri (n 9) 8–10.

[89] See, for example, DK Citron and FA Pasquale, 'The Scored Society: Due Process for Automated Predictions' (2014) 18 *Washington Law Review* 1, 14.

[90] Binns (n 2) 1.

[91] Cf the Article 29 Working Party on 'personal data', holding that the context and purpose of the processing should be taken into account in assessing whether (and at what point) data may be considered 'personal data': Article 29 Working Party, Opinion 4/2007 on the Concept of Personal Data (20 June 2007).

can infer relevant information with a reasonable degree of certainty then it's likely to be special category data even if it's not a cast-iron certainty'.[92] This seems to be more directly focused on harm-alleviation – and also fits with the language of 'revealing' or 'concerning' in art 9 GDPR. In this scenario, the focus shifts from regulating an intention, or purpose, to generate sensitive data per se to sensitive *uses* of data that, in the course of the processing, take on the character of sensitive data (or are reasonably likely to do so).[93] Presumably, where it is clear that the processing will reveal sensitive data through a process still being undertaken (the latter scenario constituting what the ICO terms 'a cast-iron certainty'), that will also be sufficient.[94] However, there can be a fertile ground for argument in practice whether and at what point inferences reach this threshold of certainty. Given that decision-making on inferences about protected attributes will often be no less harmful where inferences are uncertain or even erroneous, we suggest that a liberal approach should be adopted to this threshold issue.

Usually, a hybrid approach that combines a focus on intention, or purpose, and reasonable degree of certainty in a single inquiry makes the most sense – and again, we argue, for a liberal approach that takes into account the risk of harm and places the onus on the party responsible for the processing to make the necessary risk assessment and take precautionary measures rather than leaving costs to lie where they fall, i.e. on data subjects. Sometimes the risks can be quite subtle. For instance, a 2018 study conducted by José González Cabañas et al[95] examined how Facebook profiled users based on their interactions with Facebook, such as liking a post or using an app, and assigned so-called 'ad preferences' to them. These ad preferences allowed advertisers to target people based on inferred interests in certain issues, which included sensitive categories such as political views, sexual orientation, health conditions, religious beliefs or ethnic origin. The Cambridge Analytica scandal also highlighted the potential for a psychometric profile to be used to target an individual with political messaging on the basis of (and tailored for) that individual's perceived attitudes towards a social issue under political

---

92   Information Commissioner's Office (n 83).

93   See L Moerel and C Prins, 'Privacy for the Homo Digitalis: Proposal for a New Regulatory Framework for Data Protection in the Light of Big Data and the Internet of Things' (25 May 2016) <https://papers.ssrn.com/sol3/papers.cfm?abstract_id=2784123>, 11. Cf Simitis (n 20).

94   See Information Commissioner's Office (n 83).

95   JG Cabañas, Á Cuevas and R Cuevas, 'Unveiling and Quantifying Facebook Exploitation of Sensitive Personal Data for Advertising Purposes', Proceedings of the 27th USENIX Conference on Security Symposium (USENIX Association 2018) <http://dl.acm.org/citation.cfm?id=3277203.3277240>.

debate.[96] Facebook submitted to the UK Information Commissioner's Office (ICO) that it does 'not target advertising to EU users on the basis of sensitive personal data'.[97] This would seem to be an attempt to distinguish an interest in a particular topic, as indicated by user interactions with Facebook content, from inferences about any personal characteristics about them as a result of those interactions. However, it is difficult to see how a user's interest in, say, 'animal rights', 'climate change' or 'abortion' is not, at least to some extent, revealing of their political opinions (or their philosophical or religious beliefs). While having an interest can mean to have either a positive or negative view on the issues in question, it seems undeniable that, in these cases, 'an individual is targeted after the processing of other data sets to infer their political views'.[98]

Some authors have suggested that a liberal treatment of inferred sensitive data raises the question of the ongoing viability of the categorisation of sensitive data and the legitimacy of the heightened protections afforded to sensitive personal data, particularly in an age of big data and AI.[99] For instance, Sandra Wachter and Brent Mittelstadt argue that there is 'a fundamental problem' if '[n]on-sensitive data can become sensitive if used to infer sensitive attributes, yet the content of the data remains the same'.[100] Likewise, Paul Quinn and Gianclaudio Malgieri point out a risk that the concept of sensitive personal data might be devalued over time if enhanced computational capabilities lead to a future where an increasing amount of personal data will become sensitive in nature.[101] It cannot be denied that the advances in big data analytics,

---

[96]   See *In re Facebook, Inc*, 402 F Supp 3d 767, 784 (ND Cal 2019) and, generally, V Bakir and A McStay, 'Fake News and The Economy of Emotions: Problems, Causes, Solutions' (2018) 6 *Digital Journalism* 154.

[97]   Information Commissioner's Office, *Democracy Disrupted: Personal information and political influence* (ICO, London 2018) 39.

[98]   B Shiner, 'The Legal Landscape' in M Palese and J Mortimer (eds), *Reining in the Political 'Wild West' Campaign Rules for the 21st Century* (Electoral Reform Society, 2019) 33 <https://www.electoral-reform.org.uk/wp-content/uploads/2019/02/Reining-in-the-Political-Wild-West-Campaign-Rules-for-the-21st-Century.pdf>.

[99]   See, for instance, Moerel and Prins (n 93); TZ Zarsky (n 70), 1013; L Edwards, 'Data Protection: Enter the General Data Protection Regulation' in L Edwards (ed), *Law, Policy and the Internet* (Hart Publishing, 2018) 90; S Wachter and B Mittelstadt, 'A Right to Reasonable Inferences: Re-Thinking Data Protection Law in the Age of Big Data and AI' (2019) 2 *Columbia Business Law Review* 494. On the related concern that the concept of 'personal data' is ever-expanding, see: WK Hon, C Millard and I Walden, 'The Problem of "Personal Data" in Cloud Computing: What Information Is Regulated? – The Cloud of Unknowing – Part 1' (2011) 1 *International Data Privacy Law* 211; N Purtova, 'The Law of Everything: Broad Concept of Personal Data and Future of EU Data Protection Law' (2018) 10 *Law, Innovation and Technology* 40.

[100]   Wachter and Mittelstadt (n 99) 564.

[101]   Ibid.

combined with increasingly sophisticated uses of AI technologies, have the potential to blur the lines between the categories of 'ordinary' and 'sensitive' personal data. Maintaining the current categorisation carries the risk that sensitive data proliferates, ultimately requiring more and more data processing to follow the stricter rules applying to 'sensitive' (or 'special') data. Nonetheless, in our view, the harms associated with processing sensitive data or processing data for sensitive attributes can be very real for data subjects. Thus for now the additional protections for sensitive data still represent an appropriate response to the greater and more pointed risks of identifiable harms flowing from misuse of these categories of data, provided that these categories are appropriately delineated, as we have argued above.[102] In summary, a focus on harm-alleviation can help to inform policymakers considering the problem of AI and inferred sensitive data – whether in the EU or in other jurisdictions, such as California (especially when it introduces its new CPRA regime).

7.   CONCLUSION

A theme of this chapter has been that stricter regulation of the processing of 'sensitive' personal data under data protection laws is warranted in a time of heightened legitimate fears about sensitive data misuse and resultant harms under current socio-technological conditions. Indeed, our analysis of EU, US (especially California) and other common law jurisdictions (e.g. Australia) demonstrates a growing consensus, albeit differently manifested in the jurisdictions. We contend that what is needed now is a more concerted response to the challenge of the proliferation of machine-learning and associated AI technologies which have the potential to blur the lines between 'sensitive' and other personal data, because they allow the drawing of inferences about sensitive attributes when seemingly innocuous data are combined with other data over the course of their life. We argue that an approach that treats harm alleviation as a guiding consideration in assessing and regulating sensitive data, including with respect to inferences, offers a helpful way forward.

BIBLIOGRAPHY

Articles/Books/Reports

Bakir, V and A McStay, 'Fake News and The Economy of Emotions: Problems, Causes, Solutions' (2018) 6 *Digital Journalism* 154

---

[102]   Quinn and Malgieri (n 9) reach the same conclusion about the value of preserving the concept of sensitive data: 30.

Binns, R, 'Fairness in Machine Learning: Lessons from Political Philosophy' (2018) 81 *Proceedings of Machine Learning Research* 1

Citron, DK and FA Pasquale, 'The Scored Society: Due Process for Automated Predictions' (2014) 18 *Washington Law Review* 1

Clifford, D and J Paterson, 'Consumer Privacy and Consent: Reform in the Light of Contract and Consumer Protection Law' (2020) 94(10) *Australian Law Journal* 741

Edwards, L, 'Data Protection: Enter the General Data Protection Regulation' in L Edwards (ed), *Law, Policy and the Internet* (Hart Publishing, 2018)

Hon, WK, C Millard and I Walden, 'The Problem of "Personal Data" in Cloud Computing: What Information Is Regulated? – The Cloud of Unknowing – Part 1' (2011) 1 *International Data Privacy Law* 211

Hoofnagle, CJ, *Federal Trade Commission Privacy Law and Policy* (Cambridge University Press, 2016)

Hornung, G and C Schnabel, 'Data Protection in Germany I: The Population Census Decision and the Right to Informational Self-determination' (2009) 25 *Computer Law & Security Review* 84

Information Commissioner's Office, *Democracy Disrupted: Personal information and political influence* (ICO, London 2018)

Korff, D, *Report on the findings of the study, EC Study on Implementation of Data Protection Directive* (Study Contract ETD/2001/B5-3001/A/49) Annex 3 (July–December 2002)

Kugler, MB, 'From Identification to Identity Theft: Public Perceptions of Biometric Privacy Harms' (2019) 10 *UC Irvine Law Review* 107

Lyon, D, *The Culture of Surveillance: Watching as a Way of Life* (Polity, 2018)

McCullagh, K, 'Data Sensitivity: Proposals for Resolving the Conundrum' (2007) 2 *Journal of International Commercial Law and Technology* 190

Office of the Privacy Commissioner of Canada, *Consent and Privacy: A discussion paper exploring potential enhancements to consent under the Personal Information Protection and Electronic Documents Act*, Gatineau (2016)

Ohm, P, 'Sensitive Information' (2014) 88 *Southern California Law Review* 1125

Oostveen, M and K Irion, 'The Golden Age of Personal Data: How to Regulate an Enabling Fundamental Right?' in M Bakhoum et al (eds), *Personal Data in Competition, Consumer Protection and IP Law – Towards a Holistic Approach?* (Springer, 2017)

Perrin, S et al, *The Personal Information Protection and Electronic Documents Act: An Annotated Guide* (Irwin Law, 2001)

Purtova, N, 'The Law of Everything: Broad Concept of Personal Data and Future of EU Data Protection Law' (2018) 10 *Law, Innovation and Technology* 40

Richards, N, *Intellectual Privacy: Rethinking Civil Liberties in the Digital Age* (Oxford University Press, 2015)

Vismann, C, *Files: Law and Media Technology*, tr Geoffrey Winthrop-Young (Stanford University Press 2008)

Wachter, S, 'Data Protection in the Age of Big Data' (2019) 2 *Nature Electronics* 6

Wachter, S and B Mittelstadt, 'A Right to Reasonable Inferences: Re-Thinking Data Protection Law in the Age of Big Data and AI' (2019) 2 *Columbia Business Law Review* 494

Wacks, R, *Personal Information: Privacy and the Law* (Oxford University Press, 1989)

Wang, M and Z Jiang, 'The Defining Approaches and Practical Paradox of Sensitive Data: An Investigation of Data Protection Laws in 92 Countries and Regions and

200 Data Breaches in the World' (2017) 11 *International Journal of Communication* 3286
YongQuan, BW, 'Protection of Sensitive Personal Data' [2018] PDP Digest 19
Zarsky, TZ, 'Incompatible: The GDPR in the Age of Big Data' (2017) 47 *Seton Hall Law Review* 995
Zuboff, S, *The Age of Surveillance Capitalism: The Fight for a Human Future at the New Frontier of Power* (PublicAffairs, 2019)

Cases

Cullen v Zoom (ND Cal, filed 30 March 2020)
Federal Constitutional Court of Germany, BVerfGE 27 ('Mikrozensus')
GC, AF, BH, and ED v Commission Nationale de l'Informatique et de Libertes (CNIL), Premier ministre, and Google LLC, ECLI:EU:C:2019:773
In re Facebook, Inc, 402 F Supp 3d 767 (ND Cal 2019)
In re: Zoom Video Communications Inc Privacy Litigation, U.S. District Court, Northern District of California, No. 20-02155
Re Aviva Ltd [2018] PDP Digest 245
Re Galaxy Credit & Investments Pte Ltd [2019] PDP Digest 288
Rosenbach v Six Flags Entertainment Corp, 2019 IL 123186 (25 January 2019)
Royal Bank of Canada v Trang [2016] 2 SCR 412

Legislation

Biometric Information Privacy Act 2008 740 ILCS 14/15
California Consumer Privacy Act of 2018 (California Civil Code §§ 1798.100–1798.199)
California Privacy Rights Act of 2020 (California Civil Code §§ 1798.100–1798.199.100)
Children's Online Privacy Protection Act of 1998 Pub.L. 105–277, 15 USC §§ 6501–6506
Competition and Consumer Act 2010 (AUS)
Consumer Privacy Protection Act (contained in Bill C-11, Can, 2020)
Data Protection Act 1984 (UK)
Data Protection Act 1998 (UK)
Data Protection Act 2018 (UK)
Directive 95/46/EC of the European Parliament and of the Council of 24 October 1995 on the protection of individuals with regard to the processing of personal data and on the free movement of such data, OJ 1995 L281/31
Genetic Information Nondiscrimination Act of 2008 Pub.L. 110–233, 42 USC 2000
Gramm-Leach-Bliley Act of 1999 Pub.L. 106–102
Health Insurance Portability and Accountability Act of 1996 Pub.L. 104–191
Personal Data Protection Act 2012 (Singapore)
Personal Data Protection Bill 2021 (India)
Personal Data Protection Bill 2021 (Pakistan)
Personal Information Protection and Electronic Documents Act, SC 2000, c 5 (Can)
Privacy Act 1974 Pub.L. 93–579, 5 USC § 552a
Privacy Act 1988 (AUS)
Privacy Act 2020 (NZ)
Privacy Act, RSC 1985, c p-21 (Can)

Privacy Amendment (Enhancing Privacy Protection) Act 2012 (AUS)

Privacy Amendment (Private Sector) Act 2000 (Cth)

Regulation (EU) 2016/679 of the European Parliament and of the Council of 27 April 2016 on the protection of natural persons with regard to the processing of personal data and on the free movement of such data, OJ 2016 L119/1

Video Privacy Protection Act 1988 18 Pub.L. 100–618 USC § 2710

Treaties

Charter of Fundamental Rights of the European Union, OJ 2010 C83/389

Convention for the Protection of Individuals with regard to Automatic Processing of Personal Data, 1981, CETS No 108

Protocol amending the Convention for the Protection of Individuals with Regard to the Processing of Personal Data, 2018, CETS No 223

Other

Article 29 Working Party, *Guidelines on Automated individual decision-making and Profiling for the purposes of Regulation 2016/679* (wp251rev.01) (February 2018)

Article 29 Working Party, Opinion 4/2007 on the Concept of Personal Data (20 June 2007) Asia-Pacific Economic Cooperation (APEC), *Privacy Framework* (2015)

Attorney-General's Department, *Privacy Act Review*, Discussion Paper, Canberra (October 2021)

Australian Competition and Consumer Commission, *Digital Platforms Inquiry*, Final Report, Canberra (June 2019)

Australian Human Rights Commission, *Human Rights and Technology*, Final Report, Canberra (2021)

Council of Europe, Explanatory Report to the Council of Europe, *Convention for the Protection of Individuals with regard to Automatic Processing of Personal Data*, Strasbourg (1981)

European Commission, *Communication from the Commission to the European Parliament and the Council, Data protection as a pillar of citizens' empowerment and the EU's approach to the digital transition – two years of application of the General Data Protection Regulation*, COM(2020) 264 final, Brussels (24.06.2020)

McCullagh, K, *The Social, Cultural, Epistemological and Technical Basis of the Concept of 'Private Data'* (PhD Thesis, University of Manchester, 2011)

Organisation for Economic Co-operation and Development (OECD), *OECD Guidelines on the Protection of Privacy and Transborder Flows of Personal Data*, accompanied by an Explanatory Memorandum, Paris (1980)

Organisation for Economic Co-operation and Development, *OECD Privacy Framework*, Paris (2013)

UN Guidelines for the Regulation of Computerized Personal Data Files, adopted by General Assembly resolution 45/95 of 14 December 1990

4. Revaluing labour? Secondary data imperialism in platform economies

Mark Findlay and Josephine Seah[1]

...platforms represent a distinct type of governance mechanism, different from markets, hierarchies, or networks, and therefore pose a unique set of problems for regulators, workers, and their competitors in the conventional economy. Reflecting the instability of the platform structure, struggles over regulatory regimes are dynamic and difficult to predict, but they are sure to gain in prominence as the platform economy grows.[2]

1.   INTRODUCTION

Still in the pandemic's grip, food delivery and logistics 'gig workers' have transited from a preferred option to arguably an essential service. This reconceptualisation of functionality supports the assumption that along with global crisis conditions, even in a realm of reluctant globalised engagement and heightened localised dependencies, devalued labour must be repositioned.[3] There can be little doubt that in times of social distancing and restrictions over movement, delivery services, particularly in heavily urbanised environments, have grown in fundamental social utility.

Platform providers have aligned themselves with this commercial opportunity in a variety of market-driven ways. In many jurisdictions, they have argued special exemption status, or a waiver on the restrictions faced by other commercial service providers in terms of business activity and worker applica-

---

[1]   This research is supported by the National Research Foundation, Singapore under its Emerging Areas Research Projects (EARP) Funding Initiative. Any opinions, findings and conclusions or recommendations expressed in this material are those of the author(s) and do not reflect the views of National Research Foundation, Singapore.

[2]   S Vallas and J Schor, 'What do Platforms Do? Understanding the Gig Economy' (2020) 46(1) *Annual Review of Sociology* 273.

[3]   S Katta et al, '(Dis) embeddedness and (de) commodification: COVID-19, Uber, and the unravelling logics of the gig economy' (2020) 10(2) *Dialogues in Human Geography* 203; P Martyn, 'What does Covid-19 mean for people working in the gig economy?', *RTÉ News* (2020) <https://www.rte.ie/news/business/2020/0522/1140094 -covid-19-and-its-impact-on-the-gig-economy/>.

tion.[4] The tendency to exploit an already vulnerable workforce in situations of higher demand has been responded to by limited organised resistance.[5]

The impact of the pandemic on gig workers requires labour revaluing and empowerment in the face of many existing structural vulnerabilities for workers, as a consequence of neoliberal platform disruption of employment relations, and push-back against calls for reform. As such, whether the pandemic and its social ramifications have provided a window for worker empowerment, or is simply another context for exploitation depends on whether one is a profit beneficiary of the platform, an exploited service deliverer or someone in the public who needs a meal or a parcel.[6]

The regulatory theorising in this chapter expounds that for human workers, regulation should enable social good, along with, and above, market sustainability. This broad aspiration recognises the alternative regressive neoliberal position taken by many who argue for the introduction of AI into the workplace primarily on profit and efficiency terms. This lobby usually rejects regulatory interference in favour of some compromised belief in the neutrality and potency of competitive market forces. The intellectual poverty and the commercial duplicity of this position in platform economy oligopolies[7] are recognized and will be countered by two arguments that move beyond humanist considerations:

- As the revaluation of platform-facilitated delivery and logistics services during the social distancing and movement restrictions of COVID-19 should reveal, depressed labour pricing and disempowered labour participation are mechanically motivated internal market forces at work. A realistic understanding of labour revaluation relative to crisis utility is resisted by neoliberal pushback.
- Human provision remains the bulk of platform service delivery and to ignore work-life quality in regulatory agendas is a short-sighted appreciation of market priorities, even when neoliberal discourse conceals 'human

---

[4]   A Pardes, 'This Pandemic Is a "Fork in the Road" for Gig Worker Benefits', *Wired* (2020) <https://www.wired.com/story/gig-worker-benefits-covid-19-pandemic/>.

[5]   S Ghaffary, 'The May Day strike from Amazon, Instacart, and Target workers didn't stop business. It was still a success', *Vox* (2020) <https://www.vox.com/recode/2020/5/1/21244151/may-day-strike-amazon-instacart-target-success-turnout-fedex-protest-essential-workers-chris-smalls>.

[6]   L Chaibi, 'Pandemic is time to recognise gig workers' rights', *EUobserver* (2020). <https://euobserver.com/opinion/147902>.

[7]   FA Pasquale, 'Tech Platforms and the Knowledge Problem' (2018) *American Affairs* (Summer) 3.

capital' behind 'economic units' and conventional employment relationship disruption.

AI impacts on labour markets by augmenting and/or substituting human capital in both mundane and specialist sites for decision-making.[8] In most labour markets, the drivers for introducing AI are clearly based on profit: namely an expected reduced reliance on wage labour, and increased efficiency through mechanical predictability and reproductivity. AI technologies for managing and applying data in labour markets, outside facilitating market sustainability,[9] present risks for workers at the intersection of human agency and AI. Workers utilising platform communication markets are inextricably immersed in AI. The platform, which masks employment arrangements behind 'independent service provision', sets rates of return, constructs transactions and sells on secondary data. These automations depend on big data, machine learning and computational interface. Platform technologies enhance service delivery and customer engagement but at the cost of depersonalising the supply chain and giving market power to platform operators as exclusive agents in a variety of logistics transactions.

In the emerging context of platform facilitation, the labour market has developed in two ways. The first was an organic consequence of computerisation in traditional economies, where organisations digitised their transactions and interactions with other market players. This phenomenon is not the interest of this analysis. Rather it is with the second:

> …and potentially more consequential path of growth [which] began outside the traditional economy, as companies that have been born digital use the internet to usurp existing markets or create entirely new ones. Examples here involve e-commerce platforms, which have captured a growing share of the revenues once controlled by brick-and-mortar retail outlets; capital platforms or lodging, goods, and even machinery; service labor platforms for rides, household help, and caring labor; and video streaming and content platforms, which compete with broadcast, cable, and other media companies. The platform economy also encompasses social media firms such as Facebook and Instagram, which subsist on revenue from advertising

---

[8]   CB Frey, *The Technology Trap: Capital, Labor, and Power in the Age of Automation* (Princeton University Press, 2019). See also R Teigland et al, 'The Substitution of Labor: From Technological Feasibility to Other Factors Influencing Job Automation' (2018) <https://ssrn.com/abstract=3140364>.

[9]   Market sustainability in the context of this chapter is grounded in the observation that oligopolistic markets which operate on heavy stakeholder power disparities and exploit key vulnerable market players absent of capital interests will only continue to operate if the constituents of exploitation such as de-valued labour and regulatory distancing remain. As the COVID-19 crisis has shown with the new social valuing of some platform labour, externalities will impact on discriminatory sustainability.

and the sale of data, and internet service platforms such as Amazon Web Services, which provide the infrastructure on which other companies and platforms depend. As such, the platform economy represents an important and strategically consequential branch of global capitalism, not least because of the Schumpeterian creative destruction – or disruption, in the contemporary parlance – it has imposed across much of the economic landscape.[10]

Predatory capitalism[11] creates economic conditions that in turn feed on the vulnerabilities of many in its labour demographic, disrupting conventional employer/employee arrangements, disengaging traditional worker protections, destabilising bargaining power in any market/collective sense, and re-orienting even flexi-work[12] into employment environments devoid of predictability and certainty. The new worker world is one re-imagined by a sanitised language of 'independent contracting', 'freelancing' and 'gigging' as some supplementary labour pastime.[13] The tendency of such discourse to further erode the dignity of the oppressed[14] takes this thinking to its eventually perverted and now contested discourse.

Information deficits prevail across platform economies, and important data subjects such as drivers and customers are excluded from accessing the data they produce, or even the knowledge of what and when they are producing it. A lucrative market in the monetising of secondary data, primarily the product of surveillance, is also debarred from worker/customer benefit.[15] In these circumstances, information (or its containment) presents two regulatory challenges. The first relates to general information closure. If workers do not have access to basic data which would indicate objective measures of labour value, they are in no position to construct informed representations on wages, conditions and work-life quality measures. Disempowerment in this form is

---

[10]   Vallas and Schor (n 2) 274–275.

[11]   P Zanoni, 'Labor Market Inclusion Through Predatory Capitalism? The "Sharing Economy," Diversity, and the Crisis of Social Reproduction in the Belgian Coordinated Market Economy' in S Vallas and A Kovalainen (eds), *Work and Labor in the Digital Age, Vol. 33* (Emerald Publishing, 2019) ch 6.

[12]   T Kumar and LK Jena, 'Capital vs. Digital Labor in the Post-industrial Information Age: A Marxist Analysis' (2020) 6(1) *Emerging Economy Studies* 50.

[13]   KM Kuhn, 'The Rise of the "Gig Economy" and Implications for Understanding Work and Workers' (2016) 9(1) *Industrial and Organizational Psychology* 157.

[14]   J Prassl, *Humans as a Service: The Promise and Perils of Work in the Gig Economy* (Oxford University Press, 2018); D Kergel and R Hepp, 'Start Ups, Social Networking and Self-Tracking – The Neoliberal Freedom of the Entrepreneurial Self in the Digital Age' in T Rachwał, R Hepp and D Kergel (eds), *Precarious Places* (Springer, 2020) 139.

[15]   S Zuboff, *The Age of Surveillance Capitalism: The Fight for a Human Future at the New Frontier of Power* (PublicAffairs, 2019).

exaggerated when the alternative performance measures such as customer satisfaction ratings are managed from the employer's perspective.[16] The second intersects with automatically produced personal data (some that is monetised) over which the data subject has no control. Both information-centred challenges:

- share a common characteristic, namely that the data/information deficit on which they rely disempowers vulnerable workers in crucial market interactions;
- determine data as a commodity with monetised value rather than as personal and essential to the integrity of the data subject and her privacy; and
- each are available for AI-assisted information technologies[17] to create data loops[18] that have potential to remedy information deficits and rebalance power asymmetries.

Putting faith in a derivative of market-centred self-regulation to address information deficits and power asymmetries invites critical reflection on the somewhat-concealed neoliberal assumption concerning the market as a sufficient regulatory paradigm. In practice, market regulatory potency is blunted by structural power asymmetries in the existing labour market arrangements. As such, 'collective bargaining power' from the worker perspective is apocryphal, even illusory when labour is so individuated and undermined. That said, informed participation as the essential conditions for sustainable self-regulation is designed to counter conventional regulatory capture, powerful to powerless,[19] and obviate any reliance on illusive market competition which the regulatory model cannot totally ensure. These conditions underpin the confidence in *inclusive, participatory self-regulation.*[20]

---

[16]   S O'Connor, 'Let gig workers control their data too', *Financial Times* (2018) <https://www.ft.com/content/a72f7e56-3724-11e8-8b98-2f31af407cc8>.

[17]   By AI-assisted information technologies, we include the gamut of increasingly quotidian 'weak' AI/algorithmic processes that run in the background of technologies that we increasingly take for granted: social media news feeds, search engines, smartphones and applications.

[18]   That is, sharing aggregated user data with platform users themselves.

[19]   JL Short, 'Self-Regulation in the Regulatory Void: "Blue Moon" or "Bad Moon"?' (2013) 649(1) *The Annals of the American Academy of Political and Social Science* 22.

[20]   Much of the literature on inclusive self-regulation comes from the education sector and focuses on the classroom context with diverse student demographics. For an interesting analysis connecting self-regulation in the workplace to issues of resiliency, see M Rothstein, M McLarnon and G King, 'The Role of Self-Regulation in Workplace Resiliency' (2016) 9(2) *Industrial and Organizational Psychology* 416. There is much more discussion of participatory self-regulation in the workplace, but it has a heavy

Introducing AI to further disrupt a fictitious bargaining model is not going to be achieved through internal or external regulation alone. Even if information deficits are filled through information looping, and vulnerable market players are empowered as a consequence, there needs to develop a counter-narrative which values labour in terms of utility rather than through structurally inequitable technologised oligopolies. *AI for profit* market priorities exacerbate the fundamental power asymmetries underpinning labour devaluing. The apparent unfairness of these asymmetries is a consequence of discourses that only monetarise the value of labour as a commodity within the deregulated production model, ignoring external and predominant themes of social good such as job security.

Moving on from a more general labour force, the critique of neoliberalist devaluing and disempowerment, and its socially negative consequences for the disaffected and dispossessed, this chapter has two purposes. First is to reveal how the application of new AI technologies can both advance and ambush neoliberal market primacies, depending on the priorities which are fed into machine driven learning and application design. The special focus for AI applications is on market forces for information empowerment/disempowerment. Second is a more contentious and speculative line of thinking. Global crises more often than not promote international engagement. True it is that in the early reactions to the COVID-19 threat, parochial, state interests stood in the way of any genuinely integrated and global response, about which the UN Secretary General was scathing. But as the search for a vaccine intensified, and the realisation that economic recession could be a global reality sunk in, transnational engagement at least has come to the fore.[21] Realising

---

focus on tripartism and ideas of stakeholder engagement in the more conventional state/employer/worker paradigm: see, for example, C Estlund, 'Rebuilding the Law of the Workplace in an Era of Self-Regulation' (2005) 105 *Columbia Law Review* 319. This chapter is proposing something different – self-regulation wherein market players are included and participate in an empowered environment of information access. Self-regulation empowerment programmes again are not uncommon in a classroom setting: see, for example, TJ Cleary and BJ Zimmerman, 'Self-regulation empowerment program: A school-based program to enhance self-regulated and self-motivated cycles of student learning' (2004) 41(5) *Psychology in the Schools* 537. Empowerment is essential for inclusive participatory self-regulation. It is a novel approach in workplace engagement. The UN's Food and Agriculture Organisation has done some interesting work on self-regulation, information access and gender empowerment which resonates with our model's intentions: see S Isenberg, 'Investing in information and communication technologies to reach gender equality and empower rural women', *Food and Agriculture Organization of the United Nations* (2019) <http://www.fao.org/policy-support/tools-and-publications/resources-details/en/c/1195147/>.

[21] This statement should not down-play the unfortunate parochial politicking between the USA and China regarding responsibility and the USA and the WHO

state-centred protectionism is exacerbating both negative health and economic consequences, it is now more possible that a changed world of labour relations which cannot carelessly realise profit without social sustainability and human capital consideration could eventuate in new forms of labour valuing, even if this is not achieved in a pre-virus vocabulary.[22] Law would likely have a role in ensuring this shift from commodification to the market/social, in the face of neoliberal opportunism and regression (as Polanyi would wish).

2.   REGULATION AS MARKET STIMULUS?

John Braithwaite's work on enforced self-regulation,[23] from which we have drawn inspiration, offers a balance between internally moderated and settled compliance measures, an information pathway for highlighting intentional and recurrent non-compliance, and external oversight for correction, repositioning and, if necessary, penalty. On top of his model, a condition of automatic information sharing to lessen the internal power asymmetries that he recognises in market settings where power is a consequence of organisational hierarchies is available through AI-assisted disruption. In addition, the proposed regulatory model harnesses to follow technology which in its current form is responsible for information deficit, to provide a facility for information access and inclusion. It is assumed that AI-assisted decision-making and data-driven technologies can support and enliven self-regulatory actors or forces by ensuring wider information sharing in a climate of openness and inclusion, through information access and clearer explanations of how algorithms impact employment decisions.[24]

---

concerning complicity, both of which emerge out of anxiety governance and are the divisive discourse of populism. Also critics such as Gordon Brown believe that multi-lateral governance has failed: 'In the coronavirus crisis, our leaders are failing us', *The Guardian* (2020) <https://www.theguardian.com/commentisfree/2020/mar/13/coronavirus-crisis-leaders-failing-gordon-brown>.

[22]   Seeing gig workers as essential in the pandemic context has not produced better wages or more job security. However, as with the re-evaluation of the importance of migrant labour in Singapore as this sector has been impacted by quarantined incubation, consideration of workers as more than economic units offers new opportunities to conceive their human dignity and work life quality.

[23]   J Braithwaite, 'Enforced Self-Regulation: A New Strategy for Corporate Crime Control' (1982) 80(7) *Michigan Law Review* 1466.

[24]   Later we discuss the mechanics of information looping, the possible resistance to it from platform providers, and the inducements for eventual compliance and participation. Although it may also be a necessary eventual precondition for a more balanced information playing field, we do not envisage formal algorithm explainability or auditing in this model.

In making this assertion, it is not enough to hold that more information means more inclusion, more market power and more empowered regulatory influence. It is recognised that along with information enrichment, there is a need for enabling external market modifications that make more likely the involvement of better informed labour-force stakeholders to understand and participate in the decision processes and outcomes which are assisted by AI.[25] Through the inclusion in decision-making of a wider audience of interest, the regulatory project will be targeted at satisfying a greater range of legitimate regulatory imperatives.[26] Injecting AI-assisted information technologies into the regulatory frame as mutualised capacities for open-access information, but with the specific intentions of revealing and making accountable AI-assisted employment decision-making and data collection, will meet some of the criticisms about capture and power imbalance that reverberate through the self-regulation literature.[27] In this way, AI is a regulatory medium with a regulatory focus.

There are dangers that the common absence of accountability and participatory democracy in some forms of self-regulation,[28] and market power imbalance in labour valuing, will minimise the regulatory force and protective functions for labour at risk – hence, the intention to include facilities for greater data access and inclusivity to counteract the negative influence of market power asymmetries.[29] In addition, through enforced self-regulation, there will be facilities for exposing non-compliance and thereby seeking the assistance of an external regulatory presence.

---

[25] There is space here to detail the nature of AI information systems which we see as appropriate beyond building into surveillance technologies information loop capacities specifically framed for aggregated data access by workers and, in some cases, customers.

[26] In keeping with the 'social-good' regulatory motivation, vulnerable market participants are the subjects of inclusion and participation. It is assumed that powerful market players such as platform providers, already well serviced with employment data, will not require the model's assistance to participate.

[27] See work by Short (n 19); F Haines, *The Paradox of Regulation: What Regulation Can Achieve and What it Cannot* (Edward Elgar Publishing, 2011).

[28] N Gunningham and J Rees, 'Industry Self-Regulation: An Institutional Perspective' (1997) 19(4) *Law & Policy* 363.

[29] These market power asymmetries resultant from forces for dis-embedding have led to disputation over responsibility for anxiety and disaffection. They are also at the heart of wider regulatory challenges in ensuring better work-life quality for gig workers, which is not the focus of the present analysis.

3.   THE PRECARIAT: VISIBILITIES AND INVISIBILITIES – BLINKERING THE REGULATOR

Gig workers straddle a compounded precarity of unconventional labour standards and conditions pertaining to, for example, healthcare benefits resulting from injury sustained at work. Somewhat perversely most platform operators deny such responsibility to their workers (employees or contractors) while denying the worker a stake in capturing, digitalising, using and marketing data of their work-life experiences.[30] In the platform ecosystem, consumers of communication become data, and that data is a force both for empowering the powerful (platform providers) and dis-empowering the weak (subjects of data surveillance). Through mass digitalised surveillance, worker engagement is both mitigated as privacy dissolves (when consent to this intrusion is an irrevocable condition for access to work) and personal data monetising encapsulates Proudhon's observation that *property is theft.*[31]

The explosion of platform-centred worker engagement suggests that a combination of management/service delivery automation and better but segmented information and communication technology systems will exacerbate the 'fissured workplace'.[32] David Weil traces new labour anxieties down to the changing nature of work and its organization.[33] In a similar vein, Guy Standing notes the global rise of *the precariat* – workers who share economic and social insecurities as a function of international movements of capital away from conventional means of production to data environments.[34] More recently, the literature around precarity and gig work has started to focus on the figure of the platform worker, finding typically fragmented work-life experience through platform applications.[35]

---

[30]   An important consequence of more open data access in the regulatory frame is the inclusion of secondary data monetising as an – up until now – largely concealed feature of work-life quality.

[31]   The application of Proudhon's aphorism against the commodification of digitised property is discussed in M Findlay, *Law's Regulatory Relevance? Property, Power and Market Economies* (Edward Elgar Publishing, 2017).

[32]   D Weil, *The Fissured Workplace* (Harvard University Press, 2014).

[33]   Ibid.

[34]   G Standing, *A Precariat Charter: From Denizens to Citizens* (Bloomsbury, 2014).

[35]   V De Stefano, 'The rise of the just-in-time workforce: On-demand work, crowdwork, and labor protection in the gig-economy' (2015) 37 *Comparative Labor Law & Policy Journal* 471; Prassl (n 14).

The relationship between labour and capital has never been more open to question due to the nature of *datafication*.[36] Despite the diversification of labour commodification through datafication, evolving largely beyond the knowledge of data subjects, implications for labour are gaining traction amidst a wide if sporadic spectrum of worker pushbacks against tech companies.[37] Much of this resistance is against surveillance technologies and employer intrusion into worker privacy and personal dignity. Unfortunately from the perspective of vulnerable stakeholder empowerment, little of this mundane resistance translates into any detailed discussion of worker empowerment through access to secondary data automatically produced via surveillance. In contemporary service-delivery markets, an often-undisclosed relationship between data and profit stimulates the commodification of employment and surveillance data.[38]

From its initial conception, platform work was imagined and sold as a pathway towards greater individual freedom and autonomy.[39] Workers, it was said, would have the autonomy to choose when, where and how they wanted to work. In doing so, the platforms would expand labour opportunities to areas and communities where such openings were previously limited.[40] Accepting at best that this does not represent gig workers whose options are platform labour or nothing, the argument that these systems are merely 'digital interfaces' or 'frictionless marketplaces'[41] denies the employment relation-

---

[36] Datafication is a process whereby relationships, behaviours and essential human experiences are reduced to data, and thereby are more amenable to commodification. V Mayer-Schönberger and K Cukier, *Big Data: A Revolution That Will Transform How We Live, Work, and Think* (Houghton Mifflin Harcourt, 2013).

[37] E Smith, 'A memo to big tech: The techlash against Amazon, Facebook and Google – and what they can do', *The Economist* (2018) <https://www.economist.com/briefing/2018/01/20/the-techlash-against-amazon-facebook-and-google-and-what-they-can-do>.

[38] N van Doorn and A Badger, 'Platform Capitalism's Hidden Abode: Producing Data Assets in the Gig Economy', *Antipode* (2020) <https://onlinelibrary.wiley.com/doi/full/10.1111/anti.12641>. See also J Sadowski, 'When Data is Capital: Datafication, Accumulation, and Extraction' (2019) (6)(1) *Big Data & Society* 1.

[39] A Shapiro, 'Between Autonomy and Control: Strategies of Arbitrage in the "On-demand" Economy' (2018) 20(8) *New Media & Society* 2954.

[40] G Valenduc and P Vendramin, 'Work in the Digital Economy: Sorting the Old from the New' (2016) ETUI Research Paper – Working Paper 2016.3, *SSRN Innovation Law and Policy eJournal* <https://papers.ssrn.com/sol3/papers.cfm?abstract_id=2770405>.

[41] 'Digital platforms like Uber and Airbnb harness the power of the internet to offer a frictionless marketplace that powerfully matches supply and demand so as to make whole new sets of assets available to customers': N Radjou, 'Tackling Big Global Challenges with Low-Cost Innovation' *Harvard Business Review* (2016) <https://hbr.org/2016/02/tackling-big-global-challenges-with-low-cost-innovation>.

ship between the platform and its workers and ignores/hides/evades labour laws where they exist and have purchase. In addition, platform operators are crafting and relying on new discourses of engagement and disengagement (talking of independent contracting and new connections between provider and customer) designed to obscure the absence of conventional obligations and responsibilities of employer and employee interdependence.

More recently, critical analyses have sought to lift this mask.[42] The reality of gig workers' employment lifestyles reaches a more sanguine consensus of low wages, poor conditions and unpredictable income streams.[43] In addition to discriminatory labour terms, there are the invasions of worker space in the name of surveillance which further challenge worker dignity and the reality of free choice. While there are genuine productivity and customer satisfaction motivations for some transparency surveillance, even the best intentioned comes at a cost of privacy and worker dignity. More sophisticated surveillance devices work by human tracking – both physically and electronically – and the concealing of information thus collected through unaccountable and non-transparent algorithmic management are increasing across working environments. Particularly for gig workers, such tracking and data collection are becoming the norm in their work life experience. According to one report, 22% of platform providers[44] around the world are collecting data on their employee's movements, 17% monitor computer use, and 16% monitor their staff's calendars.[45] Amazon fulfilment centers monitor and track their employees for performance standards,[46] while Walmart patented technology that would let them listen in on customers' conversations with their employees. Cogito is an AI company whose goal is to 'make workers more effective by giving them real-time feedback'. Under efficiency justifications, the software listens in to conversations at calls centres and tallies scores onto a dashboard

---

[42]   AJ Wood et al, 'Networked but Commodified: The (Dis)Embeddedness of Digital Labour in the Gig Economy' (2019) 53(5) *Sociology* 931; Prassl (n 14).

[43]   N Srnicek, *Platform Capitalism* (John Wiley, 2017). See also J Rubery et al, 'Challenges and Contradictions in the "Normalising" of Precarious Work' (2018) 32(3) *Work, Employment and Society* 509; A Tassinari and V Maccarrone, 'Riders on the Storm: Workplace Solidarity among Gig Economy Couriers in Italy and the UK' (2019) 34(1) *Work, Employment and Society* 35.

[44]   This term covers enterprises which, through employment and service provision platforms, make money by connecting customers to a largely uncontracted and under-regulated labour force, for significant agency profit.

[45]   E Woollacott, 'Should you be monitoring your staff with AI?' *Raconteur* (2019) <https://www.raconteur.net/technology/ai-workplace-surveillance>.

[46]   Ibid.

that can then be viewed by supervisors.[47] Percolata uses sensors in stores to calculate a productivity score for workers. Earlier this year, it was revealed that DoorDash was surveilling gratuity payments and using tips to substitute for workers' base wages.[48]

Worker surveillance is not a new phenomenon: earlier motivations for worker surveillance related to delegating supervision responsibility and decentralising accountability frames (so oversight was passed on laterally and horizontally), which are still familiar today. Researchers previously made the argument that just-in-time (JIT) and total quality control (TQC) represented enhanced managerial oversight through improved surveillance technologies, and governed workers' life experience. This was said to be preferable to delegating supervisory roles to workers.[49] They argued that:

> The development and continued refinement of electronic surveillance systems using computer-based technology can provide the means by which management can achieve the benefits that derive from the delegation of responsibility to teams *while retaining authority and disciplinary control* through ownership of the superstructure of surveillance and the information it collects, retains, and disseminates.[50]

Others similarly observe:

> The tendency towards decentralization expresses itself, not in the autonomy of individuals, but in the increasing arrangement of social life by centralized systems… [since] an IT infrastructure can help overcome spatial constraints on organisations, such that it becomes possible to orchestrate widely disseminated sites of production *as if* they are centralized – flexibility is gained without loss of control.[51]

Nonetheless, what is new about surveillance in the platform/gig setting is an employment terrain where worker engagement is heavily organised through algorithmic management and communicated across high tech information platforms.[52] The platform and the surveillance are interconnected techno-systems.

---

[47]   K Roose, 'A Machine May Not Take Your Job, but One Could Become Your Boss', *The New York Times* (2019) <https://www.nytimes.com/2019/06/23/technology/artificial-intelligence-ai-workplace.html>.

[48]   K Roose, 'After Uproar, Instacart Backs Off Controversial Tipping Policy', *The New York Times* (2019) <https://www.nytimes.com/2019/02/06/technology/instacart-doordash-tipping-deliveries.html>.

[49]   G Sewell and B Wilkinson, '"Someone to Watch Over Me": Surveillance, Discipline and the Just-in-Time Labour Process' (1992) 26(2) *Sociology* 271.

[50]   Ibid 283 (emphasis added).

[51]   F Webster and K Robins, 'I'll Be Watching You: Comment on Sewell and Wilkinson' (1993) 27(2) *Sociology* 243, 247.

[52]   A Rosenblat and L Stark, 'Algorithmic Labor and Information Asymmetries: A Case Study of Uber's Drivers' (2016) 10 *International Journal of Communication* 27.

The extent and intrusion of such surveillance is profound, and the platform technology syncs it into the work-life quality of gig workers. Better seen as a dynamic to disempower worker engagement through privacy intrusion, the capture of personal data and its unauthorised commodification through algorithmic observation aligns with earlier trends of control as discipline in the workplace.[53]

In its current incarnation, and of additional and certainly not lesser importance, surveillance produces commodifiable data generating prescient concerns about data control, access, possession, portability and integrity. The algorithmic management of surveillance data about people's work-lives and working patterns also provokes issues of transparency, explainability and accountability that are at the heart of principled-based AI governance strategies.

The pandemic has realised a much more invasive and overarching surveillance society, within which notions of positive surveillance are couched in life-saving terms. As long as pandemic and post-pandemic surveillance proliferates and entrenches, justified by the specious necessity to prioritise health and safety above privacy and individual rights, it will be more difficult to call out situations of surveillance, often insidious and unseen simply because they make the platform provider wealthy at the cost of worker self-determination.

Is it possible to flip intrusive surveillance mechanisms used to monitor worker amenability into shared information repositories which equally make platform operators and corporate managers accountable for the types of behaviors that they reward and punish? The regulatory model advocated later sees this possibility as a beneficial outcome in terms of empowerment through information access and data proliferation transparency. Comprehensively, from a regulatory angle, the outcomes of algorithmic governance can be required to make visible the motivations and actions of the surveiller and the surveilled. Whether this is through algorithmic justice conventions or more specific feed-back looping that informs all stakeholders about the production of personal data and logs use (or a complementary combination of both), surveillance technology has a capacity, appropriately directed, to disrupt this one-way data streaming.

Gandini has highlighted how many gig platforms embed forms of individual/personal investment at the heart of the labour process as a result of performance evaluation such as role feedback, ranking and consumer rating systems designed to calibrate social interaction between workers and consum-

---

[53] The literature on the relationship between surveillance and disempowerment is well established, and the workplace as a space for discipline and disempowerment is generally recognised. See M Foucault, *Discipline and Punish: The Birth of the Prison* (Penguin Books, 1991). Interestingly, a better translation from the French is 'Surveillance' and punish.

ers/clients.[54] Gig work's reliance on rating systems is more than a necessary evil as part of a decentred performance system where consumer satisfaction is a crucial market variable. Rating the worth of labour on how it is received by a more empowered market player leads to an intensification of worker estrangement by tying their value to an 'economy of feeling' which might or might not be concerned with productivity.

The commodification of labour in a market model driven by profit for the owner of the means of production and by under-valued wages for the worker is presently inevitable in technologised neoliberal labour markets, if unlikely to last into the medium-term future as currently configured.[55] During this phase of transition in labour markets and the re-imagining of property relations associated with capital and production, the introduction of big data and AI into the human/machine interface has capacities either to exacerbate or resolve power imbalances inherent in recent commodification models, depending on the nature and inclusive reach of regulatory control. As such, the regulator needs to swing back the power shift within conventional market models, using regulatory technologies designed in other eras of labour arrangements, or look at new regulatory relationships and styles which, rather than being determined by advancing market profitability and minimising labour involvement, work on information transparency and inclusive access to offer new solidarities.

Ideally, if the shift to modern AI-assisted occupation environments leads to new solidarities forming across vulnerable market participants, then through stimulating the visibility of sociality forums or social media communities, more equitable solidarities can generate. In these informal regulatory realms mundane dissent builds normative pressure on platform providers to recognise the hypocrisy of denying employment arrangements, while demanding the power to intrude into worker behaviours and their personal data as if such obligatory relationships are in place.

4.   EVALUATING THE REGULATION OF LABOUR ENGAGEMENT IN THE DIGITAL ECONOMY

Despite the currently inhospitable work-life environment for many in the gig economy, the literature that has sought better prospects for workers has thus far rarely interrogated how new forms of data relations and digitalisation mediate the organisation of power in labour markets. Presently, with the broad

---

[54]   A Gandini, 'Labour process theory and the gig economy' (2019) 72(6) *Human Relations* 1039.

[55]   P Moriarty and D Honnery, 'Three Futures: Nightmare, Diversion, Vision' (2018) 74(2) *World Futures* 51.

acceptance of the digitalisation of so many aspects of life, data and politics become increasingly intertwined. The dual communication/commodification frames of data infrastructures and pathways of data access now mean that big data is employed largely for commercial profit and data is viewed as a marketable 'thing'. Shoshana Zuboff argues that this profit motivation has led to a new form of capitalism – where big technology platforms extract 'surplus data' in the form of behavioural data and trade on their proprietary analytical (predictive) value.[56] The platform, as such, sucks up profit while the user/ service provider simply generates data to be sold on. Responding to this argument, Couldry and Mejias have argued that rather than marking a new stage of capitalism, data relations run parallel with labour relations in a market for data that can never be beyond the machine.[57] The once-observed dominant role of labour as the means of production in more conventional capitalist iterations is now replaced by data commodification (through surreptitious surveillance technologies) as a primary market driver. What happens to worker engagement and work-life quality as labour value retreats in the face of encompassing data commodification?

Unlike Couldry and Mejias's envisaging of data colonialism mirroring the function of historical colonialism, it would be entirely possible for data profit to outpace labour profit in the market. This would be as a parasitic dynamic where data feeds from labour. For this to occur, data commodification needs the datafication of human experience[58] to grow as a market commodity. Data extraction necessitates the mining of human experience, which is in turn rationalised into data messages abstract from human life and thereby something which is exchangeable.[59] The digitalisation and datafication of human activity as assets thereby contributes to a significant transformation in value creation that marks the platform labour-capital relationship.

Out from these observations there are disempowering market influences operating in tandem. The first is surveillance capitalism, extracting data from life experience and commodifying it for market exchange. The second draws from Benanav's observations of a deepening economic stagnation that manifests as mass underemployment, being a natural consequence of the neoliberal wealth creation cycle but blamed as the result of globalisation.[60] The combined effect of these regressive forces sees the extraction of data for profit exploiting

---

[56]   Zuboff (n 15).

[57]   N Couldry and UA Mejias, *The Costs of Connection: How Data is Colonizing Human Life and Appropriating It for Capitalism* (Stanford University Press, 2019).

[58]   Mayer-Schönberger and Cukier (n 36).

[59]   Couldry and Mejias (n 57).

[60]   A Benanav, 'Automation and the Future of Work – I' (2019) 119 *New Left Review* 5.

that underemployment, both by decreasing labour's share of income through concentrating returns to those at the top of platform management *and* by furthering the capacity for breaking jobs into segmented tasks and thus *adding* to what Graham and Anwar have identified as the planetary labour market.[61] This notion places tasks as sub-labour forms which are disaggregated while still connected to more consolidated labour objectives. Disaggregation in this way further fractures sustainable wage labour by making workers dependent on what the platform chooses to commercialise, a decision which is driven by profit and not by socially embedding market relations.

Amir Anwar argued about the consequences of disaggregation and alienation:

> The contemporary gig economy represents the latest manifestation of the restructuring of capitalism...advancements made in digital technologies have generated new divisions of labour, defined as the specialisation or separation of tasks between different types of workers...on platforms, commodification of labour power is made possible as thousands of workers compete globally for digital tasks...for Marx, alienation of workers is at the heart of capitalist production... Alienation is even more present in the way the global gig economy is organised and controlled. Job descriptions on platforms are often vague and unspecified, the client is looking for workers with the lower rates rather than a certain skill set. Workers do not know who their client is. The fact that workers are competing for short-term gigs like these means that they have less incentive to know what they are creating, for who and to what purposes. Thus, the more work they do, the more alienated they become...[62]

If these observations hold true for engineers, technicians and other professionals throughout the AI ecosystem it may be little more than wishful thinking to talk of principled design. The attribution and distribution of ethical responsibility for AI technology and algorithm applications of big data depend on recognising and mediating client intention and product purpose.

The nature of data market relationships within digital employment arrangements highlights information deficits, surreptitious data acquisitions, and irresponsible data commodification that have become institutional features of work-life quality. Data commodification includes monetary value that might be created secondary to work being done, either emerging from surveillance technologies at places of employment, or through the collection and selling of client/service-provider data through third-party brokers. Just by one's interaction with – or perhaps in proximity to – digital platforms and their surveillance capacities, data is produced and potentially commodified. Van Doorn and

---

[61] M Graham and M Anwar, 'The global gig economy: Towards a planetary labour market?' (2019) 24(4) *First Monday*.

[62] A Anwar, 'How Marx predicted the worst effects of the gig economy more than 150 years ago', *NS Tech, New Statesman* (2018) <https://tech.newstatesman.com/guest-opinion/karl-marx-gig-economy>.

Badger have pointed out that through their production of raw data, gig workers engage in 'dual value production' in the following manner:

> ...besides extracting rent *from* each transaction they orchestrate, platforms can also extract data *about* these transactions, which means that gig workers can likewise be understood to provide an 'informational service' to platforms... [as such] the monetary value produced by the service provided is augmented by the use and speculative value of data produced before, during, and after service provision.[63]

Inverting worker productivity from labour to data, and revaluing labour worth against data marketisation, is the context from which the regulatory effort needs to reposition workers centrally within this new employment dynamic. At the very least, if data, compulsorily extracted and unaccountably commodified, remains out of the reach of work-place bargaining, then any regulatory focus on labour productivity alone will miss touching the reality of new market arrangements. Add to this anonymous human engagement across platform service provision, the human/machine interface (each dehumanising) and the position of workers in any counter regulatory frame becomes an essential consideration in its potential impact in reasserting labour value and worker integrity.

The organization of workers in the digital economy[64] is an important aspect to consider in empowerment projects. As workers on digital platforms become increasingly atomised and geographically dispersed, it is more difficult for them to organise and participate in social dialogue and collective bargaining.[65] Moreover, the concentration of global digital platforms limits workers' bargaining power which is usually temporarily and spatially bound. In this context policymakers need to ensure that the value, in terms of productivity gains that may emerge from digitalisation, is distributed in a fair manner between labour and capital, and that workers understand it as an asset of their work-life, or contain it if they do not want their personal data monetised.[66]

---

[63]   van Doorn and Badger (n 38) 1475 (emphasis in original).

[64]   This is a much-misused term. It means more now than any economy based on computing technology communication. Specifically it has come to include all forms of internet markets and web-based commerce. Digital economies feature the mobility of intangibles and business platforms. For this analysis, digital economies are focused on the commodification of data, and the central place of data transacting for economic outcomes.

[65]   AJ Wood, V Lehdonvirta and M Graham, 'Workers of the Internet unite? Online freelancer organisation among remote gig economy workers in six Asian and African countries' (2018) 33(2) *New Technology, Work and Employment* 95.

[66]   United Nations Conference on Trade and Development, *Digital Economy Report 2019: Value Creation and Capture: Implications for Developing Countries* (2019).

Recognising automation, dispersal and disempowerment, regulatory poli-cymakers need to craft styles that integrate currently isolated market players (workers in particular). The aim here is that with access to more and better information, the participation of the latter in the regulatory enterprise may be rewarding, and consequently open up greater appreciations of their labour value and their personal integrity.

Underpinning such regulatory inclusion is the necessity to respond to labour disruptions with a worker-focus for the foundational motivation of market sustainability. This is often under-emphasised in digital economy contexts, where labour is virtual and labour relations are transient and porous. Turning power dispersal intentions into policy outcomes requires mindfulness of how digital economies – and platform-based arrangements in particular – value (or devalue) labour, and how transiting labour as data to magnify market profit is achieved through concealed data processing rather than accountable and inclusive transactions.

Workers in platform arrangements are presently the largely passive objects of what is known; they are excluded from any further benefit through the com-modified valuation of their data by conscious veils of ignorance thrown around their market positioning by the platforms.[67] Reflecting on empowering forms of labour engagement in such a market of data exclusivity (through worker organisations or market cooperatives) and adapting their benefits to a platform economy will require regulation at the point that other market players acquire data about work-life behaviours and commercially act on that knowledge. The problem facing conventional organised labour solidarity as a power balance in such contexts is that the scope of ignorance about digitisation goes much further than the individual worker and their market positioning.

Minus the opportunity or likelihood of organised labour counter-movements operating in digital economies, if regulation is to rebalance market power in the direction of labour-force, the regulator should recognise and employ the importance of digital infrastructure as part of the problem and part of the solution. From such thinking, and unique in this argument, is the opportunity for turning AI-assisted information technology towards the regulatory disrup-tion of exclusionist platform power imbalance. As previously suggested, this would represent a positive regulatory development if such incorporation was for the purposes of illuminating the decision-making process that comprises the interface between human agency and AI, as well as their consequences that ought to be regulated.

---

[67] Srnicek (n 43). See also M Kenney and J Zysman, 'Work and Value Creation in the Platform Economy' in S Vallas and A Kovalainen (eds), *Work and Labor in the Digital Age, Vol. 33* (Emerald Publishing, 2018) ch 1.

In parallel with political empowerment through technological augmentation to regulatory purposes, Morozov furthered Mayer-Schönberger and Ramge's identification of 'feedback data'[68] as a future site of empowerment politics[69] by arguing that:

> We need to widen the scope of the concept and consider 'feedback infrastructure' itself: the ownership and operation of the means of producing 'feedback data' are at least as important as the question of who owns the data itself. The crucial battles ahead will involve the role of this 'feedback infrastructure' in the reinvention of the political projects of both left and right.[70]

The concept of transactional openness via feedback infrastructure is more appealing for regulatory efficiency than contested arguments about data owners. As such, productive regulatory discussions move away from confronting predatory and exclusive data ownership/control, to being involved in the active shaping of data dissemination. In this discourse, it becomes more impactful to expose resistance against data feedback, rather than engaging in debate over data ownership/control as the primary regulatory expression, and instead to create a worker-focused impetus for data openness. This is not an argument for the removal of barriers currently existing to regulate unencumbered flows of data,[71] but to highlight that in data assemblages[72] there are choices to be made in the conceptualisation of data and its subsequent movement from one set of social actors to another, which are implicated in entrenched power distributions. As has been argued by others about data valuing, 'data capture and its use to meet specific needs or interest are what makes it valuable; not data itself'.[73] It is preferable to shift the grounds for discussion away from boundary

---

[68] V Mayer-Schönberger and T Ramge, *Reinventing Capitalism in the Age of Big Data* (Basic Books, 2018).

[69] A concept that encompasses social, economic and political empowerment usually through organisational inclusion, but in this situation, more as a result of regulatory intervention with power dispersal as its political purpose.

[70] E Morozov, 'Digital Socialism? The Calculation Debate in the Age of Big Data' (2019) 116/117 *New Left Review* 33.

[71] To provide participants with masses of personalised or non-aggregated data would open up real privacy and integrity concerns which would undermine the success of efforts for information looping.

[72] R Kitchin and T Lauriault, 'Towards Critical Data Studies: Charting and Unpacking Data Assemblages and Their Work' in J Thatcher, J Eckert and A Shears (eds), *Thinking Big Data in Geography: New Regimes, New Research* (University of Nebraska Press, 2014) ch 1.

[73] AJ Lee and PS Cook, 'The myth of the "data-driven" society: Exploring the interactions of data interfaces, circulations, and abstractions' (2019) 14(1) *Sociology Compass*.

formations around data – data as a form of property – to looking at the ways in which data friction[74] might be enhanced or smoothed out when the processes of labour are increasingly datafied.

An important driver behind re-empowering worker engagement is not humanity alone, but a much harsher recognition that while its labour is further devalued through new and more vicious divisions of labour (as an appendage to an app), the commodification of work-life data about human experience argues for workers' reclaiming an essential position as a means of production. As Stewart and Stanford suggest, the thin aura of innovation surrounding pro-motional arguments for gig economies[75] can as easily be understood as some ahistorical, anti-regulation reversion. This 'innovation/liberation' discourse that speaks about freeing up under-used resources and empowering freelanced labour washes away generations of struggle against exploitation for fairer market conditions covering disempowered stakeholders. As such this battle for legitimate discourse is more than what meaning one accepts, but who wins and who loses from which side the regulator sits.

5.   INCLUSIVE, PARTICIPATORY SELF-REGULATION AS A WAY FORWARD?

Moving from information deficits and market power asymmetries which are exacerbated by algorithmic obscurity and platform containment, an important step in activating the regulatory enterprise is to provide access for stakeholders to essential information managed and manipulated by platform providers.[76] As this information revelation evolves, platform stakeholders and key market players involved in the platform's monetising of secondary data can better contribute to inclusive participatory self-regulation, turning secretive and com-bative data protection posturing into more open data sharing as the precursor to regulatory responsibility. To achieve this transition, the regulatory project may need to progress along a continuum – from command and control to enforced

---

[74]   J Bates, 'The politics of data friction' (2018) 74(2) *Journal of Documentation* 412.

[75]   This term is chosen to cover a range of employment engagements, denying (by platform operators) the conventional status of employer/employee relationships, facili-tated through computer platform technology, said to more closely connect the customer with the service provider, and to expand opportunities for freelance work.

[76]   F Di Porto and M Zuppetta, 'Co-regulating algorithmic disclosure for digital platforms' (2020) *Policy and Society* 1.

self-regulation – as the benefits of the latter become clear to those who presently oppose regulatory openness.[77]

It is anticipated that in the first stage of the regulatory model, there will be impediments to information openness. These impediments are technical and operational:

- locating and identifying automatically produced personal data on regulatory recipients (primarily vulnerable workers and their customers);
- respecting data privacy if the data is not anonymous in its feedback form or not aggregated in bulk;
- introducing AI-assisted technologies to notify regulatory recipients of data production, storage and use;
- creating convenient paths of open access which recognise commercially sensitive data that may attach to automatically produced personal data;
- ensuring internal privacy protections covering the identity of data subjects;
- educating regulatory recipients in the use and utility of AI-assisted information technologies and their data pathways;
- enabling regulatory recipients with simple tools to analyse the significance of automatically produced personal data; and in the spirit of enforced self-regulation;
- activating and enabling an 'honest broker' third party/agency to ensure that conditions covering access are complied with.

Arguments about data ownership and who bears the responsibility and cost for establishing this access and information framework will need to be settled at the 'command and control' end of the regulatory model (between a relevant state agency and the platform managers/administrators). This will require the processes of arbitration so that fundamental disputes have an orderly and legitimate resolution at the hands of an honest third party. Experience from the operation of 'data trusts'[78] no doubt would be helpful in these negotiations, where third party intervention adds legitimacy to resolutions in dispute.

In present day platform environments, the adoption and construction of information infrastructures such as those identified above concentrate and polarise power in the hands of the platform operators, while regulators and their regulated entities are largely excluded from these information pathways.

---

[77] M Findlay, 'Regulating Regulation – Who Guards the Guardian', in *Contemporary Challenges in Regulating Global Crises* (Palgrave Macmillan, 2013) ch 9.

[78] C Reed and I Ng, 'Data Trusts as an AI Governance Mechanism' (2019) <https://papers.ssrn.com/sol3/papers.cfm?abstract_id=3334527>. See also S Delacroix and N Lawrence, 'Bottom-up data Trusts: disturbing the "one size fits all" approach to data governance' (2019) 9(4) *International Data Privacy Law* 236.

In the initial stage of the regulatory enterprise, the problems facing effective engagement with disempowered market players in participatory self-regulation boil down to the likely 'capture' of ill-informed and data-starved stakeholders by more data powerful participants (including external regulators). Capture is not only a consequence of obscuring rather than revealing the nature, purpose and processes of data, but will also arise if regulatory participants do not understand and share the regulatory purpose of information emancipation. Opening up data access in a manner which encourages shared participation and trusting inclusion requires creating an information infrastructure which flattens structural imbalances by encouraging bottom-up data management models.[79] Obviously, this is more than a market structure issue. As a precondition in its development the information access technology and pathways should reflect a more equitable user-driven format.[80] The regulatory model will need to counter the current market reality that algorithmic intervention adds cash in the pockets of the information governors. The counter message against data as an exclusive commodity is more universal and widespread recognition of the need to protect automatically produced personal information from market abuse and data subject discrimination.[81] Once this message has been grounded in the regulatory enterprise, then other key players in market productivity (vulnerable regulatory recipients) need a place in an informed and inclusive decision-making interface, which will be the dispute resolution phase of the regulatory model. Only then will inclusive self-regulation grow to its potential for market power dispersal. So that this process will take root, state agencies as licensing authorities, for instance, could impose external conditions on market entry – making this dependent on arrangements for bottom-up information management and inclusive operational decision-making.

Today, not only are many platform operators denying users a place at the decision-making table, they are excluding users from information as a facility and a function for inclusive self-regulation, and thereby repudiating the need for a table around which to discuss grievances. Above this power-grab is the appetite for surveilling users as valuable data mines. If datafiction is driving such surveillance systems and contributing to information asymmetries, then it needs also to be productive for workers and self-regulatory mechanisms by

---

[79]   Delacroix and Lawrence (n 78).

[80]   An initial challenge lies in the current market reality that the platform providers claim ownership of the personal data automatically produced through commercial and surveillance technologies, and will resist any possibility that its value as a market commodity may be reduced through more open access. Data ownership determinations must not be a prohibitive precondition to the regulatory enterprise.

[81]   M Bakhoum et al, *Personal Data in Competition, Consumer Protection and Intellectual Property Law: Towards a Holistic Approach?* (Springer, 2018).

'feed[ing] such data back to users, enabling them to orient themselves in the world'.[82] Again, this highlights a very legitimate concern for regulation from a labour-force perspective. It is one thing for platform operators to surveil their workforce, justified by regulatory concerns for issues such as customer safety. It is another to use surveilled information for undisclosed commercial purposes which should be open to the subject's consent or dissent. An important by-product of the regulatory enterprise will be disseminating the information necessary for an informed debate among regulatory recipients concerning secondary data, its monetising, and possible negative impacts on work-life quality.

To complement a move away from regulatory elitism and towards participant inclusion through information access, important external players such as government agencies and labour organisations must ensure that labour-force is institutionally included in the regulatory process – both in its crafting and implementation. These are a priori external market requirements if information access is to contribute to regulatory empowerment as this analysis predicts.

BIBLIOGRAPHY

Bakhoum, M et al, *Personal Data in Competition, Consumer Protection and Intellectual Property Law: Towards a Holistic Approach?* (Springer, 2018)

Bates, J, 'The politics of data friction' (2018) 74(2) *Journal of Documentation* 412

Benanav, A, 'Automation and the Future of Work – I' (2019) 119 *New Left Review* 5

Braithwaite, J, 'Enforced Self-Regulation: A New Strategy for Corporate Crime Control' (1982) 80(7) *Michigan Law Review* 1466

Cleary, TJ and BJ Zimmerman, 'Self-regulation empowerment program: A school-based program to enhance self-regulated and self-motivated cycles of student learning' (2004) 41(5) *Psychology in the Schools* 537

Couldry, N and UA Mejias, *The Costs of Connection: How Data is Colonizing Human Life and Appropriating It for Capitalism* (Stanford University Press, 2019)

De Stefano, V, 'The rise of the just-in-time workforce: On-demand work, crowdwork, and labor protection in the gig-economy' (2015) 37 *Comparative Labor Law & Policy Journal* 471

Delacroix, S and N Lawrence, 'Bottom-up data Trusts: disturbing the "one size fits all" approach to data governance' (2019) 9(4) *International Data Privacy Law* 236

Di Porto, F and M Zuppetta, 'Co-regulating algorithmic disclosure for digital platforms' (2020) *Policy and Society* 1

Estlund, C, 'Rebuilding the Law of the Workplace in an Era of Self-Regulation' (2005) 105 *Columbia Law Review* 319

Findlay, M, 'Regulating Regulation – Who Guards the Guardian' in *Contemporary Challenges in Regulating Global Crises* (Palgrave Macmillan, 2013)

Foucault, M, *Discipline and Punish: The Birth of the Prison* (Penguin Books, 1991)

---

[82]　H Kennedy, T Poell and J van Dijck, 'Data and agency' (2015) 2(2) *Big Data & Society*.

Frey, CB, *The Technology Trap: Capital, Labor, and Power in the Age of Automation* (Princeton University Press, 2019)

Gandini, A, 'Labour process theory and the gig economy' (2019) 72(6) *Human Relations* 1039

Graham, M and M Anwar, 'The global gig economy: Towards a planetary labour market?' (2019) 24(4) *First Monday*

Gunningham, N and J Rees, 'Industry Self-Regulation: An Institutional Perspective' (1997) 19(4) *Law & Policy* 363

Haines, F, *The Paradox of Regulation: What Regulation Can Achieve and What it Cannot* (Edward Elgar Publishing, 2011)

Katta, S et al, '(Dis) embeddedness and (de) commodification: COVID-19, Uber, and the unravelling logics of the gig economy' (2020) 10(2) *Dialogues in Human Geography* 203

Kennedy, H, T Poell and J van Dijck, 'Data and agency' (2015) 2(2) *Big Data & Society*

Kenney, M and J Zysman, 'Work and Value Creation in the Platform Economy' in S Vallas and A Kovalainen (eds), *Work and Labor in the Digital Age, Vol. 33* (Emerald Publishing, 2018) ch 1

Kergel, D and R Hepp, 'Start Ups, Social Networking and Self-Tracking – The Neoliberal Freedom of the Entrepreneurial Self in the Digital Age' in T Rachwał, R Hepp and D Kergel (eds), *Precarious Places* (Springer, 2020) 139

Kitchin, R and T Lauriault, 'Towards Critical Data Studies: Charting and Unpacking Data Assemblages and Their Work' in J Thatcher, J Eckert and A Shears (eds), *Thinking Big Data in Geography: New Regimes, New Research* (University of Nebraska Press, 2014) ch 1

Kuhn, KM, 'The Rise of the "Gig Economy" and Implications for Understanding Work and Workers' (2016) 9(1) *Industrial and Organizational Psychology* 157

Kumar, T and LK Jena, 'Capital vs. Digital Labor in the Post-industrial Information Age: A Marxist Analysis' (2020) 6(1) *Emerging Economy Studies* 50

Lee, AJ and PS Cook, 'The myth of the "data-driven" society: Exploring the inter-actions of data interfaces, circulations, and abstractions' (2019) 14(1) *Sociology Compass*

Mayer-Schönberger, V and K Cukier, *Big Data: A Revolution That Will Transform How We Live, Work, and Think* (Houghton Mifflin Harcourt, 2013)

Mayer-Schönberger, V and T Ramge, *Reinventing Capitalism in the Age of Big Data* (Basic Books, 2018)

Moriarty, P and D Honnery, 'Three Futures: Nightmare, Diversion, Vision' (2018) 74(2) *World Futures* 51

Morozov, E, 'Digital Socialism? The Calculation Debate in the Age of Big Data' (2019) 116/117 *New Left Review* 33

Pasquale, FA, 'Tech Platforms and the Knowledge Problem' (2018) *American Affairs* (Summer) 3

Prassl, J, *Humans as a Service: The Promise and Perils of Work in the Gig Economy* (Oxford University Press, 2018)

Rosenblat, A and L Stark, 'Algorithmic Labor and Information Asymmetries: A Case Study of Uber's Drivers' (2016) 10 *International Journal of Communication* 27

Rothstein, M, M McLarnon and G King, 'The Role of Self-Regulation in Workplace Resiliency' (2016) 9(2) *Industrial and Organizational Psychology* 416

Rubery, J et al, 'Challenges and Contradictions in the "Normalising" of Precarious Work' (2018) 32(3) *Work, Employment and Society* 509

Sadowski, J, 'When data is capital: Datafication, accumulation, and extraction' (2019) (6)(1) *Big Data & Society* 1

Sewell, G and B Wilkinson, '"Someone to Watch Over Me": Surveillance, Discipline and the Just-in-Time Labour Process' (1992) 26(2) *Sociology* 271

Shapiro, A, 'Between autonomy and control: Strategies of arbitrage in the "on-demand" economy' (2018) 20(8) *New Media & Society* 2954

Short, JL, 'Self-Regulation in the Regulatory Void: "Blue Moon" or "Bad Moon"?' (2013) 649(1) *The Annals of the American Academy of Political and Social Science* 22

Srnicek, N, *Platform Capitalism* (John Wiley, 2017)

Standing, G, *A Precariat Charter: From Denizens to Citizens* (Bloomsbury, 2014)

Tassinari, A and V Maccarrone, 'Riders on the Storm: Workplace Solidarity among Gig Economy Couriers in Italy and the UK' (2019) 34(1) *Work, Employment and Society* 35

Vallas, S and J Schor, 'What do Platforms Do? Understanding the Gig Economy' (2020) 46(1) *Annual Review of Sociology* 273

Webster, F and K Robins, 'I'll Be Watching You: Comment on Sewell and Wilkinson' (1993) 27(2) *Sociology* 243

Weil, D, *The Fissured Workplace* (Harvard University Press, 2014)

Wood, AJ, V Lehdonvirta and M Graham, 'Workers of the Internet unite? Online free-lancer organisation among remote gig economy workers in six Asian and African countries' (2018) 33(2) *New Technology, Work and Employment* 95

Wood, AJ et al, 'Networked but Commodified: The (Dis)Embeddedness of Digital Labour in the Gig Economy' (2019) 53(5) *Sociology* 931

Zanoni, P, 'Labor Market Inclusion Through Predatory Capitalism? The "Sharing Economy," Diversity, and the Crisis of Social Reproduction in the Belgian Coordinated Market Economy' in S Vallas and A Kovalainen (eds), *Work and Labor in the Digital Age, Vol. 33* (Emerald Publishing, 2019) ch 6

Zuboff, S, *The Age of Surveillance Capitalism: The Fight for a Human Future at the New Frontier of Power* (PublicAffairs, 2019)

5. Gauging the acceptance of contact-tracing technology: an empirical study of Singapore residents' concerns and trust in information sharing

Ong Ee Ing and Loo Wee Ling[1]

1. INTRODUCTION

In 2020, the COVID-19 virus swept across the world. Given its high rate of infection, many countries,[2] including the Singapore government, emphasised the need for contact tracing.[3] In Singapore, the government encouraged the use of the local tracing app, TraceTogether[4] and

[1] The authors would like to thank Huang Tengjiao (PhD candidate, SMU School of Social Sciences) and Alicia Wee, Research Associate at the Center for AI & Data Governance (Singapore Management University) for their thorough research assistance, as well as Associate Professor Tan Hwee Hoon (Singapore Management University) and Senior Lecturer Rosie Ching (Singapore Management University) for their invaluable advice. This research is supported by the National Research Foundation, Singapore under its Emerging Areas Research Projects (EARP) Funding Initiative. Any opinions, findings and conclusions or recommendations expressed in this chapter are those of the authors and do not reflect the views of National Research Foundation, Singapore.
[2] See, eg, G De Vynck, 'The world embraces contact-tracing technology to fight COVID-19', *Bloomberg* (2020) <https://www.bloomberg.com/news/articles/2020-04 -30/the-world-embraces-contact-tracing-technology-to-fight-covid-19>.
[3] See, eg, Government of Singapore, 'Help speed up contact tracing with TraceTogether', *Gov.Sg* (21 March 2020) <https://www.gov.sg/article/help-speed-up -contact-tracing-with-tracetogether>.
[4] SK Tang and AH Mahmud, 'Singapore Launches TraceTogether Mobile App to Boost COVID-19 Contact Tracing Efforts', *CNA* (21 March 2020) <https://www .channelnewsasia.com/news/singapore/covid19-trace-together-mobile-app-contact -tracing-coronavirus-12560616>.

subsequently introduced the wearable tracking device, the TraceTogether token.[5]

The main alternative to the government-initiated contact tracing technology has been the one offered by the business organisations, Apple and Google. Apple and Google's technology provided greater privacy to individuals as users at risk were alerted without their identities being released to the authorities, allowing them discretion to volunteer the information 'when, for example, they register for a test'.[6] However, the Singapore government had ruled out using this technology on the basis (among other reasons) that the very advantage of Apple and Google's technology limited its capacity for effective identification of the source of infection and the chain of transmission.[7]

The government's promotion of its own TraceTogether technology, however, was not well accepted by Singapore residents. Since its launch in late March 2020, uptake of the app has been low;[8] by August 2020, only 2.4 million residents had downloaded it[9] although for the technology to be effective, about 75% of Singapore's 5.7 million residents must have the app on their smartphones.[10]

---

[5]   The Singapore government is also promoting the use of the TraceTogether token, which exchanges Bluetooth signals with other tokens nearby or with mobile phones that are running the TraceTogether mobile application. J Lim, 'TraceTogether token to be distributed nationwide from Sept 14; new self-check, SMS alert services to be rolled out', *Today Online* (5 October 2020) <https://www.todayonline.com/singapore/tracetogether-token-be-distributed-nationwide-sept-14-new-self-check-sms-alert-services-be>.

[6]   S Asher, 'TraceTogether: Singapore turns to wearable contact-tracing Covid tech', *BBC* (5 July 2020) <https://www.bbc.com/news/technology-53146360>.

[7]   GovTech Singapore, 'Two reasons why Singapore is sticking with TraceTogether's Protocol', *GovTech Singapore* (29 June 2020) <https://www.tech.gov.sg/media/technews/two-reasons-why-singapore-sticking-with-tracetogether-protocol>. The Singapore government also noted that the Apple and Google technology could only run on later models of smartphones and not everyone in Singapore can afford one.

[8]   See also L Lin and KP Chong, 'Singapore Built a Coronavirus App, but It Hasn't Worked So Far', *WSJ* (22 April 2020) <https://www.wsj.com/articles/singapore-built-a-coronavirus-app-but-it-hasnt-worked-so-far-11587547805>.

[9]   C Co, 'Low community prevalence of COVID-19, 0.03% of people with acute respiratory infection test positive: Gan Kim Yong', *CNA* (4 September 2020) <https://www.channelnewsasia.com/news/singapore/covid-19-singapore-low-community-prevalence-testing-13083194>.

[10]   Lin and Chong (n 8) ('But for the technology to be effective, three-quarters of the city-state's 5.7 million residents must have the app on their smartphones, officials have said. A month after its launch, Singapore is far from that target. As of last week, TraceTogether had 1.08 million users, a government spokeswoman said').

It was only in late December 2020 that the adoption rate surpassed 70% when 'more than two million people [had] downloaded the TraceTogether mobile application and 1.75 million tokens [had] been distributed'.[11] Significantly, this was after the government's October announcement that it would be mandatory to use TraceTogether (either in app or token form) in multiple venues by December 2020, and that Phase 3, a phase that allowed more freedom of movement, would not occur until there was widespread adoption of the technology.[12] Of note, while the October announcement incentivised more to collect the tokens, reports surfaced soon after that there were individuals making unauthorised modifications to prevent the tokens from working as intended and urging others to do the same.[13]

The reluctance of some residents to use the app had been attributed to practical issues,[14] especially the way the app drained iPhone batteries.[15] However, there were also significant privacy and data security concerns surrounding the app[16] which were not ameliorated by the subsequent rollout of the token.[17] In fact, the introduction of the token triggered a public petition which warned of the danger of Singapore becoming a 'surveillance state' should adoption of the

---

[11]   N Meah, 'TraceTogether adoption rate surpasses 70%, more distribution points to reopen from January 2021', *Today Online* (23 December 2020) <https://www.todayonline.com/singapore/tracetogether-adoption-rate-surpasses-70-more-distribution-points-reopen-january-2021>.

[12]   D Choo, 'Compulsory to use TraceTogether to check in at venues such as malls, schools, workplaces by December: Govt', *Today Online* (20 October 2020) <https://www.todayonline.com/singapore/compulsory-use-tracetogether-check-venues-such-malls-schools-workplaces-december-govt>.

[13]   D Sun, 'TraceTogether tokens allegedly modified by some', *The Straits Times* (29 October 2020) <https://www.straitstimes.com/singapore/tracetogether-tokens-allegedly-modified-by-some>.

[14]   For example, the need to 'hunt down the app' as it was released as a standalone app: see M Lee, 'Given low adoption rate of TraceTogether, experts suggest merging with SafeEntry or other apps', *Today Online* (9 May 2020) <https://www.todayonline.com/singapore/given-low-adoption-rate-tracetogether-experts-suggest-merging-safeentry-or-other-apps> and the lack of marketing: see D Sim and K Lim, 'Coronavirus: why aren't Singapore residents using the TraceTogether contact-tracing app?', *SCMP* (18 May 2020) <https://www.scmp.com/week-asia/people/article/3084903/coronavirus-why-arent-singapore-residents-using-tracetogether>.

[15]   M Mathews, A Tan and S Suhaini, 'Attitudes towards the Use of Surveillance Technologies in the Fight against COVID-19' (24 May 2020) <https://lkyspp.nus.edu.sg/docs/default-source/ips/ips-report-on-attitudes-towards-the-use-of-surveillance-technologies-in-the-fight-against-covid-19-240520.pdf>; Lee (n 14).

[16]   Sim and Lim (n 14).

[17]   The token merely addressed the practical issues of iPhone battery-drainage and accessibility to the contact tracing scheme by people who could not afford smartphones: see GovTech Singapore (n 7).

token be made mandatory.[18] Indeed, despite repeated government assurances about data safety (because of the promise to confine use of data collected for contact tracing only and to restrict its period of retention) and privacy (as the app or token does not track users' location),[19] some residents still harboured concerns over these issues.[20] In this respect, an academic had opined in May 2020 that there could be a trust issue in reaction to past incidents of cyberattacks on government databases that resulted in massive data breaches.[21] As it was, the issue of trust came to the fore when the government revealed in January 2021 that TraceTogether data could and had been accessed by the police for criminal investigations, as permitted by extant criminal procedural law.[22] Numerous residents expressed resentment at having been 'betrayed' even as the government sought to explain its actions. Soon after, the government took legislative action to limit the use of TraceTogether data to investigations of serious crimes only.[23]

---

[18]   W Low, 'Singapore says "No" to wearable devices for Covid-19 contact tracing', *change.org* (2020) <https://www.change.org/p/singapore-government -singapore-says-no-to-wearable-devices-for-covid-19-contact-tracing?fbclid= IwAR23WqoltvznlxK9e-xOnUGz99z_ZCitqA9amEfmo5NEewt-YGvtIpiuVJU>. As of 29 July 2021, the petition had garnered above 55,000 signatures.

[19]   See, eg, Government of Singapore (n 3). See also 'New TraceTogether token to have no GPS or internet connectivity to track user's whereabouts: Vivian Balakrishnan', *Today Online* (5 October 2020) <https://www.todayonline.com/singapore/tracetogether -token-has-no-gps-or-internet-connectivity-track-users-whereabouts-vivian>.

[20]   Sim and Lim (n 14); Lee (n 14).

[21]   See, eg, comment by Teo Yi-Ling, a senior fellow at the S. Rajaratnam School of International Studies' Centre of Excellence for National Security, cited in Sim and Lim (n 14). She highlighted the incident in June 2018 'when hackers copied the hospital records of more than 1.5 million patients, of which 160,000 had information about their outpatient dispensed medicines taken, in an incident described by authorities as the "most serious breach of personal data"'.

[22]   PIS Yip, '"Feeble" efforts by the Government to handle backlash on TraceTogether data', *Today Online* (31 January 2021) <https://www.todayonline.com/ voices/feeble-efforts-government-handle-backlash-tracetogether-data?cid=emarsys -today_TODAY%27s%20morning%20briefing%20for%20Jan%208,%202021%20 %28ACTIVE%29_newsletter_08012021_today>.

[23]   N Elangovan and YL Tan, 'Some TraceTogether users upset with Govt's revelation on police access to data, say they'll use it less', *Today Online* (7 January 2021) <https://www.todayonline.com/singapore/some-tracetogether-users-upset-govts -revelation-police-access-data-say-theyll-use-it-less?cid=emarsys-today_TODAY %27s%20morning%20briefing%20for%20Jan%207,%202021%20%28ACTIVE %29_newsletter_07012021_today>; K Chee, 'Vivian Balakrishnan says he "deeply regrets" mistake on TraceTogether data', *The Straits Times* (2 February 2021) <https://www.straitstimes.com/singapore/vivian-balakrishnan-says-he-deeply-regrets -mistake-on-tracetogether-data-first-realised-it>; K Chee, 'Bill limiting police use of TraceTogether data to serious crimes passed', *The Straits Times* (2 February 2021)

The patent data privacy and security concerns of some residents and their distrust in the government contact tracing technology (which was then exacerbated by the January 2021 revelation) provides an interesting counterpoint to the perception that Singapore residents generally trust the government, perhaps more so than they trust business organisations.[24] This phenomenon flags the need for further investigation as the issue of trust is important. The mere act of downloading the app or collecting the token does not mean that people will use the technology. As mentioned, some individuals who had collected the tokens were reported to have made modifications to prevent them from working.[25] After the initial download, people could also delete the app from their phones, as some had done even before the January 2021 revelation.[26] This would defeat the purpose of using the technology for contact tracing. For these reasons, we investigate the following questions in this chapter:

First, given the alternative offered by Google and Apple which has been adopted by a growing list of countries,[27] would Singapore residents have more trust in (that is, have less concern about) the use of contact tracing technology introduced by business organisations compared to government-initiated technology? To the degree that contact tracing technologies are perceived to collect many types of users' personal data, the level of concern about sharing (or the willingness to share) such data with the data-collecting entity provides a gauge as to the level of trust reposed in the entity. A user with a high level of concern would be less willing to share his data, indicating less trust in the data-collecting entity.

Second, even if Singapore residents do, in general, repose greater trust in the government compared to businesses, what types of personal data would they still consider important to protect from the government, whether motivated by a desire to preserve privacy (and not be subject to surveillance) or ensure safety of their data from unauthorised government use or leakage to unauthorised parties? In this connection, anecdotal evidence shows that some residents perceive that the TraceTogether technology downloaded on their phone would

---

<https://www.straitstimes.com/singapore/politics/bill-limiting-use-of-tracetogether-for-serious-crimes-passed-with-govt-assurances>.

[24]   See discussion in section 2 'Literature review'.

[25]   Sun (n 13).

[26]   For instance, in a YouGov survey conducted in December 2020, 11% of the respondents said they had downloaded the app but then deleted it: HM Chew, 'TraceTogether adoption up to more than 60% as privacy concerns wane; users still bothered about battery drain', *CNA* (14 December 2020) <https://www.channelnewsasia.com/news/singapore/tracetogether-app-token-adoption-phase-3-13748714>.

[27]   For the list of countries that have adopted the Apple and Google contact tracing app, see <https://www.xda-developers.com/google-apple-covid-19-contact-tracing-exposure-notifications-api-app-list-countries/>.

allow the government access to other information on their phones, such as their location, health history and contacts.[28]

Finally, what are some basic demographic characteristics that typify those who possess more data privacy or security concerns about government collection of their data, especially data that are of particular relevance to contact tracing technology?[29] Examination of relevant demographic factors could be helpful in the successful deployment of the technology. Conversely, investing without recognizing potential factors in adopters' willingness to use the technology 'may lead to a waste of resources'.[30]

In this respect, a survey we carried out in late 2019 provides insights into these three questions. Our survey was on the attitudes of Singapore residents towards business organisations' use of artificial intelligence (AI) in data-mining practices, focusing on their sensitivity towards ethical values as the subjects of these practices. As part of this survey, we measured residents' level of concern towards the collection of their personal data by the *Singapore government*, as compared with their reactions towards the same by *businesses*. We also assessed the specific categories of personal data that residents considered important to protect from the government. In addition, our research provides us with the opportunity to examine differences in the level of concern exhibited by certain demographic groups towards government collection of data categories that are of particular relevance to contact tracing technology.

With this study, we were able to investigate the following research questions:

RQ1: The potential differences between Singapore residents' level of concern with the *Singapore government* as compared to *business* collecting their personal data.

RQ2: The *categories* of personal data that Singapore residents consider important to protect from the Singapore government.

RQ3: The *relationships* between basic demographic characteristics and Singapore residents' concerns about the Singapore government collecting categories of personal data relevant to contact tracing technology.

---

[28]   See, eg, Appendix: Google Play Store Reviews of the TraceTogether App (and screenshots) in A Wee and M Findlay, 'AI and Data Use: Surveillance Technology and Community Disquiet in the Age of COVID-19' (Research Paper No 2020/10, 14 September 2020) 9, 52–57 <https://papers.ssrn.com/sol3/papers.cfm?abstract_id=3715993>.

[29]   See discussion in section 2 'Literature review' for what these categories of data are.

[30]   P Esmaeilzadeh, 'Use of AI-based tools for healthcare purposes: a survey study from consumers' perspectives' (2020) 20 *BMC Medical Informatics and Decision Making* 170: 1–19.

We note that there have been a number of multi or single country investigations, mainly in the US and European countries, into the attitudes of the public towards the adoption of contact tracing technology and the factors that influence acceptance.[31] On the Singapore front, such studies have been conducted, for example, by the Institute of Policy Studies[32] and YouGov.[33]

By contrast, our study preceded the COVID-19 pandemic and the introduction of tracing technology,[34] and did not purport to elicit responses to questions about the adoption of the technology. Nonetheless, our findings provide a unique perspective on the public's resistance to contact tracing technology, in that it uncovered pre-existing trust concerns and sensitivities among Singapore residents which were subsequently magnified by the chain of events precipitated by the pandemic. In addition, our results could provide insight into whether the acceptance of contact tracing technology is heavily dependent on context-specific factors such as the COVID-19 emergency and government-mandated measures.

The rest of this chapter is organised as follows: Section 2 provides a literature review on the linkage between willingness to share information (corresponding to having no or less concern about sharing information) with others, and trust. It also provides the background to our presumption of a difference between responses to data collection by government and business in Singapore. In addition, section 2 explains the categories of personal data perceived to be placed at risk in the context of contact tracing technology. It also explains our focus on the categories of health history, location and social network information in our analysis of the relationship between certain demographic characteristics and concern about government collection of contact tracing personal data. Section 3 describes our research methodology, while section 4 describes our results. In section 5 we discuss the implications of our results with respect to Singapore residents' relative trust in government and business concerning contact tracing technology, the categories of personal data that residents considered important to protect from the Singapore government, and the exploratory analyses into certain demographic characteristics and

---

[31] See, eg, G Kostka and S Habich-Sobiegalla, 'In Times of Crisis: Public Perceptions Towards COVID-19 Contact Tracing Apps in China, Germany and the US' (Institute of Chinese Studies, Freie University of Berlin, 16 September 2020) 5–6 <https://papers.ssrn.com/abstract=3693783> and the studies mentioned therein at section '2.2 Public attitudes of CTAs'.

[32] Mathews, Tan and Suhaini (n 15).

[33] See, eg, K Ho, 'Singaporeans divided on tracking token', *YouGov* (18 June 2020) <https://sg.yougov.com/en-sg/news/2020/06/18/singaporeans-divided-tracking-token/>.

[34] We completed gathering the survey responses towards the end of 2019, just as COVID-19 started making its presence known.

concerns about sharing personal data relevant to contact tracing technology with the Singapore government. Section 6 provides some concluding thoughts and implications for government data-collection undertakings, together with suggestions for further research going forward.

2.   LITERATURE REVIEW

2.1   Willingness to Share Information as a Facet of Trust

As mentioned, our survey investigated the level of concern Singapore residents had about the collection of particular categories of personal data by the government and a business, respectively, with the underlying premise that a high level of concern would reduce the willingness of residents to share information. This would in turn signal a lower degree of trust reposed in the data-collecting entity. In essence, we define willingness to share information with other parties as a facet of trust. Our definition is supported by studies into the construct of trust.

In the context of dyadic relationships within organisations, Mayer, Davis and Schoorman define trust as 'the willingness of a party to be vulnerable to the actions of another party based on the expectation that the other will perform a particular action important to the trustor, irrespective of the ability to monitor or control that other party'.[35] They further note that 'making oneself vulnerable' is to take risk and that trust involves a 'willingness to take risk'.[36] Usoro et al helpfully noted that Mayer, Davis and Schoorman's definition of trust had also been used in non-dyadic and intra-organisational studies.[37] In the context of an individual sharing personal information with an organisation, parallels can usefully be drawn to Mayer, Davis and Schoorman's definition. When one shares personal information, one places oneself in a position of vulnerability vis-à-vis the recipient of the information, insofar as one takes the risk of what the recipient may do with the information. Thus, willingness to share one's personal information inevitably involves trust.

Indeed, in the context of the 'modern networked life' that is 'mediated by information relationships', Richards and Hartzog point out that trust is an 'essential ingredient' when we share 'sensitive personal information with Internet service providers (ISPs), doctors, banks, search engines, credit card

---

[35]   RC Mayer, JH Davis and FD Schoorman, 'An integrative model of organisational trust' (1995) 20(3) *Academy of Management Review* 709, 712.

[36]   Ibid.

[37]   A Usoro et al, 'Trust as an antecedent to knowledge sharing in virtual communities of practice' (2007) 5 *Knowledge Management Research & Practice* 199, 200–201.

companies, and countless other information recipients and intermediaries'.[38] In sharing such information, they note that we trust doctors 'not to reveal information about our health and mental state' and 'ISPs and search engines not to reveal our search history'.[39]

In addition, studies show a correlation between trust and the individual's willingness to share personal information with a business.[40] For example, Waldman, in an empirical study of Facebook users, argues that 'higher levels of trust in the platform and higher levels of trust in those individuals in our networks are associated with a higher propensity to share personal information' and that 'Facebook knows this and it has designed its platform to benefit from it'.[41] More to the point, Waldman noted that '[s]cholars have shown that, with respect to e-commerce websites, higher levels of trust in the website translate into a greater willingness to share'.[42]

Against this backdrop of trust and its link to the willingness to share personal information, we note that studies generally indicated that the Singapore public reposed a high level of trust in their government. For instance, the World Values Survey Wave 2014 showed that the Singapore government distinguished itself in this regard when compared to other high-income countries: 24% of people in Singapore had a 'great deal of confidence' in their government, compared to 5.8% in South Korea, 5.5% in Germany and 3.7% in the US.[43]

Indeed, the Edelman Trust Barometer 2020 (Singapore Report), based on a survey conducted between October and November 2019, indicated that respondents generally trusted the Singapore government. Moreover, compared to the Edelman 2019 Report, trust in the government had risen to 70% from 67% in the previous year.[44] Conversely, respondents were neutral in their trust

---

[38]   NM Richards and W Hartzog, 'Taking Trust Seriously in Privacy Law' (2016) 19 *Stanford Technology Law Review* 431, 433.

[39]   Ibid 460.

[40]   See, eg, A Gupta and A Dhami, 'Measuring the impact of security, trust and privacy in information sharing: A study on social networking sites' (2015) 17 *Journal of Direct, Data and Digital Marketing Practice* 43; B Suh and I Han, 'The Impact of Customer Trust and Perception of Security Control on the Acceptance of Electronic Commerce' (2003) 7 *International Journal of Electronic Commerce* 135.

[41]   AE Waldman, 'Privacy, Sharing, and Trust: The Facebook Study' (2016) 67 *Case Western Reserve Law Review* 193, 195–196.

[42]   Ibid 233.

[43]   See http://www.worldvaluessurvey.org/WVSOnline.jsp. See also CML Wong and O Jensen, 'The Paradox of Trust: Perceived Risk and Public Compliance during the COVID-19 Pandemic in Singapore' (2020) *Journal of Risk Research* 1, 2.

[44]   Edelman Trust Barometer 2020 (Singapore) <https://www.edelman.com/ sites/g/files/aatuss191/files/2020-06/2020%20Edelman%20Trust%20Barometer %20Singapore%20Report%5b1%5d.pdf>; S Rekhi, 'Trust in Singapore Government

of businesses. In fact, trust in business decreased to 58% from 60% in the previous year.[45] Further, in comparison to businesses, the Singapore government was considered more ethical.[46]

In contrast, on a global level, the Edelman Trust Barometer 2020 showed that businesses fared better than governments, with trust at 58% compared to 49%. Even so, there had been a general decline of trust across business sectors, especially in the area of technology, with a 4% reduction from 2019.[47] This could be because, as another study noted, 'trust [in technology companies] has been eroding for a while now because of the techlash'.[48] Such sentiment was reflected in Amnesty International's observation that:

> Google and Facebook dominate our modern lives – amassing unparalleled power over the digital world by harvesting and monetising the personal data of billions of people … [t]heir insidious control of our digital lives undermines the very essence of privacy and is one of the defining human rights challenges of our era.[49]

More relevant to the issue of data collection by business for contact tracing purposes, another study found that:

> [w]hile technology companies have launched promising initiatives to track the spread of COVID-19, many consumers aren't buying it. 84% of Americans are

---

up: Edelman Poll', *The Straits Times* (22 June 2020) <https://www.straitstimes.com/asia/trust-in-singapore-government-up-edelman-poll>.

[45]   Edelman Trust Barometer 2020 (Singapore) (n 44).

[46]   Ibid.

[47]   Ibid (also reported in J Anderson, 'Trust in government now exceeds the public's faith in business', *Quartz* (8 May 2020) <https://qz.com/1851749/covid-19-has-us-trusting-government-more-than-ceos/> and S Fischer, 'Trust in business falls behind government', *Axios* (5 May 2020) <https://www.axios.com/coronavirus-government-trust-business-d045d88d-a3f9-4407-b734-55d51ea0bf69.html>. For some suggestion of a counter-trend in some countries, see ES Hestriana, 'Why Do We Trust Google More than the Government?', *The Jakarta Post* (21 November 2017) <https://www.thejakartapost.com/life/2017/11/21/why-do-we-trust-google-more-than-the-government.html>; B Zhang and A Dafoe, 'Artificial Intelligence: American Attitudes and Trends' (University of Oxford, January 2019) <https://www.ssrn.com/abstract=3312874>.

[48]   EY, 'Bridging AI's Trust Gaps: Aligning Policymakers and Companies' (July 2020)   15   <https://assets.ey.com/content/dam/ey-sites/ey-com/en_gl/topics/ai/ey-bridging-ais-trust-gaps-report.pdf>. See also II Mitroff and R Storesund, *Techlash: The Future of the Socially Responsible Tech Organization* (Springer, 2020) ch 1.

[49]   Statement by Kumi Naidoo, Secretary General of Amnesty International in 'Amnesty slams Facebook, Google over "pervasive surveillance" business model', *The Register* (21 November 2019) <https://www.theregister.com/2019/11/21/amnesty_facebook_google/>.

worried that data collection for COVID-19 containment will sacrifice too much of their privacy, and 74% of Australians say the same.[50]

In Singapore, consumers likewise had concerns over businesses' treatment of their personal data. For example, an April 2019 study reported that less than one in four (23%) of Singapore consumers believed that their personal data would be treated in a trustworthy manner by organisations offering digital services.[51]

The foregoing supports the perception that Singapore residents would be more willing to share (or be less concerned about the collection of) their personal data where the entity collecting the information is the Singapore government rather than a business. It also provides the basis for our hypothesis that Singapore residents would be more willing to share contact tracing information with the Singapore government rather than a business.

2.2   Personal Data Perceived to be Placed at Risk by Contact Tracing Technology

In a survey by Altman et al of respondents in France, Germany, Italy, the UK and the US in late April 2020, 35% indicated the fear of a contact tracing app rendering the phone vulnerable to hackers as a reason for not installing it;[52] 42% of the respondents also indicated concern about 'government surveillance at the end of the epidemic' as a reason for not installing the app.[53]

In Singapore, such fear of surveillance by the government through the use of data collected by the app or token had also been expressed.[54] In addition, the Singapore public was concerned about the possible loss of the collected data

---

[50]   Okta, 'The Cost of Privacy' <https://www.okta.com/cost-of-privacy-report/2020/>. This was an 'online survey of over 12,000 people between the ages of 18 and 75 in six countries: Australia, France, Germany, the Netherlands, the United Kingdom, and the United States. When COVID-19 changed our world, Juniper [Research] went back and asked nearly 6,000 of those original respondents how the pandemic has affected the way they think about privacy'.

[51]   Singapore News Center, 'Less than 1 in 4 Singapore consumers trust organisations that provide digital services to protect their personal data: Microsoft – IDC Study' (16 April 2019) <https://news.microsoft.com/en-sg/2019/04/16/less-than-1-in-4-singapore-consumers-trust-organisations-that-provide-digital-services-to-protect-their-personal-data-microsoft-idc-study/>.

[52]   S Altmann et al, 'Acceptability of App-Based Contact Tracing for COVID-19: Cross-Country Survey Evidence' (28 April 2020) 7 <https://papers.ssrn.com/abstract=3590505>.

[53]   Ibid.

[54]   Low (n 18). See also Sim and Lim (n 14).

to persons hacking into the servers where the data were stored.[55] Despite the Singapore government's explanations that the TraceTogether technology does not log GPS location data or connect to mobile networks, and hence cannot be used for surveillance of a person's movements,[56] this remains a valid concern:

> [One] has to acknowledge that the complex software and hardware environment of smartphones with multiple apps makes it more difficult to prevent security issues with smartphone-based contact tracing apps. Also, when it comes to privacy, anonymisation technologies exist, but also here one has to acknowledge that smartphones contain personal information, are always on and as a result their location can be traced.[57]

Thus, as applied to our survey questions, in assessing the level of trust reposed in the government or businesses, we measured the levels of concern about the collection of those categories of personal data that one might find *on a phone*:

- Personal Contact Information
- Work Contact Information
- Credit Card Information
- Demographic Information
- Government Identification
- Health History
- Location
- Purchase History
- Social Network Friends' Information
- Communication History
- Web-surfing History

To assess the particular categories of personal information that the Singapore public considered important to protect from the government, our survey question focused on the same list above.

---

[55]   See, eg, Wee and Findlay (n 28) 52. See also Sim and Lim (n 14).

[56]   TraceTogether, 'Can TraceTogether track the location of all phones installed with the TraceTogether App?', *TraceTogether FAQs* <https://support.tracetogether .gov.sg/hc/en-sg/articles/360043224874-Can-TraceTogether-track-the-location-of-all -phones-installed-with-the-TraceTogether-App>.

[57]   European Institute of Information and Technology, 'Anonymous COVID-19 contact tracing using physical tokens' (14 May 2020) <https://eit.europa.eu/our -activities/covid-19-response/solutions/anonymous-covid-19-contact-tracing-using -physical-tokens>.

Certain data categories are of especial relevance to contact tracing technology, given their sensitivity and the perception that they are collected by the technology. These data categories are:

- *Health history*: There could be concern about being stigmatised, or even harassed, if one is infected by COVID-19.[58] In addition, concern over this category of personal data may be more acute given recent incidents in Singapore that resulted in the leak of health-related information. Of note are: (1) the 2018 hacking incident into the database of Singapore's largest group of public healthcare institutions, SingHealth, where 1.5 million patients' particulars (including outpatient dispensed medicines) were stolen;[59] and (2) the 2019 leak of confidential information of HIV-positive individuals (including their medical information) that was stolen by a fraudster with the aid of his partner who had access to the HIV Registry of the Singapore National Public Health Unit.[60]
- *Social Network Friends' Information*: We took this category of information as a proxy for social contacts' information. The TraceTogether technology captures Bluetooth data of the phones of people in close proximity to the person using the app or token.[61] Naturally, this makes possible the identification of people with whom the app or token user spent time. Yet, there could be people who may wish to keep such information confidential, as for example someone who visited a brothel.[62]

---

[58] See, eg, G Sotgiu and CC Dobler, 'Social stigma in the time of Coronavirus' (2020) *European Respiratory Journal*; The Straits Times, 'Coronavirus: Social stigma, harassment undermine testing efforts across Asia', *The Straits Times* (13 May 2020) <https://www.straitstimes.com/asia/east-asia/coronavirus-social-stigma-harassment-undermine-testing-efforts-across-asia>.

[59] 'MOH News Highlights' <https://www.moh.gov.sg/news-highlights/details/singhealth's-it-system-target-of-cyberattack>.

[60] A-L Chang, F Koh and S Khalik, 'Data of 14,200 People with HIV Leaked Online by US Fraudster Who Was Deported from Singapore', *The Straits Times* (30 January 2019) <https://www.straitstimes.com/singapore/data-of-14200-singapore-patients-with-hiv-leaked-online-by-american-fraudster-who-was>.

[61] TraceTogether, 'How Does TraceTogether Work?', *TraceTogether FAQs* <http://support.tracetogether.gov.sg/hc/en-sg/articles/360043543473>. See also TraceTogether, 'How are my Possible exposures determined? Does Possible exposure mean I was a Close contact of a COVID-19 case?', *TraceTogether FAQs* <https://support.tracetogether.gov.sg/hc/en-sg/articles/360053464873-How-are-your-possible-exposures-determined->.

[62] Today, 'Covid-19: Man in Hong Kong who visited prostitute before testing positive sparks police tracking operation', *Today Online* (23 November 2020) <https://www.todayonline.com/world/covid-19-man-hong-kong-who-visited-prostitute-testing-positive-sparks-police-tracking>. See also D Sun, 'Uncovering the KTV "butterfly" effect in Singapore as Covid-19 cluster grows to 88 cases', *The Straits Times* (16 July

- *Location*: As with the concern to keep the identity of social contacts confidential, people could equally be uncomfortable revealing their location. As mentioned, despite assurances by the government that location data was not collected by the app or token, some members of the Singapore public continued to believe otherwise.[63]

Thus, in assessing the relationship between certain demographic characteristics and the level of concern about government collection of personal data, we narrowed our focus to these data categories.

2.3   Relevant Demographic Factors

The results of existing studies are generally inconclusive as to which individual demographic characteristics affect people's acceptance of technology.[64] For instance, results as to age and gender appear to vary depending on the survey used, as well as the region explored.[65] Few also have studied educational levels, or income levels.[66] As such, our aim is simply to explore whether (and how) such demographic factors would affect acceptance of contact tracing technology in Singapore.

Further, we also explore whether prior computer science or programming experience, or prior exposure to AI would have an impact on willingness to share information. For instance, recent studies in AI adoption in the health-care sector have shown that familiarity with AI could have an impact on a person's intention to use AI technology for health-care purposes.[67] Our expectation is that such prior experience or exposure will be positively correlated with concern about government collection of personal data relevant to contact tracing technology.

2021) <https://www.straitstimes.com/singapore/uncovering-the-ktv-butterfly-effect-in-singapore-as-covid-19-cluster-grows-to-88-cases>.

[63]   See, eg, Sim and Lim (n 14); and Wee and Findlay (n 28) 54.

[64]   Kostka and Habich-Sobiegalla (n 31).

[65]   Ibid.

[66]   Ibid. However, this paper also noted a 2020 Pew Research Center survey which revealed that acceptance of contract tracing apps was higher among the better educated.

[67]   Esmaeilzadeh (n 30); S Oh et al, 'Physician Confidence in Artificial Intelligence: An Online Mobile Survey' (2019) 21(3) *Journal of Medical Internet Research.*

3.　SURVEY METHODOLOGY

3.1　Measures

We carried out this survey in 2019 to determine the attitudes of Singapore residents towards business organisations' use of AI in data-mining practices, with a focus on their sensitivity towards ethical values as the subjects of these practices.

We based our questions on similar surveys on data collection and analysis.[68] We tested out initial versions of the survey questionnaire on two focus groups, one comprising data privacy practitioners (AsiaDPO) and the other comprising academics at a forum. We also tested the questionnaire on friends and family, as well as fellow academics in the law and social sciences discipline.

We first explored, as between the government and a business, which entity Singapore residents had more trust in (had less concern about) collecting their personal information (RQ1). We then investigated which categories of personal data residents considered important to protect from the Singapore government as the TraceTogether technology is government-initiated (RQ2). Finally, we explored the *relationships* between basic demographic charac-teristics and residents' concerns about the Singapore government collecting personal data relevant to contact tracing technology (RQ3).

To examine RQ1, we asked the survey respondents how concerned they were about the government or a business collecting certain categories of their personal information through the use of AI, respectively. The respondents were asked to indicate their level of concern from 1 (*not concerned at all*) to 5 (*extremely concerned*).

To examine RQ2, respondents were asked to select up to six categories of personal information that they felt were most important to protect from the government.

For each of the questions, the respondents were asked to consider the fol-lowing categories of personal information:

- Personal Contact Information
- Work Contact Information
- Credit Card Information

---

[68]　See, eg, T Morey, T Forbath and A Schoop, 'Customer Data: Designing for Transparency and Trust', *Harvard Business Review* (May 2015) <https://hbr.org/2015/05/customer-data-designing-for-transparency-and-trust>; Global Alliance of Data-Drive Marketing Associations, 'Global data privacy: What the consumer really thinks' (May 2018) <https://www.acxiom.co.uk/resources/global-data-privacy-what-the-consumer-really-thinks/>.

- Demographic Information
- Government Identification
- Health History
- Location
- Purchase History
- Social Network Friends' Information
- Communication History
- Web-surfing History

To examine RQ3, respondents were asked to answer questions on certain demographic measures, including the typical ones of age, gender, income and education, as well as prior computer science or programming experience, and exposure to AI. This would allow us to test for associations with concerns about the Singapore government collecting personal data relevant to contact tracing technology.

3.2   Participants

We analysed responses from 1,001 Singapore residents aged 18 and above.[69] As our goal was to understand the reactions of all residents, we did not limit our survey to Singapore citizens, but allowed responses from anyone who resided in Singapore, regardless of their legal status.

The respondents comprised 47.55% males and 52.45% females. The race profile was: 79.92% Chinese, 10.79% Malay, 5.39% Indian and 3.90% other races. In terms of age, there were 6.69% in the 18–23 range (Generation Z), 33.37% in the 24–39 range (Millennial), 37.36% in the 40–55 range (Generation X) and 22.58% in the 56 and above range (Boomer and above).[70]

---

[69]   Using data from the Singapore Department of Statistics <https://www.singstat .gov.sg/>, as of June 2019 the total population of Singapore was 5.7 million. The data also indicates that there were 3.44 million citizens and permanent residents aged 15 and above. Similar data is unavailable for those who reside in Singapore but are neither citizens nor permanent residents. However, data from the Statistics Division, UNESCAP <https://data.unescap.org> indicates that as of 2019, there were 5.1 million individuals in Singapore aged 15 and above. Using the data from either the Singapore Department of Statistics or UNESCAP, a sample size of 1,001 provided a confidence level of 99%, 0.5 standard deviation and approximately 4% margin of error.

[70]   The age profile breakdown corresponds to a generational breakdown provided by the Pew Research Center as of 2019: Generation Z (7–22), Millennials (23–38), Generation X (39–54), and Boomers (55–73) <https://www.pewresearch.org/fact-tank/ 2019/01/17/where-millennials-end-and-generation-z-begins/>. Based on data from the Singapore Department of Statistics <https://www.singstat.gov.sg/>, as of June 2019 the profile of Singapore citizens and permanent residents aged 15 and above is as follows: (a) males 48.56%, females 51.44%; (b) 'Chinese' 75.49%, 'Malays' 12.78%, 'Indians'

Table 5.1   *Summary of the key socio-demographic characteristics of the sample*

		Frequency	%
Gender			
	Male	476	47.55%
	Female	525	52.45%
Age (years)			
	18–23 (Generation Z)	67	6.69%
	24–39 (Millennial)	334	33.37%
	40–55 (Generation X)	374	37.36%
	56–74 (Boomer)	226	22.58%
Race			
	Chinese	800	79.92%
	Malay	108	10.79%
	Indian	54	5.39%
	Others	39	3.90%
Income			
	$0	9	0.90%
	Less than $24,999	72	7.19%
	$25,000 to $49,999	139	13.89%
	$50,000 to $74,999	165	16.48%
	$75,000 to $99,999	155	15.48%
	$100,000 to $124,999	159	15.88%
	$125,000 to $149,999	73	7.29%
	$150,000 to $174,999	47	4.70%
	$175,000 to $200,000	49	4.90%
	$200,000 or higher	81	8.09%
	Prefer not to say	52	5.19%
Education			
	Primary (i.e. PSLE and below)	8	0.80%
	Secondary (i.e. GCE 'O'/ 'N' Levels)	106	10.59%
	Post Secondary (Non-Tertiary, i.e. ITE, JC)	70	6.99%
	Diploma & Professional Qualification (i.e. Polytechnic and similar)	202	20.18%
	University Degree (i.e. Bachelor's or Equivalent)	438	43.76%
	Postgraduate – Masters (or Equivalent)	139	13.89%
	Postgraduate – Doctorate (or Equivalent)	36	3.60%
	Others	2	0.20%

	Frequency	%
Prior computer science/programming experience		
No	653	65.23%
Yes	348	34.77%
Self-perceived exposure to AI		
None at all	29	2.90%
A little	334	33.37%
A moderate amount	443	44.26%
A lot	195	19.48%

3.3   Procedure

We conducted an online, self-administered survey from late August to mid-December in 2019. The survey company, Qualtrics LLC, drew participants from their panel of respondents to match the general demographic percentages of residents in Singapore aged 18 and above, based on gender, age and race.

We began the survey with a series of questions relating to AI and data collection, including the questions mentioned above regarding respondents' concern with government and business collecting personal data, as well as the categories of personal data considered important to protect from the government. At the end of the survey, as mentioned, the respondents completed a number of demographic measures, including the typical ones of age, gender, income and education, as well as prior computer science or programming experience, and exposure to AI. Table 5.1 provides a summary of the socio-demographic characteristics of the sample.

4.   RESULTS

4.1   RQ1. The Potential Differences between Singapore Residents' Level of Concern with the Singapore Government as Compared to Business Collecting their Personal Data

First, on average, respondents were at least 'moderately concerned' about either the Singapore government or business collecting their data.[71] However,

---

8.66%, 'Others' 3.07%; and (c) 15–19 years 6.47%, 20–24 years 7.25%, 25–39 years 25.69%, 40–54 years 26.61%, and 55 years and above 33.98%. Similar data is unavailable for those who reside in Singapore but are neither citizens nor permanent residents.

[71]   The mean responses for both questions were between '(3) moderately concerned' and '(4) very concerned'.

the mean response for *concern about government collecting data* was lower (3.1409) than the mean response for *concern about business collecting data* (3.5441). This suggested a lower level of concern about government collecting personal data than business.

To further explore this potential difference, we conducted 11 Wilcoxon matched pairs signed rank tests for each of the 11 data categories. Table 5.2 reports the descriptive statistics and Wilcoxon matched pairs signed rank tests (corrected for ties). Based on this test, as compared between the two entities, respondents expressed significantly less concern with the *government* than a *business* collecting personal data.

More specifically, respondents generally expressed significantly less concern with the government than a business collecting the following data categories: personal contact information; work contact information; credit card information; demographic information; government identification; health history; location; social network friends' information; and communication history.[72] We note that there were no significant differences in the median levels of concern with the government than a business collecting respondents' purchase history and web-surfing history.[73]

4.2 RQ2. The Categories of Personal Data that Singapore Residents Consider Important to Protect from the Singapore Government

To further examine the types of information that respondents are most concerned about protecting from the government, respondents were asked to select up to six categories of information they felt were most important to protect from the government.

As seen in Table 5.3, the top three data categories most frequently considered as important to protect from the government were credit card information (65.33%), personal contact information (45.75%), and communication history (44.86%). The bottom three data categories that were least frequently considered as important to protect from the government were purchase history (26.77%), location (25.17%) and demographic information (20.88%).

---

[72] Personal contact information ($T = 176786.00$, $z = -17.32$, p < .001); work contact information ($T = 130246.00$, $z = -12.31$, p < .001); credit card information ($T = 111052.00$, $z = -15.02$, p < .001); demographic information ($T = 42123.50$, $z = -7.59$, p < .001); government identification ($T = 171942.00$, $z = -17.78$, p < .001); health history ($T = 27263.50$, $z = -13.75$, p < .001); location ($T = 37010.50$, $z = -10.13$, p < .001); social network friends' information ($T = 45771.00$, $z = -5.98$, p < .001); and communication history ($T = 54241.00$, $z = -4.53$, p < .001). See results in Table 5.2.

[73] Collecting purchase history ($T = 57880.00$, $z = -0.60$, $p = .55$); and web-surfing history ($T = 65355.50$, $z = -.15$, $p = .89$). See results in Table 5.2.

Table 5.2　*Descriptive statistics and Wilcoxon matched pairs signed rank tests for the concern with the government and a business collecting personal information for each data category*

	Median		Mean rank		Sum of ranks		Z	p-value
	Government	Business	Negative	Positive	Negative	Positive		
Personal Contact Information	3.00	4.00	213.39	335.46	21979.00	176786.00	-17.32[a]	<.001***
Work Contact Information	3.00	3.00	245.51	302.19	35354.00	130246.00	-12.31[a]	<.001***
Credit Card Information	4.00	5.00	191.51	263.78	15704.00	111052.00	-15.02[a]	<.001***
Demographic Information	3.00	3.00	234.02	272.34	42123.50	91779.50	-7.59[a]	<.001***
Government Identification	3.00	4.00	174.78	333.87	17478.00	171942.00	-17.78[a]	<.001***
Health History	3.00	4.00	216.38	298.51	27263.50	129256.50	-13.75[a]	<.001***
Location	3.00	3.00	229.88	284.41	37010.50	106369.50	-10.13[a]	<.001***
Purchase History	3.00	3.00	245.25	243.79	57880.00	61436.00	-0.60[a]	.55
Social Network Friends' Information	3.00	3.00	232.34	268.54	45771.00	83515.00	-5.98[a]	<.001***
Communication History	3.00	4.00	251.12	272.13	54241.00	84360.00	-4.53[a]	<.001***
Web-surfing History	3.00	3.00	254.30	255.71	65355.50	64439.50	-0.14[b]	.89

[a] Based on negative ranks.
[b] Based on positive ranks.
* p-value ≤ .05.
** p-value ≤ .01.
*** p-value ≤ .001.

Table 5.3   Frequency and percentage of respondents that selected
a category of information as important to protect from the
government

	Frequency	%
Credit Card Information[a]	654	65.33%
Personal Contact Information[a]	458	45.75%
Communication History[a]	449	44.86%
Social Network Friends' Information	407	40.66%
Government Identification	391	39.06%
Web-surfing History	365	36.46%
Health History	300	29.97%
Work Contact Information	292	29.17%
Purchase History[b]	268	26.77%
Location[b]	252	25.17%
Demographic Information[b]	209	20.88%

[a] Top three categories of information considered as important to protect from the government.
[b] Bottom three categories of information considered as important to protect from the government.

4.3   RQ3. The Relationships between Basic Demographic Characteristics and Singapore Residents' Concerns about the Singapore Government Collecting Categories of Personal Data Relevant to Contact Tracing Technology

We examined the relationships between a number of demographic characteristics and concern with the government collecting personal data of particular
relevance to contact tracing technology.

The socio-demographic characteristics of interest include age, gender,
annual household income, educational qualification, self-perceived AI exposure, and prior computing and/or programming experience. To determine relationships between these characteristics (excluding gender) and concern with
the government collecting forms of data relevant to contact tracing technologies, namely health history, location, and social network friends' information,
we conducted a series of Spearman's rank-order correlations (see Table 5.4).

We first examined the relationship between age and concern with the government collecting personal information relevant to contact tracing. Spearman's
rank-order correlations revealed a significant negative relationship between
age and concern with the government collecting location data. As the age of
the respondents increased, the less concern they expressed about government
collection of their location data. However, the analyses also showed that

Table 5.4　　Spearman correlations for concern with the government collecting personal information pertaining to health history, location, and social network friends' information with selected socio-demographic variables

Socio-demographic Variable	N		Concern with the Government Collecting Personal Information Pertaining to		
			Health History	Location	Social Network Friends' Information
1. Age	1001	Spearman's Rho	.007	-.10***	-.013
		p-value	(.83)	(.001)	(.68)
2. Annual Household Income	949	Spearman's Rho	.099**	.084**	.081*
		p-value	(.002)	(.009)	(.012)
3. Educational Qualification	963	Spearman's Rho	.079*	.085**	.059
		p-value	(.015)	(.008)	(.068)
4. Self-perceived AI Exposure	1001	Spearman's Rho	.083**	.11***	.13***
		p-value	(.009)	(<.001)	(<.001)
5. Prior Computing and/or Programming Experience	1001	Spearman's Rho	.057	.059	.094**
(1=No, 2=Yes)		p-value	(.071)	(.062)	(.003)

* *p*-value ≤ .05.
** *p*-value ≤ .01.
*** *p*-value ≤ .001.

respondents' age was unrelated to their concern with government collection of their health history and social network friends' information.[74]

For the relationship between annual household income[75] and levels of concern, income was positively correlated with concern about the government collecting health history, location, and social network friends' information.[76] Thus higher levels of annual household income were associated with greater concern with the government collecting all three forms of information.

Similarly, educational qualification[77] was positively correlated with concern about the government collecting health history and location data, but unrelated to the collection of social network friends' information.[78] That is, higher educational qualification levels were associated with greater concern about the government collecting health history and location data.

Interestingly, self-perceived exposure to AI was positively correlated to concern with the government collecting health history, location, and social network friends' information.[79] Thus the more exposed to AI the respondents perceived themselves to be, the greater concern they expressed about the government collecting all three forms of information.

Analyses also showed that prior computing and/or programming experience was positively correlated with concern about the government collecting social network friends' information but not with collecting health history and location data.[80] This suggests that respondents with prior computing and/or programming experience were more likely to express concern with the government collecting social network friends' information than respondents without such prior experience.

Finally, to explore potential gender differences regarding concern with the government collecting these three forms of information, we conducted Mann-Whitney U tests. Figures 5.1, 5.2 and 5.3 illustrate gender differences

---

[74] Location $(r_s(1001) = -.10, p = .001)$; health history $(r_s(1001) = .007, p = .83)$; social network friends' information $(r_s(1001) = -.013, p = .68)$.

[75] Prior to analysis, responses that indicated 'Prefer not to say' were excluded.

[76] Health history $(r_s(949) = .099, p = .002)$; location $(r_s(949) = .084, p = .009)$; social network friends' information $(r_s(949) = .081, p = .012)$.

[77] Prior to analysis, responses that indicated post-secondary and diploma and professional qualification were grouped together. Responses that indicated 'Others' were also excluded.

[78] Health history $(r_s(963) = .079, p = .015)$; location $(r_s(963) = .085, p = .008)$; social network friends' information $(r_s(963) = .059, p = .068)$.

[79] Health history $(r_s(1001) = .083, p = .009)$; location $(r_s(1001) = .11, p < .001)$; social network friends' information $(r_s(1001) = .13, p < .001)$.

[80] Social network friends' information $(r_s(1001) = .094, p = .003)$; health history $(r_s(1001) = .057, p = .071)$; location $(r_s(1001) = .059, p = .062)$.

in the concern about the government collecting health history, location, and social network friends' information respectively.

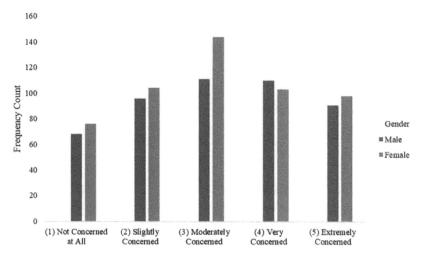

Figure 5.1   The distribution of males' (n = 476) and females' (n = 525) concern with the government collecting health history information

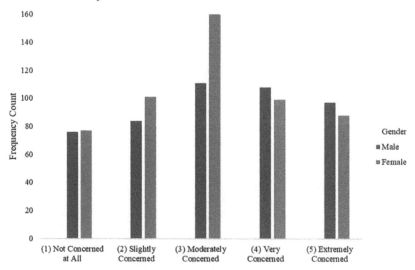

Figure 5.2   The distribution of males' (n = 476) and females' (n = 525) concern with the government collecting location information

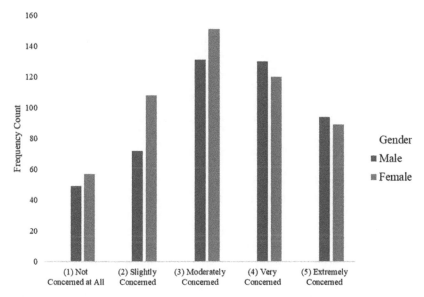

Figure 5.3   The distribution of males' (n = 476) and females' (n = 525)
                concern with the government collecting social network
                friends' information

The analyses revealed no significant difference between male and female respondents in their concern about the government collecting health history[81] or location data.[82] However, male respondents expressed significantly greater concern than female respondents about the government collecting social network friends' information.[83]

5.   DISCUSSION

We had defined the willingness to share information as a facet of trust and hypothesised that given the general perception that Singapore residents trusted

---

[81]   Male respondents (*Mean Rank* = 506.28, n = 476) compared to female respondents (*Mean Rank* = 496.21, n = 525), $\underline{U}$ = 122435.00, z = -0.56 (corrected for ties), p = .57.

[82]   Male respondents (*Mean Rank* = 513.25, n = 476) compared to female respondents (*Mean Rank* = 489.89, n = 525), $\underline{U}$ = 119119.00, z = -1.31 (corrected for ties), p = .19.

[83]   Male respondents (*Mean Rank* = 521.99, n = 476) compared to female respondents (*Mean Rank* = 481.97, n = 525), $\underline{U}$ = 114959.00, z = -2.25 (corrected for ties), p = .025.

their government more than businesses, they would be more willing to share contact tracing information with the former rather than the latter.

At a general level, our results support our hypothesis above. With regard to RQ1 (the differences between Singaporean residents' level of concern with the Singapore government as compared to a business collecting their personal data), the results show that Singapore residents were less concerned about the government, relative to a business, engaging in collection of most categories of personal data which were perceived to be placed at risk by contact tracing technology.

However, as had been noted, the reality on the ground is that some Singapore residents are reluctant to download the TraceTogether app or to use the TraceTogether token, even before the January 2021 revelation. Our results show certain trends that could account for this phenomenon. Specifically, the results for RQ3 (the relationships between basic demographic characteristics and concerns pertaining to the Singapore government collecting personal data relevant to contact tracing technology) suggest that the higher a person's income and education, the more concerned he or she would be with the government collecting such data. The results further suggest that the greater a person's self-perceived exposure to AI, the more concerned he or she would be with the government collecting such data.

In total, this suggests that residents inhabiting such demographics may be more resistant to sharing contact tracing data with the Singapore government. Thus, although our results support our hypothesis at a general level, they also provide insights into why there may be segments of the Singapore public that would resist adopting contact tracing technology.

We note that data on health history (29.97%), location (25.17%) and social network friends' information (40.66%) are not within the top three categories considered important to protect from the government. Nevertheless, the percentages of Singapore residents who considered them important to protect were certainly not insignificant. In fact, our results show that concern to protect each of the 11 categories of personal data from the Singapore government existed even in pre-COVID times.

Indeed, Singapore residents were already 'moderately concerned' about the government engaging in AI-aided collection of their personal data before the advent of COVID-19 and the use of contact tracing technology. It is thus not too far-fetched to surmise that the level of concern would only rise when privacy-compromising technology is deployed, especially when there is a prospect that its use could become the new normal even in post-pandemic times.[84]

---

[84]   M Motsenok et al, 'The Slippery Slope of Rights-Restricting Temporary Measures: An Experimental Analysis' (2020) *Behavioural Public Policy* 1.

Further reasons that could account for the resistance to the TraceTogether technology are:

- residents' data security concerns, given that there had been massive data breaches into government online portals in the recent past;[85]
- policymakers, in the face of the pandemic, treating '...civil liberties and data integrity [as] the necessary casualties of policies for a safer society';[86]
- the above phenomenon, in turn, could have triggered visceral fears of a surveillance government, as is evident from an online petition that declared: 'All that is stopping the Singapore government from becoming a surveillance state is the advent and mandating the compulsory usage of such a wearable device ...What comes next would be laws that state these devices must not be turned off [and must] remain on a person at all times – thus sealing our fate as a police state';[87] and
- the fact that such fears are naturally fed '...in times of a pandemic (when surveillance is more obvious and apparent than traditional citizen monitoring devices) [providing] a regular reminder that individuals are being tracked, logged, and aggregated in mass data-sharing practices like never before'.[88]

And the fears could be well-founded. An expert had noted that the data collected by the TraceTogether tokens would allow the 'Ministry of Health' to 'go from this cryptic, secret number that only they know, to a phone number – to an individual'.[89] Even if such fears may be overhyped, it is worth reiterating that in such situations the public's perception of the technology and how it may operate would likely have significant impact on their actions.[90]

---

[85]   In 2019 alone, there were three high profile data breaches, see: Today, 'Personal data of 808,000 blood donors compromised for nine weeks; HSA lodges police report', *Today Online* (18 March 2019) <https://www.todayonline.com/singapore/personal-data-808000-blood-donors-compromised-nine-weeks-hsa-lodges-police-report>; Chang, Koh and Khalik (n 60); H Baharudin, 'Passwords and usernames of staff from MOH, MOE and other agencies stolen and put up for sale by hackers', *The Straits Times* (21 March 2019) <https://www.straitstimes.com/singapore/compromised-log-ins-passwords-from-several-govt-agencies-on-sale-online-says-russian-cyber>.

[86]   Wee and Findlay (n 28) 5.

[87]   Asher (n 6).

[88]   Wee and Findlay (n 28) 6.

[89]   Statement of hardware developer S Cross, see Asher (n 6).

[90]   This is also supported by the idea that public trust is often perceptual and subjective rather than objective in nature. See JS Nye, 'Introduction: The decline of confidence in government' in JS Nye, P Zelikow and D King (eds), *Why People Don't Trust Government* (Harvard University Press, 1997) 1, cited in EW Welch, 'Linking Citizen

We note that the results do not necessarily imply acceptance of the Apple and Google technology, even though it offers greater privacy and autonomy to the user. As mentioned, our results show an overarching tendency for Singapore residents to be more wary of businesses collecting their personal data, including the three data categories of particular relevance to contact tracing technology.

5.1   Limitations and Future Research

Some limitations of our study are as follows: as the respondents are Singapore residents, the results may not be generalisable beyond the Singapore context. Additionally, while large sample sizes generally result in more precise estimates of population characteristics, they may also over-emphasise certain effects.[91] There are also the usual limitations of an online and self-administered survey.[92]

To address the last two problems, to the extent practicable, we endeavoured to ensure that the respondents generally represented Singapore residents in terms of age, gender and race.[93] In this regard, we noted that the younger age groups were over-represented, while the older age groups were under-represented (as compared with the number of Singapore citizens and permanent residents aged 15 and above).[94] This is consistent with research demonstrating that older individuals prefer 'non-web' modes of responding to surveys (and are hence less responsive to online surveys), while younger adults prefer to respond online.[95] Given this, future research targeting older generations (Boomer and above) could shed light on whether Singapore residents in the Millennial and Generation X cohorts would develop the same attitudes as the older age groups shown in our study or whether they have a particular relationship to trust and data sharing that will be sustained over time.

It would also be helpful to conduct research into residents' responses after the COVID-19 situation has been resolved, to determine the changes, if any, in

---

Satisfaction with E-Government and Trust in Government' (2004) 15(3) *Journal of Public Administration Research and Theory* 371, 374.

[91]   B Lantz, 'The large sample size fallacy' (2013) *Scandinavian Journal of Caring Science* 487.

[92]   See J Bethlehem, 'Selection Bias in Web Surveys' (2010) 78(2) *International Statistical Review* 161.

[93]   See also JR Evans and A Mathur, 'The Value of Online Surveys' (2005) 15(2) *Internet Research* 195 for a discussion of some of the positive aspects of conducting surveys online.

[94]   See note 70.

[95]   J Mulder and M de Bruijne, 'Willingness of Online Respondents to Participate in Alternative Modes of Data Collection' (2019) 12 *Survey Practice* 1.

residents' attitudes towards data collection by the government, and the factors that contribute to such changes. Moreover, deeper investigations could be made into the socio-demographic factors that correlate with or would foster trust in government data collection.

6.   CONCLUSION

Although our survey was conducted before the onslaught of COVID-19 and the accompanying use of privacy-compromising contact tracing technology, our findings still served to provide insights into the resistance towards the use of such technology. In particular, our findings show that there already existed concerns about government collection of personal data and corresponding trust issues before they became magnified by subsequent events. To this extent, it may be inferred that the high adoption rate[96] of the TraceTogether technology by Singapore residents at this point in time is a context-specific phenomenon, driven by the COVID-19 emergency and government-mandated measures. Once the emergency is over, it may well be that Singapore residents will revert to at least their pre-COVID-19 levels, if not higher levels of concern over the government's collection of personal data given the January 2021 revelation.

Indeed, the public outcry that followed the revelation was immediate. Some residents experienced a 'visceral feeling of betrayal' and expressed their unhappiness and fear as follows:[97]

> If you have the realisation that (the data) would not be as private as you mentioned earlier, why didn't you say something? ... It does feel like there has been a promise broken... It feels like choosing not to use TraceTogether – and to use only the other (SafeEntry system) – is the least I can do to assuage my emotions.
>
> It's kind of like the start of your worst fears happening, and it may unravel further.

Other residents have raised concerns about a breach of trust[98] including what was seen as a 'bait-and-switch' by the government.[99] While the government

---

[96]   C Wong, 'Budget debate: Contact tracing process shortened with almost 90% of S'pore residents using TraceTogether', *The Straits Times* (26 February 2021) <https://www.straitstimes.com/singapore/politics/almost-90-per-cent-of-residents-on-tracetogether-programme>.

[97]   Elangovan and Tan (n 23).

[98]   See, eg, O Rajah, 'Netizen vents frustration against TraceTogether in profanity-filled post', *The Independent* (8 January 2021) <https://theindependent.sg/netizen-vents-frustration-against-tracetogether-in-profanity-filled-post/>.

[99]   K Han, 'Broken promises: How Singapore lost trust on contact tracing privacy', *MIT Technology Review* (11 January 2021) <https://www.technologyreview.com/2021/01/11/1016004/singapore-tracetogether-contact-tracing-police/> .

quickly passed legislation restricting the use of contact tracing data in criminal investigations to only serious crimes (such as murder and terrorism), along with certain other data protection safeguards,[100] it is uncertain whether the concerns have been assuaged.

The results of our study and this turn of events should give the Singapore government pause as there are wider implications at stake beyond the acceptance of contact tracing technology. The current efforts to make Singapore an AI hub and smart nation[101] would naturally involve the need to collect large amounts of data from the population. As it is, our study shows that increased exposure to AI correlates to having greater concern about sharing personal data with the government. This implies that Singapore's push towards a more AI-savvy population[102] could simultaneously hinder its AI hub ambitions. The public disquiet highlighted above also indicates that maintaining trust is vital for the success of any government-initiative, even ones that are intended for the public good. The Singapore government would do well to heed the expressed sentiments on the ground in its push towards making Singapore a smart nation – whether the endeavour would be a smooth or rocky one would depend on this, as the experience with getting Singapore residents to adopt the TraceTogether technology has amply shown.

BIBLIOGRAPHY

Articles/Books/Reports

Bethlehem, J, 'Selection Bias in Web Surveys' (2010) 78(2) *International Statistical Review* 161

Esmaeilzadeh, P, 'Use of AI-based tools for healthcare purposes: a survey study from consumers' perspectives' (2020) 20 *BMC Medical Informatics and Decision Making* 170

Evans, JR and A Mathur, 'The Value of Online Surveys' (2005) 15(2) *Internet Research* 195

Gupta, A and A Dhami, 'Measuring the impact of security, trust and privacy in information sharing: A study on social networking sites' (2015) 17 *Journal of Direct, Data and Digital Marketing Practice* 43

Lantz, B, 'The large sample size fallacy' (2013) *Scandinavian Journal of Caring Sciences* 487

---

[100]   Chee (n 23).

[101]   See, eg, the Smart Nation Open Data Portal <https://www.smartnation.gov.sg/resources/open-data-resources>.

[102]   See, eg, National Artificial Intelligence Strategy <https://www.smartnation.gov.sg/docs/default-source/default-document-library/national-ai-strategy.pdf?sfvrsn=2c3bd8e9_4>.

Mayer, RC, JH Davis and FD Schoorman, 'An integrative model of organisational trust' (1995) 20(3) *Academy of Management Review* 709

Mitroff, II and R Storesund, *Techlash: The Future of the Socially Responsible Tech Organization* (Springer, 2020)

Motsenok, M et al, 'The Slippery Slope of Rights-Restricting Temporary Measures: An Experimental Analysis' (2020) *Behavioural Public Policy* 1

Mulder, J and M de Bruijne, 'Willingness of Online Respondents to Participate in Alternative Modes of Data Collection' (2019) 12 *Survey Practice* 1.

Nye, JS, 'Introduction: The decline of confidence in government' in JS Nye, P Zelikow and D King (eds), *Why People Don't Trust Government* 1 (Harvard University Press, 1997)

Oh, S et al, 'Physician Confidence in Artificial Intelligence: An Online Mobile Survey' (2019) 21(3) *Journal of Medical Internet Research*

Richards, NM and W Hartzog, 'Taking Trust Seriously in Privacy Law' (2016) 19 *Stanford Technology Law Review* 431

Sotgiu, G and CC Dobler, 'Social stigma in the time of Coronavirus' (2020) *European Respiratory Journal*

Suh, B and I Han, 'The Impact of Customer Trust and Perception of Security Control on the Acceptance of Electronic Commerce' (2003) 7 *International Journal of Electronic Commerce* 135

Usoro, A et al, 'Trust as an antecedent to knowledge sharing in virtual communities of practice' (2007) 5 *Knowledge Management Research & Practice* 199

Waldman, AE, 'Privacy, Sharing, and Trust: The Facebook Study' (2016) 67 *Case Western Reserve Law Review* 193

Welch, EW, 'Linking Citizen Satisfaction with E-Government and Trust in Government' (2004) 15 *Journal of Public Administration Research and Theory* 371

Wong, CML and O Jensen, 'The Paradox of Trust: Perceived Risk and Public Compliance during the COVID-19 Pandemic in Singapore' (2020) *Journal of Risk Research* 1

Legislation

Personal Data Protection Act 2012 (Singapore)

6. Regulating personal data usage in COVID-19 control conditions

Mark Findlay and Nydia Remolina[1]

1. INTRODUCTION

Concern has been widely expressed about the potential for COVID-19 control technologies and resultant data sharing negatively impacting on civil rights, invading personal privacy, undermining citizen dignity through expansive data matching and ultimately providing opportunities for data use well beyond the brief of virus mitigation. Citizen trust may be another tragic victim of the pandemic, without appropriate and proportionate regulatory intervention.[2]

This chapter offers suggestions regarding effective and inclusive regulatory responses when faced with extended surveillance, tracking/tracing, public/ private provider data sharing and any breakdown in personal data firewalls, or otherwise conventional aggregated data deviations and distortion. In doing so, the chapter explores personal data usage in the context of COVID-19 as a regulatory enterprise. Hence, the chapter addresses four fundamental features influencing the ultimate regulatory decision and direction: why, when, where and what. The chapter then presents a regulatory strategy to address the challenges of data usage in COVID-19 control conditions.

[1] The authors acknowledge the assistance of Loke Jia Yuan with research into discrimination, and sunset clauses. This research is supported by the National Research Foundation, Singapore under its Emerging Areas Research Projects (EARP) Funding Initiative. Any opinions, findings and conclusions or recommendations expressed in this material are those of the author(s) and do not reflect the views of National Research Foundation, Singapore.

[2] A Wee and M Findlay, 'AI and Data Use: Surveillance Technology and Community Disquiet in the Age of COVID-19' (SMU Centre for AI & Data Governance Research Paper No 2020/10, 14 September 2020) <https://ssrn.com/ abstract=3715993>.

2. PART 1: HOW TO REGULATE DATA USE

In approaching any regulatory enterprise there are four fundamental features influencing the ultimate regulatory choice and direction:

Why – The simple answer is that because many of the pandemic control technologies employed to fight the virus produce, use, store or disseminate personal data then this should not proceed without responsible governance.[3] Are the control justifications for employing personal data and restricting liberties valid, or indeed excessive?[4] Thus, the *why* question becomes difficult to isolate from the consent, compliance, goodwill or even reluctant acquiescence of the data subject.

When – When the emergency conditions are sufficiently relieved to return to considerations of conventional personal data protection may be more a political and economic, rather than a health sciences determination.[5] To avoid inconsequential deliberations over when is it safe enough to be concerned about personal data use, regulators can suggest that it is more productive to get protections in place as we roll out and apply intrusive technologies.[6] This thinking accepts either that there is no crisis too great or no personal data too insignificant to obviate the need for regulatory oversight.

---

[3] T Muller, 'Health apps, their privacy policies and the GDPR' (2019) 10(1) *European Journal of Law and Technology*; B Fung, 'In this time of the coronavirus, does personal data privacy get thrown out the window?', *Withers World Wide* (20 March 2020) <https://www.withersworldwide.com/en-gb/insight/in-this-time-of-covid-19-does-personal-data-privacy-get-thrown-out-the-window>; European Patients Forum, 'The new EU Regulation on the protection of personal data: what does it mean for patients?' (2018) <https://www.eu-patient.eu/globalassets/policy/data-protection/data-protection-guide-for-patients-organisations.pdf>.

[4] S Nossel, 'Don't Let Leaders Use the Coronavirus as an Excuse to Violate Civil Liberties, Foreign Policy', *Foreign Policy* (30 April 2020) <https://foreignpolicy.com/2020/04/13/governments-coronavirus-pandemic-civil-liberties/>; M Bull, 'Beating Covid-19: The problem with national lockdowns', *The London School of Political Science, EUROPP - European Politics and Policy Blog* (Blog Post, 26 March 2020) <https://blogs.lse.ac.uk/europpblog/2020/03/26/beating-covid-19-the-problem-with-national-lockdowns/>.

[5] J Bacevic, 'There's no such thing as just "following the science" – coronavirus advice is political', *The Guardian UK* (28 April 2020) <https://www.theguardian.com/commentisfree/2020/apr/28/theres-no-such-thing-just-following-the-science-coronavirus-advice-political>. In the context of the coronavirus, disagreements among scientists are evident. See R Milne, 'Architect of Sweden's no-lockdown strategy insists it will pay off', *Financial Times* (8 May 2020) <https://www.ft.com/content/a2b4c18c-a5e8-4edc-8047-ade4a82a548d>.

[6] By 'intrusive technologies' we mean any type of data-driven initiative that automatically collects and/or shares personal data that outside the crisis context of the pandemic data would likely be subject to limitations or protections.

Where – Wherever the data is produced, stored, accessed and used. There seems little doubt that the value of personal privacy is militated by access to private space, and familiarity with rights discourse.[7] A key strategy in the fight against the virus promoted by North World states[8] has been social distancing. The discriminatory resonance of that discourse for migrant workers, prisoners and mental health patients in secured facilities, residents in aged-care institutions, the poor in slums, and people living on the streets should not justify regulatory location only where personal data and individual liberties are actionable.

What – Regulatory techniques range across a continuum of command and control to the least intrusive compliance formats.[9] Where any regulatory initiative sits on that continuum will depend on the urgency for a regulatory outcome, cooperation with or resistance against regulatory intent, and the extent to which regulatory needs can be quarterised from other unconnected or competing regulatory demands. Another important determinant when choosing a preferred regulatory technology[10] is the extent to which regulatory recipients identify the need for behavioural change outcomes.[11] Take, for instance, the

---

[7]   C Raab and B Goold, 'Protecting information privacy' (Research Report No 69, Equality and Human Rights Commission, 2011) <https://www.equalityhumanrights .com/sites/default/files/research-report-69-protecting-information-privacy.pdf>;   G Greenleaf, 'The Right to Privacy in Asian Constitutions' (Draft Chapter, 4 March 2020) <https://papers.ssrn.com/sol3/papers.cfm?abstract_id=3548497>.

[8]   United States, Canada, the United Kingdom, all member states of the European Union, Russia, Israel, Japan, Singapore, South Korea, Australia, and New Zealand.

[9]   M Findlay, 'Corporate Sociability: Analysing Motivations for Collaborative Regulation' (2014) 46(4) *Administration and Society* 339.

[10]   In talking of optional regulatory 'technologies' this refers to the style of regulation (both in substance and application), not to be confused with any technology against which regulation might be directed.

[11]   B Marr, 'COVID-19 Is Changing Our World – And Our Attitude To Technology And Privacy –Why Could That Be Dangerous?', *Forbes* (23 March 2020) <https:// www.forbes.com/sites/bernardmarr/2020/03/23/covid-19-is-changing-our-world- -as-well-as-our-attitude-to-technology-and-privacy-why-could-that-be-a-problem/ #45c68cdd6dc1>; S Khalik, 'Coronavirus: Expect a new normal even if current circuit breaker measures are eased', *The Straits Times Singapore* (7 May 2020) <https:// www.straitstimes.com/singapore/expect-a-new-normal-even-if-current-measures-are -eased>; M Albani, 'There is no returning to normal after COVID-19. But there is a path forward', *World Economic Forum* (15 April 2020) <https://www.weforum.org/ agenda/2020/04/covid-19-three-horizons-framework/>; S Bhargava et al, 'Consumer sentiment evolves as the next "normal" approaches', *McKinsey & Company* (12 May 2020) <https://www.mckinsey.com/business-functions/marketing-and-sales/our -insights/a-global-view-of-how-consumer-behavior-is-changing-amid-covid-19>; CR Sunstein, 'The Meaning of Masks' (Forthcoming Article, 13 April 2020) <https://ssrn .com/abstract=3571428>.

recently introduced 'contact tracing' protocols in countries such as Singapore which require that citizens wanting to gain access to designated private and public premises may only do so if they pass certain health screening, and provide automated identity particulars.[12] Innocuous as these provisions seemed when they were activated, there is growing disquiet over what happens to the data they collect, process and share/disseminate.[13] In addition, the suggestion from the government that association and location data should be combined has strained assurances of privacy protection.[14]

Who – A common failing of regulatory overviews is to stipulate responsibility without specific attribution. This is a global pandemic, but there has been little international cooperation in the regulatory responses. Because of their responsibilities for the provision of health care at large, state agencies obviously assume an important role, or the more so when compulsory powers or enforcement potentials are required. Civil society carries reporting and community oversight functions, provided they are given sufficient information to enable potent participation in the regulatory exercise. Social and conventional media represent an important public education function and a facility for accountable debate provided reporting does not degenerate into misinformation or propaganda for any particular dogma.[15] Independent regulation

---

[12] 'What is SafeEntry?', *Safe Entry* <https://support.safeentry.gov.sg/hc/en-us/articles/900000667463-What-is-SafeEntry-> 'COVID-19: SafeEntry digital check-in system deployed to more than 16,000 venues', *Channel News Asia* (9 May 2020) <https://www.channelnewsasia.com/news/singapore/covid-19-safe-entry-digital-checkin-deployed-16000-venues-1271739>.

[13] Experts around the world have raised their concerns about similar initiatives. G Bellarchive, 'We need mass surveillance to fight covid-19 – but it doesn't have to be creepy', *MIT Technology Review* (12 April 2020) <https://www.technologyreview.com/2020/04/12/999186/covid-19-contact-tracing-surveillance-data-privacy-anonymity/>; A Hern, 'Digital contact tracing will fail unless privacy is respected, experts warn', *The Guardian UK* (20 April 2020) <https://www.theguardian.com/world/2020/apr/20/coronavirus-digital-contact-tracing-will-fail-unless-privacy-is-respected-experts-warn>.

[14] M Findlay, N Remolina, J Loo, A Wee and J Seah, 'Strengthening measures for safe reopening of activities: ethical ramifications and governance challenges' (CAIDG Research/Policy Comment 1, September 2020) <https://caidg.smu.edu.sg/sites/caidg.smu.edu.sg/files/research/20200922_Strengthening%20Measures%20for%20Safe%20Reopening-%20MFAW%20%28A1%29.pdf>.

[15] G Pennycook et al, 'Fighting COVID-19 misinformation on social media: Experimental evidence for a scalable accuracy nudge intervention' (Working Paper, MIT Initiative on the Digital Economy, 2020) <http://ide.mit.edu/sites/default/files/publications/Covid-19%20fake%20news%20ms_psyarxiv.pdf>; R Jayaseelan, D Brindha and K Waran, 'Social Media Reigned by Information or Misinformation About COVID-19: A Phenomenological Study' (2020) <https://papers.ssrn.com/sol3/papers.cfm?abstract_id=3596058>.

institutions and processes are particularly prominent when the purpose is to generate trust in the data management regime. Ultimately, and in a simple configuration when addressing regulatory attribution, the chapter progresses with this rule of thumb: *depending on who it is that advocates and promotes and administers control technologies automatically producing personal data that could be misused, or to the harm of the data subject, then the responsibility to build in regulatory strategies to avoid harm and misuse rests first with them.*

Acknowledging these peremptory questions, the regulatory agenda that follows rests on several prevailing regulatory maxims, when it comes to personal data protection and data use. In most jurisdictions, regional conventions and international instruments, there is recognition of the necessity to protect personal data, both in the interests of the data subject and for the integrity of the data itself.[16] While the limitations on personal data protection, and privacy regulation more generally, are widely understood,[17] and there is often contention surrounding what is a challenge to personal data and privacy,[18] constitutional rights of privacy and administrative/legislative activity for the protection of personal data support regulation in the case at hand. In countries where these measures have been implemented, there is a groundswell of public opinion questioning the data safety of data use measures in the pandemic and asking for guarantees that the use of personal data will be limited to the exigencies of the health crisis.[19]

Even though there are fundamental and universal characteristics which attend on human dignity, humane society and inclusive governance that should be a core aspirational focus of personal data protection, moving from that commitment, it would be naïve to ignore the differential attitudes to the regulation of data protection region-to-region. Currently, in Europe, the UK, Australia and Singapore there has been much debate surrounding the operation of smartphone tracing apps, with particular reference to voluntary versus compulsory usage, centralised versus individualised data storage, and private plus public

---

[16] G Greenleaf, 'Global Data Privacy Laws 2019: 132 National Laws & Many Bills' (2019) 157 *Privacy Laws & Business International Report* 14; PM Schwartz and K Peifer, 'Transatlantic Data Privacy' (2017) 106 *Georgetown Law Journal* 115.

[17] Greenleaf (n 16); Schwartz and Peifer (n 16).

[18] SF Winter and SF Winter, 'Human Dignity as Leading Principle in Public Health Ethics: A Multi-Case Analysis of 21st Century German Health Policy Decisions' (2018) 7(3) *International Journal of Health Policy and Management* 210.

[19] M Findlay et al, 'Ethics, AI, Mass Data and Pandemic Challenges: Responsible Data Use and Infrastructure Application for Surveillance and Pre-emptive Tracing Post-crisis' (Research Paper No 2020/02, SMU Centre for AI & Data Governance, 2020) <https://papers.ssrn.com/sol3/papers.cfm?abstract_id=3592283>.

information platform alliances.[20] This debate has raised protective options such as algorithm audits, data protection commissions, and independent recurrent evaluation.[21] Often these protection proposals are premised on pre-existing data management infrastructure, backed up by extensive enactments or protocols. Sophisticated debates about the enforcement of protective guarantees make sense in that context.[22] However, for the rest of the world, such as India, yet to legislate for general data protection, the nuances of such a regulatory discussion may be of little practical relevance when civil liberties and human dignity are at stake.

In some jurisdictions with identity card requirements for residents, tracing and tracking may not appear initially as much of a major rights intrusion. In Singapore, the SafeEntry QR code tracing protocols could not function without there being a direct reporting link to the individual's NRIC (National Registration Identity Card).[23] However, in countries such as the United Kingdom and Australia, where personal identity cards have been for decades vigorously opposed as human rights attacks by the state, this would be the foundation position from which, in those jurisdictions, data protection initiatives around such a code process would progress.

The case for regulation being complex but made out, it is now essential to give form and purpose to any proposed regulatory strategy discussed in Part 2.[24] For present purposes there are several different structural approaches that present themselves:

- Highlight an essential regulatory obligation which binds together all the possible challenges posed by surveillance technologies and consequent data use. This *central theme approach* runs the risk of down-playing or bypassing other important themes.

---

[20]   J Ryu and KM Murphy, 'Public-private partnerships for contact tracing can help stop Covid-19', *STAT* (24 April 2020) <https://www.statnews.com/2020/04/24/contact-tracing-public-private-partnerships-covid-19/>.

[21]   European Commission – E-Health Network, 'Mobile applications to support contact tracing in the EU's fight against COVID-19 Common EU Toolbox for Member States' (15 April 2020) <https://ec.europa.eu/health/sites/health/files/ehealth/docs/covid-19_apps_en.pdf>.

[22]   M Kuschewsky, *Data Protection and Privacy: Jurisdictional Comparisons* (Thomson Reuters, 2012); M Gray, *Understanding and Improving Privacy 'Audits' Under FTC Orders* (Working Paper, Stanford Center for Internet & Society, 2018) <https://papers.ssrn.com/sol3/papers.cfm?abstract_id=3165143>.

[23]   'What is SafeEntry?' (n 12); 'COVID-19: SafeEntry digital check-in system deployed to more than 16,000 venues' (n 12).

[24]   The regulatory strategy presented in Part 2 of this chapter provides solutions to address challenges posed by surveillance and control policy. For an expanded explanation of these challenges see M Findlay et al (n 19).

- Follow a more conventional pattern and link regulatory techniques to individual data-use challenges. The difficulty with this approach is that it tends to become repetitive and is too causally dependent.
- Group the challenges under 'liberty/integrity'; 'authority/legitimacy'; 'good governance/data justice' themes and from there consolidate regulatory responses. This approach seems formalist and may tend to predetermine regulatory selection.
- Reverse that approach by setting out a menu of likely and appropriate regulatory technologies and then group data challenges under these options. This approach has the advantage of identifying the regulatory sponsors (state/industry/civil society) more directly.

3.   PART 2: REGULATORY STRATEGIES AND POLICY RECOMMENDATIONS

3.1   General Regulatory Fundamentals

There will be constant and ongoing instances of where deliberations on access against protection, and extraordinary use compared with institutionalised conventional safeguards, will require evaluation around use-case necessities, as the crisis winds down. Additionally, COVID-19 will not be the only global pandemic of this type to confront human futures and there will need to be prevailing appraisal of reasonable conditions to qualify regulatory universals. These observations mean that any realistic regulatory framework should include an arbitration/conciliation facility that will responsibly weigh competing externalities and adjust regulatory requirements to reflect safety/risk imperatives which may never fully extinguish.

There will be different regulatory capacities and styles jurisdiction to jurisdiction, region to region, and across different regulatory challenges. Even so, it is necessary, for the sake of consistent regulatory attainment, to present three particular technologies/institutions/processes that reflect our concerns about enforceability, engagement and citizen empowerment. In brief summary it is proposed that these regulatory cornerstones should be created:

(a)   *COVID Personal Data Commissioner* (CPDC) – this agency would have carriage for researching potential personal data challenges transitioning out of the health crisis. It would have a public education consultation and complaints function. In addition, it would act as a personal data access arbitrator, to determine applications for access against data protection protocols. Finally, it would house a licensing function for data technologies, repositories and expiration requirements. Preferably the Commissioner would be an independent agency with legislative authority, reporting to a board of public and private sector data-harvesters and users, and representatives of other data protection instrumentalities, and civil society.

(b) *Enforced Self-regulation Units* (ESUs) – tasked with the responsible operation and eventual decommissioning of surveillance technologies, and their data repositories, on a technology-specific focus. The CPDC would act as the independent agency in the enforced self-regulatory model. These units would determine compliance guidelines in consultation with the CPDC, public and private stakeholders, and civil society.

(c) *Civil Society Empowerment Initiatives* (CSEI) – during the COVID-19 crisis many countries and communities have seen the emergence of organised and informal community endeavours designed to assist in and propagate the risk/safety control message. As a counterbalance to the negative impact strenuous data protection regulation may have on current and future pandemic control strategies, now and ongoing, this volunteer power-base needs to be enhanced and institutionalised to assist in ensuring the safety conditions of the 'new normal' as the virus crisis transits from an immediate threat to a feature of health care horizons.

There may be two initial reservations raised against the proposals above. Cost and complexity are one. The other is an overreliance on the heavy hand of the state. Responding to the cost and complexity concern which no doubt locates in (a), while we prefer the establishment of a purpose-designed authority there is nothing arguing against its location within a permanent and more generalised data-protection administration. An approach like this would protect against costly duplication, unnecessary overlap and offer economies of scale in administrative capacity and operational infrastructure. In addition, representing tightly confined duties and responsibilities the legislative super-structure for the CPDC would be simple and uncontentious.

As for an over-reliance on state sponsorship, (b) and (c) are self-regulation technologies in primary operation. Further, each of these three proposed technologies appear beneath the earlier mentioned regulatory attribution of first resort – those who are promoting the technologies for tracking, tracing, surveillance, quarantine containment and safe entry have initial responsibility to ensure that automatically produced personal data are sufficiently protected within the operation of the technology and consequent data use. As is the common understanding in enforced self-regulation models, most data use challenges will be met at the lowest level of the regulatory pyramid and this would be no exception in our view, assuming the promoters of the control technology are acting in the public interest at large.

Why would state and private sector data-harvesters and sharing data platforms want to give up windfall data access gains that the virus crisis had offered ongoing. We speculate two reasons:

• *Generation of long-term trust.* Science warns that this will not be the last global health that pandemic states and regions should plan for. A general criticism of the responses to COVID-19 has been the lack of preparedness despite years of serious forewarning.[25] Associated with this failing was a general public insufficiently equipped, informed and ready for the necessary intrusions that surveillance and movement regulation would entail. Put these two factors together and when contact tracing apps were mooted swathes of society were willing to trust neither the technology nor the promoter's assurances.[26] To avoid any tragic repeat of this resistance in future crises, if communities could be reassured by the responsible way key data players cooperated in the protection of personal data with the virus in transit, then the benefits are obvious (and considerable) for those responsible for health risk/safety administration.

• *Best-practice reputation.* The differential infection rates, horrifyingly exponential death tolls and contention over sourcing and spread have left some political (and scientific) reputations in tatters. These negative repercussions for national and regional standings will not be cured by financial bailouts or international enquiries alone. How countries come out the other side in terms of personal data protection and rejecting the temptations of a greater surveillance governance will offer hard proof of responsible regulatory commitment, ethical ascription, and a desire to show the world that universal rights and safeguards do not have to join the scale of human lives lost as the critical measure of control competence.

---

[25]   University of Wyoming, 'Lack of COVID-19 preparedness in line with previous findings, economists find', *ScienceDaily* (14 May 2020) <https://www.sciencedaily .com/releases/2020/05/200514115734.htm>; A Brzozowski, 'COVID-19 pandemic raises questions on preparedness for biological threats', *Euractive* (30 March 2020) <https://www.euractiv.com/section/defence-and-security/news/covid-19-pandemic -raises-questions-on-preparedness-for-biological-threats/>.

[26]   K Cox, 'Half of Americans won't trust contact-tracing apps, new poll finds', *Ars Technica* (30 April 2020) <https://arstechnica.com/tech-policy/2020/04/half-of -americans-wont-trust-contact-tracing-apps-new-poll-finds/>; C Cantú et al, 'On health and privacy: technology to combat the pandemic', *BIS Bulletin No 17* (19 May 2020) <https://www.bis.org/publ/bisbull17.pdf>.

3.2   Challenges Associated with Regulating for Individual Liberty/ Integrity

3.2.1   Discrimination

In order to avoid discrimination in terms of personal data use and harmful conclusions drawn, governments can implement several measures. First, it is important to reduce asymmetries of information. People are more susceptible to biases and stereotypes when they lack accurate information. Clear, concise and culturally appropriate communication – in multiple forms and in multiple languages – is needed to reach broad segments of the population, with particular focus on marginalised communities. This approach can be taken up at a civil society engagement level where prevailing community-based bias is easier to identify.

Additionally, it is relevant to portray different ethnic groups, different age demographics and different levels of physical ability in public information materials about the virus and the emphasis on the special need to protect the vulnerable. This approach has been adopted in certain situations when advertising degrees of social distancing. Images of diverse communities working together to reduce risk can powerfully communicate messages of solidarity and shared commitments to health and well-being. However, racial and gender tokenism, particularly in the portrayal of health-care workers, can have negative impacts and needs to be guarded against.

Finally, media reports which focus on individual behaviour and infected individuals' 'responsibility' for having and spreading the virus can stigmatise these individuals and the groups from which they originate. News consumers should insist on responsible media reports that emphasise prevention practices, and individualised symptoms to look out for and when to seek care rather than stigmatising certain communities. Citizen awareness and professional news oversight bodies have a role to play.

Principles to tackle possible discriminatory practices related to the fight against COVID-19 and the personal data uses should be included in the legal frameworks that regulated the infectious diseases control strategies. By so doing, anti-discrimination measures would not apply to the COVID-19 emergency alone, but also to any other form of data use in all infectious disease environments.

Quarantining control measures, usually imposed on otherwise virus vulnerable or discriminated populations such as migrant workers, confined aged care patients, prisoners and the military, can have a disease incubating effect. The consequent impact on how victim personal data is harvested, interpreted and maintained can complicate ongoing discrimination. The necessity for mass screening, ramped up medical services, humane isolation and progressive reintegration protocols is the responsibility of the quarantining authority as it operates its containment endeavours.[27] At the same time, this authority must have in place personal data protection conventions for the manner in which aggravated infection has disadvantaged particular vulnerable sectors. These conventions should be drafted in consultation with the independent data protection agency. As mentioned above, if personal data produced in the circumstances of mass incubation is then transferred to other databases and subjects are harmed as a result, compensation opportunities need to be administered by an independent data protection agency, perhaps through a public complaints initiation and regular data-use monitoring.

Established anti-discrimination regulators and their legislative powers should not be diminished in their reach during pandemic emergency conditions.

3.2.2 Grassroots transparency and accountability

The reasons behind any limitation of individual liberties and integrity should be publicly enunciated by those promoting the data-harvesting technology with this potential. Information regarding the positive and negative impacts on safety and identity should be clearly and candidly canvassed in forms and formats that are accessible and understandable to all communities that the technologies will cover (If the CPDC is adopted with licensing powers this information/communication obligation would be a condition of the licence.) As the scale and severity of the COVID-19 pandemic rose to the level of a global public health threat[28] justifying restrictions on certain rights,[29] then causal relations between threat, control policy and intended outcomes must require informed and routine monitoring by civil society effected from intrusive technologies. Civil society can only perform a potent monitoring function if it is provided with up-to-date information, and constant information looping, that details the operation of data-harvesting. Civil society monitoring should be assisted by the regular review of operational objectives for the technology against rights and liberties measures, carried out by the technology promoters (again, if the CPDC is adopted public awareness can also be facilitated within its mandate).[30] Concomitantly, careful attention to human rights such

---

[27] J Loo, J Seah and M Findlay, 'The Vulnerability Project: Migrant Workers in Singapore' (SMU Centre for AI & Data Governance Research Paper No 01/2021, 21 January 2021) <https://ssrn.com/abstract=3770485>.

[28] World Health Organization, 'Coronavirus disease (COVID-19) Pandemic' <https://www.who.int/emergencies/diseases/novel-coronavirus-2019>.

[29] For instance, those that result from the imposition of quarantine or isolation limiting freedom of movement. See A Salcedo, S Yar and G Cherelus, 'Coronavirus Travel Restrictions, Across the Globe', *The New York Times* (15 April 2020) <https://www.nytimes.com/article/coronavirus-travel-restrictions.html>.

[30] *International Covenant on Economic, Social and Cultural Rights*, opened for signature 16 December 1966, 993 UNTS 3 (entered into force 3 January 1976); United

as non-discrimination, and ethical principles like transparency and respect for human dignity can align with an effective control response even in the turmoil and disruption that inevitably results in times of crisis, when the urgent need to protect health dominates discussions of potential harm to other individual rights. For these 'rights' to have localised meaning, technology promoters must translate principles into practice through a 'use-case approach' to control benefits and liberty/integrity intrusions (if ESUs are adopted and activated they would take on this regulatory responsibility). A useful way to embed this 'awareness' regulatory atmosphere is through recurrent and structured community consultations and conversations.[31]

3.2.3 Anxiety reduction

Social and conventional media provide both positive and negative influences over community anxieties associated with the pandemic and its control. Depending on the emphasis, economic or scientific, reporting of virus control can condemn or extol the same strategies. Social distancing is a necessary measure to keep us safe or an authoritarian over-reaction that will ruin the economy. Guarding against anxiety-inducing media influence is much more than vigilance against fake news or pernicious reporting. Major news platform providers (social and conventional) in an atmosphere of anxiety and dangerous polarisation have a duty to provide balanced reporting. Unfortunately, in the COVID-19 outbreak they have patently failed to maintain even unbiased news coverage. This expectation is difficult to achieve when certain influential politicians, in particular, dispute science and prefer misguided populism to evidence-based policy.[32]

The paternalist state can suggest it will protect us from the extremities and excess of AI and big data. As such, data protection laws become preventive, and individuals are nominated within their reach as vulnerable subjects who see risk in so many third-party applications of personal information which their profligate sharing has enabled, in turn, demanding state regulatory protection. Anxiety, distrust and fear are institutionalised in this order, and it is a contemporary form of divide and rule. Perhaps there is something to be said of the predictive capacities of big data and AI, like the stories that technology can finally identify 'harmful' trends and intervene accordingly, which ensures

---

Nations, Office of the Human Rights Commissioner, 'CESCR General Comment No. 14: The Right to the Highest Attainable Standard of Health (Art. 12)' (11 May 2000) <https://www.refworld.org/pdfid/4538838d0.pdf>.

[31]   European Commission – E-Health Network (n 21).

[32]   We accept that because there are genuine scientific and control-centered disputes about information and outcomes, evidenced-based policy will always be a casualty in an emerging and evolving crisis such as the current pandemic.

the appeal of a 'saved by science' model to anxieties otherwise inevitable calamities. Such preventive imaginings complement a riven social world. This thinking returns us to Mayhew and the 'dangerous classes' of 18th-century London.[33] If the state can identify and predict sites of danger, but fails to make us safe even so, then we turn to other, more radical dualities which want to prevent the flow of humanity so that we can secure our own small safe spaces.

Two regulatory obligations arise in the climate of anxiety. First is a general responsibility on politicians and policymakers to keep the control discourse within objective and evaluative boundaries. An example of this is the daily, detailed public reporting from the Singapore Ministry of Health concerning the demographic details of infection rates, tracing programmes, hospitalisation and community reintegration. This exemplary information flow was not so well maintained when the SafeEntry QR Code strategy was rolled out (with detailed explanation about the centralisation of data only advertised on a government website).[34] Second is the obligation on social media news platform providers and press councils covering conventional media professional standards to vigilantly oversee balanced reporting and not only identify and redact fake news.

3.2.4   Individual and data integrity

It is important to ensure that data is genuine and fit for the declared purpose, particularly if that emergency purpose is meant to justify abnormal data intrusion. Its objective will be defeated, and unnecessary risk can arise if data that goes into or out of, say, a tracing app is inaccurate. Further, if the app advertises a purpose that it cannot achieve through insufficient data coverage, citizens may become complacent and ignore alternative control measures

---

[33]   H Mayhew, *London Labour and London Poor* (Wordsworth Editions, 2008).

[34]   The SafeEntry website explains the following: 'All data is encrypted, and the data can only be accessed by authorised personnel for contact tracing purposes. The data will be purged when it is no longer needed for contact tracing purposes. Under the Public Sector Governance Act, public officers who recklessly or intentionally disclose the data without authorisation, misuse the data for a gain, or reidentify anonymised data may be found guilty of an offence and may be subject to a fine of up to $5,000 or imprisonment of up to 2 years, or both. The data collected via SafeEntry is stored in the Government server, which will only be accessed by the authorities when needed for contact tracing purposes. The Government is the custodian of the data submitted by individuals, and there will be stringent security measures in place to safeguard access to personal data. Only authorised public officers involved in contact tracing will have access to the data, when the need arises. The data may also be de-identified and aggregated for analytics purposes. Contact data will be shared with the relevant authorities for the specific purpose of contact tracing.' See 'How will my data be protected', *SafeEntry* <https://support.safeentry.gov.sg/hc/en-us/articles/900000681226-
-How-will-my-data-be-protected->.

with a better record of success. Imagine the consequences for eroding trust, of sending out a hundred notifications or requests for self-quarantine on the basis of an incorrectly recorded contact, or as happened recently, notifications of positive tests when the test results were faulty. Therefore, data integrity, or the maintenance of, and the assurance of the accuracy and consistency of data over its entire life-cycle, is a critical requirement for the design, implementation and usage of any system which accesses, stores, processes or retrieves personal data like the case in point.[35]

In the preferred regulatory attribution, it would be the responsibility of the technology promoter, the data-harvester and the data user to have design requirements and data verification fail-safes so that the harmful consequences of inaccurate (or incorrectly analysed data) are minimised and monitored (if the ESU model is adapted this would be the unit's regulatory responsibility).

A completely anonymous data facility where data accuracy is not independently verified can be prone to error and possible abuse. Under the guise of anonymity, users may submit inaccurate information in bad faith, or in good faith but incompetently. To solve the problem of tainted data and the problematic consequences that it represents for individuals' liberties and integrity, data protection regulators (specifically, in the self-regulatory mode, the app promoters) should encourage and embrace the implementation of independent verifiers for the apps that are implemented in COVID-19 related controls, but at the same time not compromising the integrity of the data in use (the CPDC would provide that independent verification). This would be an ex ante measure that may help governments to preserve data integrity, achieve control purposes, and better ensure data subject trust through accountability mechanisms.

However, data integrity also requires some ex post controls once the app is functioning and a possible inaccuracy has been detected. We suggest that preferred data protection authorities (and as a first stage responsibility, app promoters) develop a set of key performance indicators (KPIs) that public and private authorities can use to assess and reflect the effectiveness of the apps in supporting contact tracing. This measure was suggested by the European Commission in April 2020. However, the European Commission does not address which authority should be in charge of this ex post measure.[36] In keeping with the specific responsibilities for promoters they should propose KPIs overseen by the CPDC.

---

[35] KH Govern and J Winn, 'Data Integrity Preservation and Identity Theft Prevention: Operational and Strategic Imperatives to Enhance Shareholder and Consumer Value' in A Jalilvand and AG Malliaris (eds), *Risk Management and Corporate Governance* (Routledge, 2012).

[36] European Commission – E-Health Network (n 21).

3.2.5   Accessibility

Much emphasis has been placed on universal application and the digital accessibility of control strategies and technology. Particularly in South World locations, reliance on smartphone technologies for participation in control efforts will discriminate against those without access to this technology, and cause anxiety if citizens believe their safety is at risk through non-participation. The same is the case with older populations that are less technologically capable. These disadvantages need to be recognised and app promoters should offer alternative manual engagement where possible.

The greatest accessibility issue at the centre of alleviating the crisis is vaccine availability and coverage. Many teams are currently at work producing a vaccine, and China has pledged a massive manufacturing capacity to make available vaccine advantage worldwide.[37] Universal access to vaccination when it eventuates is the prime example of a need for international regulatory cooperation and nation-state interventions against intellectual property barriers. Some of the best placed teams to reach vaccine certification are subsidised by large pharmaceutical companies.[38] One of these organisations at least has promised to charge out doses at cost for the life of the pandemic.[39] This on its own is insufficient assurance that the COVID-19 vaccine will not go the way of HIV-Aids medication, and be available only to the rich. International philanthropic organisations have a role to play in shaming rabid commercialisation and profiteering. National legislatures and courts have the tools of price-fixing and compulsory licensing to counter commercial inaccessibility.[40] Social justice over profit protection is recognised in international trading agreements for circumstances such as these.[41]

---

[37]   C Gretler, 'Xi Vows China Will Share Vaccine and Gives WHO Full Backing', *Bloomberg* (19 May 2020) <https://www.bloomberg.com/news/articles/2020-05-18/china-s-virus-vaccine-will-be-global-public-good-xi-says>.

[38]   A Darzi, 'The race to find a coronavirus treatment has one major obstacle: big pharma', *The Guardian* (2 April 2020) <https://www.theguardian.com/commentisfree/2020/apr/02/coronavirus-vaccine-big-pharma-data>.

[39]   Z Sherrell, 'Experts weigh in on how much a dose of a successful coronavirus vaccine could cost', *Business Insider* (4 May 2020) <https://www.businessinsider.sg/how-much-will-coronavirus-vaccine-cost-2020-5?r=US&IR=T>.

[40]   Ibid.

[41]   DP Fidler, 'Negotiating Equitable Access to Influenza Vaccines: Global Health Diplomacy and the Controversies Surrounding Avian Influenza H5N1 and Pandemic Influenza H1N1' (2010) 7(5) *PLoS Medicine.*

3.3   Challenges Associated with Authority/Legitimacy and Accountability

3.3.1   Private sector data sharing

One tool in the data privacy legislation toolbox is 'information fiduciary' rules. The basic idea is this: When you give your personal information to a data collector or data processor in order to get a service, that company should have a duty to exercise loyalty and care in how it uses that data. Professions that already follow fiduciary rules – such as doctors, lawyers and accountants – have much in common with the online businesses that collect personal data. Both have a direct relationship with customers; both collect information that could be used against those customers; and both have one-sided power over their customers or data subjects.[42]

Accordingly, some have proposed adapting these venerable fiduciary rules to apply to online companies that collect personal data from their customers.[43] New laws would define such companies as 'information fiduciaries'.[44] Some authors have even proposed abandoning the 'one-size-fits-all approach' in data governance when private organisations work with aggregated data collected from individuals who trust in these companies. For those authors, the power that stems from aggregated data should be returned to individuals through the legal mechanism of trusts. Bound by a fiduciary obligation of undivided loyalty, the data trustees would exercise the data rights conferred by the top-down regulation on behalf of the trust's beneficiaries. The data trustees would hence be placed in a position where they could negotiate data use in conformity with the trust's terms, thus introducing an independent intermediary between data subjects and data collectors. Unlike the current 'one-size-fits-all' approach to data governance, there should be a plurality of trusts, allowing data subjects to choose a trust that reflects their aspirations, and to switch trusts when needed.[45]

---

[42]   S Delacroix and N Lawrence, 'Bottom-Up Data Trusts: Disturbing the "One Size Fits All" Approach to Data Governance' (Forthcoming Article, 2018) <https://ssrn .com/abstract=3265315>.

[43]   A Schwartz and C Cohn, '"Information Fiduciaries" Must Protect Your Data Privacy, Electronic Frontier Foundation' (25 October 2018) <https://www.eff.org/ es/deeplinks/2018/10/information-fiduciaries-must-protect-your-data-privacy>;   N Richards and W Hartzog, 'Taking Trust Seriously in Privacy Law' (2016) 19 *Stanford Technology Law Review* 431.

[44]   G Gebhart, 'EFF's Recommendations for Consumer Data Privacy Laws', *Electronic Frontier Foundation* (17 June 2019) <https://www.eff.org/deeplinks/2019/ 06/effs-recommendations-consumer-data-privacy-laws>.

[45]   Delacroix and Lawrence (n 42).

Hence, when the private sector is leading the technology initiatives for controlling the pandemic, privacy can and should be thought of as enabling trust in our essential information relationships. A fiduciary duties approach may empower consumers, build trust and clarify that private companies helping to tackle the virus are also liable not only before health authorities, but as fiduciaries as well. However, this approach requires sophisticated courts and an efficient judiciary system able to adequately enforce those fiduciary duties.

Additionally, in the context of COVID-19 and pandemic control, regulators (such as the CPDC and specific application and technology ESUs) should also consider setting up a national system of evaluation/accreditation endorsement of national apps. This will add an ex ante protection mechanism for data subjects who will be able to discriminate among the multiple offers of surveillance/tracing technologies available in a specific jurisdiction.

3.3.2   State sector surveillance

The main promoters of surveillance technologies in the current crisis are state agencies in charge of controlling the pandemic. The UK and Australian experiences with rolling out contact tracing apps have highlighted two areas of state power that are contentious. The first relates to volition or compulsion when it comes to app uptake. This choice was debated at length in the Australian context and, against a variety of civil rights and community trust measures, compulsion was not preferred.[46] We concur with these arguments and hold in any case that the reality of informed and actual consent in situations such as the one in question are of themselves sufficiently problematic as to make comfort drawn from volition cold and conditional.

The second issue involves data repositories. Several models prefer that data should be stored centrally, assuming in some state repository.[47] The problems associated with this from a data protection point of view are so obvious as to not require detailing.[48] The other alternative is that all data remains on the

---

[46]   A Meade, 'Australian coronavirus contact tracing app voluntary and with "no hidden agenda", minister says', *The Guardian* (18 April 2020) <https://www.theguardian.com/technology/2020/apr/18/australian-coronavirus-contact-tracing-app-voluntary-and-with-no-hidden-agenda-minister-says>.

[47]   Under the centralised model, the anonymised data gathered is uploaded to a remote server where matches are made with other contacts, should a person start to develop COVID-19 symptoms. This is the method the UK is pursuing. Singapore and Australia adopted the centralised model as well. C Criddle and L Kelion, 'Coronavirus contact-tracing: World split between two types of app', *BBC News* (7 May 2020) <https://www.bbc.com/news/technology-52355028>.

[48]   Privacy concerns with regards to state-level repositories for contact tracing range from cybersecurity issues to data use. For instance, in terms of data use, there were initially concerns regarding 'function creep', with information being used for other law

individual device and this is said to offer maximum privacy protections. This assertion has also been disputed.[49]

The starting point for the European Data Protection Board (EDPB) Guidance for COVID-19[50] is that contact tracing apps should be voluntary and not rely on tracking individual movements based on location data but on proximity information regarding users (e.g. contact tracing by using Bluetooth). Especially noteworthy is that the EDPB stresses that such apps cannot replace but only support manual contact tracing performed by qualified public health personnel, who can sort out whether or not close contacts are likely to result in virus transmission. The proximity emphasis, and need for manual tracing to predominate, is not consistent with applications for entry screening operated by employers to track the entry and egress of employees and suppliers to places of work.

Whichever position prevails on voluntary/compulsory and centralised/individualised, state-sponsored surveillance through the application of intrusive technologies is not a regulatory challenge that can be adequately met either by self-regulation or through community activism. This is one occasion where the governance of an independent and commensurably powerful independent data protection agency is to be preferred.

---

enforcement purposes besides COVID-19 contact tracing. In Australia, these concerns were addressed by amending the Australian Privacy Act 1988. The amendment creates offences for using data collected by the COVIDSafe app for any purpose other than contact tracing. Similarly, in January 2021, the government clarified that police have the power to order anyone to produce any data, including TraceTogether data, for the purposes of a criminal investigation. The revelation sparked privacy concerns after the Government had earlier said that TraceTogether data would be strictly used for contact tracing. In February, the government introduced a Bill in Parliament to restrict the use of personal contact tracing data in police investigations. Contact tracing data could be used only to investigate serious offences (terrorism, drug trafficking, murder, kidnapping and serious sexual offences such as rape). See A Mahmud, 'Bill restricting police use of TraceTogether data introduced in Parliament, with tougher penalties for misuse', *CAN Insider* (1 February 2021) <https://www.channelnewsasia.com/news/singapore/trace-together-data-police-use-tougher-penalties-bill-parliament-14086650>; 'Contact Tracing apps: a new world for data privacy', *Norton Rose Fulbright* (February 2021) <https://www.nortonrosefulbright.com/en-sg/knowledge/publications/d7a9a296/contact-tracing-apps-a-new-world-for-data-privacy>.

[49]   J Duball, 'Centralized vs. decentralized: EU's contact tracing privacy conundrum', *International Association of Privacy Professionals* (28 April 2020) <https://iapp.org/news/a/centralized-vs-decentralized-eus-contact-tracing-privacy-conundrum/>.

[50]   European Data Protection Board, 'Guidelines 04/2020 on the use of location data and contact tracing tools in the context of the COVID-19 outbreak' (21 April 2020) <https://edpb.europa.eu/sites/edpb/files/files/file1/edpb_guidelines_20200420_contact_tracing_covid_with_annex_en.pdf>.

3.4   Challenges Associated with Good Governance and Data Justice

The foreword to this section is the universal preference that if data surveillance technologies, tracing, tracking, safe entry or quarantine processes are instituted by the state they should rest on democratically debated legislative authority. Such authority is not satisfied, except in extreme circumstances by relying on general emergency powers or by broadly enunciated health and safety, national security, immigration or public order provisions. In the present control circumstances, many of these initiatives will be augmented from pre-COVID powers to exercise health and safety protections. If so, the particular COVID-19 applications require (for transparency and accountability to be prioritised) specification and not just as administrative provisions under the broad authority of the executive.

In addition, state agencies wishing to avail themselves of such powers must recognise the force and application of constitutional rights and liberties, as well as the specific influence of domestic data protection enactments. Regional and international agreements and conventions which are binding on the activating states must also be taken into account.

As regards the exercise of extra-ordinary data sharing between the private and public data platforms, general use consent provisions, non-specific contract exclusions or commonly worded (and user reliant) privacy statements need to be revisited with special reference to the new sharing practices. These arrangements need to be brought to the individual attention of customers, clients and consumers whose personal data is affected by these sharing protocols.

Compliance with legislative power provisions, private contract obligations and international best practice are fields of review appropriate to the work of the independent data protection agency. A public complaints facility may have the capacity to sharpen this review and increase public confidence in the regulator.

3.4.1   Explainability
Much of what would be discussed under this sub-heading has already been canvassed in considerations of transparency and accountability. We see community comprehension as essential for informed consensus, voluntary participation and the active investment of trust. The first regulatory attribution here rests with the promoters of the device or data users (if ESUs are employed they would coordinate this responsibility). Explainability is more than just the provision of complex and comprehensive information. It needs to be confirmed through evaluations of genuine understanding. Civil society has an important role in testing and confirming that risks and benefits have been comprehensively explained. Many reservations on trusting control strategies and data use are based on misinformation, incomplete information, double meanings

or counter-messages. An effective way to measure whether the message is getting through and that it is the intended message is through public complaints functions. It is envisaged that this remit in the CPDC's brief will provide an important and independent verification tool when explainability is in question.

3.4.2   Avoiding bias

In some cases, biases can manifest as a result of challenges associated with data governance. For instance, certain location data is scattered among multiple commercial platforms generated by automatic location notifications, producing personal movement data about which most data subjects are not even aware. Bigtech companies can also collect location data and have enormous reach within the population.[51] Any kind of automated contact tracing that hopes to find the total array of close contacts will need to access more than a thin slice of existing data pools if the tracking is to effectively find otherwise unknown infected people. In addition, if location data is available to augment proximity data then there is a case for its limited and responsible use. However, it should be remembered that location information provided for one purpose but used for another can, and often does, generate biased analysis. For instance, if someone uses their smartphone locator to traverse Google maps and enters premises where a gay night club may also be operating, if that information is connected with health safety tracing, the nature of the data subject's contexts will carry an assumed bias until manually corrected. Data sources may represent a problem of false conclusions and unsubstantiated analysis which eventuates in misrepresentations of certain associations, thereby magnifying biases. There may also be differences in how various populations and demographics are represented in the data from one location motivation to another. Making public health decisions on such datasets could leave out entire populations, misrepresent others, and lead to a deployment of health care resources that is ineffective from a public safety standpoint.[52] The originating regulatory attribution again rests with the technology promoter and data user to work with designers in

---

[51]   C Farr, 'Facebook is developing new tolls for researchers to track if social distancing is working', *CNBC* (6 April 2020) <https://www.cnbc.com/2020/04/06/facebook-to-help-researchers-track-if-social-distancing-is-working.html>. With over 2.6 billion monthly active users as of the first quarter of 2020, Facebook is the biggest social network worldwide. In the third quarter of 2012, the number of active Facebook users surpassed one billion, making it the first social network ever to do so. 'Number of monthly active Facebook users worldwide as of 1st quarter 2020', *Statista* <https://www.statista.com/statistics/264810/number-of-monthly-active-facebook-users-worldwide/>.

[52]   J Stanley and JS Granick, 'The Limits of Location Tracking in an Epidemic', *American Civil Liberties Union* (8 April 2020) <https://www.aclu.org/sites/default/files/field_document/limits_of_location_tracking_in_an_epidemic.pdf>.

identifying possible algorithmic bias and countering it as the technology is developed. Bias generation needs then to be constantly monitored against the datasets and databases combined in mass data use from unconnected purposes, to health safety tracing objectives.

3.4.3   Data aggregation is not enough

Compared to using individualised location data for contact tracing, deriving public health insights from aggregated location data poses fewer privacy and other civil liberties risks such as restrictions on freedom of expression and association. However, even 'aggregated' location data comes with potential risks and pitfalls. Indeed, aggregation is not a synonym of anonymisation. There is a difference between 'aggregated' location data and 'anonymized' or 'deidentified' location data.[53] Information about where a person is and has been itself is usually enough to re-identify them. Someone who travels frequently between a given office building and a single-family home is probably unique in those habits and therefore identifiable from other readily identifiable sources.[54] A study from 2013 found that researchers could especially characterize 50% of people using only two randomly chosen time and location data points.[55] Will preserving privacy when using aggregated data depend on other temporal and spatial factors around when and how the data is aggregated? How large an area does each data count cover so important associations cannot be drawn but extraneous connections can be avoided? When is a count considered too low and dropped from the data set?[56] For example, injecting statistical noise into a data set preserves the privacy of data subjects, but might undermine the accuracy of the decisions taken based on the particular data set.[57] These variables should be widely known and discussed when any justification relying on aggregation or anonymity is advanced.

In order to address the potential risks and limitations of data aggregation, it is necessary to implement some high-level personal data management

---

[53]   S Stalla-Bourdillon and A Knight, 'Anonymous Data v. Personal Data – A False Debate: An EU Perspective on Anonymization, Pseudonymization and Personal Data' (2017) *Wisconsin International Law Journal* 284.

[54]   J Hoffman-Andrews and A Crocker, 'How to Protect Privacy When Aggregating Location Data to Fight COVID-19', *Electronic Frontier Foundation* (6 April 2020) <https://www.eff.org/deeplinks/2020/04/how-protect-privacy-when-aggregating -location-data-fight-covid-19>.

[55]   Y de Montjoye et al, 'Unique in the Crowd: The privacy bounds of human mobility' (2013) 3 *Scientific Reports*.

[56]   Hoffman-Andrews and Crocker (n 54).

[57]   A Nguyen, 'Understanding Differential Privacy', *Towards Data Science* (1 July 2019) <https://towardsdatascience.com/understanding-differential-privacy-85ce 191e198a>.

practices in the fight against COVID-19.[58] First, private or public companies that produce reports based on aggregated location data from users should release their full methodology as well as information about who these reports are shared with and for what purpose. To the extent they only share certain data with selected 'partners' these groups should agree not to use the data for other purposes or attempt to re-identify individuals whose data is included in the aggregation. Again, this private sector use compliance can be monitored by informed civil society and when shortfalls from best practice arise, the independent agency can investigate and intervene, particularly if any breach involves the monetising of secondary data. Second, data aggregators need to disclose how they address the trade-offs between privacy and granularity and usefulness of data sets. Third, there is often pressure imposed on data aggregators to reduce the privacy properties in order to generate an aggregate data set that a particular decision-maker claims must be more granular in order to be meaningful to them.[59] Before moving forward with plans to aggregate and share location data, aggregators should consult with independent experts approved by the protection agency about the aforementioned trade-offs. Getting input on whether a given data-sharing scheme sufficiently preserves privacy can help reduce the bias that such pressure creates.[60] Use-case evaluations on particular balancing considerations (protection of privacy and protection of public safety) would come within the independent agency's arbitration function.

3.4.4 Privacy by design is not enough

Tech solutionism and privacy-by-design might not be enough for addressing the challenges associated with good governance and data justice. The current focus of the privacy community is very much on whether such apps meet the principles of privacy by design.[61] However, privacy by design is actually embedded within the processes of most companies who have recently come under scrutiny for suspect privacy practices.[62] This begs the question whether privacy by design is enough, beyond expressions of good intent to actually translate into monitored best practice. The inadequacies of privacy by design

---

[58]   Hoffman-Andrews and Crocker (n 54).

[59]   Ibid.

[60]   Ibid.

[61]   Organisation for Economic Co-operation and Development (OECD), 'Tracking and tracing COVID: Protecting privacy and data while using apps and biometrics', *OECD Policy Responses to Coronavirus (Covid-19)* (23 April 2020) <http://www.oecd .org/coronavirus/policy-responses/tracking-and-tracing-covid-protecting-privacy-and -data-while-using-apps-and-biometrics-8f394636/>.

[62]   I Rubinstein and N Good, 'Privacy by Design: A Counterfactual Analysis of Google and Facebook Privacy Incidents' (2013) 28 *Berkeley Technology Law Journal* 1333.

speak volumes in justifying the higher positioning of an independent protection agency in the COVID-19 personal data protection pyramid, above the self-regulatory endeavours of designers, promoters and users.

The main challenge to effective privacy by design is that business concerns often compete with and overshadow privacy concerns. In other words, privacy by design only goes as far as the organisation culturally and commercially accepts it.[63] Hence, in an enforced self-regulation spirit, designers and promoters need to work with independent regulators to agree much clearer guidance about applicable design principles and how best to incorporate them into software development processes in practice. Greater guidance is also needed about how to balance privacy with business (or eventual public safety) interests, and there must be oversight mechanisms, such as an independent agency, in place. Tech-driven initiatives must be aligned with trust-based business strategies with stakeholder accountability metrics to overcome trust redaction from many citizens and consumers located on brands and institutions. Corporate culture should be part of what data protection regulators oversee from a privacy perspective, consistent with the enforced self-regulation model.

3.4.5   Cybersecurity

Ransomware attacks on hospitals and health systems have continued during the pandemic, raising key cybersecurity considerations about infrastructure disruptions.[64] COVID-19 has caused governments and private companies to spread and dilute data security priorities and resources, making it even more challenging to get attention focused on addressing cybersecurity challenges like ransomware attacks, which were significant issues to healthcare cybersecurity even before the pandemic.[65]

This tech-driven type of control for pandemics might be exposing data subjects and health system stability in ways that have not been factored into

---

[63]   L Kaufman, 'Is "Privacy by Design" Enough? Product development's privacy alibi', *Medium, Popular Privacy* (20 January 2020) <https://medium.com/popular -privacy/is-privacy-by-design-enough-12aa4fddb747>.

[64]   J Drees, 'COVID-19 cyber threats: Why data integrity is crucial & how to protect it', *Becker's Health IT* (6 May 2020) <https://www.beckershospitalreview.com/ cybersecurity/covid-19-cyber-threats-why-data-integrity-is-crucial-how-to-protect-it .html>.

[65]   For example, the most serious breach of personal data in Singapore's history took place in 2018, with 1.5 million SingHealth patients' records accessed and copied while 160,000 of those had their outpatient dispensed medicines' records taken. K Kwang, 'Singapore health system hit by "most serious breach of personal data" in cyberattack; PM Lee's data targeted', *Channel News Asia* (18 October 2018) <https:// www.channelnewsasia.com/news/singapore/singhealth-health-system-hit-serious -cyberattack-pm-lee-target-10548318>.

risk/benefit analysis. The issue at the security level is not simply whether there is a misplaced confidence in the capacity of tracing apps to balance out added health and safety compromises through a reduction in self-distancing, although this must be vigorously reviewed if automated tracing is to offer anything but a false sense of security. Governments and private organisations deploying these solutions often talk about the importance of nominated technology for saving lives. Coincidentally, there has not been in these justifications disclosure on how citizens in this new environment are exposed to insecurity more than the inherent over-expectations for the tech. It has been reported that the government's anticipated COVID-19 tracing app in the UK has failed crucial security tests and is not yet safe enough to be rolled out across the country.[66] It is understood that the system has botched all tests needed in order for it to be encompassed in the NHS Apps Library, including cyber security, clinical safety and performance.[67] Until these regulatory and quality control hurdles can be met there is little point in standardisation of cyber security protocols, when emergency exceptions avoid their universal ascription.

If governments would like people to opt into such applications, they need to address universal security concerns. To achieve this result, cybersecurity authorities should disclose to the public if the apps used for containing the pandemic comply with the same standards that other health data processing initiatives observe.

3.4.6　Expiration of the use of data

Best practices in surveillance and mass data use need to be identified along with responsible data-collection and data-processing standards at a global scale. Essential in any best practice menu is the expiration and redaction of data once the purpose for its collection has been met. In so saying we return to a fundamental expectation that emergency purposes are clearly enunciated, contained and achievable.

It is of utmost importance to have a clear plan for the permanent expunging and erasure of all personal data collected during the pandemic once it no longer serves the original need. It is important to remember that genuinely anonymous information (argued as information that can never be traced back to the data subject) is not classified in many protection instruments as personal data and, for instance, is not covered by the GDPR. Even so, such anonymised data

---

[66]　A Lynn, 'COVID-19 tracing app fails NHS and cyber security tests', *Electronic Specifier* (6 May 2020) <https://www.electronicspecifier.com/industries/medical/covid -19-tracing-app-fails-nhs-and-cyber-security-tests>.

[67]　Ibid.

will exponentially lose its emergency purpose; and therefore on that test alone it is a candidate for automatic redaction.

It might be argued that users should have the choice of whether to opt-in to every new use of their data or remain outside the strategy, but we recognise that obtaining consent for aggregating previously acquired location data to fight COVID-19 may be difficult with sufficient speed to address the public health need. Expediency also means that real and informed data subject consent may, in practice, be illusory. That is why it is especially important that users should be able to review and delete their data at any time.[68]

Whatever legislative powers are granted to generate, store access and share, either in general form, or more specifically enunciated, they should be contained through sunset clause provisions. The goal is to force the rule-maker to revisit the regulation to determine whether it should be extended or automatically expire.[69] Sunsetting is often, but not always, associated with emergency legislation that is enacted during war and other times of crises. For example, the 2001 US Patriot Act and 2005 UK Prevention of Terrorism Act include sunset clauses.[70] In line with this trend, a few countries have included or considered sunset clauses as part of their response to COVID-19.

In practice, sunsetting is not always an effective expiration device. One common shortcoming is that the targeted regulation receives 'rubber stamp' re-approval, as opposed to meaningful review. For example, Part 4 of the UK 2001 Anti-terrorism, Crime and Security Act allows for indefinite detention of non-national terrorist suspects. The Act was reviewed in 2003, but with little scrutiny.[71]

It is anticipated that use cases will arise where automatic data expiration needs to be reviewed. Provided the conditions for and consequences of the review are open, and the data subject is empowered to participate in the review, then individual evaluations of data life extension appear appropriate.

---

[68]   Gebhart (n 44).

[69]   S Ranchordas, 'Sunset Clauses and Experimental Regulations: Blessing or Curse for Legal Certainty?' (2015) 36(1) *Statute Law Review* 28; I Bar-Siman-Tov, 'Temporary Legislation, Better Regulation, and Experimentalist Governance: An Empirical Study' (2018) 12(2) *Regulation & Governance* 192.

[70]   Ranchordas (n 69).

[71]   S Molloy, 'COVID-19, Emergency Legislation and Sunset Clauses', *UK Constitutional Law Association Blog* (Blog Post, 8 April 2020) <https://ukconstitutionallaw.org/2020/04/08/sean-molloy-covid-19-emergency-legislation-and-sunset-clauses/>.

4.   CONCLUSION

This chapter offers suggestions regarding effective and inclusive regulatory responses when faced with extended surveillance, tracking/tracing, public/private provider data sharing and any breakdown in personal data firewalls, or otherwise conventional aggregated data deviations and distortion. In doing so, the chapter explores personal data usage in the context of COVID-19 as a regulatory enterprise.

The chapter addresses four fundamental features influencing the ultimate regulatory decision and direction: why, when, where and what, and presents a regulatory strategy to address the challenges of data usage in control conditions. There will be constant and ongoing instances of where deliberations on access against protection, and extraordinary use compared with institutionalised conventional safeguards will require evaluation around use-case necessities, as the crisis winds down. COVID-19 will not be the only global pandemic of this type to confront human futures and there will need to be prevailing appraisal of reasonable conditions to qualify regulatory universals. These observations mean that any realistic regulatory framework should include an arbitration/conciliation facility that will responsibly weigh competing externalities and adjust regulatory requirements to reflect safety/risk imperatives which may never fully extinguish.

The proposed regulatory model processes reflect our concerns about enforceability, engagement and citizen empowerment. In brief summary, it is proposed that this model is based on: First, the creation of an independent agency that researches potential personal data challenges transitioning out of the control situations, acts as a personal data access arbitrator and houses a licensing function for data technologies, repositories and expiration requirements. Second, Enforced Self-regulation Units tasked with the responsible operation and eventual decommissioning of surveillance technologies, and their data repositories, on a technology-specific focus. Third, Civil Society Empowerment Initiatives that act as a counterbalance to the negative impact that strenuous data protection regulation may have on current and future pandemic control strategies.

Since originally proposing this regulatory structure, many of its features have received serious consideration by those jurisdictions where their public is active in debating data use, and some pre-existing institutional and process safeguards are in place. In addition, the theoretical and policy underpinnings of the framework have resonated with those regulators who are discovering that the promises about ethical ascription are not enough on their own to generate the community trust necessary for the control efficacy of the technology.

The closing invocation for those contemplating the regulation of global crises is that no problem is so pressing or pervasive as to demand the closure of representative civil participation, or the hijacking of personal data and the diminution of human dignity that follows.

BIBLIOGRAPHY

Articles/Books/Reports

Bar-Siman-Tov, I, 'Temporary Legislation, Better Regulation, and Experimentalist Governance: An Empirical Study' (2018) 12(2) *Regulation & Governance* 192

de Montjoye, Y et al, 'Unique in the Crowd: The privacy bounds of human mobility' (2013) 3 *Scientific Reports*

Fidler, DP, 'Negotiating Equitable Access to Influenza Vaccines: Global Health Diplomacy and the Controversies Surrounding Avian Influenza H5N1 and Pandemic Influenza H1N1' (2010) 7(5) *PLoS Medicine*

Findlay, M, 'Corporate Sociability: Analysing Motivations for Collaborative Regulation' (2014) 46(4) *Administration and Society* 339

Govern, KH and J Winn, 'Data Integrity Preservation and Identity Theft Prevention: Operational and Strategic Imperatives to Enhance Shareholder and Consumer Value' in A Jalilvand and AG Malliaris (eds), *Risk Management and Corporate Governance* (Routledge, 2012)

Greenleaf, G, 'Global Data Privacy Laws 2019: 132 National Laws & Many Bills' (2019) 157 *Privacy Laws & Business International Report* 14

Mayhew, H, *London Labour and London Poor* (Wordsworth Editions, 2008)

Muller, T, 'Health apps, their privacy policies and the GDPR' (2019) 10(1) *European Journal of Law and Technology*

Ranchordas, S, 'Sunset Clauses and Experimental Regulations: Blessing or Curse for Legal Certainty?' (2015) 36(1) *Statute Law Review* 28

Richards, N and W Hartzog, 'Taking Trust Seriously in Privacy Law' (2016) 19 *Stanford Technology Law Review* 431

Rubinstein, I and N Good, 'Privacy by Design: A Counterfactual Analysis of Google and Facebook Privacy Incidents' (2013) 28 *Berkeley Technology Law Journal* 1333

Schwartz, PM and K Peifer, 'Transatlantic Data Privacy' (2017) 106 *Georgetown Law Journal* 115

Stalla-Bourdillon, S and A Knight, 'Anonymous Data v. Personal Data – A False Debate: An EU Perspective on Anonymization, Pseudonymization and Personal Data' (2017) *Wisconsin International Law Journal* 284

Winter, SF and SF Winter, 'Human Dignity as Leading Principle in Public Health Ethics: A Multi-Case Analysis of 21st Century German Health Policy Decisions' (2018) 7(3) *International Journal of Health Policy and Management* 210

Treaties

International Covenant on Economic, Social and Cultural Rights, opened for signature 16 December 1966, 993 UNTS 3 (entered into force 3 January 1976)

7. Editors' reflections

Mark Findlay and Jolyon Ford

- Coding legal norms: an exploratory essay (Will Bateman)
- Artificial intelligence and the unconscionability principle (Dilan Thampapillai)
- The possibilities of IF-THEN-WHEN (Sally Wheeler)
- Doing it online: is mediation ready for the AI age? (Nadja Alexander)

At a time when the regulation of big tech seems to be only just finding ground beyond oblique deference to ethical principles, it may seem premature – even naïve – to be placing faith in concepts like digital justice or attempts to codify legal norms. Yet the digital remains ever present, more so during the slow drag through COVID purgatory. Even for those at the periphery of emerging technologies, each new day brings reminders of e-government services, of digital finance, of cryptocurrencies, of the supposed benefits of a distributed ledger. In this context, to not ask questions of justice, fairness and equity would be disingenuous. All four chapters in this section are responding to a similar set of questions: with AI being increasingly ubiquitous, how should legal theory and practice keep pace? How can we – as practitioners, researchers and theorists – understand these changes? Whose responsibility is it to respond to these developments so that their motivation is not confined to economic pre-determinants and outcomes? How can the digital discourse embrace wide social concerns consistent with the normative frames of many legal arrangements?

Recognising insufficiencies is one way to propose arenas for change: Thampapillai's chapter invites a unique take on familiar ground: the recognition that AI has enabled gross power imbalances between those building and working in platforms – social media companies or the gig economy – and its users. His chapter breaks down contract law and the doctrine of unconscionable conduct. By highlighting examples that we are now no stranger to – the online harassment of minorities and the contractual unfairness between workers and gig platforms opened up in other contributions – Thampapillai makes a compelling argument to expand the contractual reach by making explicit transactional imbalances, or unjustified benefits, and recognising that contractual benefits can sometimes nonetheless be misappropriated by platforms. This analysis also suggests a wider inclusion of interests in the conventional understanding of contracting parties.

This examination of contract law is mirrored in Wheeler's chapter on the development of smart contracts. Where Thampapillai's chapter discusses the contractual relationships which have developed to become the default tool regulating our relationships with social media companies, and the mystification of consent gateways, Wheeler's chapter returns to a more traditional notion of contracts: an agreement between parties that is protected and enforceable under the law. Here, Wheeler reverses the question typically levied at smart contracts, not 'are smart contracts legal instruments?' but '*how* do smart contracts change relationships between contracting parties?' Examining the *Law in Action* scholarship, Wheeler notes that the first question often takes priority over the second, when in fact the reality of contracting – in effect, formalising in text only a partial reality of the existing relationship between two parties – is born from a sociality that is now expanding to include little-understood norms and institutions in which programmers and coders are enmeshed. When this happens, the issue on the table is not so much that smart contracts are inflexible – the common argument put forth by detractors – but that they are nudging the formation of new relationships that have implications for both the practising of contracting – its formation and enforcement – and how parties orientate their relationships around these contracts. At heart this is a struggle between narrow concepts such as legal certainty, and the flexibility and subjective application of legal discretions. This is a struggle between binary language and more fluid legal linguistics – a struggle that should have its roots in the social rather than technological expedition.

Bateman's contribution takes this concept of smart contracts and expands it further to look at debates around legal automation. Here, the question of formalising principles and norms – good faith, reasonable care – are the central axis upon which disagreements are most vivid. Distinguishing between 'law as rules' (deterministic and predictable) and 'law as project management' (indeterminate and accommodating for certain varieties of uncertainties), his chapter points out the affinities that exist between the first and supporters of automated systems, which understandably do not exist for the latter. State of the art systems reinforce this divide: algorithms remain mostly deterministic; concepts like good faith remain difficult to formalise in mathematical equations; machine learning models remain insufficiently robust when facing dynamic social complexities. As with Wheeler's contribution, the question of how legal automation will unfold over the coming years is not simply a technical one; instead, Bateman argues that these decisions of what to automate, and how, will be answered by existing socio-legal systems. Wheeler writes that programming and coding create specific tools that permit 'flexibility of use rather than flexibility of terms'; the same principle, it seems, applies here to legal automation. Not to be forgotten is the reality that the vast majority of contacts are performed based on general relationships of trust and not definitive terminology from which parties cannot escape. Seen in this light the incursion of technology into contracting should respect intuitive action and not enforce compulsory determinations in a context of impending breach. The lawyer might need to prevail over the technician in this regulatory frame.

All of these questions – of the codification of legal norms and the reconfiguration of institutions of trust; of power and the benefactors and losers of adapting currently inscrutable digital systems into our legal systems – come to a head in Alexander's chapter on digital mediation. Over the past years of COVID restrictions and social distancing, support for digital mediation has grown both conceptually and in practice. Here, then, Wheeler's discussion of the relevance of social relationships and Bateman's emphasis on indeterminate processes find their clearest expression in mediation's procedural flexibility. The concept of *online* mediation, seen through their lenses, becomes a minefield to navigate. As Alexander explains, digital mediation needs to be grounded in touchstones of usability, reliability and accessibility that characterise physical mediation. Like Bateman's chapter, it is the tension between support for technical solutions and the reality of embedding norms that Alexander captures most succinctly in her chapter. Her conclusion is telling: in a world tipped into digitisation by the pandemic, 'there is real risk that online mediation practice moves faster than the digital readiness of its institutional providers and in doing so compromises opportunities to transform the core characteristics of mediation in digitally compatible formats'.

'Who are the winners and losers in such a world?' Bateman asks in his discussion of a world where rule-based law has triumphed over its managerial counterpart. But the question applies to all four of these chapters. Power and critiques of it ultimately tie these chapters together. Read separately, they offer insights into the challenges of legal automation across a range of applications. But the chapters also speak to each other. In a world where contract formation and enforcement have collapsed via smart contracts, where do mechanisms of dispute resolution fit? Wheeler reminds us that smart contracts formalise only a single aspect of our sociality, but Thampapillai's chapter warns us that technological systems operating at scale can and do emphasise some modes of sociality over others. Put another way: how will smart contracts be used by social media and gig platforms? If these relationships are already characterised by significant information asymmetries, as trust shifts from people to machines running lines of code, who are we really trusting? These questions are speculative and their discussions can only be exploratory; but these chapters suggest that in order to understand, comprehend and respond to emerging technologies and their associated changes, perhaps we should be casting a wide (and deep) net. Alexander offers digital readiness as a pathway along which dispute resolution practitioners can enjoy the benefits offered through technology without compromising or indeed side-lining personal confirmation of access to justice – humans are never out of the loop.

8.   Coding legal norms: an exploratory essay[1]

Will Bateman

Legislation governing public sector service delivery and negotiated commercial contracts are (both) foundational legal institutions and prime targets for automation through algorithmic decision-systems. 'Smart contracts'[2] and 'e-government'[3] have familiar, unglamorous, upsides: they are cheap and predictable. If the content of public (legislative) and private (contractual) law norms is fixed and determinate, there are few obvious downsides to legal automation. Unfortunately, legal norms are famously diverse. Some are cast as clear commands, others are deliberately vague and unpredictable, yet others are divined by analysing reasons for judgment or the writings of scholars which express values, rather than stipulates. Further complicating the picture is the reality that different types of actors (judges, lawyers, contracting-parties, insurers, public officials, politicians) understand law differently, yet each makes decisions about the content and application of law which have momentous effects on social behaviour.

That diversity in the abstract design and institutional realities of legal norms complicates technical proposals to 'automate law'.[4] It also complicates normative critiques of legal automation. One view is that legal rules should

[1]   Deep thanks are extended to the following thinkers who generously gave their time to discussing, reading and commenting on this work: Kiara Bruggeman, Gordon Brysland, Alban Grastien, Mario Guenther, Brian Hedden, Lachlan McCalman, Leighton McDonald, Frank Pasquale, Julia Powles, Pamela Robinson and Jake Stone.

[2]   See LA DiMatteo, M Cannarsa and C Poncibò (eds), *The Cambridge Handbook of Smart Contracts, Blockchain Technology and Digital Platforms* (Cambridge University Press, 2019); M Corrales, M Fenwick and H Haapio (eds), *Legal Tech, Smart Contracts and Blockchain* (Springer, 2019).

[3]   See S Jeffares, *The Virtual Public Servant: Artificial Intelligence and Frontline Work* (Palgrave, 2021); A Gronlund (ed), *Electronic Government: Design, Applications and Management* (IGI Global, 2001).

[4]   This idea is almost as old as the use of digital computers to create 'artificial intelligence'. For the first recorded proposal, see L Mehl, 'Automation in the Legal World' (paper presented at the *Mechanization of Thought Process Symposium*, National Physical Laboratory, Teddington, Middlesex November 1958). For an intellectual

be automated because they are (or should) not be vague.[5] An opposing view is that vagueness is such an inherent part of law that attempts to eradicate it through mechanistic codification are (at best) magnets for legal risk or (more likely) nonsensical.[6] Outside the academy, where commercial pressures trump normative debates, the impressment of binary code in the administration of contracts and statutes marches on without significant reflection on variations in the design of legal norms.[7] There is little agreement on the terms of debating the question: is legal automation a good thing?

This exploratory chapter proposes some guide-posts through that analytic maze. It begins by explaining why (both) determinate and vague legal norms are valuable and ubiquitous. In some domains, determinate legal rules are useful and valuable because they clearly delineate authority and power, private and public, by providing clear guidance for action. In other domains, indeterminate legal principles, standards, policies and aspirations are more effective guides to, and regulators of, human behaviour. Together, they can be understood as part of a model of 'Law as Project Management', in which legal vagueness is a technique to govern the uncertainties associated with complex social projects.

The chapter then observes some technical features of algorithmic systems that point to the relative ease of automating rule-based legal norms and the obstacles to coding vague law. Useful algorithmic systems are deterministic, even when they incorporate probabilistic elements and machine learning technologies. Coding human language and social practices into algorithmic form is difficult whether 'symbolic' or 'connectionist' models of artificial intelligence are used. Algorithmic systems cope better in highly stationary environments and worse in highly dynamic environments. Although the technological foundation of algorithmic design can change rapidly, those technical features place large obstacles in the way of automating managerial legal regimes.

---

history of artificial intelligence, see M Boden, *Mind as Machine* (Oxford University Press, 2006).

[5]   Eg, C Coglianese and D Lehr, 'Regulating by Robot: Administrative Decision Making in the Machine-Learning Era' (2017) 105 *Georgetown Law Journal* 1147.

[6]   For sources within that spectrum, see W Bateman, 'Algorithmic Decision-Making and Legality: Public Law Dimensions' (2020) 94 *Australian Law Journal* 520; F Pasquale, 'A Rule of Persons, Not Machines: The Limits of Legal Automation' (2018) 87 *George Washington Law Review* 1; M Zalnieriute, L Bennett Moses and G Williams, 'The Rule of Law and Automation of Government Decision-Making' (2019) 82 *Modern Law Review* 425.

[7]   For a sense of the mood, see V Pivovarov, '10 Tips on How To Justify The Need To Implement Automation', *Medium* (6 June 2019) <https://medium.com/case-one-legal-tech/10-tips-on-how-to-justify-the-need-to-implement-automation-1557b899dd15>.

The chapter concludes by mooting some potential impacts of attempting to subject managerial law to machine logic. One predictable impact is an increase in the extent and accuracy of automated planning by businesses and governments. While intuitive, that development would not be entirely free of perverse outcomes, nor desirable on its own terms. Another impact would be a reduction in the capacity of legal norms to guide human behaviour, particularly in relation to complex social activities which have traditionally been governed by vague and indeterminate legal regimes. The final, related, impact would be a narrowing of law's function as a social tool which, all things considered, may not be an entirely undesirable outcome assuming that an effective substitute institution(s) could be found.

Those impacts are expressed as 'potential' (and the chapter as 'exploratory') because the field of 'law and artificial intelligence' is in its adolescence. Providing comprehensive answers to broad questions raised by the use of machine intelligence in legal reasoning and practices requires engaging with a variety of disciplines, experts and human lived experience. Those tasks require more space and time than is available. The following entrée is presented, in lieu of an undercooked banquet.

1.   LAW AS RULES

Some legal norms are highly determinate, predictable and govern people's behaviour in binary ways. They take the stylised forms:

- 'if you perform action X, then sanction Y will apply to you, unless exemption Z applies';
- 'if counterparty A delivers good C to beneficiary B by date D, then distribute divided E to bank account F'; and
- 'if person J is between age range K <-> L, then apply tax credit M'.

Concrete examples of determinate and predictable legal norms can be readily identified in public and private law contexts. Most (but not all)[8] criminal legislation is drafted in a strict, rule-based fashion. Many contractual clauses are drafted to eliminate uncertainty,[9] as is much legislation, particularly governing

---

[8]   See JC Jeffries Jr, 'Legality, Vagueness, and the Construction of Penal Statutes' (1985) 71 *Virginia Law Review* 189.

[9]   Although not invariably: KJ Crocker and SE Masten, 'Pretia Ex Machina? Prices and Process in Long-Term Contracts' (1991) 34 *Journal of Law and Economics* 69; CA Hill and C King, 'How Do German Contracts Do as Much With Fewer Words?' (2004) 79 *Chicago-Kent Law Review* 889; RJ Gilson, 'Value Creation by Business Lawyers: Legal Skills and Asset Pricing' (1984) 94 *Yale Law Journal* 239.

the distribution of social benefits (visas, unemployment insurance, health benefits).[10]

Those rule-based legal norms are venerated by some theoretical approaches to law and government. Within the analytical jurisprudential tradition, 'law as command' theories are premised on the idea that 'law' (properly so called) is composed of clear orders issued from the sovereign to the populace.[11] The same idea of law is a core 'desiderata' of proceduralised jurisprudential theories that link the 'calculability' of legal norms to the legitimacy of liberal government.[12] A similar idea can be found in broader political theoretic work, such as Pettit on republicanism and Lovett on the rule of law,[13] and in the writing of theoretically ambitious appellate judges who lean heavily on the idea that 'the rule of law, means the law of rules'.[14]

Within that eclectic mixture of thinkers, several core ideas are fixed. First, law is a distinct authoritative way to guide people's conduct within society. Secondly, people's conduct will be guided by laws with less (rather than more) textual indeterminacy and institutional complexity. Thirdly, that determinate law is a critical component of western liberalism because free people must be able to predict their legal rights and obligations without undue complication. Let us label the fusion of those ideas the 'Law as Rules' model.

Judging under the Law as Rules model is mechanical. After finding facts, judges simply apply widely accepted conventions of language (definitions, grammar, syntax) to written texts. That austere method reduces independent political and policy choice and endears the Law as Rules model to jurists and theorists at many points on the political spectrum.[15] That method is certainly identifiable in high-volume dispute resolution where time and cost pressures

---

[10]   For the complications with this proposition, see R Dickerson, 'The Diseases of Legislative Drafting' (1964) 1 *Harvard Journal on Legislation* 5; AW Seidman, RB Seidman and N Abeyeskere, *Legislative Drafting for Democratic Social Change: A Manual for Drafters* (Kluwer Law International, 2001); E Majambere, 'Clarity, Precision and Unambiguity: Aspects for Effective Legislative Drafting' (2011) 37 *Commonwealth Law Bulletin* 417.

[11]   See generally, M Freeman and P Mindus (eds), *The Legacy of John Austin's Jurisprudence* (Springer, 2013).

[12]   See L Fuller, *The Morality of Law* (Yale University Press, 1969) 46–81; K Rundle, *Forms Liberate* (Hart Publishing, 2012) 69.

[13]   See P Pettit, *Republicanism: A Theory of Freedom and Government* (Oxford University Press, 1999); and F Lovett, *A Republic of Laws* (Cambridge University Press, 2016) 210–211, who helpfully traces the importance of determinate, calculable law through the theories of Dicey, Hayek, Fuller, Rawls, Raz and Finnis.

[14]   Notably, A Scalia, 'The Rule of Law as a Law of Rules' (1989) 56 *University of Chicago Law Review* 1175.

[15]   Compare the different attitudes to the political effects and desirability of rule-based legal norms in FA Hayek, *Law, Legislation and Liberty* (Routledge,

and the simplicity of legal disputes push judges towards mechanical solutions to legal controversies.[16] It is less obviously identifiable the further up the appellate ladder a dispute proceeds.[17]

Strict rule specification and application, a core feature of the Law as Rules model, is also particularly attractive to designers and proponents of automated decision systems: software engineers, computer scientists, managers and management consultants seeking to cut labour costs; commercial parties trying to control counterparty risk; and public policy practitioners seeking to build mathematically rigorous regulatory systems.

2.   LAW AS PROJECT MANAGEMENT

The Law as Rules model has a counterpoint in the Law as Project Management model which deliberately deploys normative indeterminacy and institutional complexity to permit social co-operation under conditions of high uncertainty. The following rendering of that model draws on the insights of the 'rules vs principles' debate, particularly its conceptual ordering by Braithwaite.[18]

Within the Law as Project Management model, legal norms are a mixture of, on the one hand, rules (determinate and predictable) and, on the other hand, principles, standards, policies and aspirations (indeterminate and unpredictable). Those latter norms are deliberately vague, context dependent and interpretative. Examples familiar to academic and practising jurists include: 'The Parties shall use their best endeavours....'; 'negotiate in good faith'; 'take reasonable care'; 'act in the national interest'; 'make a grant to person suffering hardship'; and 'grant a licence only to a person of good character'.

Those nebulous norms are no less 'legal' than determinate rules. Judges, legislators and contracting parties regularly invoke them. Legal academics write extensively about them.[19] They are integral parts of Western legal systems. Legal theorists, notably Endicott, have explained why 'vague'[20]

2012) with B Scheuerman, 'The Rule of Law and the Welfare State: Towards a New Synthesis' (1994) 22 *Politics and Society* 195.

[16]   On some accounts, a mechanical process of legal reasoning premised on 'incomplete agreements' may be an inherent part of all legal systems: C Sunstein, 'Incompletely Theorised Agreements' (1995) 108 *Harvard Law Review* 1733.

[17]   See the discussion in F Schauer, 'Judging in a Corner of the Law' (1988) 61 *Southern California Law Review* 1717.

[18]   J Braithwaite, 'Rules and Principles: A Theory of Legal Certainty' (2007) 27 *Australian Journal of Legal Philosophy* 47.

[19]   See the debate canvassed by B Leiter, 'Legal Indeterminacy' (1995) 1 *Legal Theory* 481.

[20]   The literature on vague laws is very deep. For an entry point, see R Poscher, 'Ambiguity And Vagueness In Legal Interpretation' in Lawrence Solan and Peter

legal norms are both ineradicable (a brute fact) and valuable.[21] Vagueness is valuable because it 'enables the regulation of activities which simply cannot be regulated with precision and it can be a useful technique for allocating decision-making power and encouraging forms of private ordering that promote the purposes of the law'.[22]

Empirical scholarship supports that theory. Braithwaite's sociological studies indicated that (in certain domains) indeterminate, principle- or standard- like norms more effectively achieved desired regulatory objectives than precise, rule-like norms. Braithwaite's major empirical studies concerned nursing homes and concluded that broadly-framed and subjective (ie, vague) regulation outperformed strict, rule-based regulation in achieving health, safety and care-quality objectives.[23] Similar results were identified in other regulatory contexts composed of extremely precise, granular legal rules: financial services regulation and taxation.[24] A vast regulatory universe of finely-grained rules can be misunderstood, ignored or evaded by industry participants.[25] Such a universe also creates abundant opportunities for regulatory evasion and arbitrage by resource-rich entities that create commercial structure that follow the letter, while flouting the spirit, of the law.[26] In each concrete context, to use Endicott's terminology, vague law enables the governance of activities which cannot be regulated with precision (financial market misconduct, tax evasion and health and safety inside care homes) and encourages private forms of ordering that promote the purposes of the law (voluntary compliance, industry regulation, etc). In complex, high-value domains, broadly-framed legal standards provide meaningful guides to action and reduce the capacity for regulatory arbitrage.

The Law as Project Management model provides a way to think about why legislators and contracting parties would deploy a combination of determinate and indeterminate legal norms. Within that model law is a tool to govern

---

Tiersma (eds), *Oxford Handbook of Language and Law* (Oxford University Press, 2012).

[21] T Endicott, *Vagueness in Law* (Oxford University Press, 2000); T Endicott, 'The Value of Vagueness' in Andrei Marmor and Scott Soames (eds), *Philosophical Foundations of Language in the Law* (Oxford University Press, 2011).

[22] Endicott, 'The Value of Vagueness' (n 21) 28.

[23] J Braithwaite and V Braithwaite, 'The Politics of Legalism: Rules Versus Standards in Nursing-Home Regulation' (1995) 4 *Social and Legal Studies* 307; T Makkai and J Braithwaite, 'Pride, Praise and Corporate Compliance' (1993) 21 *International Journal of the Sociology of Law* 73.

[24] Braithwaite (n 18) 53.

[25] J Black, *Rules and Regulators* (Oxford University Press, 1997).

[26] D McBarnet and C Whelan, 'The Elusive Spirit of the Law: Formalism and the Struggle for Legal Control' (1991) 54 *Modern Law Review* 848.

complex social projects (bilateral and multilateral) where there are high levels of agreement about objectives at a project's core and low levels of agreement at the periphery. Determinate legal norms are used to govern the core; vague legal norms are used to govern the periphery.

On that view, 'managerial' legal regimes emerge from a process of strategic bargaining between people that rely on law to achieve common objectives by using vague legal norms to manage various types of uncertainty.[27]

Managerial regimes permit legal agents to agree on central subject-matters, while being uncertain about edge cases. 'We agree that the provision of *"electricity services to your construction yard"* requires supply through *"the wholesale grid"* [core], but have not decided whether it could require constructing a wind turbine on our land so agree to discuss the matter *"in good faith"* [periphery].' 'We (the parliament) agree to give permanent residency to people from a specified set of countries [core], but do not agree on the circumstances that will make a person undesirable due to their social circle [periphery].' Let us call this 'subject-matter uncertainty'.

Managerial law regimes also allow projects to commence where counterparties have shared short-/medium-term objectives, and conflicting/ambiguous long-term objectives. 'We can confidently say that we will continue to lease the building that houses your safety deposit box for a minimum of 10 years [core]. After that time, we are less sure and agree to use our "best endeavours" to negotiate an extension [periphery].' Let us call this 'temporal uncertainty'.

Finally, managerial law binds people despite an inability to forecast the stability of the environmental conditions necessary to carry out their projects. 'Our contract to insure your house against *"loss caused by fire"* [core] never contemplated rolling catastrophic bushfire seasons [periphery].' 'We (the constitutive power) agree to confer legislative power over *"money"* including *"gold and silver"* [core] and whatever that may mean in the future [periphery].' Let use call this 'environmental uncertainty'.

Judging under the Law as Project Management model is an exercise in hermeneutic diplomacy: interpreting vague text and contested context in a manner sensitive to litigants' epistemic and strategic limitations. When judges are resolving conflicts about core legal norms, their task is mechanical because they are applying rule-based law. When judges are resolving conflicts about peripheral legal norms, their task is rather different. They are required to interpret vague texts, which forces them to have recourse to the context from which those texts emerged, revealing the epistemic and strategic limitations of

---

[27]   Similar models have been proposed elsewhere: eg, V Fon and F Parisi, 'On the Optimal Specificity of Legal Rules' (2007) 3 *Journal of Institutional Economics* 147.

the law-makers, including the different types of uncertainty which motivate the use of vague legal norms.

Unlike rule-based law, there is no obvious affinity between managerial legal regimes (and their use of vagueness) and the set of actors who promote, develop and purchase algorithmic decision systems. Open-textured language is not obviously compatible with the strict rule specification and conceptual precision required to create and run algorithms on digital computers. That mismatch between vague law and precise code is a bad augury for managerial law in a world of automated decision systems.

3.   TRANSLATING LEGAL NORMS INTO MACHINE CODE

Asking whether legal norms can be translated into machine code is a technical question about the potential future design and operation of computer programs.

Unhappily, making confident predictions about the future technical capabilities of the algorithmic decision-systems operated by digital computers is extremely difficult. Core technologies are proprietary and confidential. Economic incentives push technology companies to make aggressively optimistic public claims about the current and future functionality of their products. Public sector fiscal constraints (and private sector lobbying) compel governments towards the aggressive adoption of algorithms and the development of national economic policy around the private sector's bold technological visions. Academic funding and professional advancement track those features of markets and the public sphere. For most pessimistic accounts of the technical potential of algorithmic law,[28] there are countervailing optimists,[29] and thinkers who walk a middle line.[30] The high noise-to-signal ratio in applied and theoretic debates about 'AI' is a formidable barrier to conclusive answers to questions like: 'can legal norms be replicated by algorithms?'

Alert to those difficulties, here are some tentative observations about the current technical state of the art.

---

[28]   Pasquale, 'A Rule of Persons' (n 6); F Pasquale, 'Four Futures of Legal Automation' (2015) 63 *UCLA Law Review Discourse* 26; J Sklaroff, 'Smart Contracts and the Cost of Inflexibility' (2018) 166 *University of Pennsylvania Law Review* 263.

[29]   Coglianese and Lehr, 'Regulating by Robot' (n 5); M Van Rijmenam and P Ryan, *Blockchain: Transforming Your Business and Our World* (Routledge, 2019).

[30]   Zalnieriute, Bennett Moses and Williams (n 6); S Wheeler, 'Modelling the Contracts of the Future' (2018) 26 *Griffith Law Review* 593.

3.1 Deterministic Algorithms

Most algorithmic systems are deterministic and are useful for that reason. Businesses and governments value algorithmic systems because they produce pre-determined outputs for a pre-determined set of inputs: allowing the predictable execution of tasks, at lower cost and higher regularity, formerly reserved to human employees. Those values are clearly replicated in rule-based automation technologies – where the basic parameters of an algorithm (inputs, outputs, logic) are manually set by a human coder.[31] Probabilistic algorithmic systems, including machine learning technologies, are less deterministic, because they can learn correlations between data inputs independently of a human coder. That potential decision-making independence drives utopian and dystopian visions about machines planning and acting in ways beyond the control of humans.[32] In reality, probabilistic algorithms are desirable because they are embedded in broader rule-based automation systems. Consider an automated credit approval system operated by a commercial bank. A 'credit scoring' algorithm assigns customer credit risk scores based on correlations between past and future customers' attributes, like default rate, age, post-code, income, employment/marital status, in a data set: a probabilistic task. Those scores are then fed into a 'credit-allocating' algorithm that approves or rejects a customer's request based on pre-set risk and pricing thresholds: a deterministic task. That fusion of probabilistic and deterministic elements is useful because it is predictable, and a credit scoring algorithm that acted in unpredictable ways would be useless.

The deterministic bent of algorithmic systems has obvious consequences for the two models of law sketched in this chapter. Deterministic systems are more likely to be able to replicate determinate legal norms and less likely to replicate indeterminate principles, standards, aspirations and institutional relationships.

3.2 Mathematisation of Language and Social Practices

Using algorithmic systems to interpret texts requires translating human language into symbolic, mathematic form or processing data about human language according to statistical relationships. There is a vast literature on the difficulties and possibilities of reducing complex texts and social practices to

---

[31] An accessible, technically rigorous description of algorithm design processes (with a slant towards robotics) can be found in M Ghallab, D Nau and P Traverso, *Automating Planning and Acting* (Cambridge University Press, 2016).

[32] Compare M Tegmark, *Life 3.0: Being Human in an Age of Artificial Intelligence* (Knopf, 2017) and M Shanahan, *The Technological Singularity* (MIT Press, 2015).

symbolic, mathematical form.[33] The less determinate the text, and the more complex the social practice it represents, the more difficult it is to code. The turn to machine learning can be seen as a way to avoid those problems with 'symbolic' artificial intelligence.[34] Rather than seeking to distil a universal symbolic logic underlying human language and behaviour, machine learning techniques attempt to identify statistical correlations between words and concepts in large datasets. It is hard to represent the concept of 'good faith' in symbolic logic; it is easier to gather data on recorded human actions that have been described as 'good faith' and then project those actions (and their derivatives) onto future behaviour. That approach relies on identifying connections between information within very large banks of reliable data about human behaviour. The confidentiality and strategising of many social behaviours associated with legal norms pose large challenges to deploying that 'connectionist' approach to subject managerial law to algorithmic systems.[35]

3.3   Stationarity

Algorithmic systems cope best when deployed in environments that are more stationary than dynamic. Coping with non-stationary data and environments is a major design challenge in robotics and machine learning.[36] Building algorithms requires coding very precise information about the state of the world, but the world constantly changes at different rates. Algorithms that fail to keep pace with changes in the world fail to meet their objectives. If the environment surrounding an algorithm is largely stationary, the algorithm can have a high level of 'stationarity' and fulfil its objective (all else being equal). If the environment is highly dynamic, the same algorithm can fail: epically.

Stationarity affects rule-based and managerial legal norms differently. Determinate legal rules are designed to operate in binary ways no matter how dynamic the environment – hence their predictability. Vague legal norms

---

[33]   Much of that research can be found in the annals of the International Association of Artificial Intelligence and Law.

[34]   P Smolensky, 'Connectionist AI, Symbolic AI, and the Brain' (1987) 1 *Artificial Intelligence Review* 95; M Garnelo and M Shanahan, 'Reconciling Deep Learning with Symbolic Artificial Intelligence: Representing Objects and Relations' (2019) 29 *Current Opinion in Behavioural Sciences* 17.

[35]   Attempts have been made to meet those challenges: N Aletras et al, 'Predicting Judicial Decisions of the European Court of Human Rights: a Natural Language Processing Perspective (2016) 2 *PeerJ Computer Science* e93; M Medvedeva, M Vols and M Wieling, 'Using Machine Learning to Predict Decisions of the European Court of Human Rights' (2020) 28 *Artificial Intelligence and Law* 237.

[36]   M Sugiyama and M Kawanabe, *Machine Learning in Non-Stationary Environments: Introduction to Covariate Shift Adaptation* (MIT Press, 2012).

are designed to be highly responsive to different environments – hence their unpredictability. A simple fix to the problems of stationarity is to build intense supervision and updating systems around an algorithm. Those systems could be mainly manual (requiring a human to input new data into the system) or mainly automated (requiring an automated and constant flow of new data into the system). Manual supervision systems may manage the ubiquitous risk of fast-scaling errors, but also reduce the extent to which algorithmic systems are truly 'automated'. Applied to vague legal rules, a manual supervision system would require large volumes of lawyers to update systems about (say) a new interpretation of a statute or an unpredicted change in the economic, social or natural environment. That variety of supervision comes with an obvious trade-off between system performance and cost. Automated systems defer but do not solve problems of stationarity.

Those tentative observations support the intuition that vague legal norms are more difficult to codify in machine logic than rule-based norms. If they harden to axioms, it will be difficult to avoid the conclusion that managerial legal regimes cannot be coded into an algorithmic system.

4.   LAW IN A WORLD OF MACHINE RULES

Let us (reasonably) assume that, despite the technical obstacles, market and political forces lead to the automation of strongly managerial legislative and contractual regimes.

In that world, vague legal norms will be codified in rule-based ways. That shift will present a number of difficult choices for legal actors. Judges must decide whether an algorithmic system, with its necessarily deterministic logic, is legally compatible with vague legal standards. For example, is a system which automatically sends five notifications over the course of 48 hours (and no more) to an email inbox following a failed payment an example of a contracting party making its 'best endeavour' to notify the other contracting party of a default? Similarly, is an automated welfare benefit distribution system that determines whether a person has suffered 'hardship' based on previous reported instances of hardship compatible with public law norms which protect individualised justice (such as procedural fairness)? Finally, would an automated system for the distribution of dividends used by an asset managing firm breach general anti-avoidance rules in taxation legislation if the system automatically directed revenue streams to (and from) jurisdictions that were likely (on a probabilistic analysis) to decrease (or increase) taxation audits against beneficiaries?

After much hand-wringing, answers to questions like these will eventually be produced by legal systems. Instead of mooting future cases, let us consider some broader questions which arise on the assumption that judges permit the translation of managerial into rule-based law: who are the winners and losers in such a world? What would be gained and lost by a domination of rule-based over managerial law?

Obvious winners include the profit-seeking enterprises that create and sell automated decision-systems, their investors, managers and employees. Obvious losers include quantitatively-challenged tertiary services professionals who are replaced by coders and system administrators. Whether the cost-saving and error-eliminating promises of automation accrue a net benefit to the enterprises and governments that buy them is less obvious, given: the fiscal impact of replacing qualitatively-skilled personnel with quantitatively-skilled personnel (given the labour shortage of the latter); distortions in pricing of technology services due to concentrations in technology markets; and regulatory risks arising from rapidly-scalable errors.

Outside the tertiary services market, identifying winners and losers from the domination of rule-based law becomes more complex. If rule-based and managerial legal models were not overlapping and ubiquitous, forecasting the effects of imposing mechanistic rules onto managerial legal regimes would be a manageable task. Inconveniently, both determinate and vague legal norms can be found in most statutes (anti-discrimination, criminal, tax, immigration, social welfare, etc), consumer contracts, the wills of poor, middle class and ultra-high-net worth people, industrial instruments, company constitutions and national constitutions. Because neither precision nor vagueness are legal techniques confined to any particular social activity, conclusive normative arguments about the merits of supplanting vague with determinate law are evasive.

Some potential impacts of that shift are, however, identifiable.

4.1   Planning

The first impact is that the intensity and accuracy of automated planning, by business groups and government, increase. Centralised planning of complex social projects (for- and non-profit) was a clear objective of the cybernetic movement and system theoretic approaches to human grouping.[37] The idea that human behaviour could (and should) be controlled or understood according to predictable, scientific models is an enduring theme of both theoretic schools.[38]

---

[37]   See PR Duffy, 'Cybernetics' (1984) 21(1) *International Journal of Business Communication* 33; R Vidgen, 'Cybernetics and Business Processes' (1998) 5(2) *Knowledge and Process Management* 118; RR Kline, 'Cybernetics, Management Science, and Technology Policy: The Emergence of "Information Technology" as a Keyword, 1948–1985' (2006) 47(3) *Technology and Culture* 513.

[38]   Canonical texts in the cybernetic tradition are N Weiner, *Cybernetics or Control and Communication in the Animal and the Machine* (MIT Press, 2nd ed, 2019); N

The same theme pervades cybernetic and system theoretic approaches to legal systems,[39] and is a foundational element of the automation of contract administration and legislation.

From the perspective of commercial enterprises, higher predictability in the operation of legal norms implies lower regulatory risk (increased ability to forecast risks arising from legal non-compliance) and a lower cost of capital (as the certainty of risk forecasts increases, the risk premium of capital decreases).[40] This undoubted benefit would need to be balanced with various costs, including those arising from rapidly-scaling negative externalities. From the perspective of government agencies, higher legal predictability implies more accurate public policy interventions and enforcement action. Society becomes controlled by a vast set of finely-tuned rules, and the discretionary powers of public officials are mostly eradicated. That may be a good thing on some liberal and republican accounts of government, assuming state action is democratically legitimate. Some perverse outcomes are, however, foreseeable, chief amongst which is a higher frequency of legal disputes arising from the stationarity of algorithmic systems and the highly dynamic state of the world.

4.2   Reduced Guidance Capacity

The second potential impact of replacing managerial with rule-based legal norms is a reduction in the guidance capacity of law.

That impact flows from the idea that '[w]ith complex actions in changing environments where large economic interests are at stake, principles are more likely to enable legal certainty than rules'.[41] Using algorithms to administer contracts and distribute public services does nothing to change the cognitive and social attributes of the people affected by those mechanistic legal regimes. Blocks to legal effectiveness experienced by people failing to understand vastly complex rule-based legal norms will remain, as will the psychological and economic drivers of regulatory arbitrage where economic rewards are momentous.

Weiner, *The Human Use of Human Beings: Cybernetics and Society* (Free Thinking Press, 1988); N Weiner, *God and Golem Inc* (MIT Press, 1966).

[39]   See generally, Wiener, *The Human Use of Human Beings* (n 38) 106; N Luhmann, *A Sociological Theory of Law* (Routledge, 2013); G Teubner, *Law as an Autopoietic System* (Blackwell Publishers, 1993); DA Kerimov, 'Future Applicability of Cybernetics to Jurisprudence in the USSR' (1963) 4 *Modern Uses of Logic in Law* 153; DA Kerimov, 'Cybernetics and Law' (1963) 1 *Soviet Law and Government* 4.

[40]   P Burkhard, *Regulatory Risk and the Cost of Capital* (Springer, 2010).

[41]   Braithwaite (n 18) 53.

It is also worth observing that substituting an algorithm for a human as the agent that executes a rule-based legal regime is likely to have only marginally positive impacts on law's guidance capacity. If human behaviour is more likely to be guided by legal norms framed in determinate language, then the administration of such norms by machines (rather than humans) should be mostly neutral. It is not clear why people who make strategic or passionate decisions to ignore determinate legal rules will be less likely to do so if those norms are administered by a machine rather than a human being. Nor is it clear why good faith disagreements about the meaning of an ostensibly rule-based law would be less pervasive for the simple reason that a machine or a human being is applying the rule.

4.3   Narrower Legal Governance

The third potential impact of supplanting managerial law with mechanistic rule-based legal regimes is that law's function as an institution to govern complex social projects may become narrower.

Contracting parties have a number of choices if they cannot use vague norms ('good faith', 'best endeavours', 'reasonableness') to govern the peripheral aspects of their deals. They can limit their legal relations to the absolute core of their projects, adjusting the economics of their deals to reflect the jettisoning of peripheral objectives. They can choose not to contract at all. They can govern the same deal using entirely rule-based norms. The attractiveness of each choice will depend on the parties' attitudes to the different types of uncertainty (subject-matter, temporal and environmental) that may affect their bargain.

The same set of decisions confronts legislatures. A legislative system of (say) visa regulation may use vague legal techniques to manage uncertainties arising from: the successful visa applicant developing relationships with serious criminal actors (subject-matter uncertainty); new information coming to light regarding the applicant's suitability for the grant of the visa (temporal uncertainty); or an unforeseen disaster requiring the urgent remove of non-citizen residents lawfully present in the country (environmental uncertainty). If all those uncertainties have to be accurately forecast and reduced to precise rules, the legislature may decide to reduce the rights attached to the initial visa, not to create the visa class at all or simply to cast their entire visa system in rule-based norms.

It is difficult to understand why a lawmaker (contractor or legislator) would choose either of the last two options: refuse to conclude the contract/ enact legislation; or use entirely rule-based norms. The 'refuse to contract/ legislative' option assumes that people see no value in law as an institution for governing complex social projects. That would be an extraordinary jettisoning of a core governance mechanism with no identifiable replacement.[42] The 'entirely rule-based norms' option was available before the hypothetical world in which managerial law was replaced with rule-based algorithmic law. It was not used because the lawmakers (legislatures and contracting parties) could not reach sufficient consensus to govern the totality of their relationships using rule-based norms. Perhaps their level of consensus would be changed by the non-availability of vague law due to its indigestibility by algorithmic systems, although it is not clear why technical drafting considerations would have such a fundamental impact on personal preferences and interpersonal dynamics.

The intuitively likely outcome is the first: lawmakers choose to shrink the scope of their legal relations to their core objectives which can easily be coded in rule-based norms. Such an outcome would preserve the use of legal norms as a mechanism to govern cooperative projects. It would accommodate the attenuated scope of their design in the world of mechanised rule-based law. It would also reflect a (rational) attitude to uncertainty: there is no consensus about peripheral objectives of the contract/legislation; that lack of consensus is driven by uncertainty; that uncertainty would have been managed by vague legal norms which are no longer available; thus, peripheral objectives should not be governed by legal norms.

In that way, law's function as a tool to manage complex social projects may be narrowed, with a diversity of ramifications. The legitimacy of legal institutions may be reinforced, as vague (bad) law is replaced by determinate (good) law. People's trust in law may rise: predictability increases, arbitrariness disappears and the monopoly of 'a professional elite who may have no special insight into justice or politics but who are experts in the manipulation of fine-grained rules' (ie, lawyers) dissipates.[43] Alternatively, the inability of mechanistic rule-based law to accommodate the ineradicable messiness of human life may cause a loss of faith in legal institutions: the useful scope of legal institutions narrows; rule-based law grinds against social and environmental conditions; and people lament the loss of a professional body of advocates and its replacement with computer scientists. All things considered, that may not be a negative outcome but it would leave a significant gap in the structure of normative tools available to govern cooperative projects in an increasingly complex world.

---

[42]   A similar, but broader, point is made in M Hildebrandt, 'Law *as* Information in the Era of Data-Driven Agency' (2016) 79 *Modern Law Review* 1.

[43]   C Eisgruber, 'Judicial Supremacy and Constitutional Distortion' in SA Barber and RP George (eds), *Constitutional Politics: Essays on Constitution Making, Maintenance and Change* (Princeton University Press, 2001) 71.

BIBLIOGRAPHY

Articles/Books/Reports

Aletras, N et al, 'Predicting Judicial Decisions of the European Court of Human Rights: a Natural Language Processing Perspective' (2016) 2 *PeerJ Computer Science* e93

Bateman, W, 'Algorithmic Decision-Making and Legality: Public Law Dimensions' (2020) 94 *Australian Law Journal* 520

Black, J, *Rules and Regulators* (Oxford University Press, 1997)

Boden, M, *Mind as Machine* (Oxford University Press, 2006)

Braithwaite, J, 'Rules and Principles: A Theory of Legal Certainty' (2007) 27 *Australian Journal of Legal Philosophy* 47

Braithwaite, J and V Braithwaite, 'The Politics of Legalism: Rules Versus Standards in Nursing-Home Regulation' (1995) 4 *Social and Legal Studies* 307

Burkhard, P, *Regulatory Risk and the Cost of Capital* (Springer, 2010)

Coglianese, C and D Lehr, 'Regulating by Robot: Administrative Decision Making in the Machine-Learning Era' (2017) 105 *Georgetown Law Journal* 1147

Corrales, M, M Fenwick, H Haapio (eds), *Legal Tech, Smart Contracts and Blockchain* (Springer, 2019)

Crocker, KJ and SE Masten, 'Pretia Ex Machina? Prices and Process in Long-Term Contracts' (1991) 34 *Journal of Law and Economics* 69

Dickerson, R, 'The Diseases of Legislative Drafting' (1964) 1 *Harvard Journal on Legislation* 5

DiMatteo, LA, M Cannarsa and C Poncibò (eds), *The Cambridge Handbook of Smart Contracts, Blockchain Technology and Digital Platforms* (Cambridge University Press, 2019)

Duffy, PR, 'Cybernetics' (1984) 21(1) *International Journal of Business Communication* 3

Eisgruber, C, 'Judicial Supremacy and Constitutional Distortion' in SA Barber and RP George (eds), *Constitutional Politics: Essays on Constitution Making, Maintenance and Change* (Princeton University Press, 2001)

Endicott, T, *Vagueness in Law* (Oxford University Press, 2000)

Endicott, T, 'The Value of Vagueness' in Andrei Marmor and Scott Soames (eds), *Philosophical Foundations of Language in the Law* (Oxford University Press, 2011)

Fon, V and F Parisi, 'On the Optimal Specificity of Legal Rules' (2007) 3 *Journal of Institutional Economics* 147

Freeman, M and P Mindus (eds), *The Legacy of John Austin's Jurisprudence* (Springer, 2013)

Fuller, L, *The Morality of Law* (Yale University Press, 1969)

Garnelo, M and M Shanahan, 'Reconciling Deep Learning with Symbolic Artificial Intelligence: Representing Objects and Relations' (2019) 29 *Current Opinion in Behavioural Sciences* 17

Ghallab, M, D Nau and P Traverso, *Automating Planning and Acting* (Cambridge University Press, 2016)

Gilson, RJ, 'Value Creation by Business Lawyers: Legal Skills and Asset Pricing' (1984) 94 *Yale Law Journal* 239

Gronlund, A (ed), *Electronic Government: Design, Applications and Management* (IGI Global, 2001)

Hayek, FA, *Law, Legislation and Liberty* (Routledge, 2012)

Hildebrandt, M, 'Law *as* Information in the Era of Data-Driven Agency' (2016) 79 *Modern Law Review* 1

Hill, CA and C King, 'How Do German Contracts Do as Much With Fewer Words?' (2004) 79 *Chicago-Kent Law Review* 889

Jeffares, S, *The Virtual Public Servant: Artificial Intelligence and Frontline Work* (Palgrave, 2021)

Jeffries Jr, JC, 'Legality, Vagueness, and the Construction of Penal Statutes' (1985) 71 *Virginia Law Review* 189

Kerimov, DA, 'Cybernetics and Law' (1963) 1 *Soviet Law and Government* 4

Kerimov, DA, 'Future Applicability of Cybernetics to Jurisprudence in the USSR' (1963) 4 *Modern Uses of Logic in Law* 153

Kline, RR, 'Cybernetics, Management Science, and Technology Policy: The Emergence of "Information Technology" as a Keyword, 1948–1985' (2006) 47(3) *Technology and Culture* 513

Leiter, B, 'Legal Indeterminacy' (1995) 1 *Legal Theory* 481

Lovett, F, *A Republic of Laws* (Cambridge University Press, 2016)

Luhmann, N, *A Sociological Theory of Law* (Routledge, 2013)

Majambere, E, 'Clarity, Precision and Unambiguity: Aspects for Effective Legislative Drafting' (2011) 37 *Commonwealth Law Bulletin* 417

Makkai, T and J Braithwaite, 'Pride, Praise and Corporate Compliance' (1993) 21 *International Journal of the Sociology of Law* 73

McBarnet, D and C Whelan, 'The Elusive Spirit of the Law: Formalism and the Struggle for Legal Control' (1991) 54 *Modern Law Review* 848

Medvedeva, M, M Vols and M Wieling, 'Using Machine Learning to Predict Fecisions of the European Court of Human Rights' (2020) 28 *Artificial Intelligence and Law* 237

Pasquale, F, 'Four Futures of Legal Automation' (2015) 63 *UCLA Law Review Discourse* 26

Pasquale, F, 'A Rule of Persons, Not Machines: The Limits of Legal Automation' (2018) 87 *George Washington Law Review* 1

Pettit, P, *Republicanism: A Theory of Freedom and Government* (Oxford University Press, 1999)

Poscher, R, 'Ambiguity And Vagueness In Legal Interpretation' in Lawrence Solan and Peter Tiersma (eds), *Oxford Handbook of Language and Law* (Oxford University Press, 2012)

Rundle, K, *Forms Liberate* (Hart Publishing, 2012)

Scalia, A, 'The Rule of Law as a Law of Rules' (1989) 56 *University of Chicago Law Review* 1175

Schauer, F, 'Judging in a Corner of the Law' (1988) 61 *Southern California Law Review* 1717

Scheuerman, B, 'The Rule of Law and the Welfare State: Towards a New Synthesis' (1994) 22 *Politics and Society* 195

Seidman, AW, RB Seidman and N Abeyeskere, *Legislative Drafting for Democratic Social Change: A Manual for Drafters* (Kluwer Law International, 2001)

Shanahan, M, *The Technological Singularity* (MIT Press, 2015)

Sklaroff, J, 'Smart Contracts and the Cost of Inflexibility' (2018) 166 *University of Pennsylvania Law Review* 263

Smolensky, P, 'Connectionist AI, Symbolic AI, and the Brain' (1987) 1 *Artificial Intelligence Review* 95

Sugiyama, M and M Kawanabe, *Machine Learning in Non-Stationary Environments: Introduction to Covariate Shift Adaptation* (MIT Press, 2012)

Sunstein, C, 'Incompletely Theorised Agreements' (1995) 108 *Harvard Law Review* 1733

Tegmark, M, *Life 3.0: Being Human in an Age of Artificial Intelligence* (Knopf, 2017)

Teubner, G, *Law as an Autopoietic System* (Blackwell Publishers, 1993)

Van Rijmenam, M and P Ryan, *Blockchain: Transforming Your Business and Our World* (Routledge, 2019)

Vidgen, R, 'Cybernetics and Business Processes' (1998) 5(2) *Knowledge and Process Management* 118

Weiner, N, *God and Golem Inc* (MIT Press, 1966)

Weiner, N, *The Human Use of Human Beings: Cybernetics and Society* (Free Thinking Press, 1988)

Weiner, N, *Cybernetics or Control and Communication in the Animal and the Machine* (MIT Press, 2nd ed, 2019)

Wheeler, S, 'Modelling the Contracts of the Future' (2018) 26 *Griffith Law Review* 593

Zalnieriute, M, L Bennett Moses and G Williams, 'The Rule of Law and Automation of Government Decision-Making' (2019) 82 *Modern Law Review* 425

Other

Mehl, L, 'Automation in the Legal World' (paper presented at the *Mechanization of Thought Process Symposium*, National Physical Laboratory, Teddington, Middlesex, November 1958)

9. Artificial intelligence and the unconscionability principle

Dilan Thampapillai

1. INTRODUCTION

There is an abundance of scholarship about the impact of artificial intelligence on the field of intellectual property. For the most part, this scholarship has examined the question of whether AI can be accommodated within IP regimes.[1] However, the real battleground sits within the broader realm of private law. It is here that commercial actors have rapidly embraced the use of the AI technologies in commercial practice.[2] This is an interesting development because it finds the law at a particularly curious stage in its own evolution. There is at this point no consensus at all on whether artificial intelligence entities could be granted legal personality in their own right.[3] This state of being within the law automatically rules out the possibility that agency law might apply to the things that an AI entity might do.[4] In the absence of the applicability of agency law, with its set rules on liability and responsibility, the broader field

---

[1] See A Guadamuz, 'Do Androids Dream of Electric Copyright? Comparative Analysis of Originality in Artificial Intelligence Generated Works' (2017) 2 *Intellectual Property Quarterly* 169. See also J Ginsburg and L Budiardjo, 'Authors and Machine' (Working Paper) 2 <https://papers.ssrn.com/sol3/papers.cfm?abstract_id=3233885>. See also, A Bridie, 'Coding Creativity: Copyright and the Artificially Intelligent Author' (2012) *Stanford Technology Law Review* 5, 69.

[2] This process has begun with the use of smart contracts. See E Mik, 'Smart Contracts: Terminology, Technical Limitations and Real World Complexity' (2017) 9(2) *Law, Innovation and Technology* 269. It has moved into the sphere of artificial agents. See also D Johnson and M Verdicchio, 'AI, agency and responsibility: the VW fraud case and beyond' (2019) 34 *AI & Society* 639.

[3] See S Chesterman, 'Artificial Intelligence and the Limits of Legal Personality' (2020) 69 *International and Comparative Law Quarterly* 819.

[4] In turn, this obviates the possibility that agency law can serve as a mechanism for attributing liability between one of two relatively innocent parties where a loss has been occasioned by a third party. See *First Energy (UK) v Hungarian International Bank* [1993] 2 Lloyd's Rep 194.

of contract law emerges as the default regime to regulate issues of fairness and obligation in commercial and contractual settings.

However, contract law has its own doctrinal problems. A law of contracts is the field of law that houses both common law and equitable doctrines. In essence, this means that the law of contracts is caught between the imperatives of the bargain principle and the demands of the unconscionability principle.[5] While these two principles ordinarily run together and do not necessarily compete for primacy within the law, there is still a discernible tension between them. This is evident in the broad jurisprudence within Australia around unconscionable conduct.

Unconscionable conduct has emerged as a central regulating doctrine within Australian contract law. As has become apparent, the Parliament of Australia has used the concept of unconscionable conduct both as principle and as doctrine to regulate the commercial morality in a range of spheres.[6] This has resulted in a rather puzzling situation within which commercial transactions under the Australian consumer law are designed to be governed by rules concerned with fairness,[7] which is in turn arguably a byword for good faith,[8] but ordinary non-commercial transactions are subject to no such generalised standard of fairness. In reality, the courts have interpreted the law to mean that in order to be set aside the commercial transactions must have a higher

---

[5] M Eisenberg, 'The Bargain Principle and Its Limits' (1982) 95 *Harvard Law Review* 741, 742.

[6] See Schedule 2 to the Competition and Consumer Act 2010 (Cth) which houses s 20 of the Australian Consumer Law ('the ACL'), s 12CA of the Australian Securities and Investment Commission Act 2001 (Cth) ('the ASIC Act') and ss 90K and 90KA of the Family Law Act 1975 (Cth).

[7] See *Australian Securities and Investment Commission v Kobelt* (2019) 267 CLR 1 [295] (Edelman J) ('*Kobelt*'). In *Kobelt*, Edelman J noted, 'Like other open-textured criteria, such as "unfair" or "unjust", there is no clear baseline moral standard for what constitutes "unconscionable" conduct within s 12CB of the *ASIC Act*'.

[8] See P Finn, 'Commerce, the Common Law and Morality' (1989) 17 *Melbourne University Law Review* 87, 89. Finn noted that equity served a role as 'the sometimes moral policeman of the law' and also noted the emergence of the unconscionability principle as 'becoming as imperialistic in equity as the neighbourhood principle in tort law'. The unconscionability principle is the central informing principle of the doctrine of unconscionable conduct. The status of good faith within Australian contract law is rather more indifference. There has been support from some courts. See *Renard Constructions (ME) Pty Ltd v Minister for Public Works* (1992) 26 NSWLR 234, 263–265 (Priestley JA). While made obiter, the comments of Priestley JA in *Renard* were supportive of an implication of a term of good faith as a corollary of reasonableness. In contrast, see *CGU Workers Compensation (NSW) Ltd v Garcia* (2007) 69 NSWLR 680 [131]–[137] (Mason P). See also *Key Infrastructure Australia Pty Ltd v Bensons Property Group Pty Ltd* [2019] VSC 522 [291]–[294] and *Growthbuilt Pty Ltd v Modern Touch Marble & Granite Pty Ltd* [2021] NSWSC 290.

standard of capriciousness than those contested under equity or the unwritten law. As the doctrine of unconscionable conduct is the exemplar of the unconscionability principle, this is a delicate and contentious position in which the law now resides.

Elsewhere, in Singapore and in England – jurisdictions which themselves are also concerned with contractual and commercial morality – these matters are dealt with in a manner that is rather more subtle and diffuse. Rather than place all of their eggs in one basket these jurisdictions rely upon a range of laws which, in turn, are informed by base principle by the concept of unconscionability. These are doctrines such as mistake, economic duress, misrepresentation, estoppel and even undue influence. It is noticeable that in these jurisdictions, unlike Australia, the settled position on contract construction has centred around the notion of the objective commercial bystander for quite some time. Given the likelihood of contract construction being a ground for disputation, this approach is likely to yield fairer results. In stark contrast, Australia has as yet no settled position on contractual ambiguity – the so-called true rule in the *Codelfa* decision being no more than a mirage.

It is into this uneasy and uncertain doctrinal mix that the new and complex variable of artificial intelligence enters. The early signs are not promising. The *Quione Pte Ltd v B2C2 Ltd*[9] decision is highly controversial. Likewise, in Australia the Robodebt payments scandal still reverberates as an instance of technology gone awry and on unjust enrichment through payments wrongfully procured.[10]

The base problem is quite simple. AI technologies, while being extraordinarily useful in some instances, are quite capable of doing unforeseen, unpredictable and problematic things. The question is whether the commercial convenience outweighs the risk that something could go catastrophically wrong. In the event that it does there is the unanswered question of what the law of contracts will do to resolve the matter.

This chapter looks at how contract law might respond to artificial intelligence through the unconscionable conduct doctrine. In this chapter I argue that the law is going to have to restructure itself in order to answer the questions posed by new technologies. The problem is that the use of artificial intelligence technology dramatically and drastically reconfigures the contractual landscape such that a transactional imbalance is almost always present in any dealings between an AI-enhanced party and an ordinary human being. This confounds

---

[9] [2020] SGCA (I) 02.

[10] T Carney, 'Robo-debt illegality: The seven veils of failed guarantees of the rule of law?' (2019) 44(1) *Alternative Law Journal* 4; A James and A Whelan, 'Ethical artificial intelligence in the welfare state: Discourse and discrepancy in Australian social services' (2022) 42 *Critical Social Policy* 22.

the ordinary paradigm upon which the unconscionability principle has been built. Instead of a transaction in which the two parties are in close proximity, such that knowledge, intention and exploitation are all discernible features of the procurement of the transaction and its outcome,[11] AI technologies bring in a degree of distance, a level of inscrutability and an inability to form the desire to act in a bad faith manner in a human sense. Technology and commerce will move quickly such that the law in its present form is unsustainable.

In section 2 of this chapter, I address the issues of possibilities and paradigms of exploitative situations involving AI entities in commercial and consumer transactions. In section 3, I examine the issue of transactional imbalance and information asymmetry. In section 4, I evaluate the contested territory of exploitation within unconscionability. Section 5 concludes that the law must develop new concepts within existing paradigms in order to meet the exigencies of transactional imbalance and exploitation.

2.   BETWEEN CODE AND CONSCIENCE

There are a wide variety of ways in which AI technologies can affect contractual dealings in a manner that would implicate conscience. To begin with, an AI technology is an autonomous tool used by one of the parties either to create a legal relationship (contract) or to regulate dealings within an existing contractual relation.[12] The ordinary dichotomy used to describe conscience in this context pertains to procedure and substance.[13] Here, procedure means acts done in the procurement of a contract. In other words, this denotes defects in formation that would warrant vitiation of the contract. In contrast, substance refers to the imbalance or improvidence of the bargain taken as a whole. This is important conceptually because the existence of substantive unconscionability is often evidence of procedural unconscionability. However, in the presence of AI used to manage a contractual relationship, the dichotomy of procedure and substance is not entirely helpful. Instead, we need a concept that explains why defects in post-formation conduct might be against conscience.[14]

---

[11]   See *Thorne v Kennedy* (2017) 263 CLR 85 (*'Thorne'*).
[12]   I Giuffrida, F Lederer and N Vermeys, 'A Legal Perspective on the Trials and Tribulations of AI: How Artificial Intelligence, the Internet of Things, Smart Contracts, and Other Technologies Will Affect the Law' (2018) 68(3) *Case Western Reserve Law Review* 747.
[13]   See *Commercial Bank of Australia v Amadio* (1983) 151 CLR 447, 461 (*'Amadio'*); *Louth v Diprose* (1992) 175 CLR 621; and *Bridgewater v Leahy* (1998) 194 CLR 457.
[14]   To some extent, the extended statutory form of unconscionability that exists under ss 21 and 22 of the ACL and ss 12CB and 12CC of the ASIC Act do already address this issue of behaviour within an existing contractual relationship. See *Jams*

For the most part, this is new ground. Defects in post formation conduct have ordinarily been regulated through the termination for breach and remedies doctrines. These doctrinal rules around conditions, intermediate terms and repudiation are subject to common law rules, but they are not necessarily devoid of equitable principles. The question then is whether a wholly equitable concept can be developed to identify and define the type of advantage-taking that emerges through the use of AI technologies in a manner that substantially and materially deprives the counter-party of the benefit of the relationship for which they have contracted.

At present, the closest form of quasi-equitable legal rule that best describes this idea is that contained within statutory unconscionable conduct in Australia across the Australian Consumer Law ('the ACL') and the Australian Securities and Investments Commission Act 2001 (Cth) ('the ASIC Act').[15] What sits here is a species of unconscionable conduct, whose boundaries are the subject of some debate,[16] that might arguably extend to systems of commercial practice that deprive other parties of the benefits that they reasonably anticipate obtaining through contract performance.

The role of conscience here would be no different to that of the termination doctrines. It must seek to make the plaintiff whole.[17] However, conscience provides a different vehicle of contractually informed explanation for why a remedy is to be provided. This issue is not a deliberate and wilful breach of contract, which in turn acknowledges that parties do have a lawful right to breach a contract, particularly if it is efficient to do so. Instead, what matters in this context is the propensity and ability of AI technology to operate in a manner that systematically deprives the other of a substantial part of the value of the contract.

The question is whether we have rules in place within the conscience-based doctrine of unconscionable conduct, but also perhaps within undue influence and duress, to manage that process. New technologies require new rules, but those new rules do not necessarily need to be entirely original. Instead, it is possible that the new rules can be drawn from existing rules which are recon-

---

2 *Pty Ltd v Stubbings* [2020] VSCA 200 (*'Stubbings'*); *Australian Competition and Consumer Commission v Quantum Housing Group Pty Ltd* [2021] FCAFC 40 (*'Quantum Housing'*); *Good Living Company Pty Ltd as trustee for the Warren Duncan Trust No 3 v Kingsmede Pty Ltd* [2021] FCAFC 33 (*'Good Living Company'*).

[15] See Schedule 2 to the Competition and Consumer Act 2010 (Cth), which houses s 22 of the ACL and s 12CC of the ASIC Act.

[16] See *Stubbings* (n 14) [78]. At the time of writing *Stubbings* has been granted special leave by the High Court of Australia. See also *Good Living Company* (n 14) [4] (Allsop CJ); *Quantum Housing* (n 14); M Delany, 'Statutory unconscionable conduct: The search for rational criteria' (2020) 14 *Journal of Equity* 206.

[17] *Luna Park (NSW) Ltd v Tramways Advertising Pty Ltd* (1938) 61 CLR 286.

ceptualised and reformulated to meet the needs of new paradigm situations. This means breaking those rules down to their fundamental purposes, constituent concepts and evaluative steps.

2.1   Two Paradigmatic Situations

How can we best illustrate the impact of AI on contractual relationships? The best strategy to do so has to lie with developing a taxonomy out of the current uses of AI within contractual relationships.

2.1.1   AI as regulator of conduct and benefit under the contractual relationship

At present, social media companies use AI technologies to curate content on their platforms. Though the users of these sites do not ordinarily conceive of themselves as consumers and as party to a contractual relationship, there is an exchange taking place. The users trade data in exchange for access to and usage of the platform. In turn, their usage and the base exchange at play is regulated through the terms and conditions of the site. This meets the requirements of the formation doctrines of the law of contracts.

What then happens when an AI technology that has been employed to moderate the site does something unpredictable and removes content which otherwise meets the requirements of the terms and conditions? What happens when users are wrongly excluded from the site? There is at present a very substantial debate about regulating the ability of social media companies to govern their platforms. AI technologies are very heavily implicated in this process.

If a particularly problematic user is removed from a site, it would have a noticeable impact on activity on that site. The use of such technologies has a subtle coercive effect. This is difficult to measure, but there would be a ripple effect on the use of these technologies resulting in users feeling less free to express themselves on the platform. However, would this necessarily rise to the level of conduct that affects conscience? This seems rather unlikely because the substantive value of the bargain remains intact. Instead, it might be a situation within which the implied duty to cooperate arises.[18]

What happens when the AI technology is largely ineffectual and fails to remove human users who are trolling legitimate users and bots that are doing the same? If this has the consequence of failing to protect legitimate users from psychological harm, such that they are forced to leave the platform, then this would be something that does affect conscience.

---

[18]   See *Bensons Property Group Pty Ltd v Key Infrastructure Australia Pty Ltd* [2021] VSCA 69 [102].

Of our three candidate doctrines, only unconscionable conduct in its broader statutory form seems to be immediately relevant. The argument would be that the existence of a contractual relationship within a platform context gives rise to a duty incumbent upon the platform operator to ensure that users have an acceptable experience on the platform. A systematic failure to do so, either by failing to effectively enforce the rules against bad faith actors or by ignoring valid complaints, would give rise to a situation that tacitly affects conscience, particularly if it affects a large and definable section of the user base. For example, if women and minorities are routinely exposed to harassment and bullying online, but the platform fails to effectively intercede where it can, then it is retaining the benefit of numerous contracts (in the form of user data) in a situation where it is tacitly complicit in the deprivation of anticipated benefits to an identifiable group.

2.1.2   AI as contract negotiator and manager

Platform companies within the gig economy are increasingly using AI technologies to regulate the work of their employees.[19] If AI manages the contractual relationship, then it is the tool that drives this disadvantage. The particular strengths of AI in terms of information asymmetry and computational power would likely deprive the contractual relationship of any semblance of parity. Indeed, AI can use nudge tactics to manipulate human subjects, thereby impacting upon autonomy within the contractual relationship. Similarly, the gamification of work on the platform, a significant factor within the gig economy, opens up the possibility for manipulation and exploitation between vulnerable workers and platform owners who use AI tech as a means of managing their workforce.

3.   TRANSACTIONAL IMBALANCE

The decision of the Supreme Court of Canada in *Uber Technologies v Heller*[20] represents a radical reconfiguration of the doctrine of unconscionable conduct. In *Heller*, a majority of the Supreme Court of Canada found that an arbitration in an adhesion contract for Uber drivers was unconscionable. The arbitration clause served as the mechanism for dispute resolution within the contract

---

[19]   E Bucher, P Schou and M Waldkirch, 'Pacifying the algorithm – Anticipatory compliance in the face of algorithmic management in the gig economy' (2021) 28(1) *Organization* 44.

[20]   2020 SCC 16 (*'Heller'*). See also M McInnes, 'Uber and unconscionability in the Supreme Court of Canada' (2021) 137 *Law Quarterly Review* 30; J Gardner, 'Being Conscious of Unconscionability in Modern Times: *Heller v Uber Technologies*' (2021) 84(4) *Modern Law Review* 874.

and thereby represented the gateway to the driver's rights under the contract. However, the clause required that all arbitration take place in Amsterdam. The Court calculated that it would cost the driver at least $14,500 to access arbitration; and the majority opinion of Abella and Rowe JJ, delivered with the concurrence of Wagner CJ and Moldaver, Karakatsanis, Martin and Kasirer JJ, found that the clause requiring arbitration in Amsterdam was unconscionable.[21]

The *Heller* model simply requires transactional imbalance between the parties and improvidence on the part of the plaintiff.[22] The model of unconscionable conduct developed by the majority in *Heller* is extraordinarily different to that which operates in Australia under the *Amadio* principle.[23] In turn, it is different again to the version that operates in Singapore pursuant to *BOM v BOK*[24] and in England after the *Alec Lobb*[25] decision.

The question is whether this model is better equipped to deal with situations where there is significant information asymmetry between the parties because of the involvement of AI technologies. The multifactorial models of unconscionable conduct that have been developed in Australia, Singapore and England are all premised upon interactions between human beings. If one were to consider the leading cases in these jurisdictions, these cases have all involved relationships in which a degree of trust and confidence has existed. It is a very different thing when AI technologies enter into the commercial contracting sphere and begin to affect contractual relationships between parties who do not necessarily have any such pre-existing relationship.

It follows then that the law must seek out some new model of attribute in liability where any loss has occurred. However, contract law has long recognised that not all losses must be compensated. Some further causative elements are required before liability can be attributed to a loss. In its present form in Australia, the doctrine relies heavily upon the concept of exploitation. It begs the question of whether we need some bad faith element to exist before liability can accrue to the party using the AI technology.

If we look at our two paradigms situations, the first being subtle exploitation and the second being algorithmic management, transactional imbalance works in both situations. However, it has the immediate effect of nullifying any commercial activity within these contexts. They cannot necessarily be a desirable

---

21   *Heller* (n 20) [93]–[94].
22   Ibid.
23   Ibid.
24   [2018] SGCA 83 ('*BOM*').
25   *Alec Lobb (Garages) Ltd v Total Oil GB Ltd* [1983] 1 WLR 87. See also *Multiservice Bookbinding Ltd v Marden* [1979] Ch 84. See further N Enonchong, 'The Modern English Doctrine of Unconscionability' (2018) 34 *Journal of Contract Law* 211.

outcome. What we must do is to recognise exactly what it is at the core of both paradigm situations that is identifiable as being problematic.

Realistically, our concern has to lie with the ability of one party to obtain unjustified benefits from the other and to retain them. Perhaps then, the doctrine needs to develop the concept of unjustified benefit to sit alongside the notion of transactional imbalance. The current safeguard that exists within the Heller doctrine of improvidence is positioned from the plaintiff's perspective. However, what needs to be in place is the fault element that draws attention to the conduct of the defendants either in or during the benefit or entertaining. Again, this stretches the doctrine somewhat, because the doctrine has always looked at procedural steps taken to procure a bargain rather than at the overall substance of that bargain. However, the emergent extended statutory form of unconscionable conduct within the ACL and the ASIC Act does look to the transactional relationship as a whole.

4. EXPLOITATION

The *Amadio* principle has not yet defined a settled notion of exploitation. The case law has oscillated between modes of active and passive exploitation.[26] In *Bridgewater*, the dominance of the nephew over the uncle was enough to procure from the latter the sale of property at a considerable undervalue. There was no deception, coercion or undue pressure. Instead, the nephew enjoyed a significant degree of influence over the uncle such that the latter was particularly and peculiarly vulnerable to suggestions made by the former. In contrast, in *Louth v Diprose*,[27] manipulation and deception were significant factors in a finding of unconscionable conduct.

The problem is that exploitation via algorithm, as is starting to emerge within sectors such as the gig economy, is both subtle and cumulative. It begins from a position of disadvantage, as the AI technology has the ability to develop significant and powerful information asymmetries, but it might never manifest itself in one single noticeable transaction. Indeed, cases like *B2C2* might turn out to be something of a rarity in the broader field of contracts.

Nonetheless, there is something about algorithmic management that has the potential to be unconscionable. The doctrine needs to develop a pattern of conduct theory that examines how benefits under a contract can be withheld or misappropriated by the counterparty. There are precedents that do exist in the

---

[26] R Bigwood, 'Still Curbing Unconscionability: *Kakavas* in the High Court of Australia' (2013) 37 *Melbourne University Law Review* 465, 507.

[27] (1992) 175 CLR 621.

form of *ACCC v Simply No-Knead*[28] and *ACCC v Keshow*,[29] where overt bad faith conduct was found to be unconscionable. However, these cases involved very blatant acts of moral obloquy. In contrast, in *ASIC v Kobelt*, a racially discriminatory system of consumer credit and control over purchases at a store in a remote part of Australia which applied to Indigenous customers was found not to be unconscionable.[30] Crucially, the intentions in *Kobelt* were not entirely bad, the control element was necessitated by a desire to avoid a local practice known as 'humbugging'. However, such a system was regarded by Edelman J as a 'Hobbesian choice' and resulted in a degree of financial disadvantage to Indigenous customers.[31]

5.   CONCLUSION

The doctrine of unconscionable conduct is going to have to readjust itself to meet the new and emerging capabilities of AI within the sphere of contracts. No doctrine within private law is frozen in time and a time-bound doctrine would soon lose its relevance. Such a fate has befallen the postal rule within the law of contracts. Instead, the doctrine needs to meet AI in three critical phases: (i) contract formation; (ii) contract management; and (iii) the adjudication of contractual rights (algorithmic oversight over compliance and dispute resolution processes). There is some overlap between the second and third of these processes, but the crucial distinction lies in the way in which AI can select tasks in the contract management phase and thereby 'nudge' the human party to its preferred outcomes. The doctrine has to adjust its rules to meet the potential for unfairness in these situations. This might require new rules. Identifying those rules is an important theoretical task for scholars of both technology and jurisprudence.

BIBLIOGRAPHY

Articles/Books/Reports

Bigwood, R, 'Still Curbing Unconscionability: *Kakavas* in the High Court of Australia' (2013) 37 *Melbourne University Law Review* 465
Bridie, A, 'Coding Creativity: Copyright and the Artificially Intelligent Author' (2012) *Stanford Technology Law Review* 5

---

[28]   *Australian Competition & Consumer Commission v Simply No-Knead (Franchising) Pty Ltd* [2000] FCA 1365.
[29]   *Australian Competition and Consumer Commission v Keshow* [2005] FCA 558.
[30]   *Kobelt* (n 7).
[31]   Ibid [295] (Edelman J).

Bucher, E, P Schou and M Waldkirch, 'Pacifying the algorithm – Anticipatory compliance in the face of algorithmic management in the gig economy' (2020) 00 *Organization* 1

Carney, T, 'Robo-debt illegality: The seven veils of failed guarantees of the rule of law?' (2019) 44(1) *Alternative Law Journal* 4

Chesterman, S, 'Artificial Intelligence and the Limits of Legal Personality' (2020) 69 *International and Comparative Law Quarterly* 819

Cohen, J, 'Law for the Platform Economy' (2017) 51(1) *UC Davis Law Review* 133

De Stefano, V, 'The Rise of the Just-In-Time Workforce: On-Demand Work, Crowdwork, and Labor Protection in the Gig Economy' (2016) 37(3) *Comparative Labor Law & Policy Journal* 471

Delany, M, 'Statutory unconscionable conduct: The search for rational criteria' (2020) 14 *Journal of Equity* 206

Eisenberg, M, 'The Bargain Principle and Its Limits' (1982) 95 *Harvard Law Review* 741

Enonchong, N, 'The Modern English Doctrine of Unconscionability' (2018) 34 *Journal of Contract Law* 211

Finn, P, 'Commerce, the Common Law and Morality' (1989) 17 *Melbourne University Law Review* 87

Gardner, J, 'Being Conscious of Unconscionability in Modern Times: *Heller v Uber Technologies*' (2021) 84(4) *Modern Law Review* 874

Giuffrida, I, F Lederer and N Vermeys, 'A Legal Perspective on the Trials and Tribulations of AI: How Artificial Intelligence, the Internet of Things, Smart Contracts, and Other Technologies Will Affect the Law' (2018) 68(3) *Case Western Reserve Law Review* 747

Guadamuz, A, 'Do Androids Dream of Electric Copyright? Comparative Analysis of Originality in Artificial Intelligence Generated Works' (2017) 2 *Intellectual Property Quarterly* 169

James, A and A Whelan, 'Ethical artificial intelligence in the welfare state: Discourse and discrepancy in Australian social services' (2021) 00 *Critical Social Policy* 1

Johnson, D and M Verdicchio, 'AI, agency and responsibility: the VW fraud case and beyond' (2019) 34 *AI & Society* 639

McInnes, M, 'Uber and unconscionability in the Supreme Court of Canada' (2021) 137 *Law Quarterly Review* 30

Mik, E, 'Smart Contracts: Terminology, Technical Limitations and Real World Complexity' (2017) 9(2) *Law, Innovation and Technology* 269

Stewart, A and J Stanford, 'Regulating Work in the Gig Economy: What are the Options?' (2017) 28 *Economic & Labour Relations* Review 420

Cases

Alec Lobb (Garages) Ltd v Total Oil GB Ltd [1983] 1 WLR 87

Australian Competition and Consumer Commission v Keshow [2005] FCA 558

Australian Competition and Consumer Commission v Quantum Housing Group Pty Ltd [2021] FCAFC 40

Australian Competition & Consumer Commission v Simply No-Knead (Franchising) Pty Ltd [2000] FCA 1365

Australian Securities and Investment Commission v Kobelt (2019) 267 CLR 1

Bensons Property Group Pty Ltd v Key Infrastructure Australia Pty Ltd [2021] VSCA
    69
Bom v Bok [2018] SGCA 83
Bridgewater v Leahy (1998) 194 CLR 457
CGU Workers Compensation (NSW) Ltd v Garcia (2007) 69 NSWLR 680
Commercial Bank of Australia v Amadio (1983) 151 CLR 447
First Energy (UK) v Hungarian International Bank [1993] 2 Lloyd's Rep 194
*Good Living Company Pty Ltd as trustee for the Warren Duncan Trust No 3 v
    Kingsmede Pty Ltd* [2021] FCAFC 33
Growthbuilt Pty Ltd v Modern Touch Marble & Granite Pty Ltd [2021] NSWSC 290
Jams 2 Pty Ltd v Stubbings [2020] VSCA 200
Key Infrastructure Australia Pty Ltd v Bensons Property Group Pty Ltd [2019] VSC
    522
Louth v Diprose (1992) 175 CLR 621
Luna Park (NSW) Ltd v Tramways Advertising Pty Ltd (1938) 61 CLR 286
Multiservice Bookbinding Ltd v Marden [1979] Ch 84
Quione Pte Ltd v B2C2 Ltd [2020] SGCA (I) 02
Renard Constructions (ME) Pty Ltd v Minister for Public Works (1992) 26 NSWLR
    234
Thorne v Kennedy (2017) 263 CLR 85
Uber Technologies v Heller 2020 SCC 16

Legislation

Australian Securities and Investment Commission Act 2001 (Cth)
Competition and Consumer Act 2010 (Cth) ('Australian Consumer Law')
Family Law Act 1975 (Cth)

10. The possibilities of IF-THEN-WHEN

Sally Wheeler

The world of contract exists in a variety of different cultural contexts. This chapter looks at two of those contexts: how contract exists as text and how contract might exist as code. It considers whether the medium of code can replace text and then whether contract as code can be a device for structuring relationships in the business world. IF...THEN embodies the conditionality of contract expressed either as text or code, noting that the legitimacy of IF... THEN propositions in text might be derived from, and are at least ultimately testable before, recognised state actors in the form of the judiciary; whereas IF...THEN propositions that come from code are both currently created and adjudicated upon by private actors. The addition of WHEN points to issues of uncertain temporality around technological development, user adoption and adaption and legal and quasi-legal determination. Some of these issues are more significant than others and this chapter reflects this significance pattern in the treatment that it affords them.

Contract as code is a reference to smart contracts which are agreements written in code, say Python or Solidity, that self-execute exactly as they are written when particular pre-determined conditions occur; the if-then proposition.[1] There are conflicting views on what defines a smart contract[2] and whether smart contracts are contracts in the sense in which legal doctrine uses the word 'contract'.[3] These are not debates that this chapter pursues with any

---

[1] Two rather different worked examples are provided by J Bernstein, 'Smart Contract Integration in Professional Sports Management: The Imminence of Athlete Representation' (2018) 14 *DePaul Journal of Sports Law* 88 and K Griggs et al, 'Healthcare Blockchain System Using Smart Contracts for Secure Automated Remote Patient Monitoring' (2018) 42 *Journal of Medical Systems* 130.

[2] For a summary of possible definitions, including ones that have been passed into legislation in a variety of US States, see R de Caria, 'The Legal Meaning of Smart Contracts' (2019) 27 *European Review of Private Law* 731.

[3] The first definition of smart contracts came originally from Szabo who was not a lawyer <https://nakamotoinstitute.org/the-idea-of-smart-contracts/>. His definition of a smart contract was that it was a machine-readable protocol that created a contract with pre-determined terms. This is a long way from a definition of contract that would resonate with those immersed in legal doctrine.

vigor as they are well documented elsewhere.[4] The key point is that whilst smart contracts might not entirely fulfill the required legal niceties of doctrines such as formation and consideration,[5] they are nevertheless arrangements entered into voluntarily by the parties which when executed alter 'their rights and obligations'.[6] Rather, what this chapter adds to the literature is a reading of the possibilities of smart contracts in the light of the observations provided by empirical studies of contracting behavior.

The step change from merely electronic contracts that is occurring is the expression of the contract itself as code rather than as text. Execution of the smart contract's terms occurs through the deployment of blockchain technology that creates a record of transactions mounted on a distributed ledger (shared infrastructure) that cannot then be altered.[7] A new block is added to the ledger each time a transaction is recorded so creating a fixed and locked list of transactions which are visible to all participants in the chain. Smart contracts can pull large amounts of quantifiable data from nominated external sources known as Oracles and so work best when contract performance is subject to the achievement of identifiable and quantifiable goals. Algorithmic condition rules (IF…THEN) operate sequentially to determine whether execution occurs.

The presentation of smart contracts in the literature to date holds out to the business world[8] a promise of a frictionless and low transaction cost trading

---

[4]   See generally the excellent work of Eliza Mik, in particular, 'Smart Contracts: Terminology, technical limitations and real world complexity' (2017) 9 *Law, Innovation and Technology* 269.

[5]   A Savelyev, 'Contract Law 2.0: "Smart" Contracts as the beginning of the End for Classical Contract Law' (2017) 26 *Information and Communications Technology Law* 116.

[6]   K Werbach and N Cornell, 'Contracts Ex Machina' (2017) 67 *Duke Law Journal* 313, 341. Interestingly, Werbach and Cornell support the view that smart contracts might lack consideration but are prepared to classify them as contracts on the basis of the proposition quoted therein.

[7]   S Fernandez-Vazquez, 'Blockchain and Smart Contracts: Uses and Challenges' (2019) *International Conference on Artificial Intelligence* 394.

[8]   There are numerous possibilities for smart contracts in the consumer world: frictionless transactions for hotel rooms, micro-finance transactions, peer to peer lending, car rental etc. However transaction cost savings in the business to consumer world can be made very effectively through the earlier innovation of electronic contracts. The scaleable destination for smart contracts lies in the business to business world; examples would be supply chain management contracts around issues such as inventory, provenance and labour regulation and mainstream financial transactions: see A Sulkowski, 'Blockchain, Business Supply Chains, Sustainability, and Law: The Future of Governance, Legal Frameworks, and Lawyers?' (2018) 43 *Delaware Journal of Corporate Law* 303; and M Orcutt, 'The Pandemic has messed up Global Supply Chains. Blockchain could help' (2020) *MIT Technology Review*, 7 April <https://www.technologyreview.com/2020/04/07/998602/blockchains-covid19-supply-chain-wef/>.

environment that eliminates issues surrounding trust in the form of reliance on third party intermediaries such as financial institutions, good faith, and reputation both personal and professional.[9] For some commentators smart contracts represent the ultimate 'flat' market free of state intervention as there will no longer be a need for parties to resort to state-backed sanctions for the enforcement of obligations.[10] The extent to which either of these propositions, without considerable qualification, is an accurate representation of current or future reality is open to debate.[11] Nevertheless, smart contracts are increasingly being used for some relatively simple transactions in a variety of industries; and as knowledge, experience and technology all increase and develop this usage is likely to grow and become more sophisticated. Blockchain technology, of which smart contracts are an application, underpins the trading and payment systems of cryptocurrencies and is increasingly in use in the financial industry. There are also possible new applications – for example the creation of platforms that might deliver for multinational business the ability to track modern slavery, human rights and environmental compliance by business partners and sub-contractors.[12]

Whilst contract as text and contract as code share in common that they are both 'literacies' existing through written language and form,[13] that commonality is threatened by the apparent (in)ability to apply to contract as code, either as a fact finding and remedy providing tribunal such as a court or arbitration process, or as the parties through negotiation, adaptability and interpretation.

---

[9] M Swan, *Blockchain: Blueprint for a New Economy* (O'Reilly Media, 2015) 9–26, 94; and generally D Tapscott and A Tapscott, *Blockchain Revolution* (Penguin, 2016).

[10] Much of what we might term the extreme anti-authoritarian view and libertarian view of the possibilities afforded by smart contracts derives from the early views that were taken of blockchain technology and its disruptive potential: see R Herian, 'Taking Blockchain Seriously' (2018) 29 *Law and Critique* 163.

[11] V Shermin, 'Disrupting Governance with Blockchains and Smart Contracts' (2017) 26 *Strategic Change* 499.

[12] See, for example, the Modern Slavery Act 2015 (UK) s 54, which requires all businesses registered in the UK with a turnover of more than £36m to produce a statement that details the steps they are taking to eliminate human trafficking and modern slavery from their supply chain. Smart contracts that require proof of certified working environments and employment practices before payment is made are attractive here: see J Zhao, 'Extraterritorial Attempts at Addressing Challenges to Corporate Sustainability' in B Sjåfjell and C Bruner (eds), *The Cambridge Handbook of Corporate Law, Corporate Governance and Sustainability* (Cambridge University Press, 2019) 29.

[13] G Buchholtz, 'Artificial Intelligence and Legal Tech: Challenges to the Rule of Law' in J Wischmeyer and T Rademacher (eds), *Regulating Artificial Intelligence* (Springer, 2020) 175.

Contract as text is a broad category. It might represent the doctrinal form of contract which has shown itself to be capable of dealing with new fashions in contract – the emergence of dependence on standard terms of business, developing norms such as good faith and changing technologies such as the emergence of writing and the wonders that were fax machines and telex machines now superseded by email, e-commerce and, of course, the smart contract. Alternatively, it might be the outward facing manifestation of the lived world of contract that can be constructed from various empirical accounts of the role of contract in business practice.

The proponents of Law in Action do not dispute that the doctrinal rules of contract matter.[14] Their position is, rather, pointing to the declining number of litigated contract cases across common law jurisdictions,[15] that they are useful to solve only a small subset of disputes. Private ordering[16] through industry codes and industry adjudication,[17] relations between the parties and post litigation revisions to standard terms are all more likely to provide routes to both dispute avoidance and dispute resolution. That said, doctrinal rules, both real and imagined,[18] enter the world of business practice through the idea of 'bargaining in the shadow of the law'[19] which underlies many strategic choices

---

[14]   S Macaulay, 'The Real Deal and the Paper Deal: Empirical Pictures of Relationships, Complexity and the Urge for Transparent Simple Rules' (2003) 66 *Modern Law Review* 44.

[15]   S Macaulay, 'Freedom from Contract: Solutions in Search of a Problem' (2004) *Wisconsin Law Review* 777.

[16]   S Macaulay, 'Contract, New Legal Realism, and Improving the Navigation of *The Yellow Submarine*' (2006) 80 *Tulane Law Review* 1161, 1169–1170. Here Stewart Macaulay provides a wonderful but characteristically understated summation of the forms that private ordering in contract takes.

[17]   L Bernstein, 'Private Commercial Law in the Cotton Industry: Creating Cooperation Through Rules, Norms and Institutions' (2001) 99 *Michigan Law Review* 1724 ('Private Commercial Law').

[18]   S Macaulay and W Whitford, 'The Development of Contracts: Law in Action' (2015) 87 *Temple Law Review* 793, 805.

[19]   The original idea for 'Bargaining in the Shadow of the Law' comes from the seminal work of R Mnookin and L Kornhauser, 'Bargaining in the Shadow of the Law: The Case of Divorce' (1979) 88 *Yale Law Journal* 950. This piece is the nineteenth most-cited US Law Review piece of all time and the most cited piece in the Family Law category: see F Shapiro and M Pearse, 'The Most-Cited Law Review Articles of All Time' (2012) 110 *Michigan Law Review* 1483. Despite being used as an operational framework for fields of legal research from criminal law to international law, its sophistication is rarely captured. It depends on the interaction of five elements: party preference; the bargaining endowments created by the legal rules that a court will apply if a party negotiated settlement is not reached; the degree of uncertainty that pertains to the legal outcome which is also inextricably linked to the parties' appetite for risk; transaction costs that can be both financial; and emotional and strategic behaviour

and behaviours in the lived experience of contracting;[20] so, indirectly, perhaps, they form a frame of reference for some of what is reported by Law in Action researchers.

Section 1 of this chapter offers a reading of the journey that contract as text has taken from the first forays into writing through to its presentation as standardised terms and conditions. This section is concerned with demonstrating how the doctrinal rules of contract have been shown to be adaptable, either through the claim of functional equivalence or the claim of analogy,[21] to changes in technology and business practice even if subsequent analyses cannot determine with certainty the basis for that adaption and question whether ex post facto it was the most logical way to have proceeded.[22] Section 2 considers what Law in Action scholarship tells us: contract relationships are structured around informal 'relationship preserving norms' and 'end-game norms' in circumstances where the contracting parties want certainty from adjudicating bodies such as courts and arbitration settings rather than flexibility and adaptability.

The stories of contract as text are important for the discussion that follows in section 3 because, whilst most engagement with the possibilities of smart contracts from a non-technical computational standpoint has come from doctrinal lawyers, Law in Action scholarship offers an interesting interface with the world of business practice that needs to be engaged. In section 3 I consider in what respects contract as code, where code is defined as the 'operational technical systems and instructions that configure and govern machines',[23] might develop in similar ways to that of text based contracts. I am interested in questions around the control and direction of the code drafting process, whether standard code segments might emerge for inclusion as quasi standard contract terms and how code might develop new elements of conditionality.

---

based on the transmission of information by one party to the other. See Mnookin and Kornhauser (ibid) 966–973.

[20] L Bernstein, 'Beyond Relational Contracts: Social Capital and Network Governance in Procurement Contracts' (2015) 7 *Journal of Legal Analysis* 561 ('Beyond Relational Contracts').

[21] D Harvey, *Collisions in the Digital Paradigm* (Hart Publishing, 2017) 55f. Cf C Reed, 'Online and Offline Equivalence: aspiration and achievement' (2010) 18 *International Journal of Law and Information Technology* 248.

[22] E Mik, 'The Effectiveness of Acceptances Communicated by Electronic Means, or – Does the Postal Acceptance Rule Apply to Email?' (2009) 26 *Journal of Contract Law* 68.

[23] A McCosker and E Milne, 'Coding Labour' (2014) 20 *Cultural Studies Review* 4.

1.   SECTION 1

Writing is the first iteration of law expressed as code. When law moved from an existence only in oral form, it ceased to be based around custom, ceremony, participation and context to the same extent; if these features remain in the print era and beyond it is because they have been intentionally preserved[24] or reintroduced.[25] The advent of writing and other later technologies of communication were transformational for the legal systems of States and for the transactions of individuals. After writing with scribes as the transmitters, came the printing press, which was followed by new forms of communication for individual transactions, inter alia the postal service,[26] telephone,[27] telex. From these developments in communication there was a shift into new technologies for conducting transactions themselves: e-commerce, AI and now blockchain. Some of these technologies have been short lived compared with others[28] or have developed in a rather different way from that which was first envisaged[29] but each one has added a new dimension to how we think about adjudicating and constructing legal validity. As a general proposition, law, in the way it is expressed and practised, outside perhaps the talisman of the trial, has become a heavily textual enterprise. Contract law is no exception to this, even though contract within the system of legal classification has a stronger grip on orality[30] than other doctrines.

---

[24]   See the examples provided in W Jethro Brown, 'Customary Law in Modern England' (1905) 5 *Columbia Law Review* 561.

[25]   Restorative justice is a practice that played a role in pre-modern societies and has now been endorsed in a variety of legal or quasi-legal settings as a method for achieving victim and offender mediation or repairing community relationships. It has a somewhat contested back story: see K Daly, 'Restorative Justice: The Real Story' (2002) 4 *Punishment and Society* 55.

[26]   E MacDonald, 'Dispatching the Dispatch Rule? The Postal Rule, Email, Revocation and Implied Terms' (2013) 19 *Web Journal of Current Legal Issues*.

[27]   Telephone offers a winding back to an earlier era of orality for contract but that is very much the exception to what have otherwise been entirely text-based communication interventions.

[28]   Telex and fax are two technologies that revolutionised communication at the time of their invention and adoption but became obsolete relatively quickly: see J Coopersmith, 'Old Technologies Never Die, They Just Don't Get Updated' (2010) 80 *International Journal for the History of Engineering & Technology* 166.

[29]   See, for example, the future predicated for video technology in R Collins and D Skover, 'Paratexts' (1992) 44 *Stanford Law Review* 509.

[30]   Contract for example is still taught within the academy with a high dependence on the oral scenario. Concepts such as offer, acceptance, consideration, mistake and misrepresentation are illustrated through imagined oral exchanges between protago-

It is not intended to give a detailed historical account of how societies moved from legal arrangements made in oral form to printed texts and then supplemented their communications methods with nineteenth- and twentieth-century inventions. There are numerous accounts of this process[31] from those that look at these developments from the standpoint of the historical evolution of legal structures[32] to those that consider them from an anthropological[33] or sociological[34] and sociolinguistic perspective.[35] Rather, the point here is to look at how writing in its generic form and then subsequently printing have changed the nature of contractual arrangements. Understanding the features of this transformation and what contracts as text represent as compared with contracts underpinned only by speech acts might provide a lens for looking at the possibilities for contract as code.

Arrangements that are made in oral form encourage a focus on the intentions of the speaker, but, when the speaker finishes, those words (and necessarily the intentions they conveyed) are lost because speech is transient. The speaker's tone, gesture and volume – what linguistics calls prosodic and paralinguistic features – might have enhanced the contemporaneous meaning of the words.[36] Speech is a dynamic process in which the speaker observes the listener and can assess whether they are being understood. If the listener does not appear to understand, the speaker can rephrase and repeat. The listener can ask the speaker to give further explanation.[37] At the time of speaking what is expressed is something that is uniquely contextual and situated within a particular locality[38] but to summon those words to mind again relies on fragile memory and faulty recall. The tie to context and memory blocks innovation and

---

nists: see P Tiersma, 'The Language of Offer and Acceptance: Speech Acts and the Question of Intent' (1986) 74 *California Law Review* 189.

[31] See the extensive literature review provided by R Collins and D Skover (n 29) 514f.

[32] E Carawan, 'Oral "Agreement", Written Contract, and the Bonds of Law at Athens' in C Cooper (ed), *Politics of Orality: Orality and Literacy in Ancient Greece* (Brill, 2006) 321; and L Roach, 'Law codes and legal norms in later Anglo-Saxon England' (2013) 86 *Historical Research* 46.

[33] J Goody and I Watt, 'The Consequences of Literacy' (1963) 5 *Comparative Studies in Society and History* 304.

[34] For Weber, for example, conducting official business in writing was a depersonalising characteristic of bureaucracy: M Weber, *The Theory of Social and Economic Organization*, tr T Parsons (Free Press, 1947) 330–332.

[35] R Harris, *Rethinking Writing* (Athlone Press, 2000).

[36] R Finnegan, 'Communication and Technology' (1989) 9 *Language and Communication* 107, 119–120.

[37] P Tiersma, 'Textualizing the Law' (2001) 8 *Forensic Linguistics* 73.

[38] H Berman, 'The Background of the Western Legal Tradition in the Folklaw of the Peoples of Europe' (1978) 45 *University of Chicago Law Review* 553, 577.

development in rules and norms because to develop and innovate signals an acknowledged failure to remember.[39] It is typical of Maine's claim that what bound societies together in the pre-text era was the idea of status within groups and status maintained by groups such as the family rather than the exercise of individual agency through the mechanism of contract.[40]

Writing and, even more so, printed text are durable and span time and distance.[41] Written texts, unlike speech, are designed to be autonomous instruments in that they use language that stands without the support of a specific social context.[42] Rendering writing into printed text brings consistency as the copyist's error is eliminated and the standardised typeface and layout remove all semblance of human experience. The ready availability and use of printed text mark the start of societal transition to industrialisation; the transfer from status to contract in which the economy moves beyond the domestic to one based on manufacturing and trading at scale.[43] When a text is read there is unlikely to be any information on who wrote it and why;[44] hence interpretation is required. There is no need, as there would be with speech, to focus on the intentions of the speaker but rather on what a reasonable person knowing what the parties knew of the context of the contract would understand from the text. Contracts expressed as text are longer and syntactically denser than oral contracts and they will have been intricately planned in perhaps a way that it is not possible to achieve with speech.[45] This does not mean that speech is necessarily clearer and more transparent; the contract drafter will have tried to foresee all possible meanings and their text will have been rewritten and

---

[39]   V Boehme-Neßler, *Pictorial Law* (Springer, 2011) 21–23.

[40]   H Maine, *Ancient Law* (John Murray, 1861) 170.

[41]   W Ong, *Interfaces of the Word: Studies in the Evolution of Consciousness and Culture* (Cornell University Press, 1997) 234f.

[42]   P Kay, 'Language Evolution and Speech Style' in B Blount and M Sanches (eds), *Sociocultural Dimensions of Language Change* (Academic Press, 1977) 20.

[43]   J Goody, *The Logic of Writing and the Organization of Society* (Cambridge University Press, 1986) 144–147.

[44]   See the discussion of pari passu clauses in sovereign debt contracts: M Gulati and R Scott, *The Three and a Half Minute Transaction: Boilerplate and the Limits of Contract Design* (University of Chicago Press, 2013).

[45]   P Tiersma, *Parchment, Paper, Pixels* (University of Chicago Press, 2010) 20f.

edited repeatedly,[46] carefully crafted so as to give organisation and shape to the document and cues for any future interpretation exercise.[47]

The accessibility and durability of printed text is only sustainable if we assume literacy on the part of the contracting parties. Literacy creates a power dynamic between those who possess it and those who do not. This can occur within the contractual bond; and as the doctrinal rules of contract took shape the courts did not hesitate to support the power of literacy by assuming an ability to read and that this ability would have been deployed in relation to the contract in question on behalf of contracting parties,[48] and further that literate contracting parties would indeed read a contract before signing it, as affixing their signature to printed terms effectively locked them into the contract.[49] The issue of literacy arose most obviously in the context of risk planning through contract by the inclusion in it of clauses purporting to exclude liability in particular scenarios. The balancing factor to the Court's assumption of literacy in these cases (prior to legislative intervention on the contents of the clause[50] itself) was its simultaneous insistence on sufficient notice of the existence of

---

[46]   To paraphrase Lord Hoffmann in *Chartbrook Ltd v Persimmon Homes Ltd* [2009] UKHL 38, the first step in the interpretation of contract documents is to decide whether something has gone wrong with the language used. Only if that question is answered in the affirmative can the courts apply red ink, verbal correction and rear-rangement to the contract.

[47]   D Olsen, 'Oral Discourse in a World of Literacy' (2006) 41 *Research in the Teaching of English* 136, 139–141.

[48]   The most striking examples of this are *Parker v SE Railway Co* [1877] 2 CPD 416 and *Thompson v London, Midland and Scottish Rly* [1930] 1 KB 41, known as the 'ticket cases'. In *Parker* Mellish LJ expressly asserts (at 423) the right of the railway company to assume literacy and the exercise of literacy by those it contracts with, subject to the knowledge that there was writing on the documentation handed over and this writing might contain conditions. In *Thompson* (where *Parker* is cited with approval) only one judge in the Court of Appeal (Lord Hanworth MR) referred to the plaintiff's illiteracy and then it was to dismiss it as a relevant factor because of the authorities (presumably *Parker*) and the 'condition of education in this country' (at 46).

[49]   *L'Estrange v Graucob* [1934] 2 KB 394. The only positions open to Miss L'Estrange, despite the sympathy the Divisional Court felt for her (per Maugham LJ at 405), were to claim fraud, *non est factum*, or misrepresentation on the part of Graucob Ltd; see further J Spencer, 'Signature, Consent, and the Rule in *L'Estrange v Graucob*' (1973) 32 *Cambridge Law Journal* 104.

[50]   Most jurisdictions exercise some statutory control over the contents of exclu-sion clauses, for example in the UK the Unfair Contract Terms Act 1977 (UK) and the Consumer Rights Act 2015 (UK); and in Australia s 64 of the Competition and Consumer Law 2010 (Cth) Sch 2 ('Australian Consumer Law').

contract conditions being given to the party against whom the clause was being enforced.[51]

The robustness of contract as text is reinforced by the parol evidence rule that has the effect of sealing text off from other extrinsic evidence and ascribing to text a role as representative of the entire relationship between the parties.[52] It places the parties' agreement beyond 'the reach of future controversy, bad faith or treacherous memory'.[53] Contract as text systematises the relationship between the parties. It creates an opportunity for each party to guard against uncontrolled or unplanned behaviour on the part of the other. Further the parties might decide to include a *merger* clause or an *entire agreement clause* as part of their contract text. A provision of this sort allows the contracting parties to claim that the contract documents are the only source of terms between them. Whilst the presence of such clauses does not influence interpretation of the contractual terms by the courts, they do prevent additional obligations being sourced from the wider context of the parties' dealings and being imposed.[54]

2.   SECTION 2

The debates that have consumed commentators on smart contracts have largely been about their fit with legal doctrines and whether 'smart contracts' as a conceptual category are legal instruments in the sense that we currently understand these. There has been little consideration of whether smart contracts can

---

[51]   For the majority of the Court of Appeal in *Parker* the giving of sufficient notice of the existence of contract conditions was a question of fact. *Thompson* was factually more complicated in that the 'writing' on the back of the ticket referred to contract terms being located in another document – the timetable. The Court found that having received a ticket for travel on which it was made clear that travel was subject to conditions and also where these conditions could be found, the plaintiff could not adduce evidence that all that was reasonably necessary to draw attention to the conditions had not been done.

[52]   Most jurisdictions have a form of the parol evidence rule (which in reality is not a rule but a rebuttable presumption). For an overview of the UK and US position, see G Klass, 'Parol Evidence Rules and the Mechanics of Choice' (2019) 20 *Theoretical Inquiries in Law* 457.

[53]   *Shogun Finance v Hudson* [2003] UKHL 62 per Lord Hobhouse, quoting from *Phipson on Evidence* (19th edn, Sweet & Maxwell 2017) [49].

[54]   See C Mitchell, 'Entire Agreement Clauses: Contracting Out of Contextualism' (2006) 22 *Journal of Contract Law* 222. Mitchell situates discussion of these clauses within the debate around formalism and contextualism as interpretative strategies for judicial oversight of claims in contract in her very engaging and scholarly treatment of interpretation, C Mitchell, *Interpretation of Contracts* (Routledge, 2nd ed, 2019) (*Interpretation of Contracts*).

accommodate the way in which commercial parties to a contract currently use this relationship. The social practices and norms that we know have grown up around the inner core of contracts created as printed text are largely invisible in the discussions of smart contracts.[55] If we begin at the beginning of Law in Action scholarship in relation to contract structures then we begin with the work of Stewart Macaulay, as that is the starting point[56] for most accounts of the lived world of contract, despite his seminal work being nearly 60 years old.[57] For Macaulay a contract has to do two things: it has to include elements of rational planning by offering a risk based solution to future contingencies and it must include legal sanctions to either induce performance or compensate for non-performance.[58]

The manufacturers that Macaulay studied wanted to plan their contractual arrangements by using a formal process but not one that they necessarily intended to rely upon. Planning for contingencies was largely absent. Written contracts existed as standardised documents that were only very occasionally used to adjust or enforce exchanges. Adjustments or enforcement took place informally with legal sanctions resorted to only after careful consideration of the possible implications of such a course of action. Macaulay mapped the non-contractual relations, the bonds of sociality, that existed between commercial contracting parties; ideas of good faith in business, such as industry-wide customs, past dealings and personal friendships. Also present were ideas of trust, reciprocity and reputation, personal and professional. Some 20 years after his original research, based on his own further work and that of others, Macaulay added power, dependence and exploitation as additional relationship dynamics.[59]

---

[55] See K Levy, 'Book-Smart, Not Street-Smart: Blockchain-Based Smart Contracts and the Social Workings of Law' (2017) 3 *Engaging Science, Technology, and Society* 1, on face value perhaps the one exception to the invisibility of contract as existing in a wider frame of reference than merely doctrine. However, the account of contract given there is not recognisable as one which engages with the richness of the various available empirical accounts of contracting behavior.

[56] S Wheeler, 'Law in Action' in W Swain and D Campbell (eds), *Reimagining Contract Law Pedagogy* (Routledge, 2019) 79, 82–86; and J Braucher, J Kidwell and W Whitford (eds), *Revisiting the Contracts Scholarship of Stewart Macaulay* (Hart Publishing, 2013).

[57] S Wheeler, 'Visions of Contract' (2017) 44 *Journal of Law and Society* 74.

[58] S Macaulay, 'Non-Contractual Relations in Business: A Preliminary Study' (1963) 28 *American Sociological Review* 55, 57.

[59] S Macaulay, 'An Empirical View of Contract' (1985) *Wisconsin Law Review* 465.

Some 30 years later Esser undertook a study to see if he could replicate Macaulay's findings.[60] What he found was that the demands of the market around flexible production of specialised products at short notice, which required a constantly retooled manufacturing process rather than mass market production line items, resulted in the creation of long-term exclusive supply contracts. These long-term supply contracts were founded on cooperation and information sharing on issues such as raw material costings and price, with any notion of adversarial position taking and arm's-length bargaining abandoned.[61] Macaulay and Esser's findings are culturally and contextually contingent on the settings they were studying. Just as we saw doctrinal structures in section 1 adapt to the advent of practices such as trading on standard terms and conditions of sale through the parol evidence rule and assume the literacy of contracting parties as extended compulsory education made this more likely than not, it would not be surprising if different contracting settings gave rise to other practices and other social norms between the parties.[62] Thus it seems that in relationships that include an element of innovation such as joint product development or collaborative service systems, say, the contracting parties, whilst still not using formal legal sanctions to resolve disputes, do rely heavily on formal contracts and legal advice to create the relationship and then manage behaviour during it.[63]

We know, drawing on Law in Action scholarship, that in many instances contracting parties leave large parts of their business relationship to be governed by extra-legal commitments and sanctions which include not only social norms that have developed between them and within their industry but also well-established and formalised industry-based dispute resolution mechanisms. Contracting parties do not prefer extra-legal arrangements because

---

[60] J Esser, 'Institutionalizing Industry: The Changing Forms of Contract' (1996) 21 *Law and Social Inquiry* 593.

[61] This chimes with Badawi's suggestion that formal contract structures are preferred where 'transactions are frequent and certain because those situations present optimal cultures for drafting nearly complete contracts, which parties would want enforced by the agreement's express terms': see A Badawi, 'Interpretative Preferences and the Limits of the New Formalism' (2009) 6 *Berkeley Business Journal* 1, 5–6. Even within these relationships, however, contract doctrine can accommodate contextual factors through, for example, the division of express terms into conditions, warranties and innominate terms. Innominate terms create the space to examine the context of the contract and the breach that is alleged to give rise to the right to terminate.

[62] For an account of the historical development of contract doctrine in the light of prevailing cultural norms see J Fineman, 'Critical Approaches to Contract Law' (1983) 30 *UCLA Law Review* 829.

[63] G Hadfield and I Bozovic, 'Scaffolding: Using Formal Contracts to Support Informal Relations in Support of Innovation' (2016) *Wisconsin Law Review* 981.

the transaction costs of negotiating and then drafting legally enforceable agreements are too high. Commercial contracts are often used repeatedly, so the set-up costs of including in the original contract these extra-legal heads of agreement and operating principles would reduce accordingly over time.[64] Transaction costs, largely in the form of acquiring sufficient information to determine the trustworthiness[65] of the other party, are also present in extra-legal arrangements.[66] Instead, contracting parties prefer what they see as the certainty of approach and conservative interpretation of terms applied by private arbitration systems.

Trustworthiness derived from reputation is also key to deciding at what level within the relationship commitments and sanctions sit; the legal relationship includes provisions that will provide the best result if the contracting partner turns out to be untrustworthy and extra-legal commitments are made that will become self-enforcing agreements if the contracting partner is trustworthy.[67] Trust in a smart contract situation becomes, as section 3 explains, trust in technology rather than personal trustworthiness. Reputation is largely forged through behavior reinforced by community ties, geographical proximity and repeated dealing. Bernstein examines contracting behavior in the cotton industry. There, the contractual relationship sits not only in the shadow of contract law but also in that of long- and well-established industry-based arbitral structures. The best reputation to have as a contracting party is as a flexible business partner who can deal positively and quickly with unexpected circumstances, keeps their word, is open to renegotiation if necessary, pays debts on time and does not 'lay down on the contract'.[68] Contracting parties are working towards performance of their agreement rather than a breach and pay scenario, even being prepared to take a loss on a transaction or split the difference in circumstances where they feel sure that their contracting partner would do the same in future transactions.[69]

---

[64] Mitchell, *Interpretation of Contracts* (Routledge, 2007) 108–110.

[65] The notion of trust is much more complex and multi-layered spanning organisational and personal relationships than the Law in Action scholarship discussed here admits: see S Mouzas, S Henneberg and P Naudé, 'Trust and Reliance in Business Relationships' (2007) 41 *European Journal of Marketing* 1016.

[66] L Bernstein, 'Opting Out of the Legal System: Extralegal Contractual Relations in the Diamond Industry' (1992) 21 *Journal of Legal Studies* 115, 132–133.

[67] L Bernstein, 'Beyond Relational Contracts' (n 20).

[68] L Bernstein, 'Private Commercial Law' (n 17). The work that Bernstein did was qualitative in nature. The reality of Law in Action scholarship is that it is overwhelmingly quantitative: see Z Eigen, 'Empirical Studies of Contract' (2012) 8 *Annual Review of Law and Social Science* 291.

[69] L Bernstein, 'Private Commercial Law' (n 17) 1756; and D Campbell and D Harris, 'Flexibility in Long-term Contractual Relationships: The Role of Co-operation' (1993) 20 *Journal of Law and Society* 166.

These activities are labeled by Bernstein as 'relationship preserving norms' (RPNs). These norms she splits into two groups: 'performance norms' and 'dispute resolution norms'. Performance norms capture the extra-legal relationship between the parties which they have agreed to remain in as long as they continue to trust each other and wish to enter into repeat transactions.[70] Dispute resolution norms are the processes that commercial actors follow to resolve disputes when, notwithstanding the current hiatus in their trading relationship, they wish to deal with the other party again. RPNs will often be very different from the ones that are contained in the legally enforceable contractual agreement between the parties because the terms there will reflect, according to Bernstein, the norms that the parties would want a neutral third-party adjudicator of their dispute to apply. If the parties reach the stage of third party adjudication then they have gone past the point at which RPNs are relevant; their relationship needs radical attention and the relevant norms are 'end-game norms' (EGNs).[71] The use of EGNs occurs in two instances: where the events that have occurred mean that the parties will not deal with each other again; and where, while not relationship ending, the party allegedly in breach of the agreement needs to be sent a credible threat to secure cooperation.

Law in Action scholarship offers us two answers, which become relevant when we turn to look at the possibilities for interpretative approaches to code as contract, to the question of why contractual disputes are often not litigated. One answer is that it is important to avoid using an EGN in a situation where an RPN is more appropriate.[72] The second rather more sophisticated answer is that contracting parties prefer strict interpretation of their agreed terms when they resort to third party adjudication rather than the application of open textured standards. They want flexibility from each other to make their relationships work (RPNs) and they are prepared to negotiate for that flexibility but they require certainty from the judicial process.[73] Thus they will only engage with

---

[70]   E Fehr, S Gätcher and G Kirchsteiger, 'Reciprocity as a Contract Enforcement Device: Experimental Evidence' (1997) 65 *Econometrica* 833 demonstrate that many individuals do not behave opportunistically when it would be in their interests to do so and there is no threat of sanction or retaliation facing them.

[71]   L Bernstein, 'Merchant Law in a Merchant Court: Rethinking the Code's Search for Immanent Business Norms' (1996) 144 *University of Pennsylvania Law Review* 1765, 1796, 1797. See also A Schwartz and R Scott, 'Contract Theory and the Limits of Contract Law' (2003) 113 *Yale Law Journal* 541.

[72]   S Macaulay, 'Non-Contractual Relations in Business: A Preliminary Study' (1963) 28 *American Sociological Review* 55; and J Esser, 'Institutionalizing Industry: The Changing Forms of Contract' (1996) 21 *Law and Social Inquiry* 593.

[73]   L Bernstein, 'Copying and Context: Tying as a Solution to the Lack of Intellectual Property Protection of Contract Terms' (2013) 88 *New York University Law Review Online* 1.

formal adjudication if it is at least more likely than not to adopt a textualist or formalist rather than contextualist stance to interpretation.[74]

3.   SECTION 3

Contract as text creates a relationship between the contracting parties that each can control up to the point of seeking an externally arbitrated remedy. There is an assumption that seeking remediation in this way will occur if either of the parties is dissatisfied with the performance of the other in some respect. Law in Action scholarship suggests however that such a remedy is sought only in limited circumstances, for example one of the parties no longer wishes the business relationship to continue, because adjudication introduces the prospect of uncertain interpretation being applied to open textured terms and contextual factors. What the reluctance to use formal dispute resolution structures to achieve a remedy and the reliance instead on informal discussions and negotiations tell us is that social norms play a huge role in and around contractual practices and contractual events. Indeed this is the whole basis of relational contract scholarship – the Macneilian account of co-operation and reciprocal obligations based upon bottom up theorising and thick description.[75] The possibilities of contract as, and through, code need to be considered in the light of these complimentary but distinct narratives.

If we consider the properties of code then we see that code driven applications are tied to pre-determined building blocks, as are all computational systems. Code is presented to us as precise and rigid; immutable. As language, it wraps words and actions together.[76] It should result in a specified action or no action (as in ambiguity is impossible) when it authorises an event rather than

---

[74]   Uri Benoliel points to the presence of entire agreement clauses, often accompanied by clauses seeking to exclude oral variation or assignment, in 75% of the 1521 commercial contracts he examines as evidence that most parties actively bargain for textualist interpretation in the event of having to use third party adjudication: see 'The Interpretation of Commercial Contracts: An Empirical Study' (2017) 69 *Alabama Law Review* 469. For criticisms of Benoliel's position see Mitchell, *Interpretation of Contracts* (n 54) 131–133.

[75]   I Macneil, 'Other sociological approaches' in B Bouckaert and de G Geest (eds), *Encyclopaedia of Law and Economics* (Edward Elgar, 2000) 694. Against this we might set the work of the neoformulists who advocate the separation of contract as a social institution from contract law. Thus they exclude both open textured standards such as 'reasonableness' and social norms: see R Scott, 'The case for formalism in relational contract' (2000) 94 *Northwestern University Law Review* 847.

[76]   L Diver, 'Law as a User: Design, Affordance, and the Technological Mediation of Norms' (2018) 15 *SCRIPTed* 4.

suggesting behaviours that need to be interpreted or teased out.[77] Code collapses contract formation and contract enforcement into one ex ante moment, rather than the two separate mechanisms (one ex ante and one ex post) enjoyed within contract as text. Code is very clearly not just a translation or encoding of contractual terms, in that it is not a simple reversible process to move from code back to traditional written contract terms. Code, just like contract, has its own materiality[78] and its own power. The writers of code follow strict syntactical rules, often based around the placement of single symbols such as hash tags, or punctuation marks such as colons, in order to produce editable source code that sets out the functions and process required to complete the particular computer operations pursuant to the contract.[79]

As smart contracts can be operationalised and concluded without human intervention we might take the view that there is no room within them or around them for social norms. Indeed we might go further than that and assert that there is no longer any need for adjudicative interpretation of contract scenarios because ambiguous phrases such as 'good faith' or circumstance based ex post clauses such as force majeure will not survive the rigidity imposed by code.[80] Self-help remedies such as liquidated damages clauses will no longer be of use to the parties but instant and costless monitoring of performance will be available. For some commentators this is a welcome appeal to efficiency and transparency.[81] What this view offers is a reading of smart contracts that sees them as accessible as business processes without the need for potentially expensive contract drafting. As a frictionless schema they do not require lawyers or legal knowledge, or any other intermediary. Access to code and programmers is however key.

The converse argument to the efficiency and transparency of contract as code is that contracts expressed this way then lose both the inherent flexibility of contract doctrine that section 1 above referred to, and 'the power of human judgment' that allows, for example, one of the parties to decide that

---

[77]   J Grimmelmann, 'Regulation by Software' (2005) 114 *Yale Law Journal* 1719.

[78]   F Cramer, 'Language' in M Fuller (ed), *Software Studies/A Lexion* (MIT Press, 2008) 168. Critical Code Studies would view code not as a text in metaphorical terms but as a text that creates a sign system with its own rhetoric and as a verbal communication with a significance that is more than mere functionality: see M Marino, *Critical Code Studies* <http://electronicbookreview.com/essay/critical-code-studies>.

[79]   D Berry, 'The Relevance of Understanding Code to International Political Economy' (2012) 49 *International Politics* 277.

[80]   E Tjong Tjin Tai, 'Force Majeure and Excuses in Smart Contracts' (2018) 26 *European Review of Private Law* 787.

[81]   A Wright and P De Filippi, 'Decentralised Blockchain Technology and the Rise of Lex Cryptographia (2015) <https://ssrn.com/abstract=2580664> or <http://dx.doi.org/10.2139/ssrn.2580664>.

they no longer wish to fulfil the obligations that they had previously promised to undertake.[82] An argument that contract expressed as code screens out
ambiguity[83] and drafting costs also fails to capture the idea that, rigidity and
inflexibility notwithstanding, both code and coding are fundamentally social
institutions and practices,[84] underpinned by norms and informal customs in the
same way that Macaulay's and Bernstein's businessman and business practices
are. It is impossible to see smart contracts as a major technological advance
without thinking about how they are written, who writes them and in what
circumstances they might be used.[85] There is a growing understanding of this
last point; we do know something of the industries and circumstances in which
smart contracts are used but we know very little of the processes of contract
drafting and contract construction. We need to think about how smart contracts
fit into the relationships that parties have previously enjoyed and whether it is
possible to establish and further relationships in circumstances where trust is
to be placed not in individuals or even in other business entities but in machine
readable code, algorithms[86] and blockchain.[87] These are questions that point
to a fundamental *sociality*. In Grimmelmann's[88] terms this sociality is most
clearly expressed through locating the layer of sociality on which the technical
layer of programming language sits. It is the social layer that determines limits
and attributes meaning; code has a 'fixed objective syntax' in the technical

---

[82]   J Sklaroff, 'Smart Contracts and the Cost of Inflexibility' (2017) 166 *University
of Pennsylvania Law Review* 263, 286. Whilst we might view the decision by a contractual party to offer compensatory damages rather than performance as a perfectly acceptable exercise of the option of efficient breach, there are doubts as to the empirical reality
of this as a course of action in the light of society's normative expectations of contract:
see T Wilkinson-Ryan and J Baron, 'Moral Judgment and Moral Heuristics in Breach
of Contract' (2009) 6 *Journal of Empirical Legal Studies* 405; and T Wilkinson-Ryan,
'Legal Promise and Psychological Contract' (2012) 47 *Wake Forest Law Review* 843.
[83]   M Raskin, 'The Law and Legality of Smart Contracts' (2017) 1 *Georgetown Law
Technology Review* 305, 325.
[84]   See N Waldrip-Fruin, *Expressive Processing: Digital Fictions, Computer
Games, and Software Studies* (MIT Press, 2009) 4, where computational processes are
seen as connected to 'histories, economies, and schools of thought'.
[85]   Harvey, building on the work of Johns and McKitterick, makes a similar point
about the invention of the printing press and its effect upon both lawyers and legal
culture: see D Harvey, *The Law Emprynted and Englyssed* (Bloomsbury, 2015).
[86]   J Allen, 'Wrapped and Stacked: "Smart Contracts" and the Interaction of Natural
and Formal Language' (2018) 14 *European Review of Contract Law* 307.
[87]   K Werbach, 'Trust, But Verify: Why the Blockchain Needs the Law' (2018) 33
Berkeley Technology Law Journal 489.
[88]   J Grimmelmann, 'All Smart Contracts Are Ambiguous' (2019) 2 *Journal of Law
and Innovation* 1.

layer but the meaning of that syntax is conferred outside the code as part of a social process involving semantics.[89]

Just as lawyers, when drafting a contract, adopt a particular style in the construction of the terms so that it is clear within each, in their view, where risk and liability sit, so the programmer of source code drafts such code aiming to be a literate programmer,[90] choosing the names of variables carefully and explaining what each means. If lawyers are concerned to conceptualise and draft contracts term by term, then programmers are concerned with constructing the whole enterprise mentally as an abstract entity,[91] whilst working mainly in procedural rather than logic-based languages.[92] Source code sets out the processes and functions that are necessary for a computer to follow to achieve a particular goal. This source code is then rendered into a machine-readable code which is uploaded onto the blockchain. Human errors are possible in both coding scenarios (source code construction and the movement from source code to binary language); indeed some would assert that errors are not just possible but frequent.[93] Errors can result in non-execution or incorrect execution, or can create a security vulnerability. Unlike a text contract where there are rules to ensure that it is the definitive governing document between the parties, the source code behind the contract may not be shared, making review impossible,[94] in the same way that we can no longer determine the intentions of the speaker when contract terms move from being expressed orally to being expressed in writing.

Programming languages develop within a community of practice that is often multidisciplinary and multitalented in that it might contain academics, commercial programmers, freelance open source programmers and engi-

---

[89]   Ibid 11. The example that is used is 2**3 in Python. ** denotes to the power of in Python, explained, using natural language, as the left argument is raised to the power of the right argument. The conclusion that 2**3 = 8 is reached through applying meaning drawn from outside the programme itself.

[90]   D Berry, *The Philosophy of Software* (Palgrave Macmillan, 2015) 29.

[91]   R Miller, 'ML' in F Biancuzzi and S Warden (eds), *Masterminds of Programming: Conversations with the Creators of Major Programming Languages* (O'Reilly, 2009) 203.

[92]   For a discussion of the significance of this difference, see C Poncibò and L DiMatteo, 'Smart Contracts' in L DiMatteo, M Cannarsa and C Poncibò (eds), *The Cambridge Handbook of Smart Contracts, Blockchain Technology and Digital Platforms* (Cambridge University Press, 2020) 118, 128.

[93]   K Low and E Mik, 'Pause the Blockchain Revolution' (2020) 69 *International & Comparative Law Quarterly* 175, 173.

[94]   Y Zhou et al, 'Erays: Reverse Engineering Ethereum's Opaque Smart Contracts' (2018) *Proceedings of the 27th USENIX Security Symposium* <https://www.usenix.org/system/files/conference/usenixsecurity18/sec18-zhou.pdf>.

neers.[95] The one obvious potential participatory group that is missing is lawyers, and their absence at the innovation and formation stage is likely to create two problems: one is that legal *audit*, for want of a better term, of smart contract terms is likely to occur very late in the process, thus diminishing the prospect of genuine co-design and exchange;[96] and the other is that the acceptability of smart contracts as legitimate and accessible business practice progresses more slowly.[97] Coders are not the backroom genius loners or anarchic disrupters that we might perhaps think they are.[98] Much of what they do, whilst clearly skilled and requiring great attention to detail, is done in teams, where building involves rote actions, reusing trusted fragments of code from other programmes and online repositories or libraries of code[99] and developing norms around how the code should look in terms of presentation. Github is host to more than 3,000 open source collaborative blockchain projects. Not all of these will concern smart contracts, but many will. Projects emerge most frequently from discussion between the coding community and project owners with code review, integration and testing of functionality being identified as the key tasks.[100] It is the norm to be unable to identify a single author or single source of authorship in code development: 'code work' [has] 'extremely important social and sharing dimensions'.[101]

---

[95]　B Stroustrup, 'C++' in F Biancuzzi and S Warden (eds), *Masterminds of Programming: Conversations with the Creators of Major Programming Languages* (O'Reilly, 2009).

[96]　The development of templates that support contract design with their own language (CLACK – a Common Language for Augmented Contract Knowledge) have been suggested as a way to overcome these difficulties: see C Clack, V Bakshi and L Braine, 'Smart Contract Templates: foundations, design landscape and research directions' (2016) arxiv:1608.00771.

[97]　W Tsai et al, 'Beagle: A New Framework for Smart Contracts Taking Account of Law' (2019) *IEEE International Conference on Service-Oriented System Engineering (SOSE)* 134-13411.

[98]　C Thompson, *Coders* (Picador, 2019); and P Rushworth and A Hackl, 'Writing Code, decoding culture: digital skills and the promise of a fast lane to decent work among refugees and migrants in Berlin' (2021) *Journal of Ethnic and Migration Studies.*

[99]　T Hewa and M Liyanage, 'Survey on Blockchain based Smart Contracts: Technical Aspects and Future Research' (2016) 4 *IEEE Access* 1. The authors are of the view (at 13) that access to third party libraries and syntax improvements will make smart contract design possible for 'business stakeholders' with 'minimal knowledge of programming'.

[100]　P Chakraborty et al, 'Understanding the software development practices of blockchain projects: a survey' (2018) *Proceedings of the 12th ACM/IEEE International Symposium on Empirical Software Engineering and Measurement* <http://amiangshu .com/papers/esem2018-blockchain.pdf>.

[101]　Berry (n 90) 40.

It seems that the sociality that Law in Action scholarship reports around the use of text contracts is currently located at one step removed from the contracting community, lying as it does in the programming and coding domain. It will be sometime before we see a trickle down of smart contract adoption in the way we have seen individual text based contract terms trickle down through business communities.[102] Interventions that will progress smart contract adoption and thus support their development into more sophisticated tools are likely to lie in further innovation in the technical sphere rather than the legal sphere. Templates for standard terms and decompliers[103] which allow source code to be re-engineered from the binary code that is stored on the blockchain offer distinct opportunities for contract users to input into design. This intelligence would allow the alignment of RPN norms, and EGN in the form of appropriate terms, within an automatically executable contract. This would permit flexibility of use rather than flexibility of terms. The creation of a legal source code language[104] would allow lawyers and professional associations that are responsible for producing and advising on industry standard contracts to participate in smart contract creation more easily. The industry level arbitration, so beloved of Bernstein's research participants precisely because it offers certainty rather than interpretive flexibility, might be created to include representatives from the multi-professional smart contract community and adjudicate on contract design as well as contract terms.

4.   CONCLUSION

In this chapter I have endeavoured to bring together the various narratives that are used to explain contractual relationships and consider them against the proposition that smart contracts currently offer frictionless auto-executing business relationships. When we map the development of contract law from a purely oral proposition to text we can see that it (or rather a subset of its users) has evolved strategies to maintain opportunities for flexibility in application. Alongside this, communities of contract users have developed their own social norms around their formal legal relationship and have accorded

---

[102] S Wheeler, *Reservation of Title Clauses: Impact and Implications* (Oxford University Press, 1991); and J Davey and C Kelly, '*Romalpa* and Contractual Innovation' (2015) 42 *Journal of Law and Society* 358.

[103] See D Drummer and D Neumann, 'Is code law? Current legal and technical adoption issues and remedies for blockchain-enabled smart contracts' (2020) 35 *Journal of Information Technology* 337 for a discussion of projects such as Accord, Legalese and OpenLaw.

[104] R Cohen et al, 'Automation and blockchain in securities issuances' (2018) 33 *Butterworths Journal of International Banking and Financial Law* 144.

only a small place to official dispute adjudicatory bodies. If smart contracts are to become part of business practice and not confined solely to particular transactions in particular industries, then they need to be able to fit within this rather disjointed frame. This means being able to see how programmers and coders acquire sufficient legal knowledge, or work with other professional groups that supply it, to be able to construct business relationships that both doctrinal law and Law in Action scholarship can identify within their respective schema as transactions that exchange goods or services for value.

BIBLIOGRAPHY

Articles/Books/Reports

Allen, J, 'Wrapped and Stacked: "Smart Contracts" and the Interaction of Natural and Formal Language' (2018) 14 *European Review of Contract Law* 307

Badawi, A, 'Interpretative Preferences and the Limits of the New Formalism' (2009) 6 *Berkeley Business Journal* 1

Benoliel, U, 'The Interpretation of Commercial Contracts: An Empirical Study' (2017) 69 *Alabama Law Review* 469

Berman, H, 'The Background of the Western Legal Tradition in the Folklaw of the Peoples of Europe' (1978) 45 *University of Chicago Law Review* 553

Bernstein, J, 'Smart Contract Integration in Professional Sports Management: The Imminence of Athlete Representation' (2018) 14 *DePaul Journal of Sports Law* 88

Bernstein, L, 'Opting Out of the Legal System: Extralegal Contractual Relations in the Diamond Industry' (1992) 21 *Journal of Legal Studies* 115

Bernstein, L, 'Merchant Law in a Merchant Court: Rethinking the Code's Search for Immanent Business Norms' (1996) 144 *University of Pennsylvania Law Review* 1765

Bernstein, L, 'Private Commercial Law in the Cotton Industry: Creating Cooperation Through Rules, Norms and Institutions' (2001) 99 *Michigan Law Review* 1724

Bernstein, L, 'Copying and Context: Tying as a Solution to the Lack of Intellectual Property Protection of Contract Terms' (2013) 88 *New York University Law Review Online* 1

Bernstein, L, 'Beyond Relational Contracts: Social Capital and Network Governance in Procurement Contracts' (2015) 7 *Journal of Legal Analysis* 561

Berry, D, *The Philosophy of Software* (Palgrave Macmillan, 2015)

Boehme-Neßler, V, *Pictorial Law* (Springer, 2011)

Braucher, J, J Kidwell and W Whitford (eds), *Revisiting the Contracts Scholarship of Stewart Macaulay* (Hart Publishing, 2013)

Buchholtz, G, 'Artificial Intelligence and Legal Tech: Challenges to the Rule of Law' in J Wischmeyer and T Rademacher (eds), *Regulating Artificial Intelligence* (Springer, 2020) 175

Campbell, D and D Harris, 'Flexibility in Long-term Contractual Relationships: The Role of Co-operation' (1993) 20 *Journal of Law and Society* 166

Carawan, E, 'Oral "Agreement", Written Contract, and the Bonds of Law at Athens' in C Cooper (ed), *Politics of Orality: Orality and Literacy in Ancient Greece* (Brill, 2006) 321

Clack, C, V Bakshi and L Braine, 'Smart Contract Templates: foundations, design landscape and research directions' (2016) arxiv:1608.00771

Cohen, R et al, 'Automation and blockchain in securities issuances' (2018) 33 *Butterworths Journal of International Banking and Financial Law* 144

Collins, R and D Skover, 'Paratexts' (1992) 44 *Stanford Law Review* 509

Coopersmith, J, 'Old Technologies Never Die, They Just Don't Get Updated' (2010) 80 *International Journal for the History of Engineering & Technology* 166

Cramer, F, 'Language' in M Fuller (ed), *Software Studies/A Lexion* (MIT Press, 2008) 168

Daly, K, 'Restorative Justice: The Real Story' (2002) 4 *Punishment and Society* 55

Davey, J and C Kelly, '*Romalpa* and Contractual Innovation' (2015) 42 *Journal of Law and Society* 358

de Caria, R, 'The Legal Meaning of Smart Contracts' (2019) 27 *European Review of Private Law* 731

Diver, L, 'Law as a User: Design, Affordance, and the Technological Mediation of Norms' (2018) 15 *SCRIPTed* 4

Drummer, D and D Neumann, 'Is code law? Current legal and technical adoption issues and remedies for blockchain-enabled smart contracts' (2020) 35 *Journal of Information Technology* 337

Eigen, Z, 'Empirical Studies of Contract' (2012) 8 *Annual Review of Law and Social Science* 291

Esser, J, 'Institutionalizing Industry: The Changing Forms of Contract' (1996) 21 *Law and Social Inquiry* 593

Fehr, E, S Gätcher and G Kirchsteiger, 'Reciprocity as a Contract Enforcement Device: Experimental Evidence' (1997) 65 *Econometrica* 833

Fernandez-Vazquez, S, 'Blockchain and Smart Contracts: Uses and Challenges' (2019) *International Conference on Artificial Intelligence* 394

Fineman, J, 'Critical Approaches to Contract Law' (1983) 30 *UCLA Law Review* 829

Finnegan, R, 'Communication and Technology' (1989) 9 *Language and Communication* 107

Goody, J, *The Logic of Writing and the Organization of Society* (Cambridge University Press, 1986)

Goody, J and I Watt, 'The Consequences of Literacy' (1963) 5 *Comparative Studies in Society and History* 304

Griggs, K et al, 'Healthcare Blockchain System Using Smart Contracts for Secure Automated Remote Patient Monitoring' (2018) 42 *Journal of Medical Systems* 130

Grimmelmann, J, 'Regulation by Software' (2005) 114 *Yale Law Journal* 1719

Grimmelmann, J, 'All Smart Contracts Are Ambiguous' (2019) 2 *Journal of Law and Innovation* 1

Gulati, M and R Scott, *The Three and a Half Minute Transaction: Boilerplate and the Limits of Contract Design* (University of Chicago Press, 2013)

Hadfield, G and I Bozovic, 'Scaffolding: Using Formal Contracts to Support Informal Relations in Support of Innovation' (2016) *Wisconsin Law Review* 981

Harris, R, *Rethinking Writing* (Athlone Press, 2000)

Harvey, D, *The Law Emprynted and Englyssed* (Bloomsbury, 2015)

Harvey, D, *Collisions in the Digital Paradigm* (Hart Publishing, 2017)

Herian, R, 'Taking Blockchain Seriously' (2018) 29 *Law and Critique* 163

Hewa, T and M Liyanage, 'Survey on Blockchain based Smart Contracts: Technical Aspects and Future Research' (2016) 4 *IEEE Access* 1

Jethro Brown, W, 'Customary Law in Modern England' (1905) 5 *Columbia Law Review* 561

Kay, P, 'Language Evolution and Speech Style' in B Blount and M Sanches (eds), *Sociocultural Dimensions of Language Change* (Academic Press, 1977) 20

Klass, G, 'Parol Evidence Rules and the Mechanics of Choice' (2019) 20 *Theoretical Inquiries in Law* 457

Levy, K, 'Book-Smart, Not Street-Smart: Blockchain-Based Smart Contracts and the Social Workings of Law' (2017) 3 *Engaging Science, Technology, and Society* 1

Low, K and E Mik, 'Pause the Blockchain Revolution' (2020) 69 *International & Comparative Law Quarterly* 175

Macaulay, S, 'Non-Contractual Relations in Business: A Preliminary Study' (1963) 28 *American Sociological Review* 55

Macaulay, S, 'An Empirical View of Contract' (1985) *Wisconsin Law Review* 465

Macaulay, S, 'The Real Deal and the Paper Deal: Empirical Pictures of Relationships, Complexity and the Urge for Transparent Simple Rules' (2003) 66 *Modern Law Review* 44

Macaulay, S, 'Freedom from Contract: Solutions in Search of a Problem' (2004) *Wisconsin Law Review* 777

Macaulay, S, 'Contract, New Legal Realism, and Improving the Navigation of *The Yellow Submarine*' (2006) 80 *Tulane Law Review* 1161

Macaulay, S and W Whitford, 'The Development of Contracts: Law in Action' (2015) 87 *Temple Law Review* 793

MacDonald, E, 'Dispatching the Dispatch Rule? The Postal Rule, Email, Revocation and Implied Terms' (2013) 19 *Web Journal of Current Legal Issues*

Macneil, I, 'Other sociological approaches' in B Bouckaert and de G Geest (eds), *Encyclopaedia of Law and Economics* (Edward Elgar, 2000) 694

Maine, H, *Ancient Law* (John Murray, 1861)

McCosker, A and E Milne, 'Coding Labour' (2014) 20 *Cultural Studies Review* 4

Mik, E, 'The Effectiveness of Acceptances Communicated by Electronic Means, or – Does the Postal Acceptance Rule Apply to Email?' (2009) 26 *Journal of Contract Law* 68

Mik, E, 'Smart Contracts: Terminology, technical limitations and real world complexity' (2017) 9 *Law, Innovation and Technology* 269

Miller, R, 'ML' in F Biancuzzi and S Warden (eds), *Masterminds of Programming: Conversations with the Creators of Major Programming Languages* (O'Reilly, 2009) 203

Mitchell, C, 'Entire Agreement Clauses: Contracting Out of Contextualism' (2006) 22 *Journal of Contract Law* 222

Mitchell, C, *Interpretation of Contracts* (Routledge, 2007)

Mitchell, C, *Interpretation of Contracts* (Routledge, 2nd ed, 2019)

Mnookin, R and L Kornhauser, 'Bargaining in the Shadow of the Law: The Case of Divorce' (1979) 88 *Yale Law Journal* 950

Mouzas, S, S Henneberg and P Naudé, 'Trust and Reliance in Business Relationships' (2007) 41 *European Journal of Marketing* 1016

Olsen, D, 'Oral Discourse in a World of Literacy' (2006) 41 *Research in the Teaching of English* 136

Ong, W, *Interfaces of the Word: Studies in the Evolution of Consciousness and Culture* (Cornell University Press, 1997)

Poncibò, C and L DiMatteo, 'Smart Contracts' in L DiMatteo, M Cannarsa and C Poncibò (eds), *The Cambridge Handbook of Smart Contracts, Blockchain Technology and Digital Platforms* (Cambridge University Press, 2020) 118

Raskin, M, 'The Law and Legality of Smart Contracts' (2017) 1 *Georgetown Law Technology Review* 305

Reed, C, 'Online and Offline Equivalence: aspiration and achievement' (2010) 18 *International Journal of Law and Information Technology* 248

Roach, L, 'Law codes and legal norms in later Anglo-Saxon England' (2013) 86 *Historical Research* 46

Rushworth, P and A Hackl, 'Writing Code, decoding culture: digital skills and the promise of a fast lane to decent work among refugees and migrants in Berlin' (2021) *Journal of Ethnic and Migration Studies*

Savelyev, A, 'Contract Law 2.0: "Smart" Contracts as the beginning of the End for Classical Contract Law' (2017) 26 *Information and Communications Technology Law* 116

Schwartz, A and R Scott, 'Contract Theory and the Limits of Contract Law' (2003) 113 *Yale Law Journal* 541

Scott, R, 'The case for formalism in relational contract' (2000) 94 *Northwestern University Law Review* 847

Shapiro, F and M Pearse, 'The Most-Cited Law Review Articles of All Time' (2012) 110 *Michigan Law Review* 1483

Shermin, V, 'Disrupting Governance with Blockchains and Smart Contracts' (2017) 26 *Strategic Change* 499

Spencer, J, 'Signature, Consent, and the Rule in *L'Estrange* v *Graucob*' (1973) 32 *Cambridge Law Journal* 104

Stroustrup, B, 'C++' in F Biancuzzi and S Warden (eds), *Masterminds of Programming: Conversations with the Creators of Major Programming Languages* (O'Reilly, 2009) 1

Sulkowski, A, 'Blockchain, Business Supply Chains, Sustainability, and Law: The Future of Governance, Legal Frameworks, and Lawyers?' (2018) 43 *Delaware Journal of Corporate Law* 303

Swan, M, *Blockchain: Blueprint for a New Economy* (O'Reilly Media, 2015)

Tapscott, D and A Tapscott, *Blockchain Revolution* (Penguin, 2016)

Thompson, C, *Coders* (Picador, 2019)

Tiersma, P, 'The Language of Offer and Acceptance: Speech Acts and the Question of Intent' (1986) 74 *California Law Review* 189

Tiersma, P, 'Textualizing the Law' (2001) 8 *Forensic Linguistics* 73

Tiersma, P, *Parchment, Paper, Pixels* (University of Chicago Press, 2010)

Tjong Tjin Tai, E, 'Force Majeure and Excuses in Smart Contracts' (2018) 26 *European Review of Private Law* 787

Tsai, W et al, 'Beagle: A New Framework for Smart Contracts Taking Account of Law' (2019) *IEEE International Conference on Service-Oriented System Engineering (SOSE)* 134-13411

Waldrip-Fruin, N, *Expressive Processing: Digital Fictions, Computer Games, and Software Studies* (MIT Press, 2009)

Weber, M, *The Theory of Social and Economic Organization*, tr T Parsons (Free Press, 1947)

Werbach, K, 'Trust, But Verify: Why the Blockchain Needs the Law' (2018) 33 *Berkeley Technology Law Journal* 489

Werbach, K and N Cornell, 'Contracts Ex Machina' (2017) 67 *Duke Law Journal* 313

Wheeler, S, *Reservation of Title Clauses: Impact and Implications* (Oxford University Press, 1991)

Wheeler, S, 'Visions of Contract' (2017) 44 *Journal of Law and Society* 74

Wheeler, S, 'Law in Action' in W Swain and D Campbell (eds), *Reimagining Contract Law Pedagogy* (Routledge, 2019) 79

Wilkinson-Ryan, T, 'Legal Promise and Psychological Contract' (2012) 47 *Wake Forest Law Review* 843

Wilkinson-Ryan, T and J Baron, 'Moral Judgment and Moral Heuristics in Breach of Contract' (2009) 6 *Journal of Empirical Legal Studies* 405

Zhao, J, 'Extraterritorial Attempts at Addressing Challenges to Corporate Sustainability' in B Sjåfjell and C Bruner (eds), *The Cambridge Handbook of Corporate Law, Corporate Governance and Sustainability* (Cambridge University Press, 2019) 29

Cases

Chartbrook Ltd v Persimmon Homes Ltd [2009] UKHL 38

L'Estrange v Graucob [1934] 2 KB 394

Parker v SE Railway Co [1877] 2 CPD 416

Shogun Finance v Hudson [2003] UKHL 62

Thompson v London, Midland and Scottish Rly [1930] 1 KB 41

Legislation

Competition and Consumer Law 2010 (Cth) Ach 2 ('Australian Consumer Law')

Consumer Rights Act 2015 (UK)

Modern Slavery Act 2015 (UK)

Unfair Contract Terms Act 1977 (UK)

11. Doing it online: is mediation ready for the AI age?

Nadja M Alexander[1]

1.   INTRODUCTION

This chapter places the spotlight on mediation and examines the considerations that institutional service providers (ISPs) of mediation need to take into account in making the shift to digitizing mediation services. The central question explored is: How can the transition from live[2] to online mediation practice take place in a manner that upholds the integrity of the mediation process? What efforts should be made in this transition to enhance the user experience beyond the technical exigencies that externalities impose on personalized engagement? The analysis culminates in a call to action to include both the service providers and the users themselves in the larger narrative surrounding this conscious endeavour to see technology and digitizing move beyond expedience and embrace contextual mediation imperatives.

The chapter begins by setting out the reasons why the process of mediation is more likely than other dispute resolution processes to be altered in fundamental ways that potentially impact its core characteristics. With the focus firmly on mediation, it then examines the potential impact of digitization on

[1]   This research is supported by the National Research Foundation, Singapore under its Emerging Areas Research Projects (EARP) Funding Initiative and the Singapore International Dispute Resolution Academy (SIDRA) at Singapore Management University. Any opinions, findings and conclusions or recommendations expressed in this material are those of the author and do not reflect the views of National Research Foundation, Singapore or other funding bodies. The author wishes to acknowledge Allison Goh's work on digital readiness in arbitration, which formed the inspiration for this chapter. Many thanks to Bhumika Billa and Terence Yeo for their excellent research contributions and to the editors of this volume for their patience and guidance. In particular, thank you to Mark Findlay for his insights, which have helped to shape this chapter in its final form.
[2]   In this chapter 'live' mediation refers to mediation conducted in a physical, face-to-face setting.

this dispute resolution process with a view to identifying the factors critical to transitioning to online mediation in a manner that aligns with mediation's underlying values and principles. The analysis culminates in a framework for exploring the digital readiness for mediation practice.

By its very definition, mediation is a user-centric process in the sense that parties directly participate together with their legal advisers in a mutualized resolution process. Therefore, any exploration of how digitization impacts mediation requires the perspective of both client users and 'repeat player' legal users, the latter often referring their clients to mediation in the first place. Further, as with other private dispute resolution procedures such as arbitration, the perceptions and experiences of client and legal users – referred to simply as users in this chapter – of mediation remain critically important for ISPs in the race for a slice of the global market. For these reasons the chapter is ultimately addressed to mediation ISPs and draws on the academic and empirical literature of the user experience.

2. PROCESS, PROVIDERS AND A PANDEMIC

Dubbed the pandemic-proof process, mediation has shown itself to be highly adaptable to legal, economic, political and socio-cultural changes. As a dispute resolution mechanism, mediation is characterized by its procedural agility, cultural responsiveness, focus on party autonomy, and collaborative principles of negotiation and decision-making. Mediation offers a client-centred dispute resolution procedure, which features diverse practice models and the capacity for parties and their lawyers to have input into the design of each mediation process; significantly it is the parties who take centre stage in mediation, negotiate with each other and decide on how to resolve their dispute (or not). The time and cost efficiencies of mediation have been confirmed to be highly attractive to clients.[3] Accordingly, mediation is well-suited to managing disputes that have emerged through no fault of either party, but rather due to the consequences of COVID-19, such as disruptions within supply chains and the frustration of a wide range of business arrangements. During the pandemic period, survival for many businesses continues to depend on timely and affordable solutions to complex problems. Further, international travel restrictions and local lockdowns have increased reliance on socially-distanced and technologically-enhanced communications from workplace meetings to court hearings. These contextual necessities led to a period of rapid digitiza-

---

[3]   Singapore International Dispute Resolution Academy, 'SIDRA International Dispute Resolution Survey: 2020 Final Report' (2020) 46 <https://sidra.smu.edu.sg/sidra-international-dispute-resolution-survey-final-report-2020>.

tion of institutional and court-based mediation as well as an increase in online mediation offerings by individual mediators. As a well-known international commercial mediator exclaimed during a webinar in 2020, 'you should see my chambers now. It's wired up like a NASA station – who would have imagined this a year ago?' At the interface between mediation technology and mediation users, ISPs are playing a key role in shaping mediation processes of the future, for example through investments in technology and development of protocols. For example, the Singapore International Mediation Institute and their counterparts in Japan have moved quickly to establish COVID-19 mediation protocols that offer disputants timely, cost effective and commercially sensible resolutions of their disputes. In this way ISPs are playing a gatekeeping role in terms of what aspects of mediation are digitized, and how. They select the technology and online platforms for various aspects of mediation services, such as case filing, case management, the mediation process itself, and the recording and documentation of mediated settlement agreements.

Mediation is certainly not the only dispute resolution process to have experienced rapid digitization as a result of COVID-19. Litigation and arbitration have also increased their exposure to digital technology as the increase in remote hearings indicates.[4] However these are determinative dispute resolution processes in which the third-party judge or arbitrator, as the case may be, imposes a decision upon the disputing parties. They are considerably more formal, structured and legalistic with detailed rules of procedure and evidence compared with the flexible facilitated negotiation approach of mediation. As such there is less scope for technology to challenge the fundamental nature of these processes. Lawyers (as legal users of international dispute resolution) have mostly shrugged their shoulders in response to questions about what has changed in terms of the digitization of litigation and arbitration.[5] Remote hearings are not new; it is just that they are fast becoming the new normal in cross-border matters. In the case of procedurally flexible mediation, however, technology has been referred to as the 'fourth' party[6] with the potential to influence fundamental aspects of how the process is conducted (procedural), how parties communicate with one another (relational and cultural) and how the substance of the dispute is perceived (substantive), and the extent to which lawyers and other experts are involved. If live mediation is considered procedurally flexible, online mediation increases that flexibility multiple times over.

---

[4]   Singapore International Dispute Resolution Academy, 'User Interviews from Qualitative Phase of SIDRA International Dispute Resolution Survey' (November–December 2020) (unpublished raw data).

[5]   Ibid.

[6]   D Rainey, 'The Culture in the Code', *Mediate* (March 2009) <https://www.mediate.com/articles/culture_in_code.cfm>.

Online mediation offers many opportunities: it has the potential to bring parties together despite travel restrictions, to bridge geographical distances where parties live in different jurisdictions or remote regions, and in doing so reduces costs associated with mediation. Technology can offer further cost reductions with the assistance of negotiation support systems, blind bidding software, and automated case management. In situations in which parties may not be comfortable sitting in the same room,[7] online mediation can offer a safe haven. With the countless procedural variations available via technology, parties who can articulate their interests better with time and space to think about their response to a communication from the other party may be better off in an asynchronous text-based procedure and can choose one of the many message-based online mediation systems. Alternatively, someone who feels they can be more persuasive responding in the moment verbally may prefer a video-based platform. At the same time, there are potential risks associated with the digitization of mediation. Issues related to digital accessibility, for example access to the required hardware, software and network, need to be factored in, as do issues relating to digital literacy, availability of technical support and trust in the technology (or lack thereof). There are real risks to confidentiality linked to issues of authenticity and security including the implications of there being a record of mediation proceedings (which is not the case in physical settings). Further, online mediation may affect the relational dynamics between the parties in (un) anticipated ways. For example, choices in relation to synchronous or asynchronous communication, and text-based, audio or audio-visual platforms for the mediation may impact the dynamics of the parties' interaction with each other and the mediator, and the power relations 'in the room', thereby influencing decision-making and mediated outcomes.[8] These shifts have implications for the well-established mediation principle of party autonomy and the capacity for mediation to help parties maximize their interests.

This discussion highlights the vulnerability of highly flexible and culturally-responsive dispute resolution procedures when subject to rapid digitization. In particular, the impact of various aspects of AI-assisted information and communication technologies on the integrity of, and values underpinning, mediation processes and outcomes remains to be fully realized. Even at this early stage in the digital revolution for mediation it is worth reflecting on the essential values on which mediation thrives, and to regularly evaluate their

---

[7]　For example, this may occur where one party feels intimidated in the presence of the other and therefore less able to be comfortable articulating their interests for the purposes of negotiating a settlement.

[8]　Further illustrations of how digitization can affect the process of mediation are found throughout this chapter.

recognition and protection when the attractions of technological solutions seem pervasive.

As indicated previously, ISPs play a critical role in shaping mediation processes during this period of technological transition. Yet the digital readiness on the part of ISPs is in its infancy as many of them begin to set parameters for online mediation principles and practice on a case-by-case basis, often without an adequate understanding of (1) the technological resources available and (2) the ethical implications of what they are doing.[9] In the midst of this global real-time experiment in digitizing various aspects of mediation,[10] we must ask ourselves what it means to be digitally ready. The response to this question is offered in two parts: first, by outlining mediation-relevant technology with a view to establishing a digital baseline; and, second, by identifying core mediation values that must survive, and thrive, in digital transition for mediation to remain relevant in tomorrow's dispute resolution world.

However, readiness cannot be cut free from sustainability, resilience and the contextual differences that characterize different capacities to embrace technological modernization across the globe. While the steps towards improved readiness for change can be generalized, it is equally important to factor in the practical and principled influences over adaptation.

3.   MEDIATION AND TECHNOLOGY IN PRACTICE

Online mediation is at a critical juncture in terms of its development and acceptance as a mainstream form of dispute resolution. In a survey conducted in 2020 in the midst of the COVID-19 pandemic by UK's Independent Mediators (IM),[11] more than 90 per cent of respondents (primarily lawyers) who had already taken part in an online mediation would do so again. More than 80 per cent of those who had not yet taken part in an online mediation would be prepared to do so. These are staggeringly high figures which appear to indicate a confident preparedness to engage in online mediation. But what is online mediation, really? The main technologies that institutions are using for mediation are the general online meeting platforms of Zoom, followed by

---

[9]   This becomes evident through the 'zoomification' of mediation without consideration of the sophisticated and dedicated online mediation services that is currently available.

[10]   Further illustrations of the various ways in which aspects of mediation can be digitized are offered in section 3 below.

[11]   Independent Mediators Limited, 'Online Mediation Survey Results July 2020' (2020) 3 <http://www.independentmediators.co.uk/wp-content/uploads/2020/08/IM-Online-Mediation-Survey-Results-July-2020.pdf>.

Skype and Microsoft Teams.[12] Yet, as the following paragraphs demonstrate, diverse technologies can be applied to mediation processes.[13] The discussion will include online negotiation services as these may be offered with or without the assistance of a human mediator, and may be a prelude to 'online' mediation insofar as no settlement is reached by the parties.

Facilitated negotiation involves the provision of secure websites such as virtual collaborative workspaces or e-rooms for parties to exchange messages, share and store documents and engage in synchronous or asynchronous direct negotiations. Private e-rooms can be set up for side meetings (or in the case of mediation, caucuses). Facilitation is usually provided by the technology and the process rules established by the e-room provider, although sometimes a human mediator may assist. This service is offered by a number of providers as part of their service portfolio. Providers of facilitated negotiation include Modria,[14] Smartsettle[15] and eBay's Dispute Resolution Centre.[16] Software not dedicated to dispute resolution such as Zoom, Skype and Microsoft Teams also offers some of these features and is being used for mediation as outlined below. As an illustration, parties could negotiate online using a combination of video, audio and text communication. They could also upload and share documents such as existing contracts and share screens to work on settlement proposals. Some platforms allow previous messages to be searched using key words or organized according to different threads or themes. Further, there may be online options to sign and upload documents such as a negotiated (or mediated) settlement agreement. Should parties not be able to reach resolution, they may consider bringing in a mediator and continue using the same software program.

Automated negotiation makes use of automated software systems such as blind-bidding procedures. Automated negotiation is mainly used for monetary

---

[12] A Goh, 'Law Society Survey Results of Mediation Experiences During COVID-19', *Singapore Law Gazette* (September 2020) <https://lawgazette.com .sg/news/updates/survey-results-of-mediation-experiences/>. See also A Limbury, 'Mediating online – is it time to move from improvising to a dedicated platform?', *Kluwer Mediation Blog* (22 April 2020) <http://mediationblog.kluwerarbitration.com/ 2020/04/22/mediating-online-is-it-time-to-move-from-improvising-to-a-dedicated -platform/>; A Goncalves and D Rainey, 'Mediating Online is Much More Than Doing It on Zoom', Kluwer Mediation Blog (28 February 2021) <http://mediationblog .kluwerarbitration.com/2021/02/28/mediating-online-is-much-more-than-doing-it-on -zoom/>.

[13] Parts of this overview are adapted and updated from N Alexander, *The Hong Kong Mediation Manual* (Lexis Nexis, 2014) ch 11.

[14] See <https://www.tylertech.com/products/modria>.

[15] See <https://www.smartsettle.com>.

[16] See <http://resolutioncenter.ebay.com>.

Table 11.1   Disputes on quantum

Party A	Party B
$20 000	$1000
$12000	$2500
$5000	$4000

claims where only quantum is disputed. Participants can make consecutive bids that are independent settlement offers, without knowing the bids of the other party. Most providers offer three consecutive rounds of bidding in which claimants and respondents enter bids into a secure online website, unaware of the offers made by the other party. If the offers fall within a predetermined range – for example, 20 per cent to 30 per cent of each other – automatic settlement ensues and the difference between the offers is split. No human intervention is required. If the offers do not come within the settlement range, some providers recommend the parties to online mediation; others simply end the procedure.[17] Blind bidding is most suitable for disputes on quantum. By way of illustration, party A has a financial claim against party B. The parties may insert the following bids into the automated negotiation program, which has been coded so that if they make bids no more than $1000 apart, the amount will be split 50/50 and that will be the settlement figure, see Table 11.1.

Here the final bids are $1000 apart, so the automated negotiation software would split the difference so that party B pays party A $4500 as a final settlement figure. Online dispute resolution (ODR) providers that offer variations on automated negotiation include the International Centre for Dispute Resolution[18] and SmartSettle.[19]

Negotiation support systems allow the manipulation of negotiation variables for participants and can provide an overview of negotiation stages and expert advice on strategies and outcomes. The blueprint for a generic negotiation support system capable of being adapted to any negotiation domain in any country is said to be a three-step process:[20]

---

[17] E Katsh and J Rifkin, Online Dispute Resolution: Resolving Conflicts in Cyberspace (Jossey-Bass, 2001) 61.

[18] See the ICDR Manufacturer/Supplier Online Dispute Resolution Protocol at <www.icdr.org>.

[19] DA Larson, '"Brother, Can You Spare A Dime?" Technology can reduce dispute resolution costs when times are tough and improve outcomes' (2011) 11(2) Nevada Law Journal 523, 538–540. See also <www.smartsettle.com> for visual blind bidding.

[20] AR Lodder and J Zeleznikow, 'Developing an Online Dispute Resolution Environment: Dialogue Tools and Negotiation Support Systems in a Three-Step Model' (2005) 10 Harvard Negotiation Law Review 287, 287–388.

(1)   construction of a negotiation tool which provides feedback on the likely outcome of the dispute should the negotiation fail (that is the calculation of the BATNA[21]);

(2)   use of the tool to attempt to resolve existing disputes using dialogue techniques; and

(3)   for issues not resolved in (2), using the negotiation tool to develop bargaining strategies to facilitate resolution of the dispute.[22]

Some negotiation support systems, also called *multivariable resolution optimisation programs* (MROPs), work without the input of a human facilitator. Here, parties provide information and personal views about key issues in the dispute which are coded into values. The program then tracks these values throughout the ensuing negotiation process. MROPs generally give parties the ability to generate proposals to be presented to the other side and allow value swaps between different negotiable items. After several proposals, the program can deliver a mathematically-optimal solution to the dispute, which – relevant to the data input – maximizes the benefit for both parties.[23]

In Australia, for example, pre-trial mediation has been made compulsory in family matters and mediation services have evolved to leverage the benefits of technology.[24] Family Winner is a software package that assists people going through divorce to create rational options for trade-offs of assets and compensation. This can be done provided that:

* the issues can be described;
* the issues remain static; and
* points can be allocated to issues.

The inventors, Bellucci and Zeleznikow, concede that this bargaining-type negotiation support system has its limitations as it does not consider all relevant parameters in family dispute resolution. For example, where disputants' preferences conflict with the interests of children and notions of justice, the negotiated outcome is unlikely to be approved by a court. Other family medi-

---

[21]   BATNA is the acronym for best alternative to a negotiated agreement, first coined by R Fisher and W Ury in *Getting to Yes* (Penguin, 1983).

[22]   See C Irvine, 'Brexit Negotiated? Online Dispute Resolution Will be More Than an Alternative', *Kluwer Mediation Blog* (16 December 2018) <http://mediationblog .kluwerarbitration.com/2018/12/16/odr-will-be-more-than-an-alternative/>   for   an example of these negotiation methodologies in real-world application.

[23]   C Rule, Online Dispute Resolution for Business: B2B, E-Commerce, Consumer, Employment, Insurance, and Other Commercial Conflicts (San Francisco, 2002) 58.

[24]   See N Augar and J Zeleznikow, 'Developing Online Support and Counseling to Enhance Family Dispute Resolution in Australia' (May 2013) *Springer Science and Media Dordecht* 523–526.

ation platforms are Family Mediator (based on Family Winner with the additional input of a human mediator) and Asset Divider. Unlike Family Winner, Asset Divider allows users to input negative values as well as positive ones and recommends a percentage property split.[25]

Building on these dispute resolution systems, a new development named IMODRE uses multiple web-based intelligent agents to coordinate a negotiation and achieve fairer outcomes. According to the inventors:

> [O]ne agent uses a Bayesian Belief Network expertly modelled with knowledge of the Australian Family Law domain to advise disputants of their Best Alternatives to Negotiated Agreements (BATNAs). Another agent incorporates the recommended percentage split of marital property into an integrative bargaining process and applies heuristics and game theory to equitably distribute marital property assets and facilitate further trade-offs.[26]

The system is said to add greater fairness to family property negotiations. It has an educative function in that it helps parties prepare for negotiations and can also help mediators draft settlement agreements. Along with improved access, affordability and time management this approach has been developed with an extant and conscious prioritizing of fairness above functionality.

Increasingly, human mediators are engaged to assist parties using MROP in their negotiations across a range of practice areas. Family Winner and IMODRE are two examples of this development. Another illustration is SmartSettle, which offers a structured negotiation support system in which a mediator uses a special online interface to help parties identify the key issues and their interests in the dispute. The platform features integrative bargaining principles, the provision of graphical representations of parties' best and worst case scenarios, bargaining zone identification, option generation, concession-making, benefit maximization and agreement frameworks.[27] In yet another illustration, Modria's Fairness Engine[28] includes a diagnosis module that gathers relevant documentation about an issue and suggests potential

---

[25] See B Abrahams and J Zeleznikow, 'A Multi-Agent Architecture for Online Dispute Resolution Services' (Fifth International Workshop on Online Dispute Resolution Proceedings, 2008) <http://sunsite.informatik.rwth-aachen.de/Publications/CEUR-WS/Vol-430/Paper7.pdf>.

[26] B Abrahams, E Bellucci and J Zeleznikow, 'Incorporating Fairness into Development of an Integrated Multi-agent Online Dispute Resolution Environment' 21 *Group Decision and Negotiation* 3.

[27] See <www.smartsettle.com/products>.

[28] See <https://techcrunch.com/2012/11/19/modria-launches-a-fairness-engine-for-online-dispute-resolution/>.

solutions and a negotiations module that summarizes areas of disagreement and facilitates direct on-the-record discussions.

These brief examples of AI-assisted technology in resolving disputation through digitized mediation paint an encouraging picture. At the same time, it cannot be overstated that in deeply cognitive and affective human settings AI is still in its infancy. Recognition of the destructive potentials of bias in AI-driven predictive decision-making are well known and depend essentially on the vigilance of data enablers, outcome interpreters and the expectations demanded of automation in prediction. While ethics and principled design rely on an empathetic relationship developing between technology and humanity, AI as a solution for automatically analysing human emotions is both aspirational and deeply problematic. In the current context of the science AI is nowhere close to being able to realistically unpack complex human feelings, particularly in charged relational settings. Recognizing the limitations of technology is also important in the readiness recipe so that expectations do not outstrip the need for humans in the loop for the foreseeable future.

With this caveat in mind, the above overview shows that diverse and sophisticated technologies are readily available to support mediation and continue to develop and be tailored to mediation processes. Yet, there appears to be a lack of awareness among many ISPs – the gatekeepers of online mediation – about the state of mediation-relevant technology.[29] As much of the world moved online in 2020, a popular refrain was that mediation parties simply needed access to a computer, webcam and broadband Internet connection. The 'Zoom mediation'[30] wave of the early 2020s has largely ignored dedicated online dispute resolution platforms and the availability of AI-supported tools such as negotiation support systems. This development can conceivably be explained by the familiarity principle,[31] namely that people are more comfortable with the familiar and are reluctant to move to other options with which they are unfamiliar even if those options represent rationally better choices.[32] In other words, as user familiarity with Zoom soared during 2020, it became the go-to platform for meetings, social communication and mediation, over and above

---

[29]   Singapore International Dispute Resolution Academy (n 3) 58–60. See also Goncalves and Rainey (n 12).

[30]   G Matteucci and Stelios Asproftas, 'ODR in 30 Countries, 2020 mediation in the COVID-19 Era' <http://cisarbitration.com/wp-content/uploads/2020/05/ODR -in_30-Countries_2020-Mediation-in-the-COVID-19-Era.pdf>. See also Goh (n 12); Limbury (n 12); Goncalves and Rainey (n 12).

[31]   Also referred to as the status quo bias, namely that people have a bias for the current state of affairs: see W Samuelson and R Zeckhauser, 'Status Quo Bias in Decision Making' (1988) 1 *Journal of Risk and Uncertainty* 7.

[32]   The familiarity principle applies to mediators just as much as to users. But perhaps the tide is starting to turn: see Limbury (n 12).

dedicated online dispute resolution platforms such as CREK[33] and Modron,[34] which promised better security, opportunities not just to share documents but also to upload and store them, case management functions, a range of text/ audio/visual communication technologies, and online execution functions for settlement agreements and other options.

While pre-COVID scepticism towards online mediation[35] has given way to new experiences,[36] a growing acceptance of, and in some cases even enthusiasm for, digital disputing, online mediation is much more than just doing it on zoom. Looking forward, the question for ISPs and parties cannot be whether or not to 'zoom-mediate'. A more useful question could be: how can technology be integrated into the mediation in a manner that reflects the procedural and relational needs of the parties and upholds the integrity of the mediation process?

> As technology – AI – is irreversibly here in the world, as we cannot avoid it, we should, instead, use it. Instead of complaining about it, we should set it to work for us. Why not? We simply have to know how to use technology in order to capitalise on it, to see the ways it can enhance the principles, process and practice we call mediation.[37]

ISPs and other gatekeepers cannot make informed choices about online mediation – what it is (it is more than just zoom); how it operates, and how to roll it out – without adequate knowledge of technologies on offer, and more importantly, a better sense of characteristics and categories of mediation that would be enhanced by employing technology. Therefore, readiness is steeped in much more than technical capacity. It must also involve a deep and critical familiarity with when (and when not) technology, such as that described above, achieves the best mediated outcomes for stakeholders. Moreover, the question

---

[33]   See <https://crekodr.com/>.

[34]   See <https://www.modron.com/>.

[35]   Singapore International Dispute Resolution Academy (n 3) 58–60.

[36]   Experiences have been mixed. For examples, see the comments of a user that online mediation was a poor substitute for in-person mediation and fails to replicate the latter experience. Examples of online mediation being conducted solely by audio conferencing, or worse by 'shuttle diplomacy', were cited as contributing to less effective mediation processes: NM Alexander, SC Goh, and R Lee, 'Users' Perspectives on Mediation: Hybrids, Investor-State Disputes and Technology', *Kluwer Mediation Blog* (17 March 2021) <http://mediationblog.kluwerarbitration.com/2021/03/17/whats-happening-in-international-mediation-in-2021/>.

[37]   These lines are inspired by Mary Parker Follet's comments on conflict published in 1925: EM Fox and L Urwick (eds), *Dynamic Administration: The Collected Papers of Mary Parker Follet* (Pitman, 1973). In the text here, technology replaces conflict.

of how to translate the integrity of the mediation process to an online setting (it is more than just doing it online) is another challenge, which is explored next.

4. DOING MEDIATION ONLINE: IT STARTS WITH MEDIATION VALUES

As Goncalves and Rainey write, 'every one of the ethical principles and standards of practice for mediation are affected by working online. How do we guarantee self-determination when working online? How do we assess our own and party competence to engage in mediation? How do we explain and guarantee privacy and confidentiality online?'[38] A transition from live to online mediation requires recognition of how specific technologies can impact the values that underpin mediation. Consider, for example, the impact of concurrent caucusing online as opposed to the traditional approach of mediators conducting caucus meetings with each party, one at a time. Concurrent caucusing may influence the transparency of the process and how procedural fairness is perceived by the parties. Having simultaneous caucuses will most certainly influence the type of interventions mediators make and questions they ask; it also impacts upon confidentiality of the caucus sessions and shifts an enormous amount of power to the mediator.

Transitioning to online applications of mediation demands a sophisticated application of technology so as to preserve and potentially enhance the core values of (live) mediation that make it an attractive and compelling proposition for users, and therefore for ISPs. Accordingly, an examination of the critical appeal factors of online mediation must be grounded in an understanding of the values of mediation within the broader context of why users choose mediation – independent of technology. The 2020 SIDRA Survey Report on International Dispute Resolution shows that more than 80 per cent of mediation users identify impartiality, confidentiality, procedural flexibility, speed and cost as absolutely crucial or important factors in selecting mediation.[39] Further, the Report highlights factors that users consider important in relation to choice of mediators, mediation institutions and venues. In terms of mediator selection, users consider as absolutely crucial or important factors such as good ethics (87 per cent), dispute resolution experience (86 per cent), language (83 per cent), efficiency (78 per cent), industry/issue specific knowledge (77 per cent), cultural familiarity (72 per cent), and cost (72 per cent). Top factors

---

[38]   Goncalves and Rainey (n 12).

[39]   Singapore International Dispute Resolution Academy (n 3) 46. Other factors highlighted were flexibility in choice of institutions/venues and mediators (77 per cent), clarity in rules and procedures (76 per cent), enforceability (67 per cent) and finality (65 per cent).

for selection of mediation institutions include efficiency (83 per cent), cost (74 per cent), cultural familiarity of panel (72 per cent), size and expertise of panel and mediators (68 per cent), availability of information about the panel (65 per cent), and geographical proximity (64 per cent). The top five factors relevant to choice of mediation venue are convenience of location (82 per cent), efficiency (77 per cent), quality of administrative support (76 per cent), geographical proximity (72 per cent) and quality of facilities/technology support (69 per cent), although the importance of the final factor has likely increased since COVID-19. The identification of these bundles of factors is congruent with other relevant studies[40] and the academic literature.[41] Taken collectively, these factors fall into three categories: usability, reliability and accessibility. A closer examination of these categories reveals the core values and principles underlying mediation practice.

(1)   Usability: mediation is characterized by its ability to maximize user (party) autonomy. Aspects of mediation service provision that contribute towards this user-orientation fall into this category, including impartiality, confidentiality, efficiency and procedural flexibility.

(2)   Reliability: here notions of quality, competency, integrity, ethics and regulatory robustness are relevant to mediation services that users feel they can rely on.

(3)   Accessibility: accessibility can mean different things for users, depending on their needs. It can refer to users' ability to access mediation services in terms of geography, infrastructure, venue facilities, cost, language and (digital) literacy. Accessibility reflects the democratic nature of the mediation process that promises access to participatory, inclusive and informal justice.

These touchstones of usability, reliability and accessibility transcend the boundaries of the physical world and have also been identified in relation to online mediation – although terminology and categorizations may differ. By way of example, the International Council for Online Dispute Resolution

---

[40]   See, for example, SI Strong, 'Realizing Rationality: An Empirical Assessment of International Commercial Mediation' (2017) 73 *Washington and Lee Law Review* 1973; International Mediation Institute, 'The 2016 Census of Conflict Management Stakeholders and Trends' <https://www.imimediation.org/wp-content/uploads/2018/02/2016_Biennial_Census_Survey_Report_Results.pdf>.

[41]   See, for example, S Cole et al, *Mediation: Law Policy and Practice* (Thomson Reuters, 2020–2021); N Alexander, J Lee and K Lum, *Singapore Mediation Handbook* (LexisNexis, 2019).

(ICODR) Standards, drawing on the work of Leah Wing[42] and the US-based National Center on Technology and Dispute Resolution on principles for ODR practice,[43] state that ODR platforms must be:[44]

- Accessible: easy to find and participate in; available through diverse devices; accessible in terms of cost, physical ability and geography.
- Accountable: accountable, on an ongoing basis, to the institutions, legal systems and stakeholders, and user communities that they serve.
- Competent: ISPs and mediators must have the relevant expertise in dispute resolution, legal, technical execution, language and culture to deliver their ODR services.
- Confidential: confidentiality of mediation communications in line with norms that are transparent in terms of who sees the data, and how that data can be used.
- Equal: All participants in ODR must be treated with respect and dignity and enable silenced or marginalized voices to be heard.
- Fair/Impartial/Neutral: Parties must be treated equally and in line with due process requirements.
- Legal: ODR services must be legally compliant in all relevant jurisdictions.
- Secure: Data collected including mediation communications must remain secure among those authorized to access it; users must be informed of any breaches in a timely manner.
- Transparent: ODR providers must disclose the form and enforceability of dispute resolution processes and outcomes, and the risks and benefits of participation.

For the purposes of this chapter, party-orientation in the sense of *usability* encompasses ICODR's impartiality and fairness, equality, transparency and confidentiality factors; *reliability* addresses ICODR's security, legality, competency and accountability; finally, *accessibility* in this chapter aligns with ICODR's definition of accessibility but arguably goes further by linking it to access to justice. Other scholars who have acknowledged the relevance of these factors in the online space include Singaporean writer–practitioners, Eunice Chua and Asha Hemrajani.[45] They set out the following criteria for an ODR platform: reliability, usability, efficiency, maintainability and security.

---

[42] L Wing, 'Ethical Principles for Online Dispute Resolution: A GPS Device for the Field' (2016) 3(1) *International Journal of Online Dispute Resolution* 12.

[43] See <http://odr.info/ethics-and-odr/>.

[44] The ICODR Standards are summarized here. For the full text, refer to <https://icodr.org/standards/>.

[45] E Chua and A Hemrajani, 'Effectively Leveraging Technology in Mediation – Suggestions for a Way Forward in Asia' (2018–2019) 35 *Singapore Law Review* 208.

In this chapter, efficiency contributes to usability, while maintainability and security are relevant to the reliability of an online mediation service. While Chua and Hemrajani define usability as including accessibility, in this chapter these factors are treated separately because accountability should be the caveat over all purposes for technological development.

As this discussion suggests, the categories of usability, reliability and accessibility may not always be clear cut. For example, language is an *accessibility* factor in the sense that users' capacity to effectively access mediation services is hampered without the requisite language and literacy skills. However, at what point does language become a factor relevant to *usability*? Consider the situation where parties, all fluent in business English, may nevertheless wish to have the mediation conducted in more than one language, on the basis that it will make them more comfortable to express themselves about difficult issues and manage the nuances of negotiation. And what of confidentiality? Confidentiality is relevant to *usability* insofar as it supports full and frank negotiations between disputing parties. At the same time, confidentiality is closely connected with online security, which needs to be robust and reliable. Accordingly, the framework developed here bundles confidentiality with security as part of the *reliability* cluster. *Accessibility* is explained here in a way that reflects the inclusive and democratic nature of mediation processes, a characteristic that overlaps with the equality aspect of *usability*. A final illustration relates to the enforceability of mediated outcomes: on one hand this can be perceived as an aspect of usability and efficiency; on the other hand, it is essential to the regulatory reliability of an ODR system. With these different perspectives in mind, a deeper discussion of the three touchstones of usability, reliability and accessibility, as defined in this chapter, follows.

4.1   Usability

Mediation is characterized by a broad notion of party autonomy that allows parties to communicate directly with one another as well as indirectly through a mediator, to craft outcomes that reflect non-legal priorities whether of a personal, commercial, cultural, familial or other nature. As the term suggests, usability represents the user-centric nature of the mediation process with its focus on party autonomy supported by key characteristics of an impartial forum, procedural flexibility, time efficiency, and cultural responsiveness. To the best of their professional ability, mediators must provide an impartial forum; they must ensure that parties are treated fairly and have the opportunity to articulate what is important to them. Implicit in the duty of impartiality is an obligation to be transparent[46] about potential conflicts of interest, procedural choices, and consequences of settlement and non-settlement. A mediator's duty of impartiality is vital to supporting due process and party autonomy so that parties can make informed choices that address their interests. Procedural flexibility is enhanced when parties get to choose their own mediator and have a say in the way the procedure is designed, including the design of mixed-mode procedures. Efficiency is a factor that emerges as relevant in relation to the users' choice of mediators, mediation institution and mediation venue.[47] Finally, the facilities at mediation venues can also contribute to user orientation: options for staggered entry of disputing parties, break-out rooms, ability to customize seating arrangements, and digital infrastructure which allows parties to manage phone and wifi access, for example, the ability to block out calls and emails during parts or all of the mediation.[48]

Shifting to online mediation, usability focuses on the extent to which the online mediation service is user friendly, intuitive and customizable.[49] In terms of procedural flexibility and the ability to customize, the extent to which users can exercise their autonomy is as follows:

- co-designing the mediation process;
- crafting rules about confidentiality to meet user needs and expectations;
- maintaining the right to legal representation during mediation, unless both parties agree that legal representatives will not take part in the online mediation;
- moving back and forth between different stages in the mediation processes;
- working through the mediation at their preferred pace;[50]
- shifting between synchronous/asynchronous and text-based/verbal communication technologies;

---

[46] See, for example, the mediator's duty of disclosure in § 9(2)(c) of the Uniform Mediation Act (United States).

[47] Singapore International Dispute Resolution Academy (n 3) 49–60.

[48] In choice of mediation venues, users identified quality of facilities and technology support as one of the most important factors: Singapore International Dispute Resolution Academy (n 3) Exhibit 7.2.2; 72 per cent of users identified quality of administrative support as absolutely crucial or important in this regard.

[49] User friendliness of mediation platform is important for intake: E Wilson-Evered, T Casey and S Aldridge, 'Mediator readiness for online mediation: Application of a modified Unified Theory of User Acceptance of Technology' (Paper presented at the Fourth NADRAC Research Forum: Brisbane 2010). The study was conducted under the auspices of Relationships Australia (Queensland). It comprised qualitative interviews with 20 mediators and an online survey of 100 user practitioners.

[50] Independent Mediators Limited Survey 2020 (n 11) indicates that cost efficiency was one of the top two advantages of online mediation for users.

- moving in and out of caucus meetings with the mediator and side meetings with their advisers.

4.2   Reliability

Reliability embraces notions of quality and robustness. Specifically, reliability refers to mediation services that:

- are conducted by experienced, ethical, qualified, impartial dispute resolution professionals;[51]
- are supported by a robust legal framework that supports confidentiality and enforcement of mediated settlement agreements;[52]
- are accountable to the institutions, legal frameworks and communities that they serve;
- operate within tried and tested procedural protocols;[53] and
- are responsive to user feedback in terms of client communications and ongoing improvements.

In online environments, reliability additionally measures the extent to which the e-space is secure and private for mediation communications, and also for storage of documents including confidential mediated settlement agreements. Reliability in terms of technology also means providing users with the assurance of troubleshooting assistance. Authenticity is another factor that emerges here. To what extent can the software ensure that the person at the other end of the ODR application is really the other party to the dispute and that no one else is 'present' in the e-space without the permission of the parties?

4.3   Accessibility

Accessibility to mediation as a dispute resolution mechanism is vital for mediation to remain relevant within its broader narrative of access to justice. User accessibility includes physical, geographical, financial, linguistic and

---

[51]   Singapore International Dispute Resolution Academy (n 3) Exhibit 7.3.1.

[52]   Confidentiality was one of the top factors that users identified in choosing mediation: Singapore International Dispute Resolution Academy (n 3) Exhibit 7.1.1. Enforceability of outcomes was the top factor in choice of dispute resolution mechanism generally; however, it did not rank highly in mediation selection due to the absence of an international framework.

[53]   In choice of mediation venues, users identified quality of administrative support as one of the most important factors: Singapore International Dispute Resolution Academy (n 3) Exhibit 7.2.2; 72 per cent of users identified quality of administrative support as absolutely crucial or important in this regard.

dimensions of accessibility related to infrastructure, venue facilities and IT, as confirmed by empirical evidence.[54] For example, is the mediation venue easily accessible from major transport hubs such as bus interchanges, train stations and airports? Are the mediation services cost efficient (affordable) and proportionate to the value of the dispute?[55] Do the mediator(s) speak the preferred languages of the participants (parties, lawyers and other experts or persons who may attend)? Further, mediation service providers can enhance accessibility to mediation by providing easy-to-access resources for clients such as FAQs, preparation tools including risk assessments and user guides.

Online mediation claims to offer a new kind of accessibility. It can provide virtual meeting spaces for users to mediate using personal computers, tablets and smartphones. Available technology can connect people regardless of their physical locations and physical (dis)abilities. In terms of geography, online mediation can be helpful for many kinds of disputes. For example, online mediation may provide a cost-effective and practical way to handle cross-border disputes, where at least one party is a small or medium-sized business owner with limited resources to travel and attend an overseas mediation or where the costs associated with travel and physical meetings may exceed the value of the dispute. Even in local disputes, the new geography of online mediation can offer accessibility benefits that conventional mediation cannot, for example where parties wish to take advantage of expertise not available locally. Here, online mediation may enable mediators, advisers and other specialist professionals in different geographical locations to take part in the process.

4.4   The Path to Digital Readiness in Mediation

The exploration of the mediation touchstones of usability, reliability and accessibility has shown the enormous scope for online mediation practice and identified the need for a more thoughtful and systematic approach to digital transitioning from live mediation to online mediation. The idea of *digital readiness*, foreshadowed in the introduction to this chapter, is outlined next and is to be read against the expressed importance of further critical reflection

---

[54]   In relation to selection of mediation venues, users' top ranking factors included the following accessibility indicators: convenience of location, quality of facilities, technology support and geographical proximity; linguistic accessibility ranks highly in choice of mediator: Singapore International Dispute Resolution Academy (n 3) Exhibit 7.2.1 and Exhibit 7.3.1 [the factors require weighting percentages, for example for 'efficiency' (x %) or 'impartiality' (x %)].

[55]   Independent Mediators Limited Survey 2020 (n 11) indicates that cost efficiency was one of the top two advantages of online mediation for users.

on the many dimensions of readiness beyond those we encounter here, and the prevailing commitment to advance through readiness the importance of contextual sensitivity and cultural/community relevance.

5. TOWARDS DIGITAL READINESS IN MEDIATION

The idea of digital readiness recognises the challenges facing ISPs – and the professional mediation community at large – in competently and ethically taking forward resilient mediation processes that can navigate the post-COVID-19 technologically-enhanced dispute resolution landscape. These challenges, as mentioned earlier, are not contained either within the constraints of global crises or the inevitability of technology. For mediation ISPs, digital readiness means more than acquiring the technological bells and whistles to offer mediation online. It demands familiarity with the online terrain of mediation, its texture and dimensions as manifested through diverse technologies; it requires the knowledge and skill to create online spaces that allow mediators (whether human or AI-based) to manage conflict and negotiation dynamics, shifting power relations and cultural nuances. The path to this kind of digital readiness begins with key mediation values embedded in the touchstones of usability, reliability and accessibility. The journey continues with an offering of initial exploratory ideas about what these value indicators might mean in online settings. These ideas are presented in tabular form.

Table 11.2 sets out a framework for digital readiness based on the above considerations. The left-hand column identifies the touchstone factor – usability, reliability or accessibility; the middle column sets out relevant value indicators for each touchstone; and the right-hand column offers some aspirational ideas for the digital implementation of each value.

6. MOVING TOWARDS DIGITAL READINESS – BEYOND A CONCLUSION?

What follows are some brief reflections on pathways to achieve digital readiness and the conditions under which sustainability can be considered. Online mediation has been given a major boost by COVID-19 social distancing and reliance on digitizing all aspects of dispute resolution and justice service delivery. Recognizing that this could be confused with pragmatic and non-reflexive momentum, it is vital to remember that the practice of mediating online, in all its variations, remains in its infancy. At the start of the 2020s, there is a real risk that online mediation practice moves faster than the digital readiness of its institutional providers and in doing so compromises opportunities to trans-

Table 11.2   Digital readiness framework for mediation

Touchstone	Mediation value indicator (e.g. value/principle/goal)	Aspiration level
Usability	Impartiality of forum	The online mediation system:
		– treats all parties equally and in line with due process
		– treats all participants with respect and dignity
		– operates without bias or benefits for or against individuals, groups or entities
		– enables often silenced or marginalized voices to be heard
		– ensures that offline privileges and disadvantages are not replicated in the online mediation process
		– does not limit users' rights to legal representation
		– makes provision for cultural differences and needs
		– uses technology to maximize party autonomy and informed decision-making
	Transparency	The online mediation provider explicitly discloses in advance:
		– the form and enforceability of dispute resolution processes and outcomes
		– the risks and benefits of participation
		– their privacy and confidentiality policy,* i.e. about who will see what data, and how that data can be used
		– conflicts of interest of providers, participants, and system administrators
	Efficiency (procedure and output)	Online mediation services:
		– are timely
		– use participant time efficiently
		– offer integrated case management that allows for online case filing and payment where users can efficiently manage their cases digitally

Touchstone	Mediation value indicator (e.g. value/principle/goal)	Aspiration level
	Procedural flexibility	The online mediation system offers: – a range of process features that permit procedural variations – users the ability to customize procedure, mediator selection and other features – maintains the confidentiality of parties – communications in line with parties' wishes (and the applicable law).** This may involve variations from mediation to mediation
Reliability	Security and confidentiality	The online mediation service provider: – ensures that data collected and communications between those engaged in online mediation are not shared with any unauthorised third parties without explicit consent of the parties involved – ensures that data is gathered, managed and presented in ways to ensure it is not misrepresented or out of context – informs users of any unintended breaches in a timely manner – has in place appropriate cybersecurity and data protection protocols
	Regulatory robustness and accountability	The online mediation system: – complies with the applicable law – has the ability to automate compliance with mediated settlement agreements*** or the outcomes are recognized by courts for enforcement purposes – is accountable to the institutional mediation service provider and the users
	Maintenance and responsiveness	The online mediation provider has a system to: – monitor online mediation system performance – collect user feedback – review and respond to user feedback – offer technical support for users in mediation

Touchstone	Mediation value indicator (e.g. value/principle/goal)	Aspiration level
	Competency	The online mediation provider offers or makes available: – relevant expertise in dispute resolution (e.g. selection of mediators) and, if applicable, law (e.g. facilitates access to legal information or advice), required to deliver competent, effective services to their users
Accessibility	Cost	Online mediation services: – have clear and transparent costs protocols available to users – maximize opportunities through technology for users to save costs, e.g. use automated technology for case filing and management functions, or other aspects of mediation service
	User-friendly interface	Online mediation services have a user interface that is intuitive and easy to navigate
	Digital literacy (and accessibility)	The online mediation provider offers or makes available: – relevant technical expertise required for users to participate effectively in online mediation – technology that allows users with physical disabilities to participate, e.g. voice recognition where a person cannot type – widely accessible hardware and software requirements, e.g. can online mediation be accessed from a personal computer, tablet and smartphone using any operating system? Do the bandwidth requirements limit accessibility?
	Linguistic accessibility	The online mediation provider offers or makes available: – relevant linguistic expertise required to deliver competent, effective mediation services to their users

Touchstone	Mediation value indicator (e.g. value/principle/goal)	Aspiration level
	User capacity building	The online mediation provider offers or makes available: – access to information, guidance and training about (online) mediation and related topics, e.g. FAQs, user manuals, pre-mediation training in the ODR system – preparation and dispute analysis tools

Notes:

* See also the indicator 'security and confidentiality'.

** Regulatory compliance is examined under the indicator of 'regulatory robustness and accountability'.

*** The most successful ODR services have been those with the ability to automatically enforce their outcomes, citing the ODR schemes of ICANN, with its power to change domain name registries, and PayPal, with its ability to freeze and move funds to enforce ODR outcomes: see UNCITRAL, 'Possible future work on online dispute resolution in cross-border electronic commerce transactions', Note by the Secretariat, A/CN.9/706 (2010) para 43.

form and sustain the core characteristics of mediation in digitally compatible formats. As discussed previously, confidence in the relative sophistication of current technologies that can help optimize for factors such as benefit maximization should be balanced against the contemporary and express limitations of emotion AI, which at this point is mostly unreliable as a predictive paradigm.

Along the path to digital readiness there are numerous tensions to be navigated. The (live) mediation literature is filled with discourse that highlights how communities of mediation professionals and other stakeholders have navigated, and continue to navigate, the tensions between the core principles of mediation, on one hand, and the inevitable diversity of mediation practice that follows from the inherent flexibility of the mediation process, on the other.[56] It is the tension between maximizing parties' interests and mediator neutrality, between party autonomy and the extent to which mediators can offer advice, between confidentiality and accountability, between private settlement and open justice – and the list goes on.

In the post pandemic 'new normal' it would be tempting to advocate for online mediation expansion based on essential expediency, short-term efficacy and considerable cost saving. But the same evaluators could have been applied as the primary criterion to the development of mediation systems before digital options were at the fore.[57] Users/practitioners who value human-centric mediation and view recent online developments as just the start down a slippery slope to automation will not be placated by readily quantifiable efficiencies alone, such as costs, time and settlement rates. The resolution of tensions between diverse stakeholder goals needs to work from a common language of expectation and evaluation consistent with the core of mediation ideals. Access to justice would be high on the list of shared expectations. Access in this sense means more than usability because it is access for specific parties to a specific quality of outcome. Cost saving is tagged to access and equity but it represents a tension insofar as cost saving is just another way of corner cutting and service minimization.

---

[56] See National Alternative Dispute Resolution Advisory Council, 'The Resolve to Resolve: Embracing ADR to improve access to justice in the federal jurisdiction' (Report to the Attorney-General of the Commonwealth of Australia, September 2009) <https://apo.org.au/sites/default/files/resource-files/2009-09/apo-nid67039.pdf>.

[57] Of course (live) mediation has been, and continues to be, evaluated by various criteria including settlement rate, costs and time. However, these are certainly not the only criteria; and empirical studies on user satisfaction consistently point to the importance of parties having a voice, feeling heard and being able to shape outcomes that meet their real (non-legal) needs and priorities. See, for example, J Bercovitch, 'Mediation Success or Failure: A Search for the Elusive Criteria' (2007) 7 *Cardozo Journal of Conflict Resolution* 289.

Then there are essential concerns for subjectivity and sensitivity which can also fall victim to the routinizing that goes along with digital conversion. Some essential considerations come with their own strains and tensions. For instance, recognizing the cultural fluency of online mediation technology brings with it translation resourcing and the costs associated with ensuring equitable access when language and location may represent barriers. Then there is the issue of familiarity with the operational environments for technology that may vary relative to particular social demographics and for some disadvantaged or vulnerable groups, and require technical support, training and the provision of ancillary services.

As with all emerging technologies, initial inefficiencies can be expected as providers and users adjust to new methods and processes. Most people have stories to share about software incompatibilities, platform crashes, lags and other technological challenges. Personal anecdotes of the author include an online mediation platform crashing during a mediation and the online help desk being unavailable for frustrated parties in three continents. Technology is constantly developing with regular requirements for upgrading software and hardware. Mediators and users alike are being required to improve their technological skills continuously – thereby adding indirect costs to those involved in online mediation, at least initially. These costs may not only be viewed in financial terms but may have ramifications for user confidence and trust.

Importantly, the global reach of online mediation is premised on the existence of accessibility to, and literacy in, online technologies. The limitations of computer-based online dispute resolution are pronounced in the Global South where mobile telephony and community Internet radio are the primary links to technology for most people. In addition, bandwidth restrictions in some geographical regions may effectively make online mediation inaccessible or, at a minimum, negate its cost advantages.

These are some of the many tensions that mediation technology designers and the ISP offering such technology must tackle as they move to become digitally ready in ways that facilitate user benefit. In the context of transnational commercial mediation, which will become much more in demand as data trade features in socio economic development, readiness becomes a global conversation.

The framework developed in this chapter represents the initial phase of a larger research project that aims to support online mediation providers develop their digital offerings in a way that maximizes usability, reliability and accessibility. Future research connected to this project anticipates critical discussions about how technologies are being developed for mediation practice in order to deepen understandings of what their increasing availability means, beyond a readiness to support mediation and continue purpose-tailoring mediation processes in some general sense. Further, the project envisages a richer discussion about how these technologies have been – and can be – evaluated, and how they might (have) change(d) expectations for mediation now and in the future. Empirical studies into how they aid some aspects of mediation but diminish others in the process would be informative for advocates and sceptics alike. In terms of mediation practice, a number of institutional case studies will be analysed according to a framework for digital readiness based on the ideas presented in this chapter. Following that there will be a pressing need to critically evaluate this evolution against user satisfaction, efficacy and principled consistency.

Ultimately, how we define mediation, so as to sustain the integration of technology in ways we may not yet imagine, while at the same time remaining true to the essence of live mediation, presents challenges not only for advocates of the technology revolution, but for all those committed to reflective readiness for change that is upon us. These challenges will proceed in unwanted directions if we are not alive to augmenting core mediation values in online platforms.

BIBLIOGRAPHY

Articles/Books/Reports

Abrahams, B, E Bellucci and J Zeleznikow, 'Incorporating Fairness into Development of an Integrated Multi-agent Online Dispute Resolution Environment' 21 *Group Decision and Negotiation* 3

Alexander, N, *The Hong Kong Mediation Manual* (Lexis Nexis, 2014)

Alexander, N, J Lee and K Lum, *Singapore Mediation Handbook* (LexisNexis, 2019)

Augar, N and J Zeleznikow, 'Developing Online Support and Counseling to Enhance Family Dispute Resolution in Australia' (May 2013) *Springer Science and Media Dordecht*

Chua, E and A Hemrajani, 'Effectively Leveraging Technology in Mediation – Suggestions for a Way Forward in Asia' (2018–2019) 35 *Singapore Law Review* 208

Cole, S et al, *Mediation: Law Policy and Practice* (Thomson Reuters, 2020–2021)

Fisher, R and W Ury, *Getting to Yes* (Penguin, 1983)

Fox, EM and L Urwick (eds), *Dynamic Administration: The Collected Papers of Mary Parker Follet* (Pitman, 1973)

Katsh, E and J Rifkin, *Online Dispute Resolution: Resolving Conflicts in Cyberspace* (Jossey-Bass, 2001)

Larson, DA, '"Brother, Can You Spare A Dime?" Technology can reduce dispute resolution costs when times are tough and improve outcomes' (2011) 11(2) *Nevada Law Journal* 523

Lodder, AR and J Zeleznikow, 'Developing an Online Dispute Resolution Environment: Dialogue Tools and Negotiation Support Systems in a Three-Step Model' (2005) 10 *Harvard Negotiation Law Review* 287

Rule, C, *Online Dispute Resolution for Business: B2B, E-Commerce, Consumer, Employment, Insurance, and Other Commercial Conflicts* (San Francisco, 2002)

Samuelson, W and R Zeckhauser, 'Status Quo Bias in Decision Making' (1988) 1 *Journal of Risk and Uncertainty* 7

Strong, SI, 'Realizing Rationality: An Empirical Assessment of International Commercial Mediation' (2017) 73 *Washington and Lee Law Review* 1973

Wilson-Evered, E, T Casey and S Aldridge, 'Mediator readiness for online mediation: Application of a modified Unified Theory of User Acceptance of Technology' (Paper presented at the Fourth NADRAC Research Forum: Brisbane 2010)

Wing, L, 'Ethical Principles for Online Dispute Resolution: A GPS Device for the Field' (2016) 3(1) *International Journal of Online Dispute Resolution* 12

Legislation

Uniform Mediation Act (United States)

12. Editors' reflections

Mark Findlay and Jolyon Ford

- Ethical AI frameworks: the missing governance piece (Jolyon Ford)
- The accountability of algorithms on social media platforms (Philippa Ryan)
- Models and data trade regulation and road to an agreement (Henry Gao)

Facial recognition software used for identity verification in unemployment benefits determinations have been working inconsistently. Algorithms being used to screen tenant applications have been accused of entrenching housing discrimination. Data sets employed to train computer vision models were found to have racist and misogynistic labels for people of Black and Asian descent. As artificial intelligence (AI) and machine learning (ML) become increasingly common, particularly in otherwise-mundane public service delivery, we are constantly reminded that these systems are frail and brittle, and prone to authoritatively articulating human bias. Unrepresentative data, failures in goal optimisation, and adversarial attacks all contribute to failure modes that might lead these systems to automatically and surreptitiously discriminate against vulnerable data subject populations. Still, a simple search of 'AI for X' initiatives reveals that our expectations for AI/ML continue to remain high: AI for health, AI for autonomous and assisted driving, AI for socio-economic development. The reasons behind such uncritical concessions to the encroaching of problematic AI decision platforms should be of interest to regulators.

The chapters that make up this section speak directly to this tension between our heightened awareness of AI/ML's fallibility and our desire to keep on this road to digitising by addressing ongoing efforts that one might categorise under AI governance. In these different contexts of governance challenges, all four authors ask: how exactly is the regulation of big data and AI progressing in light of what we know about their uses and failure modes? What new forms of regulation have emerged that reflect such evolving knowledge? What essence of regulatory discussions is missing?

Ford's chapter examines Australia's release of its 'Ethical AI Framework' in light of the global trend of 'responsible AI' initiatives. In doing so, his chapter lays the groundwork for us to reflect on the questions listed above. Against the enthusiasm that gave rise to multiple AI enunciations of principles over the past handful of years (Jobin, Ienca and Vayena 2019), Ford poses a simple and revealing inquiry, 'What is the role of the law?' Where other emerging critiques have pointed out the difficulties of putting principles – accountability, transparency, privacy – into practice (Schiff et al. 2020), Ford's chapter takes up a different challenge: why haven't we grounded these principles into law-based mechanisms? Why, given the largescale consequences of AI, has there been an unwillingness to attach concepts of liability and responsibility to the development and deployment of these models and systems? Given recent developments – Google's ousting of two high-profile researchers from their ethical research team, along with increasing concern about the independence of AI research (Simonite 2021; Jurowetzki et al 2021) – these are prescient questions. We are, as Ford rightly argues, missing a more sophisticated discussion around the 'governance of AI governance' and the 'regulation of self-regulation' in failing to connect normative governance through ethics and institutional/process protections through rule of law as a governance consortium.

Ryan's chapter on the glaring absence of public accountability mechanisms within social media platforms becomes the empirical counterpart to Ford's theoretical contribution. Today, in our discussions of the pervasiveness of AI/ML, it is nearly impossible to ignore the intrusive influence of these platforms: from the use of image recognition models on Facebook and Instagram, to recommender systems on Amazon, to content engagement algorithms on Twitter. Yet in any meaningful regulatory sense, ignorance seems the prevailing constant. In each deployment, we are also, as Ryan details, witnessing different varying forms of algorithmic misconduct: from problems of bias in news coverage that feeds into the selective exposure to news we see on our timelines, to the live-streaming of violent acts, misinformation, the misuse of personal information, and the consequences of context collapse. The larger question, echoed largely in Ford's chapter, is as such: how might we hold private companies accountable for their uses of AI/ML systems when their downstream impacts have proven to be pervasive and socially harmful? Relying only on notions of corporate social responsibility at this point would be a fool's errand: '[It] is arguably not difficult for larger firms to find [their "True North"] without needing some "steer" or "nudge" from government on basic societal values', Ford reminds us. Yet as Ryan details in her chapter, self-regulation on social media platforms is riddled with complex challenges on multiple fronts – one might also suggest that it has also failed on multiple fronts. Ryan's argument for the injection of principles such as transparency and accountability into the functioning of algorithms onto these platforms is welcome, albeit unsurprising. The real challenge, she argues, is about aligning incentive systems across multiple stakeholders,

> The notion of ensuring that the values of the government and society generally are reflected in the way that algorithms behave will resonate with ethicists. However, this presupposes that the designers and developers of algorithms in all domains will hold these values. The values need to be hardwired into the code for the outcomes to be consistent with these expectations.

Incentive alignment, then, is perhaps ultimately on what AI governance ought to be focused. Ryan hints at this in the queries such as what we expect AI developers to prioritise. Commercial interests, innovation drives, public good outcomes... How might AI governance initiatives encourage discussions around these themes and who decides which takes priority? Rather than frame it combatively, Ryan's chapter urges us to look at the role sandboxes might play in these discussions of AI governance. Sandboxes – a term familiar to those in the financial services sector – are emerging as the policy equivalent of 'safe explorations' in reinforcement learning. Given the difficulties of understanding, anticipating and forecasting the downstream harms of AI/ML, sandboxes alleviate many anxieties for eventual full-scale application by carving out dedicated 'safe' spaces where regulatory compliance is loosened in exchange for ramping up internal oversight mechanisms. Perhaps, then, sandboxes might offer an answer to Ford's speculation that more regulatory approaches ought to be crafted to 'ensure that the existing body of law can be enforced adequately to address the risks that AI systems create, or whether adaptation of the legal mechanisms are needed'. Still, it may be too early to say whether the experiments with sandboxes convincingly experiments with more rigorous regulatory options, and Ryan cautions that even innovative forms of regulatory architecture can fall prey to capture and failure.

Gao's exploration of the differences between the United States', European Union's and China's models of data regulations in trade agreements returns the discussion of regulation to established global regulatory fora, and hegemonic interpretations. His chapter's detailing of the three blocs' distinct approaches to data trade regulations nonetheless reminds us that issues orthogonal to AI governance – data rights, data sovereignty, even globalisation – inadvertently shape the landscape upon which governance initiatives unfold. The chapter proceeds on certain assumptions that may have been criticised in the earlier chapters, such as the primacy of data trade, and the inevitability of global power blocks in its interpretation. That said, Gao's interest is in the way established trade regulation can be adapted and not lost in confronting and co-ordinating the ubiquitous phenomenon of data trading. The discussion here between commercial priorities and histories of regulatory approaches chosen by each bloc will have consequences for types of data-driven services (and, in the long run, AI/ML systems) created, as well as the nature and reach of their commodification. Yet, perhaps more importantly, this chapter also serves as a case study about the political and economic realities at play when any internationalising of data regulation is to meet the market. His chapter reminds us that discussions of *international* AI governance are still very much in their infancy, contingent on a patchwork of multinational institutions that may just condition the trajectory of AI governance in the years to come. In addition, as has been seen in responses to the pandemic, 'global' or 'international' responses to regulation will all be mitigated by more deep-seated power analyses that underpin national interests.

The chapters in this part are examples of case-study applications conjecturing on the future of regulatory theory. To differing empirical degrees, they drill down into political, economic and social problems that plague the application of AI and big data in their chosen contexts. They share a commitment to comparative analysis, address the local and the global, and each engage in policy prediction. None offers definitive solutions to regulatory challenges. Each confronts why such answers require considered research foundations if they are to be forthcoming.

BIBLIOGRAPHY

Jobin, Anna, Marcello Ienca and Effy Vayena, 'The Global Landscape of AI Ethics Guidelines' (2019) 1(9) *Nature Machine Intelligence* 389

Jurowetzki, Roman, Daniel Hain, Juan Mateos-Garcia and Konstantinos Stathoulopoulos, 'The Privatization of AI Research(-Ers): Causes and Potential Consequences – From University-Industry Interaction to Public Research Brain-Drain?', *ArXiv:2102.01648 [Cs]* (February 2021)

Schiff, Daniel, Bogdana Rakova, Aladdin Ayesh, Anat Fanti and Michael Lennon, 'Principles to Practices for Responsible AI: Closing the Gap', *ArXiv:2006.04707 [Cs]* (June 2020)

Simonite, Tom, 'What Really Happened When Google Ousted Timnit Gebru', *Wired* (8 June 2021) https://www.wired.com/story/google-timnit-gebru-ai-what-really-happened

13. Ethical AI frameworks: the missing governance piece

Jolyon Ford

1. INTRODUCTION

In late 2019, after a period of public consultation, the Australian government released its 'Ethical Artificial Intelligence (AI) Framework'.[1] This advanced eight entirely voluntary principles to 'encourage organisations using AI systems to strive for the best outcomes for Australia and Australians'.[2] The summary of consultation inputs records the position that law and regulation have only a 'supplementary' role to play in governing socially responsible AI and that new regulation should only be considered where failure by the 'market' to give effect to the Framework's values showed up 'clear gaps' for intervention.[3] This was not the government's own formal position as such, but in effect its AI governance strategy[4] is based on this approach.

This chapter critiques this regulatory meta-posture, understood as the unjustifiable abdication of a government's fundamental responsibility to attempt more deliberately and through law-based mechanisms (rather than just self-regulation on ethical precepts) to govern the social impact of the development and use by private actors of the bundle of technologies that combine data, algorithms and computing power, and that we might, for now, call AI/ML (machine learning).[5] Apart from anything else, such an explicit after-the-fact

---

[1]   D Dawson et al, 'Artificial Intelligence: Australia's Ethics Framework' (Discussion Paper, Data61 CSIRO, 2019).

[2]   Ibid.

[3]   Ibid.

[4]   S Hajkowicz et al, 'Artificial intelligence: solving problems, growing the economy and improving our quality of life' (Research Report, CSIRO Data61, 2019) ('AI Roadmap').

[5]   European Commission, 'White Paper on AI' (19 February 2020) 2 ('AI White Paper'). For one representation of this bundle of technologies and techniques as science (cf regulatory) domains, see 'AI Roadmap' (n 4) 17 (fig. 3). For apt discussion of the challenges for non-technical experts with conceiving of AI/ML technolo-

approach to foreseeable social harm and to the diagnosis of regulatory gaps is hard to reconcile with the repeated reiteration (for example in the Australian process) of how profoundly transformative these technologies are likely to prove. If AI/ML is such a truly significant phenomenon (as such reports state over and again),[6] why wait to see whether the market fails to govern behaviour or impact before coming up with a regulatory intervention that relies on something more than 'the market'?

On this basis, this chapter uses the Australian example to offer a far broader critique of the prevailing trend globally of resorting to ethics-based frameworks as the principal modality for governing the responsible development and use of AI. It is critical of the relative paucity, in the context of this trend, of approaches with respect to governing private and corporate activity that are adequately and appropriately grounded in law and regulation. Section 2 below charts the proliferation of ethical frameworks in this area. Section 3 identifies the missing governance dimension in this approach: how is it envisaged that the broad ethical concepts or principles (e.g. 'fairness', 'transparency') advanced in prevailing frameworks are to be connected, if at all, to mechanisms for giving effect to those principles or for providing consequences for lack of adherence to these? What is at stake in the prevailing approach – why does it matter that this piece of the governance puzzle appears, for the most part, to be missing? Section 4 explores some of the broad considerations that might shape policy choices on appropriate regulatory approaches. Section 5 briefly concludes.

2.   PROLIFERATION OF ETHICAL FRAMEWORKS

The Australian approach reflects the prevailing one of governments (and inter-governmental bodies) around the world in the 2018–2019 period. By far the dominant governance approach by state actors to the societal risk and impact issues[7] associated with private sector AI/ML development and use (and

---

gies as a subject of regulatory intervention, see LB Moses, 'How to Think about Law, Regulation and Technology: Problems with "Technology" as a Regulatory Target' (2013) 5 *Law, Innovation and Technology* 1.

⁶   'A powerful technology with risks for negative outcomes': 'AI Roadmap' (n 4) 51.

⁷   This chapter does not endeavour to catalogue the various forms and vectors of adverse impact (or risk thereof), howsoever framed (e.g. in human rights terms or alternative frames). For one overview among many, see the European Commission's 'AI White Paper' (n 5) 1, 10–13 (eg opaque decision-making, gender-based or other kinds of discrimination, privacy intrusions, safety and liability-related issues). The nature of risk is highly relevant to what regulatory approach or technique is adopted, but this

related big-data governance)[8] has been to resort to frameworks articulating broad, universalistic ethical principles. So the 2019 Australian 'Ethical AI Framework' comprises eight principles,[9] the European Commission's April 2019 'Trustworthy AI' framework comprises seven principles, the 2019 OECD one five principles[10] (adapted in part by the G20 in its June 2019 outcome document),[11] and so on. Some governments have issued sector-specific guidance rather than general principles, for example Singapore in 2018 in relation to the financial sector.[12] For its part, Beijing in 2019 also issued eight 'governance principles for responsible AI'[13] and sponsored a simultaneous ethical AI framework of 15 principles on AI development, use and governance.[14]

Alongside these government-backed frameworks (and a parallel process of technical standardisation, notably in the International Standards Organisation),[15] one sees in recent years a wave of corporate/industry self-regulatory ethical AI frameworks and guidelines (from some of the biggest technology firms 'belonging' to both OECD and non-OECD jurisdictions) intended to shape internal decision-making and strategy while also responding to external stakeholders' expectations or demands. Thus across 2018–2019 we saw Google's four principles and six recommended practices,[16] Microsoft's six principles,[17]

---

chapter's concern is with the promotion of ethical voluntarism as a non-regulatory approach, or at least an unarticulated one.

[8]   Consideration of approaches to governing public sector use of AI systems (eg UK Government 'Guidance on AI use in the Public Sector' developed with the Alan Turing Institute, published 10 June 2019) is beyond this chapter's scope, notwithstanding that such systems are typically procured from or developed with private sector actors.

[9]   Dawson et al (n 1). The principles are 'Generates net-benefits'; 'Do no harm'; 'Regulatory and legal compliance'; 'Privacy protection'; 'Fairness'; 'Transparency and explainability'; 'Contestability'; 'Accountability'.

[10]   See <https://www.oecd.org/going-digital/ai/principles/> (OECD Council Resolution Legal/0449, Paris, 22 May 2019). For the European framework, see <https://digital-strategy.ec.europa.eu/en/library/ethics-guidelines-trustworthy-ai>.

[11]   See <https://www.mofa.go.jp/files/000486596.pdf> (Tokyo, 8–9 June 2019).

[12]   'Principles to Promote Fairness, Ethics, Accountability and Transparency in the Use of AI and Data Analytics in Singapore's Financial Sector' (Monetary Authority of Singapore, 18 November 2018).

[13]   'Governance Principles for a New Generation of AI: Develop Responsible AI' (Translation), National New Generation Artificial Intelligence Governance Expert Committee, Beijing, 17 June 2019.

[14]   See <https://www.baai.ac.cn/news/beijing-ai-principles-en.html> (Beijing Academy of AI, 25 May 2019).

[15]   ISO/IEC JTC 1/SC 42 – Artificial Intelligence (Technical Committee, with national-level counterparts).

[16]   See <https://ai.google/responsibilities/responsible-ai-practices/>.

[17]   See <https://www.microsoft.com/en-us/ai/responsible-ai>.

IBM's guidance on five principles,[18] and so on. Meanwhile, Chinese tech firms collaborated with the national government in 2019 to issue an 18-principle 'Joint Pledge on AI Industry Self-Discipline'.[19] Alongside industry and corporate frameworks are various initiatives both of technical professional and AI/ML researcher bodies[20] and of civil society-academia (often endorsed by actors across societal sectors).[21] This proliferation has spawned platforms devoted to tracking the various instruments and frameworks being issued by state or multilateral, corporate, professional, civic and other organisations.[22]

The apparent intention behind such exercises (when sponsored or promulgated by governmental actors in respect of private sector AI development and use) is to elicit and encourage responsible corporate behaviour among developers and users of AI platforms and tools: such voluntary frameworks are 'designed to prompt organisations to consider the impact of using AI-enabled systems'.[23] The wave of guidelines and frameworks has generated a scholarly literature around comparing the choice and framing of ethical principles, their degree of convergence or divergence, etc.[24] Likewise, there is a rich research agenda around the cultural specificities of supposedly simple and universal

---

[18]   See <https://www.research.ibm.com/artificial-intelligence/trusted-ai/>.

[19]   AI Industry Alliance (Beijing, 31 May 2019). Translation: <https://www .newamerica.org/cybersecurity-initiative/digichina/blog/translation-chinese-ai-alliance -drafts-self-discipline-joint-pledge/>.

[20]   Notably the five core principles of the Institute of Electrical and Electronics Engineers and its work around ethically-aligned design: <https://standards.ieee.org/ industry-connections/ec/autonomous-systems.html>.

[21]   Notably, for example, the 23 principles of the 2017 'Asilomar AI Principles' (Future of Life Institute): <https://futureoflife.org/ai-principles/>; and the seven principles of the 2017+ 'Montreal Declaration' (<https://www.montrealdeclaration -responsibleai.com/>). There are various others, eg the 12 principles of the guidelines by 'Public Voice' (Electronic Privacy Information Center), October 2018. The Partnership on AI, originally established by a handful of large tech companies, is now made up of a wide variety of stakeholders, including governments. It does not have a comprehensive ethics framework but has stipulated eight tenets that members commit to uphold: <https://www.partnershiponai.org/>; see too the 'OpenAI' initiative: <https://openai.com/>.

[22]   See for example this attempted inventory of ethical AI guidelines: <https:// algorithmwatch.org/en/project/ai-ethics-guidelines-global-inventory/>; and see the OECD's 'AI Policy Observatory': <https://oecd.ai/>.

[23]   Dawson et al (n 1) (that is, this is how the Australian government's 2019 Framework is explained by the governmental organisation that designed it).

[24]   For example, see T Hagendorff, 'The Ethics of AI Ethics: an Evaluation of Guidelines' (2020) 30 *Minds and Machines* 99; A Jobin et al, 'The global landscape of AI ethics guidelines' (2019) 1 *Nature: Machine Intelligence* 389; R Calo, 'AI Policy: a primer and roadmap' (2017) 51 *UC Davis Law Review* 399.

terms such as 'transparency'.[25] Yet the issue here is not how these normative systems align with or compare to each other. It is whether and how these ethical frameworks are or can be tied to or grounded in law-based mechanisms and regulatory schemes. In addition is the wider question of what the preference for approaching AI governance by reference to voluntaristic ethics-based principles might entail in terms of the relative role of law and legal frameworks in the governance of this phenomenon.

Simply to identify the spread of national, transnational or corporate AI policies or frameworks tells us little or nothing about their effectiveness in meeting the public policy objective of addressing and remedying risks of social harm potentially involved in use of AI systems. Moreover, scholars ought perhaps to use the term 'framework' cautiously, even if this is what the Australian government calls its 'scheme': typically, such frameworks are simply promulgated *lists* (arrived at with or without consultation) of principles. Section 3 now turns to this point: all legislation ultimately involves the promulgation of words, but the ethical AI phenomenon has quite literally involved simply listing concepts or values or principles: 'fairness'; 'transparency'; 'explainability'; and so on. Part of the question is whether sponsoring or producing cascading lists of words – without any explicit link to mechanisms (law-based or other) to govern their uptake or 'breach' – constitutes 'governance' (through the implicit decision to 'prompt' or promote self-regulation by reference to broad norms). Alternatively, can it instead be seen as a decision to decline to govern, or at least to outsource governance entirely post-promulgation.

3.   THE MISSING GOVERNANCE PIECE/S

The 2019 Australia framework followed a consultative process that asked stakeholders to comment on whether the draft principles advanced were the 'right' ethical principles. However, the consultation did not ask the more important and prior question: whether responsible AI development and use is best approached principally as a question of voluntaristic ethics, rather than as a question of law and regulation (including, conceivably, mechanisms to ground ethical principles and related dialogic methodologies in legally consequential frameworks). The question is not whether there ought to be six or 12 or 23 principles, and which ones ought to be included or not. Nor is the question – at least in this chapter – about the quality of the consultative or other

---

[25]   For example, J Whittlestone et al, 'Ethical and societal implications of algorithms, data, and artificial intelligence: a roadmap for research' (Research Report, Nuffield Foundation, 2019) examines the inherent ambiguity and context-specificity of the principles that occur in the various frameworks.

processes by which such lists are arrived at (even if the process of adoption has obvious implications for the efficacy and legitimacy of such frameworks whatever the final content selected). Instead, the question that arises is one about how it is envisaged and intended that free-standing ethical frameworks and principles are intended to take or be given effect. This is a question not of 'principles for ethical AI' but of '*the governance of* principles for ethical AI'.

All this norm-making or norm-articulating activity (conducted in a discourse of universally unobjectionable broad principles such as 'fairness') only highlights the general lack of national-level mechanisms to attach liability and responsibility concepts and legal consequences. Aside from some frameworks noting the need to respect existing law, the prevailing preference for ethics-based self-regulation does not seem to contemplate a role for law (and the rule of law), despite law and legal techniques and institutions (and imperatives) being heavily implicated by concepts such as 'fairness' or 'non-discrimination'. Recent articulations of principles, like the Australian process, appear to envisage a self-executing ethical discourse among stakeholders or within organisations, and so tend not to be accompanied by any reference to ideas on how these normative structures might be linked to or underpin regulatory schemes to give them effect.[26]

Yet much as the public health risks around new biotechnologies resulted in a whole legal architecture of drug approval and certification, the risks raised by AI systems and platforms (whether understood as human rights risks or otherwise) suggest that reliance on industry self-regulation is not sufficient.[27] A regulatory orientation (rather than a corporate ethics one) is required because of the nature and significance of the potential impacts of such technologies. What, otherwise, are the consequences of 'non-compliance' with ethical codes? If there are potential *market* consequences for a firm involved in such, what are the consequences *in law* of an unethical decision or design that creates adverse impact or injustice? Any regulatory approach is not just negatively focussed on the risks relating to some uses of AI, but the policy imperatives in promoting investment in and uptake of these transformative technologies.

---

[26] See the 'AI Initiative' (Harvard Kennedy School) recommendations on shaping a global AI framework for one exception that overtly considers how national and transnational rules and regulations might be required to give effect to normative ethical standards that have now emerged.

[27] See for example C Corinne 'Governing artificial intelligence: ethical, legal and technical opportunities and challenges' (2018) 376(2133) *Philosophy Transactions of the Royal Society A: Mathematical, Physical and Engineering Sciences* 1. See too Hagendorff (n 24) for one argument about the lack of mechanisms to transform AI ethics from a 'discursive exercise' into one that is connected to substantive legal frameworks, including for remedy.

Yet it must involve a regulatory orientation, not an abdication of regulatory power in favour of voluntaristic codes of ethics: the use of AI/ML systems in making decisions that may adversely affect people and profoundly shift or entrench power relations needs to be based in the rule of law, not simply an ethical code.[28]

The disconnect between the promulgation of norms and the design of mechanisms to link these to legal systems has not gone unnoticed. In a 2018 statement,[29] the influential European Group on Ethics in Science and New Technologies suggested that a global standard of fundamental principles for ethical AI *supported by legislative action* is required to ensure the safe and sustainable development of AI. An end-2018 article in *The Economist* observed the need for regulators, hitherto on the sidelines of the ethical AI wave, to become engaged on responsible AI governance, and for policymakers to start 'applying real thought to artificial intelligence'.[30] Harari put far more starkly this sense of urgency to reclaim and resituate (within the state and its laws) the governance of AI – and the very power to govern AI – from its current pattern of drifting and vague voluntarism:

> We cannot continue this debate indefinitely ... [v]ery soon someone will have to decide how to use this power [AI] – based on some implicit or explicit story about the meaning of life [and, in this context, of dignity in a human rights sense]... engineers are far less patient, and investors are the least patient of all. If you do not know what to do with the power [of these technologies, but also the power of how to govern them], market forces will not wait a thousand years for ... an answer. The invisible hand of the market will force upon you its own blind reply...[31]

At the heart of the ethical AI and data governance debates are questions of power in society, its distribution, abuse and non-accountability.[32] AI-specific

---

[28]   P Alston, 'Statement on visit to the UK' (UN Special Rapporteur on Poverty and Human Rights) (London, 16 November 2018). Alston's remarks were particularly directed to AI-assisted administrative or judicial decisions, but seen through the social impact lens (not the 'identity of the decision-maker' one) surely apply to analogous private sector uses too.

[29]   'Statement on AI, Robotics and Autonomous Systems' (Brussels, 13 March 2018) <https://ec.europa.eu/info/publications/ege-statements_en>.

[30]   T Standage, 'Regulating Artificial Intelligence' in 'The World in 2019', *The Economist* (December 2018) 22.

[31]   YN Harari, *21 Lessons for the 21st Century* (Jonathan Cape, 2018) xiv. See too M Risse, 'Human Rights & Artificial Intelligence: an urgently needed agenda' (Working Paper RWP18-015, Harvard Kennedy School, May 2018).

[32]   See for example M Lodge and A Mennicken, 'Regulation of and by algorithm' in L Andrews et al, 'Algorithmic Regulation' (Discussion Paper No 85, Centre for Risk Analysis, London School of Economics, 2017) 2; K Yeung, 'Algorithmic regulation: a critical interrogation' (2018) 12(4) *Regulation and Governance* 505; C van Veen and

regulation might not be necessary or viable.[33] However, to note the paucity of law-backed mechanisms in prevailing approaches to governing responsible AI is not the same as arguing that each country needs specific let alone singular AI law. It is to argue that the benefits (ie to achieving regulatory aims) of the state promulgating ethical principles for private sector development and use of AI are not necessarily undermined by connecting performance on engaging with those principles to legislated mechanisms that, if nothing else, signal that the private power or privilege to make internal ethical calculations about acceptable levels of risk of harm to others is subject to public law.

4.   REGULATING ETHICAL AI GOVERNANCE FRAMEWORKS

A research agenda on broad design approaches to how socially responsible AI might be governed (other than via the prevailing 'ethical AI' approach) might conceivably cover a wide terrain. How would one design a coherent, legitimate and effective framework? What role do the now-entrenched ethical frameworks and guidelines play in such a scheme/s? What are the ideal attributes of a responsive, responsible and realistic regulatory scheme,[34] and how does one account for the intrinsically international dimension? How distinctive is algorithmic-based activity in terms of what we might learn from regulatory approaches in non-tech/pre-tech spheres?[35] That is, what lessons exist from diverse experiences in other fields about how one might design a scheme for the change-neutral governance of ethical AI that, for example, avoids both the generality of principles (at least where disconnected from mechanisms that entail legal consequences) and the prescriptiveness of rules?

This chapter does not itself address these challenges, nor the important issue of what sort of law-based mechanisms – if ethical AI is to be grounded in them – are most appropriate. There, considerable work remains to explore the merits, viability etc of potential compliance mechanisms against which private sector performance on ethical principles (or performance on the quality of methodologies for ethics-based design and other choices) might be regulated

---

C Cath, 'Artificial Intelligence: What's Human Rights Got To Do With It?', *Data & Society Points* (Blog Post, 14 May 2018).

[33] 'AI in the UK' (House of Lords Select Committee on AI, 2017–19), 18 April 2018, 116 [386].

[34] J Ford, *Regulating Business for Peace* (Cambridge University Press, 2015) Chapter 5.

[35] See in this regard the various contributions to Andrews et al (n 32). Also A Defoe, 'AI Governance: a Research Agenda' (Future of Humanity Institute, Oxford, 2018).

in a more mandatory way based on legal requirements. Such work would draw on decades of experience in other fields with most of the techniques or models being advanced in the AI context, from auditable impact statements to due diligence risks assessments to specialised expert review processes.[36] Some of these interventions will require 'ex-post' enforcement by public bodies and effective remedial avenues.[37]

Any such work must also account for the argument, again put aside here, that whatever the mechanisms to give effect to ethical AI principles, these are not the appropriate principles. That is the argument, for the rule of law reasons stated earlier, that it may be *human rights* norms and their associated comprehensive legal infrastructure (from prevention to remedy), and not *ethical* principles and methodologies, that should govern responsible AI development and use.[38] Such human rights arguments have their own limitations; ethical and human rights framings are not necessarily mutually exclusive; and practically speaking the latter have limited traction in this field, with most state and corporate responses to the 'responsible AI' governance challenge making relatively little use of human rights framings at all, let alone frameworks such as the 2011 *UN Guiding Principles on Business and Human Rights*.[39] Still, the human rights-based approach continues to have some conceptual and political traction.

4.1   A Short Answer?

These issues put aside, the focus here is merely on appreciating the need for a regulatory orientation at all (rather than a voluntaristic ethics-based approach), whatever the particular regulatory posture adopted. The introduction asked the question of how it is envisaged, by state and other sponsors of prevailing ethical frameworks, that their broad ethical principles might be

---

[36]   Or, as in the mooted European approach, 'prior conformity' assessment and verification mechanisms for higher-risk AI applications with procedures for testing, inspection or certification, combined with voluntary or other labelling schemes for lower-risk applications: 'AI White Paper' (n 5) 23.

[37]   'AI White Paper' (n 5) 24.

[38]   Australian Human Rights Commission, *Human Rights and Technology: Issues Paper* (July 2018); Risse (n 31); van Veen and Cath (n 32). See too F Raso et al, *Artificial Intelligence & Human Rights: Opportunities & Risks* (Berkman Klein Center, Harvard, September 2018); L MacGregor et al, 'International Human Rights Law as a Framework for Algorithmic Accountability' (2019) 68 *International and Comparative Law Quarterly* 309; M Latonero, 'Governing AI: upholding human rights and dignity' (Data and Society, 2018).

[39]   Adopted by the United Nations Human Rights Council, Resolution 17/4, 16 June 2011. For one attempt to frame AI by reference to the UNGPs, see Raso et al (n 38).

connected to mechanisms for giving effect to those principles or for providing consequences for lack of adherence to these. There is one very short possible answer to this question. It is that there is no lack of regulatory approach and no missing governance piece, at least in the Australian context used as an example here, because an overall regulatory position and accompanying mechanism *has* been selected. There *is* a regulatory orientation. It is simply not one that involves law or formal legislated activity (except perhaps incidentally), nor does it involve the state as the principal regulator. Instead the 'design' of governance relies, in a fairly familiar way, on non-state and market mechanisms to advance private actors' uptake of and compliance with ethical principles (as expressions of public values). If so, what is involved here is not 'mere' corporate (etc) self-regulation by reference to non-binding norms, but the regulation ('outsourced' to the market, 'licensed' to regulatees) of self-regulation.

This preference to largely refrain from state- and law-based regulation is ultimately, of course, a political-ideological one, even if often couched in economic policy terms (typically, the need to avoid regulatory intervention that might stifle innovation). Still, the short answer to the question is that this is simply a preference, and that instead of the prevailing status quo being 'no mechanisms for governance' it is that 'there is a deliberate mechanism of governance, it just relies on non-law approaches'. AI is not under-regulated, on this perspective, it is just regulated lightly and differently, with the intention to shape behaviour primarily through corporations and others designing and using AI systems acting on a voluntary basis by reference to broad ethical values (and relying, presumably, on non-state actors and 'institutions' such as investors and consumers to monitor and respond to unethical products or usages). It might in addition be argued that frameworks with six or eight or 12 broadly-stated principles are intended to shape behaviour in the way explored by theorists of 'principles-based regulation'. Principles-based regulation has considerable merits: where rule-based orders can be gamed (especially by well-resourced players), are too restrictive, or are quickly-outdated in fast-changing areas, the articulation of broad standards and values means that regulatees are forced to engage meaningfully to interpret these within their own context, and by doing so they might also internalise those values.[40]

---

[40]   See for example J Black, *Rules and Regulators* (Oxford University Press, 1997); J Braithwaite, 'A Theory of Legal Certainty' (2002) 27 *Australian Journal of Legal Philosophy* 38; also C Sunstein, 'Problems with Rules' (1995) 83 *California Law Review* 953. See also the AHRC Issues Paper 2018 (n 38) 23, 32 (citing the work of J Black referred to in the Australian Law Reform Commission's *Privacy Law* report (Report 108, 2009). See too C Ford, 'New Governance, Compliance, and Principles-Based Securities Regulation' (2008) 45(1) *American Business Law Journal* 1, 5: 'pragmatic, information-based, iterative and dialogue mechanisms to gather, distil,

Notwithstanding the 'rule of law' imperative (above), on one view we must avoid calling for mandatory law-based regulation of the 'ethical AI' phenomenon for its own sake (ie as the only regulatory type that 'counts') or at least in ways that obscure the underlying question. That question ought always to be 'how best to benefit from AI systems while appropriately managing and remedying risks associated with these'. It is a question that ought, in some ways, to be agnostic as to mode of regulation. In this sense we ought to be comfortable with the reality of a messy, multi-actor, multi-level pluralistic ethical AI governance scene, and even embrace this regulatory multiplicity and polycentricity. It may be desirable, not just inevitable, to use existing non-state orderings and systems to achieve the state's public policy goals.[41] Thus any regulatory orientation and deliberate strategy falling from it must not only account for regulatory plurality as an empirical fact, but seek (as a normative proposition) to take advantage of it and the multiple entry-points that a rich, plural, networked governance ecosystem provides for a smart and considered regulatory strategy. In this area, as in so many others, internal corporate, industry and quasi-private normative and even 'adjudication' systems are part of the regulatory scene, and are not necessarily a challenge to governmental regulation, but potentially an opportunity for such.[42] Also key to the regulatory landscape and scene are various private (or hybrid) and typically transnational normative systems capable of considerable influence on corporate behaviour, such as ISO standards. Policymaking is able to navigate the legitimacy concerns of explicitly harnessing private orderings in pursuit of public ends.[43]

This 'short answer' is not necessarily easy to dismiss if one is interested in securing regulatory objectives (and not blindly committed to any one way, state-led or other, to do so). The diffusion and pace of change and heterogeneity of such technologies and systems in the context of the state's limited regulatory resources mean that there are very sound reasons, in principle, for a regulatory strategy that deliberately seeks to stimulate, condition and harness or enrol the ordering power of internal corporate systems in pursuit of the wider social/public policy objective. In this sense 'self-regulation' is not a dirty word, but might be part of a considered policy design choice.

---

and leverage industry learning in the service of a still-robust but better designed, that is, more effective and less burdensome, public regulatory mandate'.

[41]   In the vein of various so-called 'new governance' approaches, including notably a responsive regulatory approach (eg I Ayres and J Braithwaite, *Responsive Regulation* (Oxford University Press, 1992)).

[42]   See Ford (n 34) which draws in particular on the work of John Braithwaite. See too the reference to corporations as 'enigmatic regulators' of their internal value systems, in the AHRC Issues Paper 2018 (n 38) 23.

[43]   Ford (n 34) Chapter 6.

4.2   Critiquing the 'Short Answer'

On one view, regulators should only be concerned with 'what works' in addressing risk and adverse social impact, and on this criteria formal, state-based binding legal frameworks do not necessarily have a claim to precedence: it depends what mechanism or set of them (even if not grounded in law) is coherent, legitimate and effective. Yet this chapter has nevertheless attempted to critique this approach. For one thing, there is a difference between the de facto 2019 Australian government position (that law and regulation only play a supplementary role to fill gaps once the market has failed to do so) and the position that AI-specific regulation at national level may not be necessary or viable.[44] The latter position does not, as such, necessarily privilege non-law and voluntaristic measures above mandatory ones with legal grounding and consequence.

The problem with the 'short answer' is that the same theorists that support a strategy for drawing on regulatees' own self-governance resources emphasise that what is involved is not just promoting self-regulation but *the regulation of self-regulation*;[45] and the license to self-regulate on activities that hold social risks is conditional on regulatees demonstrating that they are deserving of this autonomy, including by internalising the regulatory objective. This regulatory choice is very different from a non-regulatory approach that looks to intervene with law only once the market has failed. A framework might include a 'no regulation' position, for example a strategy that is tailored to AI-system risks or impacts and includes no regulation at one end of a risk or impact spectrum that extends all the way to a complete ban.[46] Yet the 'no regulation' element in this, because it is a considered part of a spectrum of responses, does not meet with the objections one might raise to a relatively hands-off approach such as the Australian one described or stylised in this chapter.

The European Commission is exploring options and key elements for a future regulatory framework on AI, policy and regulatory options 'towards an ecosystem for excellence and trust'.[47] This is towards a 'horizontal regulatory proposal' in 2021–2022 which will aim to safeguard fundamental values and rights and user safety by 'obliging high-risk AI systems to meet mandatory

---

[44]   See 'AI in the UK' (n 33).

[45]   C Parker, *The Open Corporation: Effective Self-regulation and Democracy* (Cambridge University Press, 2002).

[46]   For example, the five-level risk-based system proposed by the German Data Governance Commission.

[47]   'AI White Paper' (n 5).

requirements' related to their trustworthiness.[48] This 'clear regulatory framework' is explicitly pitched as being 'on top of' the non-binding guidelines in the European context.[49] Indeed alongside some adjustment to existing legislation, the European Commission in 2020 contemplated that new legislation 'specifically on AI' may be needed.[50]

What is becoming clearer is that while in any one geography there may not necessarily be a need for new substantive legislative provisions (eg on rights protections) because the involvement of an AI dimension does not necessarily render national law inapplicable, a regulatory approach and mechanisms may be required to ensure that the existing body of law can be enforced adequately to address the risks that AI systems create, or whether adaptations or new legal mechanisms are needed.[51] The obvious reason is that the peculiar attributes of AI technologies ('opacity, complexity, unpredictability and partially autonomous behaviour') may make it 'hard to verify compliance with, and may hamper the effective enforcement of' existing protective and other rules.[52] Moreover, as the European approach rightly notes, since many different actors are involved in the 'lifecycle' of any AI system, consideration needs to be given to how legal obligations are to be distributed among the different actors involved.[53]

The European Commission's AI White Paper notes that in any new legal instrument, the definition of AI will need to be 'sufficiently flexible to accommodate technical progress while being precise enough to provide the necessary legal certainty'[54] – but this is true not just of definitional issues but of the entire overall regulatory approach and framework, too. Of course we ought to avoid the premise that one must choose from among a smorgasbord of various regulatory theories or approaches.[55] In this sense the 'governance of ethical AI' debate can sometimes lack a sense of regulatory sequencing, of the co-existence (indeed co-dependence) of different regulatory approaches working together. A set of higher-order principles can sit behind and above any attempt, including at a later point in time, at more granular, contextualised (etc) rule-making in particular sectors, contexts or in respect of particular concerns,

---

[48]   See <https://digital-strategy.ec.europa.eu/en/policies/european-approach-artific ial-intelligence>; 'AI White Paper' (n 5) 3.
[49]   'AI White Paper' (n 5) 9. See the European ethical AI framework (n 10).
[50]   'AI White Paper' (n 5) 16.
[51]   Ibid 12–13.
[52]   Ibid 10, 12–13, 14.
[53]   Ibid 22.
[54]   Ibid 16.
[55]   For one binary articulation of this, see @ruchowdh (R Chowdhury), 'No one set of AI rules will be granular enough to be applied [yet] high-level enough to be universal' (Twitter, 6 March 2019).

or can be the basis for due diligence, audit, review or reporting that is required by law.[56] Yet the 'short answer' argument that the prevailing ethics-led strategies have a theoretical basis in 'principles-based regulation' is difficult to make. This is first because principles are not always enough,[57] and prevailing state approaches do not create any compliance (or even 'comply or explain') mechanisms accompanying the promulgation of principles;[58] at most we have the 'innovation' of a hands-off variant of principled regulation attached to unarticulated premises around market-based 'enforcement'.

Secondly, the argument that principles-based regulation underpins prevailing approaches is difficult to make because states – such as Australia in articulating its 2019 framework – have not themselves tried to make it. At the very least, then, policy-oriented scholarship ought to address positions such as Australia's in terms of their tendency not to be explicit about articulating the theoretical basis and public policy rationale for this 'voluntary ethical norms + market enforcement' design preference, especially relative to other possible approaches, and the trade-offs and opportunity costs and risks involved. If the intention was that the state's regulatory role was to set principles and co-opt the market into monitoring and enforcement of their uptake/implementation, why is this regulatory intent not simply made explicit? Instead, the AI governance regime has the appearance of an unjustified (ie both inappropriate, and not rationalised) state deference to technology firms notwithstanding the social risks involved in those technologies.

Likewise, the European approach to a future regulatory framework is focussed around risk-based regulation, with a proportionality-based focus on high-risk uses and processes and the mitigation of that risk.[59] While this is an

---

[56]   As one development from the binary 'principles-based regulation' vs 'rules-based systems' debate, perhaps there is scope in the medium term for some meso-level standards that give more substance than general principles, but do not purport to be as prescriptive and detailed as rules: an intermediary or mezzanine level of principles-based non-rule standards for conditional self-regulation? Contrast Gasser and Almeida's 'layered governance' approach: U Gasser and V Almeida, 'A Layered Model for AI Governance' (2017) 21(6) *IEEE Internet Computing* 58 (although this did not seek to draw upon regulatory theory of the sort considered here).

[57]   See in particular J Black, 'The Rise, Fall and Fate of Principles-Based Regulation' (Law, Society and Economy Working Paper 17, London School of Economics, 2010).

[58]   Compare William Bateman's chapter in this collection (principles-based regulation within public law administrative settings). More generally see I Szekely, MD Szabo and B Vissy, 'Regulating the Future? Law, Ethics, and Emerging Technologies' (2011) 9 *Journal of Information, Communication and Ethics in Society* 180.

[59]   'AI White Paper' (n 5) 10, 17. This will require criteria to enable regulators and regulatees to distinguish between 'high-risk' and 'low-risk' applications of AI, with considerations about the scale of the company developing or perhaps more relevantly using the application.

improvement on the Australian approach (which does not outline its regulatory compliance rationale), the European Commission does not explain or justify risk-based regulation relative to other design approaches, or acknowledge that we now have plenty of experience with this approach that will need to be accounted for. Scholars and others ought to demand more explicit engagement, in regulatory policy design 'white papers', with the empirical and theoretical literature around the advantages or limits of proposed approaches, whether they be 'risk-based'[60] or 'principles-based'.[61] The European 'beyond ethics' regulatory proposal involves compliance monitoring that is 'part of a continuous market surveillance scheme'.[62] Such a sentence and the extensive oversight it entails is easier to write in a White Paper than it is to design in reality, at least (in the context of mooted ethical AI reporting schemes) without explicitly taking into account the plethora of studies on the difficulties of regulation in systems that require the production of even more information and its insertion into an already data-saturated society.

In this regard, including in terms of policymakers being more explicit about the 'theory of change' or regulatory rationale for their approach to ethical AI (or, in Europe, the regulation of ethical AI), considerable scope remains for a research agenda around the continuities between the pre- and post-tech eras of corporate responsibility. As Harari has written:

> Since the corporations and entrepreneurs who lead the technological revolution naturally tend to sing the praises of their creations, it falls to sociologists, philosophers and historians ... [etc] to sound the alarm and explain all the ways that things can go terribly wrong.[63]

Likewise, Big Tech is (on one hand) inclined to prefer a default voluntaristic, self-regulatory approach by states to AI technologies. The whole modern history (1960s–)[64] of corporate environmental responsibility stands as a reminder that this is not the first time ethics-based voluntarism and

---

[60]   See for example M Sparrow, *The Regulatory Craft* (Brookings, 2000); J Black and R Baldwin, 'Really Responsive Risk-Based Regulation' (2010) 32 *Law and Policy* 181; F Haines, *The Paradox of Regulation* (Edward Elgar, 2012). For a recent overview, see J van der Heijden, 'Risk Governance and Risk-Based Regulation', State of the Art in Regulatory Governance Research Paper Series, 2019-02, June 2019 <http://dx.doi.org/10.2139/ssrn.3406998>.

[61]   See the examples in n 40 above.

[62]   'AI White Paper' (n 5) 24.

[63]   Harari (n 31) xiii.

[64]   See eg L Agudelo et al, 'A literature review of the history and origin of corporate social responsibility' (2019) 4 *International Journal of Corporate Social Responsibility* 1.

self-regulatory approaches have been advanced as if (a) this is the sole or main regulatory approach for balancing significant societal risk with concerns not to stifle innovation, productivity and competition, and (b) these are necessary precursors to subsequent 'hard law' regulation (rather than potentially displacing the space for this).[65]

There is (and on the other hand) another possible response to this chapter's premise that the legal-regulatory governance 'piece' is missing in prevailing patterns around responsible AI governance. This is that, on the contrary, Big Tech firms at least in the West can be heard, especially since about 2018–2019, calling for more proactive national and other regulation over and above the patchwork of ethical and self-regulatory frameworks. As Microsoft's chief told an AI summit in 2019, 'we do not want to see a commercial race to the bottom. Law is needed'.[66] Also in 2019, Google released a policy document noting how, thus far, self- and co-regulatory approaches 'have been largely successful at curbing inopportune AI use' and that 'in the vast majority of instances such approaches will continue to suffice ... within the constraints provided by existing governance mechanisms (e.g., sector-specific regulatory bodies)'.[67] However, Google's paper was produced on the basis that this 'does not mean that there is no need for action by government'.[68] Such calls are somewhat vague, and do not necessarily imply legislative action. For example, Google's piece called for governments to make a 'substantive contribution to the AI governance discussion' and play a role in 'clarifying expectations' and 'provide greater guidance'.[69] This is not necessarily an invitation to legislate. Nevertheless, and contrasted as it is in that paper with self-regulatory approaches hitherto, this call by such a significant firm for greater governmental proactivity on AI governance was a notable shift from the preceding half-decade.

Yet it ought to be entirely unsurprising that Big Tech might take this 'law is needed' line, if for no more sinister reason than that transnational firms may well prefer predictable and consistent regulatory schemes to a real or per-

---

[65]   See also Calo (n 24) on how internal ethical frameworks send the message to legislators that laws are not required to address risk and adverse impact arising from AI use.

[66]   Quoted in C Metz, 'Is Ethical AI even possible?', *New York Times* (1 March 2019). See also the statements of the CEOs of Uber, Salesforce, Facebook and Apple quoted in the Foreword to Australian Human Rights Commission, *AI Governance and Leadership White Paper* (2019) 5 nn 4–7 (that state regulation is desirable, inevitable, and/or needs to be more demanding).

[67]   'Perspectives on Issues in AI Governance' (Google, 2019): <https://ai.google/static/documents/perspectives-on-issues-in-ai-governance.pdf>.

[68]   Ibid 2.

[69]   Ibid 2.

ceived regulatory vacuum. It is natural that companies are concerned by legal and regulatory uncertainty,[70] and the 'ethical AI' phenomenon has not given them this. Still, it also ought to be unsurprising that market-dominant players with monopolistic tendencies are not necessarily threatened by regulation and indeed might seek to reinforce their dominance (and the legitimating effect of 'being regulated') by inviting the erection of law-based mechanisms that largely reflect the status quo. This is particularly so where such actors feel so confident that they are capable of shaping any resulting legislative and other schemes. The challenge for scholarship in this area in the 2020s is thus not simply about 'what models, mechanisms and techniques might tie the ethical AI project to public law' but – as the missing governance piece is replaced by piecemeal regulatory schemes – 'who are these models (etc.) for, how are they being shaped and by whom, for whom?' One goal of regulation in this area is to use public regulatory power to govern, in appropriate ways, how access to and use of AI technologies might radically transform power relations in society in potentially irreversible ways. Yet it is not just the design of those technologies but the design of the governance of those technologies that matters in this regard.

4.3 The 'True North' Concept

Finally, I noted above how the preference for an ethical framework approach at the national level (as illustrated by the 2019 Australian position) might – if cast as one kind of regulation rather than an instance of non-regulation – be more agreeable if some rather more explicit attempt was made to rationalise the approach in terms of regulatory theory. 'Principles-based regulation' is at least one basis on which one might conceivably try to justify this approach. Another is that it would be an entirely defensible position, in the sense of having a grounding in established theories of regulation, if a government's position was initially to eschew law-based mechanisms and erect a voluntaristic ethical framework for governance of private sector conduct (aware of other processes such as industry standardisation), but explicitly indicate that this was only a transitional or provisional or contingent approach. If so, the government would be signalling not 'self-regulation' but 'conditional self-regulation'[71] and its clear intent to escalate intervention should subjects prove unable or unwilling to internalise the ethical framework in a way that obviates the need for law-based regulation and related compliance measures.[72] This is somewhat

---

[70] 'AI White Paper' (n 5) 9.
[71] See Parker (n 45).
[72] Ayres and Braithwaite (n 41).

different from the position adopted in the 2019 Australian report, which cannot really be interpreted as a forward intention-signalling approach.

Yet even if one generously interprets government sponsorship of ethical frameworks as a form of regulation through virtue signalling, or some sophisticated deliberate form of principles-based self-regulation, a further question remains. Harari has talked of the abdication of responsibility, in the sense that authority in society might come to be derived from an algorithmic source and only indirectly from a human source.[73] Yet there is another risk of abdication involved in the rhetoric of tech company CEOs calling, more recently, for greater regulation. This is especially because some have indicated that they only seek a broad steer. In 2018, Salesforce's Marc Benioff stated that 'the point of regulators and government [is] to come in and point [to] True North'.[74] While this might excite those persuaded by the merits of principles-based regulation that only sets broad value parameters and orientations, it is a somewhat demoralising statement. It either reads like a form of abdication ('we cannot figure this out ourselves') or suggests a corporate or management culture that still has very far to mature in social responsibility terms ('we just do not know which societal values matter, point us to them'). Notwithstanding this chapter's argument for bringing the missing law-and-regulation piece back into the governance of ethical AI, Benioff's statement is troubling because 'True North' in social impact terms (whether framed as ethical or human rights values or something else) is arguably not difficult for larger firms to find without needing some 'steer' or 'nudge' from government on basic societal values. At this late hour in human history and in the story-arc of corporate social responsibility it is hardly as if larger corporations building and using AI platforms and systems and related data-sets cannot, even if just in the interim, discern and operationalise these basic values and legal parameters without top-down clearance or advice from a central government.

5.   CONCLUSION

With the exception now of the European Commission and some EU member states, most governments (and groups of them, in a multilateral context) have chosen to approach the governance of responsible private sector development and use of AI through the promulgation of formal voluntary ethical frameworks, or acceptance of self-imposed corporate ones. This is a defensible approach in the sense that it can conceivably be given a rational justification in

---

[73]   Harari (n 31) 47, 57ff.
[74]   Remark at the World Economic Forum, Davos, January 2018, quoted in the AHRC White Paper (n 66) 5.

terms of theories of 'what works' in regulating social impact risks associated with innovative multi-context technology. In particular, it is entirely defensible for a state to regulate a complex, fast-changing issue by setting broad principles (rather than prescriptive rules) and requiring regulatory subjects to interpret and apply and comply with these; it is defensible – again in the sense that it has a basis in regulatory theory – to leave the policing of that compliance to non-state actors; it is also defensible to promote voluntary self-regulation as an initial strategy and refrain from any state regulatory or enforcement intervention unless the subject has shown that they are unable or unwilling to self-regulate.

Yet there are two problems with this argument. First, none of these regulatory situations really describes the current approach, as exemplified in this chapter by the Australian 2019 framework. At the very least, a regulatory approach that is not explicit about its rationale is easy to mistake for an approach that lacks a considered basis, or that is in denial about preferences (ideological and other) that it has chosen and power relations it has thereby accepted. Future scholarship on the governance of responsible AI ought to analyse the apparent basis for various approaches, but also critique the drawbacks of regulatory strategies that are not openly articulated (with their alternatives explained away).

Secondly, prevailing approaches are disconnected from national-level law and legal systems – the foundations of regulatory governance and of remediation of social harm – in ways that are hard to reconcile with all we hear about how profound the social impacts of AI may be. As one prominent 'responsible AI' scholar has said, 'no amount of #AI4Good replaces good #AIRegulation'.[75] Considerable scope exists for future scholarship to explore innovative ways in which the ethical AI normative architecture can be plugged into the mechanisms and institutions (the regulatory architecture) of the rule of law. In particular, and since Europe's practice has led the way in data governance and may do so on AI, a ripe research agenda exists in exploring how the 'ethical AI' phenomenon will be connected to Brussels' preferred risk-based approach to regulatory design, and how theory around risk-based regulation may need adaptation to AI-related contexts and with what empirical requirements or implications. The complexity, diversity and increasing ubiquity of things described as 'AI' makes a 'law-based regulation of responsible AI' agenda a daunting task. In approaching it, there is not necessarily an either/or (ethics vs law) dilemma. That is, perhaps the Holy Grail in this area is somehow to retain the deliberative, self-reflective and contextualised methodologies that we associate with ethics-based conversations (different conceptions of an

---

[75]   @j2bryson (J Bryson) (Twitter, 18 April 2021) <https://ai4good.org/>.

agreed concept, eg 'fairness') yet ensure that these are institutionalised within and connected to legal regulatory and remedial frameworks that reflect the fundamental principle that any power to adversely impact other people systematically and at scale ought to be accountable under law.

BIBLIOGRAPHY

Articles/Books/Reports

Agudelo, L et al, 'A literature review of the history and origin of corporate social responsibility' (2019) 4 *International Journal of Corporate Social Responsibility* 1

Alston, P, 'Statement on visit to the UK' (UN Special Rapporteur on Poverty and Human Rights) (London, 16 November 2018)

Australian Human Rights Commission, *Human Rights and Technology: Issues Paper* (July 2018)

Ayres, I and J Braithwaite, *Responsive Regulation* (Oxford University Press, 1992)

Black, J, *Rules and Regulators* (Oxford University Press, 1997)

Black, J, 'The Rise, Fall and Fate of Principles-Based Regulation' (Law, Society and Economy Working Paper 17, London School of Economics, 2010)

Black, J and R Baldwin, 'Really Responsive Risk-Based Regulation' (2010) 32 *Law and Policy* 181

Braithwaite, J, 'A Theory of Legal Certainty' (2002) 27 *Australian Journal of Legal Philosophy* 38

Calo, R, 'AI Policy: a primer and roadmap' (2017) 51 *UC Davis Law Review* 399

Corinne, C, 'Governing artificial intelligence: ethical, legal and technical opportunities and challenges' (2018) 376(2133) *Philosophy Transactions of the Royal Society A: Mathematical, Physical and Engineering Sciences* 1

Dawson, D et al, 'Artificial Intelligence: Australia's Ethics Framework' (Discussion Paper, Data61 CSIRO, 2019)

Defoe, A, 'AI Governance: a Research Agenda' (Future of Humanity Institute, Oxford, 2018)

European Commission, 'White Paper on AI' (19 February 2020)

Ford, C, 'New Governance, Compliance, and Principles-Based Securities Regulation' (2008) 45(1) *American Business Law Journal* 1

Ford, J, *Regulating Business for Peace* (Cambridge University Press, 2015)

Gasser, U and V Almeida, 'A Layered Model for AI Governance' (2017) 21(6) *IEEE Internet Computing* 58

Hagendorff, T, 'The Ethics of AI Ethics: An Evaluation of Guidelines' (2020) 30 *Minds and Machines* 99

Haines, F, *The Paradox of Regulation* (Edward Elgar, 2012)

Hajkowicz, S et al, 'Artificial intelligence: solving problems, growing the economy and improving our quality of life' (Research Report, CSIRO Data61, 2019)

Harari, YN, *21 Lessons for the 21st Century* (Jonathan Cape, 2018)

Jobin, A et al, 'The global landscape of AI ethics guidelines' (2019) 1 *Nature: Machine Intelligence* 389

Latonero, M, 'Governing AI: upholding human rights and dignity' (Data and Society, 2018)

Lodge, M and A Mennicken, 'Regulation of and by algorithm' in L Andrews et al, 'Algorithmic Regulation' (Discussion Paper No 85, Centre for Risk Analysis, London School of Economics, 2017)

MacGregor, L et al, 'International Human Rights Law as a Framework for Algorithmic Accountability' (2019) 68 *International and Comparative Law Quarterly* 309

Moses, LB, 'How to Think about Law, Regulation and Technology: Problems with "Technology" as a Regulatory Target' (2013) 5 *Law, Innovation and Technology* 1

Parker, C, *The Open Corporation: Effective Self-regulation and Democracy* (Cambridge University Press, 2002).

Raso, F et al, *Artificial Intelligence & Human Rights: Opportunities & Risks* (Berkman Klein Center, Harvard, September 2018)

Risse, M, 'Human Rights & Artificial Intelligence: an urgently needed agenda' (Working Paper RWP18-015, Harvard Kennedy School, May 2018)

Sparrow, M, *The Regulatory Craft* (Brookings, 2000)

Sunstein, C, 'Problems with Rules' (1995) 83 *California Law Review* 953

Szekely, I, MD Szabo and B Vissy, 'Regulating the Future? Law, Ethics, and Emerging Technologies' (2011) 9 *Journal of Information, Communication and Ethics in Society* 180

Whittlestone, J et al, 'Ethical and societal implications of algorithms, data, and artificial intelligence: a roadmap for research' (Research Report, Nuffield Foundation, 2019)

Yeung, K, 'Algorithmic regulation: a critical interrogation' (2018) 12(4) *Regulation and Governance* 505

Other

Metz, C, 'Is Ethical AI even possible?', *New York Times* (1 March 2019)

Standage, T, 'Regulating Artificial Intelligence' in 'The World in 2019', *The Economist* (December 2018)

14. The accountability of algorithms on social media platforms

Philippa Ryan

1. INTRODUCTION

Technology giants depend on users remaining glued to their devices.[1] As at 2021, the social media giants are Facebook, Instagram, LinkedIn, Pinterest, Snapchat and Twitter.[2] The core income of these social media companies is derived from advertising. According to Statista,[3] Facebook's advertising revenue in the United States in 2019 was USD29.92 billion. This is three times the revenue of its nearest rival, Instagram (which is also owned by Facebook). By comparison, advertising revenue for all 7,357 print magazines in the US was just USD9.68 billion.[4] What makes social media advertising so valuable – and therefore lucrative – is the way that these platforms strategically and accurately target consumers based on data analysis about individuals as well as

---

[1] G Zichermann, 'I've worked in tech for 22 years – and it's clear we're living in an "addiction economy"', *Business Insider Australia* (15 December 2017) <https://www.businessinsider.com.au/tech-addiction-product-of-an-addiction-economy-2017-12#oZgDezzCOLBLr8yM.99>.

[2] Statista Research Department, 'Social network advertising revenue in the United States in 2019, by company', Statista.com (14 January 2021) <https://www.statista.com/statistics/1103339/social-media-ad-revenue-platform/>. By February 2020, TikTok had captured more than 2% of the US teenage market. In a September 2019 survey by YouGov, 2% of US teens aged 13–17 said TikTok was the social media platform they use most often. See, A Meola, 'Analyzing TikTok user growth and usage patterns in 2020', *Business Insider* (13 Feb 2020) <https://www.businessinsider.com/tiktok-marketing-trends-predictions-2020?mc_cid=a4463fe9e8&mc_eid=[a9d877ecbe]&r=AU&IR=T>.

[3] Statista is a German company specialising in market and consumer data. According to the company, its platform contains more than 1,000,000 statistics on more than 80,000 topics from more than 22,500 sources and 170 different industries, and generates a revenue of about €60 million. Source: <https://www.eui.eu/Research/Library/ResearchGuides/Economics/Statistics/DataPortal/Statista>.

[4] A Watson, 'U.S. magazine industry – statistics & facts', Statista.com (18 February 2021), <https://www.statista.com/topics/1265/magazines/>.

cohorts of users. They scrape, store and analyse personal details, demographics, political persuasions, online purchasing habits, opinions, expressions, relationships and sentiments. They also track user attention.

Users express their 'attention' through a variety of metrics and interactions, including posts, shares, links, @mentions, and impressions. Social media companies design algorithms that keep users engaged with their platform. News services achieve this by producing a coloured banner on our screen that reads 'Breaking news'. By way of contrast, the news feed on social media platforms includes advertisements that may look like news content, but may in fact be selling a product or service. Advertisers post images of things that we searched for only hours earlier. In this way, our attention is constantly being hijacked and this keeps us online.[5] However, data sets do not necessarily yield objective and reliable information. Indeed, there is evidence that algorithms embedded in social technologies can encode societal biases, accelerate the spread of rumours and disinformation, and amplify echo chambers of public opinion.[6] Left unchecked, algorithms may be used for misleading or deceptive purposes. Such uses include the creation of data sets and inferences gleaned from their analysis for sale to third parties to support their decision-making (for example, recruiting staff or providing credit). Without accountability, it would be impossible to determine whether an algorithm is behaving accurately or fairly, and – if so – whether the fault lies in poor design or nefarious intent.[7]

This chapter examines the nature of algorithms and how they can be used on social media platforms to gather and analyse personal data that may inform or manipulate sentiment and decision-making. It explores some recent examples of wayward algorithms and proposes steps for making algorithms accountable for their behaviour. It tentatively concludes that while thoughtful auditing of algorithms may improve their conduct, these concerns still raise broad societal questions about bias, fairness, and truth.

2.   THE NATURE OF ALGORITHMS

An algorithm is a step-by-step logical method of solving a problem. It is commonly used for data processing, calculation and other related computer and mathematical operations. Autonomous algorithms rely on data analysis and

---

[5]   J Guszcza et al, 'Why We Need to Audit Algorithms', *Harvard Business Review* (28 November 2018) <https://hbr.org/2018/11/why-we-need-to-audit-algorithms>.

[6]   The Economist, 'Fake news: you ain't seen nothing yet', *The Economist* (1 July 2017)   <https://www.economist.com/science-and-technology/2017/07/01/fake-news -you-aint-seen-nothing-yet>.

[7]   J Guszcza et al, 'Why We Need to Audit Algorithms', *Harvard Business Review* (28 November 2018) <https://hbr.org/2018/11/why-we-need-to-audit-algorithms>.

artificial intelligence to replace human controls and decision-making.[8] Not all automation is algorithmic, but all algorithms automate. The extension of algorithmic automation from purely mathematical and computational terrains to extended sociotechnical infrastructures has produced profound, ongoing, and open-ended transformations in the organisation and function of contemporary social worlds.[9] This transformation has occurred quickly, while governance models have struggled to keep up. In June 2018, Google CEO Sundar Pichai published an essay on Google's principles for AI, setting forth the objectives that guide Google's artificial intelligence strategies.[10] Then, in February 2019, the company issued a white paper arguing that governments need to take action to govern artificial intelligence.[11] While this proposal makes sense from a regulatory perspective, social media platform providers do not need regulation to take steps to improve their ethical and transparent use of AI in their algorithms.

Increasingly, algorithms implement institutional decision-making based on analytics, which involves the discovery, interpretation, and communication of meaningful patterns in data. There is growing evidence that some algorithms and analytics can be opaque, making it impossible to determine when their outputs may be biased or erroneous.[12] Organisations are increasingly relying on algorithm-based decision-making to supplant their human equivalents. In some cases, platform providers will be using AI and algorithms in novel ways that have no analogue equivalent process. This lack of historical use (albeit in a manual form) means that the use of the algorithm is with precedent or understanding of how it will impact users of the platform. This trend to use new programs to gather and analyse data has been promoted and reinforced by the technology industry and its claims that decision-making tools bring efficiency and objectivity to data analysis and decision-making, downplaying the potential bias of algorithmic outputs.[13]

It is a feature of algorithmic decision-making that it can be either probabilistic or deterministic. Deterministic algorithms produce predictable results,

---

[8]   PA Ryan, *Trust and Distrust in Digital Economies* (Routledge, 2019) 6.
[9]   I Lowrie, 'Algorithms and Automation: An introduction' (2018) 33(3) *Cultural Anthropology* 349.
[10]   S Pichai, *AI at Google: Our Principles* (Blog, 7 June 2018) <https://www.blog .google/technology/ai/ai-principles/>.
[11]   Google AI, *Artificial Intelligence at Google: Our Principles* (February 2021) <https://ai.google/principles/?>.
[12]   USACM, 'Statement on Algorithmic Transparency and Accountability', Association for Computing Machinery US Public Policy Council (USACM) (12 January 2017) <https://www.acm.org/binaries/content/assets/public-policy/2017usac mstatementalgorithms.pdf>.
[13]   U Leicht-Deobald et al, 'The Challenges of Algorithm-Based HR Decision-Making for Personal Integrity' (2019) 160 *Journal of Business Ethics* 377, 377.

because all data upon which the algorithm relies is known at the outset. With probabilistic behaviour there is an element of chance involved in the outcome, because not all data is known. So-called deep learning algorithms are on the whole – by design – not comprehensible to the software developers who designed them. This opacity arises from a lack of human control over how an algorithm might respond to new data sets and changing trends. It produces a situation where algorithms are – intentionally by design – out of control. This aspect of algorithmic behaviour may have profound consequences when they run on a social media platform like Facebook – a domain in which individuals constantly and publicly work on creating self-identities, characterised by the 'technologisation' of human interaction.[14] The personal data of social media are monitored, classified and monetised. Algorithmic insights are gained from massive volumes of information that activate and populate digital networks.[15]

One way to manage risk and to improve the integrity of algorithms is to increase the complexity of the conditional logic to account for known problems with the data. However, this higher level of complexity makes the operation of the algorithm harder to explain and to manage from a governance perspective. Add to user self-determination the allure and impact of influential bloggers and celebrity Twitter account-holders, and the algorithm becomes a powerful mediator control mechanism via which marketers and lobbyists can curate content to individual news feeds.

3.   HOW ALGORITHMS MANIPULATE ONLINE BEHAVIOUR AND SENTIMENT

Facebook members once assumed that news feeds are populated by a chrono-logical representation of activity posted by our friends, groups, and advertisers. However, it is now apparent that Facebook uses algorithms to curate what we see. These algorithms are programmed to keep our attention as long as possible by promoting only what we are most likely to click, like, and share. The data that Facebook gathers about our activity is then provided to marketers so that they can target advertising to individual users. The content that we are likely to click on and the level of our activity dictates the price that Facebook can charge for marketing to specific users. Content is created without control over

---

[14]   L Scaife, 'Learning from the Laws of the Sea, Foucault and Regulatory Theory: Proposing a Regulatory Harbour Model for the Regulation of Social Media that Serves Rather than Rules the Waves' (2018) 69(4) *Northern Ireland Legal Quarterly* 433, 433–436.

[15]   See S Livingstone, 'Audiences in an Age of Datafication: Critical Questions for Media Research' (2019) 20(2) *Television & New Media* 170.

its accuracy or purpose. The nature or quality of that content is not scrutinised to determine whether it is appropriate or safe for the user.

The algorithms that control social media content are automated to manage massive volumes of data and activity. A problem with automation is that it may skew political views, manipulate social perspectives, and entrench historical unfairness. Industry forecasters believe software programs incorporating automated decision-making will only increase in the coming years as artificial intelligence becomes more mainstream. One of the major challenges of this emerging reality is to ensure that algorithms do not reinforce harmful or unfair biases. Algorithms have the capacity to replicate and amplify human bias. Bias of several kinds can significantly distort social media data and reduce its representativeness.

Some algorithms know more than their developers could ever know. This is because they can be programmed to analyse numerous data sets and then reach conclusions about causal relationships between types of data; or to use those data sets to make predictions about outcomes or trends. The explosive growth of data collection, coupled with increasingly sophisticated algorithms, has resulted in a significant increase in automated decision-making.[16]

When Facebook delivers us clickbait and conspiracy theories, it uses an algorithm that determines our interests. A manipulative algorithm can force favoured results further to the top of our news feed, so that we read it first. If that feed includes an opinion, more people will read it. This will increase the number of people who hold that opinion. This is because increased exposure to an opinion increases the likelihood that readers will adopt that opinion as their own.[17]

Developers can control an algorithmic function by setting rewards for achieving predetermined levels of optimisation. Research demonstrates that successful versions of these programs have exhibited either competitive or cooperative behaviour, or variations of these two actions.[18] The key traits of these algorithms can then be exploited to control whether the algorithm will be 'greedy' or 'prudent', as well as its appetite for risk-taking. In the context of

---

[16]   R Dopplick (ACM Director of Public Policy), 'New Statement on Algorithmic Transparency and Accountability by ACM U.S. Public Policy Council', *United States Association for Computing Machinery* (14 January 2017) <https://techpolicy.acm.org/2017/01/new-statement-on-algorithmic-transparency-and-accountability-by-acm-u-s-public-policy-council/>.

[17]   ME Stucke and A Ezrachi, 'How Digital Assistants Can Harm Our Economy, Privacy, and Democracy' (2017) 32 *Berkeley Tech LJ* 1239, 1274–1275. See also BJ Horton, 'Malign Manipulations: Can Google's Shareholders Save Democracy' (2019) 54(3) *Wake Forest Law Review* 707, 731.

[18]   H Chia, 'In Machines We Trust: Are Robo-Advisers More Trustworthy than Human Financial Advisers?' (2019) 1(1) *Law, Technology and Humans* 129, 137.

advertising on social media, such an algorithm could promote a risky invest-ment product to a vulnerable user (for example, someone whom data analysis has determined has a gambling addiction).

For online marketers, people's attention is a resource just like time or money. Facebook has established a platform on which we are always connected with people we know, as well as friends of friends. Until we read a post and look at the pictures, we do not know whether we are interested, and yet, the news feed has our attention in any event. Meanwhile, advertisements appear in the feed via paid content from marketers, or friends sharing and liking paid content. All of this information and advertising is curated by algorithms to ensure that it suits our age, interests, and online activity. Using predictive analytics, the system decides what our interests might be.

Facebook's algorithm re-orders our news feed to ensure that the most 'liked', active, and connected of our 'friends' are appearing as the most preva-lent posts on our feed. This data informs which advertisements would be most lucrative, so that it can be used to market Facebook to advertisers. At the heart of this entire business model is our attention.

4. TYPES OF ALGORITHMIC MISCONDUCT

There are many ways in which algorithms can run amok. In financial markets, big data and artificial intelligence (AI) are used to make important business decisions, including which loans to approve, how to set prices, and when to trade stock.[19] The dangers that arise from the use of automated systems are that – when designed to achieve certain outcomes – they may opt for or 'learn' to collude or fix prices.

Beyond collusion and price fixing, algorithms have been known to display new forms of anti-competitive behaviour. For example, algorithms 'co-opt' consumers into using certain platforms or to click on an image. Users believe in the popularity of a product or service because an advertisement has been dressed up as a shared social engagement. The reason why algorithms succeed in achieving these outcomes is because they are designed to operate in the background and they are optimised for engagement. When the post is not an

---

[19] M Hurley and J Adebayo, 'Credit Scoring in the Era of Big Data' (2016) 18 *Yale JL & Tech* 148, 190–193; E Calvano et al, 'Artificial Intelligence, Algorithmic Pricing, and Collusion', *Vox* (3 February 2019) <https://voxeu.org/article/artificial-intelligence-algorithmic-pricing-and-collusion>. See also ME Diamantis, 'The Problem of Algorithmic Corporate Misconduct' (16 September 2019), Compliance and Enforcement, Program on Corporate Compliance and Enforcement at NYU School of Law <https://wp.nyu.edu/compliance_enforcement/2019/09/16/the-problem-of-algorithmic-corporate-misconduct/>.

advertisement, it may be a proxy for a data-gathering algorithm. Consumers feel as though their interaction with a particular website or app is serving their needs (that is, the consumer's needs). However, it hides the reality that the product or service is just a sideline in their vendor's actual business model: the trade in data. The wisdom of crowds has been hijacked by algorithms that behave on a large scale via fake identities or manipulated likes, shares, and ratings.

Smoke screen algorithms operating on social media platforms are designed and deployed to operate with a purpose of baiting users to engage with a platform or advertiser. However, there are other algorithmic behaviours that can lead to or amplify anti-social, unethical, or unfair consequences. Examples of such mischief abound on most social media forums, including bias, live-streaming violence, fake news, and misuse of personal information.

5. ALGORITHMIC BIAS

Algorithmic bias is a phenomenon observed in various contexts. The use of social media to access news reports has grown significantly over the past decade. However, data indicates that the use of social media to represent news events fairly is unreliable. The problem is twofold. First, traditional news services produce formal reports of events, but geographic and demographic coverage is uneven. Secondly, users of social media platforms informally report their personal experiences with the same events, but do so inaccurately or without providing context. For example, Twitter, Facebook, and WhatsApp allow ordinary members of the public to use their mobile phones or other digital devices to broadcast their personal reports of violent events widely, or to narrowcast them to private, shared interest groups.[20]

Algorithmic parameters are not value neutral. They are imbued with the values of their designers and the data sets upon which they rely. As Anna Lauren Hoffman reminds us: 'ontologies are not born in a vacuum. Instead, they emerge from (and are shaped by!) the active, open-ended, and everyday practices of the world they purport to describe.'[21]

Over the past two decades, there has been a disproportionate increase of social media and digital technology use, favouring the more developed countries of the Northern Hemisphere, compared to the Global South. Uneven dis-

---

[20] See T Roberts and G Marchais, 'Assessing the Role of Social Media and Digital Technology in Violence Reporting' (2018) 10(2) *Contemporary Readings in Law and Social Justice* 9, 9–10.

[21] AL Hoffmann, 'Science Will Not Save Us: Medicine, Research Ethics, and My Transgender Body', *Autostraddle* (16 July 2014) <http://www.autostraddle.com/science-will-not-save-us-medicine-research-ethics- and-my-transgender-body-240296/>.

tribution of access to the internet is evidenced both internationally and within individual countries.[22] Internet access is provided via physical fibre-optic or copper cable networks as well as by satellite or cellular networks. These now essential services are more developed in capital cities and commercial centres than remote and rural areas. This imbalance is reflected in formal and informal reporting of significant political and natural events. This imbalance can introduce biases into collected data.

While algorithms may seem to rely on objective data,[23] software is not free of human influence. Algorithms are written and maintained by people, and machine-learning algorithms adjust what they do based on people's attitude, interests, preferences, and behaviour. As a result, algorithms can reinforce human prejudices.[24] Since the early 2010s, concerns have been growing about how machines interpret data and optimise outcomes. For example, pre-programmed prejudices that were present in existing and historical data may inform the way that the particular machine or algorithm will determine a correct outcome or optimise its own functionality.

An important consideration for the discussion of algorithmic bias is the phenomenon of 'selective exposure' that prevails on social media: people prefer information that confirms their pre-existing attitudes (selective exposure), view information consistent with their pre-existing beliefs as more persuasive than dissonant information (confirmation bias), and are inclined to accept information that pleases them (desirability bias). In addition to these inherent biases, research indicates that people are more likely to believe misinformation if it is repeated.[25] These combinations of propensities mean that there are general biases in the population ready to be exploited and manipulated by those who know how.

---

[22] T Roberts and G Marchais, 'Assessing the Role of Social Media and Digital Technology in Violence Reporting' (2018) 10(2) *Contemporary Readings in Law and Social Justice* 9, 18.

[23] CC Miller, 'Can an algorithm hire better than a human?', *The New York Times* (25 June 2015) <https://www.nytimes.com/2015/06/26/upshot/can-an-algorithm-hire -better-than-a-human.html?module=inline>; H Devlin, 'Discrimination by algorithm: scientists devise test to detect AI bias', *The Guardian* (19 December 2016) <https:// www.theguardian.com/technology/2016/dec/19/discrimination-by-algorithm-scientists -devise-test-to-detect-ai-bias>.

[24] CC Miller, 'When Algorithms Discriminate', *The New York Times* (9 June 2015) <https://www.nytimes.com/2015/07/10/upshot/when-algorithms-discriminate.html>.

[25] JI Goldenziel and M Cheema, 'The New Fighting Words?: How U.S. Law Hampers the Fight against Information Warfare' (2019) 22(1) *University of Pennsylvania Journal of Constitutional Law* 81, 105.

6.   LIVE-STREAMING VIOLENCE

Social media now plays a prominent role in broadcasting violence and tragedy. Facebook Live was launched in 2016. Just months later, in July 2016, Philando Castile's shooting was live-streamed. Castile – a 32-year-old African American – was fatally shot during a traffic stop by police officer Jeronimo Yanez of the St. Anthony police department. The shooting of Philando Castile was streamed as it happened on Facebook Live.[26] The trauma that this video caused was widespread.[27]

Facebook was still grappling with the implications of its live-streaming feature when a gunman live-streamed the shooting of 100 people at a mosque in Christchurch, New Zealand, in March 2019. Facebook argued that it could not stop the Christchurch murderer from streaming his actions because it cannot control content in general and there is not enough 'abhorrent' content to properly train its AI.[28] For this reason, Facebook says that it is unable to identify or exclude misinformation, even when it is dressed-up to look like news.

Facebook warns potential live-streamers 'Content that violates our policies will be removed'.[29] The problem is that Facebook is unable to remove the content until after the damage has been done. Online violence causes trauma to unsuspecting viewers and has the potential to incite violence. The covert way in which algorithms can micro-target content means that divisive propaganda is steered towards the most likely audience to be manipulated. This 'weaponizing' of AI systems is not to be underestimated; it has proven very successful in the case of recent elections and referenda.[30]

---

[26]   T Wayne, 'The trauma of violent news on the Internet', *The New York Times* (10 September 2016) <https://www.nytimes.com/2016/09/11/fashion/the-trauma-of-violent-news-on-the-internet.html>.

[27]   F Ritchin, 'In the live-streaming era, the trauma is widespread', *Time* (11 July 2016) <https://time.com/4400930/philando-castile/>.

[28]   Z Doffman, 'Facebook Admits It Can't Control Facebook Live – Is This The End For Live Streaming?', *Forbes* (24 March 2019) <https://www.forbes.com/sites/zakdoffman/2019/03/24/could-this-really-be-the-beginning-of-the-end-for-facebook-live/?sh=2db94bc2ac8b>.

[29]   Facebook, 'Facebook Business Help', *Facebook* (Retrieved 14 March 2021) <https://www.facebook.com/business/help/626637251511853>.

[30]   CN Radavoi, 'The Impact of Artificial Intelligence on Freedom, Rationality, Rule of Law and Democracy: Should We Not Be Debating It?' (2020) 25(2) *Texas Journal on Civil Liberties & Civil Rights* 107, 121.

7.   FAKE NEWS

In an increasingly digital setting, concerns over free expression are pervasive in discussions about the role of social media in democracy.[31] While free expression is widely discussed in conversations about potential regulation of social media platforms, the need to secure free elections has recently become a key cause for concern among technological and governmental stakeholders. Social media allows for the rapid spread of information. While much of this information can be useful and informative, growing concerns relate to how false information may misinform and deceive voters by being circulated on social media.[32]

A problem arises when propaganda or misinformation that is being fed into social media news feeds is 'dressed-up' as news. Also troubling is the practice of presenting as the views of a real person, but is actually a fake account created to generate trust in the information that leads to distrust in an institution, idea, or group of people. This sort of activity has been revealed on Facebook and other social media platforms, particularly during the 2016 United States presidential election and the United Kingdom's Brexit referendum. Data reveals that Russia used hundreds of fake accounts to tweet about Brexit. These tweets were shared on other social platforms, including Facebook. Accounts run from a St Petersburg 'troll farm' deployed algorithms to target Britons and to sow discord over the referendum.[33]

It soon became apparent that algorithms were feeding fake news to manipulate the opinions of voters. It did this by analysing social media posts to determine sentiment. These sorts of algorithms are being used in a way that negatively impacts on our democracies, our justice systems, and our

---

[31]   E Shattock, 'Rights Based Principles: Protecting Free Elections and Free Expression in Irish Policy Responses to Fake News Online' (2020) 1(1) *Dublin Law and Politics Review* 1, 2. See also 'Fake news is fooling more conservatives than liberals. Why?', *The Economist* (6 June 2020) <https://www.economist.com/international/2020/06/03/fake-news-is-fooling-more-conservatives-than-liberals-why>; 'Censorious governments are abusing "fake news" laws', *The Economist* (11 February 2021) <https://www.economist.com/international/2021/02/11/censorious-governments-are-abusing-fake-news-laws>.

[32]   BAI, 'Use of social media for news amongst Irish consumers declines while understanding of how news appears in their social media feeds remains low', *Broadcasting Authority of Ireland* (14 June 2018) <https://www.bai.ie/en/use-of-social-media-for- news-amongst-irish-consumers -dectines-w~le-understanding-of -how-news-appears-in-their-social-media-feeds -remains-low/>.

[33]   R Booth et al., 'Russia used hundreds of fake accounts to tweet about Brexit, data shows', *The Guardian* (15 November 2017) <https://www.theguardian.com/world/2017/nov/14/how-400-russia-run-fake-accounts-posted-bogus-brexit-tweets>.

well-being. This erodes trust in others and opens up communities and societies to a risk of cyber-attack and a threat to the integrity of the electoral process.[34]

Balancing rights to free speech with attempts to curb misinformation remains an ongoing challenge. Social media platforms once claimed that they would promote and assist democratic processes. However, the lesson of recent history teaches us that individuals and state actors can easily manipulate information with powerful and corrosive consequences.

The use of manipulative algorithms on social media platforms is a type of corruption. Manipulative algorithms introduce covert, synthetic, and contrived influences into decision-making process that mediate online content, communications, relationships, and sentiment. As with most processes that occur on social media platforms, the outcomes are amplified. This amplification arises from the phenomenon of fake accounts created to generate profiles or 'avatars' that interact and post messages to deceive other members of the community. Autonomous algorithms gather and disseminate this information with the same respect for fake identities as is afforded information generated by real users. Twitter, Instagram, and Facebook are overwhelmed by the number of fake accounts operating on their platforms and struggle to detect and delete them.[35] Online scams should be treated with a particularly high level of caution. Further, this technology is developed by a small handful of companies and, due to their control and the sheer scale of the problem, the public and government do not have the tools or resources to hold the algorithms accountable.

8.   MISUSE OF PERSONAL INFORMATION

In any analysis of types of algorithmic misconduct, it is important to keep in mind that some novel (and questionable) uses of social media data are starting to creep into lending and hiring practices. Even if an algorithm that is used to analyse social media data for these purposes is reliable, transparent, and fair, the practice may be questionable as it may breach hard-fought financial and industrial codes of conduct. For example, laws in most developed economies forbid lenders and employers from discriminating on the basis of race, gender, and sexuality.[36] Yet banks and other financial organisations can refuse to give

---

[34] M Surman, 'How to keep AI from turning into the Terminator', *CNN.com* (15 January 2019) <https://www.google.com.au/amp/s/amp.cnn.com/cnn/2019/01/15/opinions/artificial-intelligence-ethical-responsible-programming-surman/index.html>.

[35] R Levinson-Waldman, 'Government Access to and Manipulation of Social Media: Legal and Policy Challenges' (2018) 61(3) *Howard Law Journal* 523, 542.

[36] The United Kingdom protects the rights of employees, consumers, borrowers, renters, students, and members of private associations via the Equality Act 2010 (UK). In the United States, title VII of the Civil Rights Act, as amended, pro-

credit to people if (for example) their LinkedIn resumé does not match the details in their loan application; or if a computer algorithm judges them to be an undesirable applicant. These regulatory gaps exist because laws have not kept up with technology; and such are widening in every digital domain.[37] Similarly, employers can get into legal trouble if they ask interviewees about their religion, sexual preference, or political affiliation. However, they may instead glean this information by simply searching the candidate's social media activity. By reviewing a candidate's posts, likes and shares, an employer can filter-out applicants based on their beliefs, looks, and habits, as revealed in their online interactions.

An important mischief in the use of algorithms to cull applicants in this way lies in the fact that it becomes impossible for a job or loan applicant to discover the misconduct that has resulted in their rejection. The lack of transparency in the process means that the offending organisation may be able to hide what is otherwise a breach of important legislation. Anti-discrimination legislation exists to improve allocation of credit and employment opportunities for those who have traditionally been unserved or underserved.

As the conventional credit scoring models mostly rely on the past financial information of borrowers, it is perceived to be inadequate to capture borrowers with a thin or new credit file.[38] However, the development of technological innovations has paved the way for credit scoring systems to exploit a wide variety of non-traditional data, such as social media footprints and other online behavioural data.

For the effectiveness of anti-discrimination, civil rights, and equality legislation to be measurable, its impact needs to visible. Namely, inclusion needs to be made visible. One challenge is that whereas diversity is relatively

---

tects employees and job applicants from employment discrimination based on race, color, religion, sex, and national origin. In Australia, borrowers and employees are protected by a number of Commonwealth Acts, including: Age Discrimination Act 2004, Australian Human Rights Commission Act 1986, Disability Discrimination Act 1992, Racial Discrimination Act 1975, and Sex Discrimination Act 1984. The following laws operate at a state and territory level, with state and territory equal opportunity and anti-discrimination agencies having statutory responsibilities under them: Discrimination Act 1991 (ACT), Anti-Discrimination Act 1977 (NSW), Anti-Discrimination Act 1996 (NT), Anti-Discrimination Act 1991 (Qld), Equal Opportunity Act 1984 (SA), Anti-Discrimination Act 1998 (Tas), Equal Opportunity Act 2010 (Vic), and Equal Opportunity Act 1984 (WA).

[37] V Wadhwa, 'Laws and Ethics Can't Keep Pace with Technology' *MIT Technology Review* (15 April 2014) <https://www.technologyreview.com/s/526401/laws-and-ethics-cant-keep-pace-with-technology/>.

[38] World Bank, *Credit Reporting Knowledge Guide 2019* (Financial Sector Study, 6 June 2019) <https://openknowledge.worldbank.org/handle/10986/2185>.

easy to measure, inclusion is typically described in qualitative, often subjective terms.[39] Furthermore, there will always be an element of subjectivity in determining credit-worthiness or fitness to fill a position in an organisation. Indeed, subjectivity may explicitly support inclusion and diversity in access to financial and employment opportunities.[40] However, this issue is heightened in the case of alternative credit scoring models that rely on several data points for assessing the creditworthiness of a prospective borrower. The increasing amount of data relied on by alternative data scoring systems raises concerns about the quality and veracity of such data, uncertainty on the use of the data, opacity of scoring methodologies, the ability of such data to predict the creditworthiness of a person, and its potential to discriminate.[41]

The use of social media data to inform decision-making is risky. The data may be unreliable for a number of reasons including the unreliability of identifying the origin of the data, its currency, accuracy, or analysis. The analysis may have been tainted by existing known or unknown biases in rating and scoring unstructured data sets. As well as disadvantaging those who are discriminated against, this conduct undermines credit information and candidate assessment systems. Trustworthy systems are an essential part of any financial or industrial infrastructure. They can address asymmetry of information between applicants and decision-makers that may lead to 'adverse selection'.[42] But the main problem with algorithms is how to establish, maintain, and assess their trustworthiness. Prior to implementation, algorithms are 'trained' and then tested against existing data sets. This training enables the algorithm to determine correlations between variables and to assess results against specific classes. Ensuring that an algorithm optimises its results without repeating pre-existing biases and exclusive behaviours is highly problematic.

In perhaps its biggest scandal to date, Facebook announced in 2017 that it had handed more than 80 million user profiles to Cambridge Analytica – an election strategy firm. While Facebook was excoriated for its behaviour and

---

[39]   P Gaudiano, 'Inclusion is invisible: How to measure it', *Forbes.com* (23 April 2019) <https://www.forbes.com/sites/paologaudiano/2019/04/23/inclusion-is-invisible -how-to-measure-it/?sh=7e1c4411a3d2>.

[40]   See TC Licsandru and CC Cui, 'Subjective social inclusion: A conceptual critique for socially inclusive marketing' (2018) 82 *Journal of Business Research* 330; P Huxley et al, *Development of a social inclusion index to capture subjective and objective life domains (Phase II): Psychometric development study. Health technology assessment* (Winchester, 2018) 16.

[41]   World Bank, *Credit Reporting Knowledge Guide 2019* (2019) <http://documents .worldbank.org/curated/en/262691559115855583/pdf/Credit-Reporting-Knowledge -Guide-zo19.pdf>.

[42]   S Ahmed, 'Alternative Credit Scoring – A Double Edged Sword' (2020) 11(2) *Journal of Indian Law and Society* 1, 1.

suffered a major stock loss, there was no corresponding drop in the number of user accounts.[43] It seems that losing the trust of your users does not immediately make them flee your business.

9.   MAKING ALGORITHMS ACCOUNTABLE

A major problem with algorithms, algorithmic bias, and technology generally is that in many domains, they are held to a higher standard than humans undertaking similar functions. This is readily understood when thinking about automated vehicles: people will not adopt or trust self-driving vehicles until they can guarantee the safety of passengers and pedestrians. This is in stark contrast to the acceptance of human drivers of vehicles, notwithstanding the global annual road toll.

The propensity to hold technology to account at a higher standard than humans can manifest as a disproportionate lack of trust in technology, when in fact, it is performing at a superior level to humans. Indeed, the same algorithmic technology that is used to propagate misinformation may be used to assess and signal 'source quality'. For example, Facebook is trialling the use of fact-checked articles to assess the quality of disputed ones. Once an article has passed assessment, Facebook proposes to add 'trust indicators' to the content. These trust indicators would include information about the publication, any corrections, and relevant ethics policies.[44] According to Facebook, trust indicators were established by an international consortium of news and digital companies collaborating to build a more trustworthy and trusted press known as the Trust Project. This endeavour is apparently part of Facebook's ongoing effort to 'enhance people's understanding of the sources and trustworthiness of news on [Facebook's] platform'.[45]

While the Trust Project aims to use technology to tackle misinformation and to increase transparency around political advertising during the United States 2020 election,[46] this effort has not deflected criticism levelled against the tech giant by New York's attorney-general, Letitia James. James described

---

[43]   M Green, 'Why I'm worried about Google', *Slate* (3 October 2018) <https://slate.com/technology/2018/10/google-is-losing-users-trust.html>.

[44]   A Polyakova and D Fried, 'Democratic Defense Against Disinformation 2.0' (June 2019) *Atlantic Council* 2, 15. See also JI Goldenziel and M Cheema, 'The New Fighting Words?: How U.S. Law Hampers the Fight against Information Warfare' (2019) 22(1) *University of Pennsylvania Journal of Constitutional Law* 81, 164.

[45]   A Anker, S Su and J Smith, 'New Test to Provide Context About Articles', *Facebook App* (5 October 2017) <https://about.fb.com/news/2017/10/news-feed-fyi-new-test-to-provide-context-about-articles>.

[46]   Facebook, 'Election Integrity', *Facebook* (25 January 2021) <https://about.fb.com/news/category/election-integrity>.

her State's December 2021 antitrust case against the world's biggest social network as stemming from its use of vast troves of data and money to suppress potential threats to its dominance. The accusations include reducing choices for consumers, stifling innovation, and degrading privacy protections for millions of Americans.[47] Forty-five US states have joined the bipartisan proceedings. The proceedings represent the latest attempt by regulators to force change in order to combat Facebook's privacy practices, the spread of fake news and conspiracy theories, and its exploitation of authoritarian regimes.

When considering the behaviour of algorithms, transparency and accountability should be regarded as linked concepts. Accountability necessitates 'openness' and therefore should be open to public scrutiny. It is a principle that should be available to the general public and its application should be available for scrutiny. Openness through accountability means that the account-giving is done in public, rather than in a shadow.[48]

There are examples of algorithms that are designed to help reduce human bias in decision-making. For example, predictive judicial-analytics technologies, which can assess extra-legal factors that influence decisions, have been developed with a view to increasing efficiency and fairness in the law. Judicial analytics can assess extra-legal factors that influence decisions.[49] Big data and data science transform organisational decision-making. We increasingly defer decisions to algorithms because machines have earned a reputation of outperforming us. These developments signal hope for the development of algorithms that can identify and address bias in user-content and news reporting on social media platforms.

Australia's *Digital Service Standard* suggests that programmers should make all new source code open by default.[50] The Standard regards as important the value of making sure that the code is open, so that others can re-use it. Making code 'open source' will reduce the costs of projects (for developers and others), prevent duplication of work, increase transparency, and add bene-

---

[47]   NY Attorney General, 'Attorney General James Leads Multistate Lawsuit Seeking to End Facebooks Illegal Monopoly' (Press Release, 9 December 2020) <https://ag.ny.gov/press-release/2020/attorney-general-james-leads-multistate-lawsuit -seeking-end-facebooks-illegal>.

[48]   E Ferlie, *The Oxford Handbook of Public Management* (Oxford University Press, 2005). See also E Shattock, 'Rights Based Principles: Protecting Free Elections and Free Expression in Irish Policy Responses to Fake News Online' (2020) 1(1) *Dublin Law and Politics Review* 1, 10.

[49]   D Chen, 'Judicial Analytics and the Great Transformation of American Law' (2019) 27(1) *Journal of Artificial Intelligence and the Law* 15, 18.

[50]   Australian Digital Codes, 'Digital Service Standard – 8 Make source code open' (1 May 2016) <https://guides.service.gov.au/digital-service-standard/8-make-source -code-open/>.

fits (including improvement of the code by other developers). Developers are also encouraged to test the code in a beta environment,[51] and to be explicit with users about licensing and how bugs and fixes will be handled.[52]

The Public Policy Council of the United States Association for Computing Machinery proposes seven principles for Algorithmic Transparency and Accountability: Awareness; Access and Redress; Accountability; Explanation; Data Provenance; Auditability; and Validation and Testing.[53] These seven principles have in common transparency and human oversight. They contemplate a regime in which there are formal and informal processes to deliver transparency in relation to the data upon which algorithms rely, the way the algorithm is tested, and whether it can be audited. These functions combine to deliver a more trustworthy system.

Algorithms and artificial intelligence have been a recent focus of the Organisation for Economic Co-operation and Development Competition Committee and the International Competition Network's Unilateral Conduct Working Group, which has for some time been addressing online competition issues.[54] These issues arise in all online market places, including social media. Given their pervasive nature, the United States Association for Computing Machinery Public Policy Council has also acknowledged that it is imperative to address 'challenges associated with the design and technical aspects of algorithms and preventing bias from the onset'.[55]

A number of countries around the world are working on the problems of accountability of algorithms and the ethical use of artificial intelligence. The New York City mayor's office established a new artificial intelligence watchdog panel. Mayor de Blasio observed that as data and technology become more

---

[51] A beta environment is a test version of a platform that will not affect production data. It is a way of running live code in real time, but with minimal risk. They are usually provided for free or significantly reduced rates to low-risk users. Automated and manual feedback systems provide reports on bugs and errors that can be fixed to improve the alpha version. See RM Lee, 'Beta-Testing the Particular Machine: The Machine-or-Transformation Test in Peril and Its Impact on Cloud Computing' (2013) 11(2) *Duke Law & Technology Review* 175.

[52] Australian Digital Codes, 'Digital Service Standard – 8 Make source code open' (1 May 2016) <https://guides.service.gov.au/digital-service-standard/8-make-source -code-open/>.

[53] USACM, 'Statement on Algorithmic Transparency and Accountability', *Association for Computing Machinery US Public Policy Council* (12 January 2017) <https://www.acm.org/binaries/content/assets/public-policy/2017usacmstatement algorithms.pdf>.

[54] See R Sims (Conference Chair), 'Can Robots Collude?', *ACCC Conference* (16 November 2017) <https://www.accc.gov.au/speech/the-accc%E2%80%99s-approach -to-colluding-robots>.

[55] USACM, 'Statement on Algorithmic Transparency and Accountability' (n 53).

central to the work of city government, the algorithms used to aid in decision making must be aligned with the city's goals and values.[56] The governments of Canada and France have announced a joint initiative to examine the intersection of artificial intelligence and ethics. Interestingly, both countries stressed the need to embed their common values into the behaviour of autonomous systems.[57] This embedding will ensure that social media users who click on official content will be protected by the algorithms running on the government platform. The notion of ensuring that the values of the government and society generally are reflected in the way that algorithms behave will resonate with ethicists. However, this presupposes that the designers and developers of algorithms in all domains also hold those values. The values need to be hardwired into the code for the outcomes to be consistent with these expectations.

Recent years demonstrate a growing use of algorithmic law enforcement by online intermediaries. Copyright law has been at the forefront of algorithmic law enforcement since the early 1990s when it conferred *safe harbour* protection to online intermediaries who remove allegedly infringing content upon notice under the Digital Millennium Copyright Act 1998. Algorithmic enforcement by online intermediaries reflects a fundamental shift in our traditional system of governance. It effectively converges law enforcement and adjudication powers in the hands of a small number of mega platforms. The best way to support trust in the law is to enforce it.

Accountability refers to the extent to which decision-makers are expected to justify their choices to those affected by these choices, to be held answerable for their actions, and to be held responsible for their failures and wrongdoings. This applies equally to decisions made by humans and algorithms.

10.   CONCLUSION

Even thoughtful design and auditing of algorithms raise broad societal questions about bias, fairness, and truth. One approach towards combatting bias and misinformation is to design and deploy algorithms that are programmed to detect incorrect or offensive content and conduct. Social media sites commonly use algorithms to 'flag' accounts that might need to be suspended. However, this is a sophisticated and complex process. Algorithms may strug-

---

[56]   'Mayor de Blasio Announces First-In-Nation Task Force To Examine Automated Decision Systems Used By The City', NYC.gov (Press Release, 16 May 2018) <https://www1.nyc.gov/office-of-the-mayor/news/251-18/mayor-de-blasio-first-in-nation-task-force-examine-automated-decision-systems-used-by>.

[57]   W Knight, 'Canada and France plan an international panel to assess AI's dangers', *MIT Technology Review* (7 December 2018) <https://www.technologyreview.com/s/612555/canada-and-france-propose-an-international-panel-to-assess-ais-dangers/>.

gle to distinguish between certain types of legitimate and illegitimate content. For example, a news clip from CNN could have the same identifiers as an ISIS video. Furthermore, voters need to be made aware of the risk that they are being fed fake news. This awareness should improve demand for trustworthy sources.

Making algorithms accountable is a desirable aim, but the notion of this accountability as a behaviour control mechanism is predicated on a belief that there are universally accepted rules and conventions by which social media users might elect to conduct themselves. Self-government has long been upheld as an ideal for use of the Internet. To this end, algorithms could support 'de-personalising' social media content by ensuring that all users are exposed to information and news that they would not have chosen themselves. Programming randomness or serendipity may sound oxymoronic, but random information generation has proven reliable in many commercial and educational applications.

While systems and regulations evolve over time through a process of review, they only matter if the community for which they are established recognises them. Imposing rules and standards of conduct may play a role in regulating some social media content and behaviour, but it cannot regulate opinion, free speech, prejudice, cultural sensitivities, and inclusion.

By allowing users to publish freely, social media platforms have proven popular with and revealing of the nature of previously 'unheard citizenry'. While this chapter argues that social media algorithms could be made accountable for their behaviour if they were simply more transparent, the same does not seem to apply to humans. Transparency only provides a window into how something behaves. The bigger challenge is to prevent that behaviour in the first place.

BIBLIOGRAPHY

Articles/Books/Reports

Ahmed, S, 'Alternative Credit Scoring – A Double Edged Sword' (2020) 11(2) *Journal of Indian Law and Society* 1
Anker, A et al, 'New Test to Provide Context About Articles', *Facebook App* (5 October 2017) <https://about.fb.com/news/2017/10/news-feed-fyi-new-test-to-provide-context-about-articles>
Australian Digital Codes, 'Digital Service Standard – 8 Make source code open' (1 May 2016) <https://guides.service.gov.au/digital-service-standard/8-make-source-code-open/>
BAI, 'Use of social media for news amongst Irish consumers declines while understanding of how news appears in their social media feeds remains low', *Broadcasting Authority of Ireland* (14 June 2018) <https://www.bai.ie/en/use-of-social-media-for

- news-amongst-irish-consumers -dectines-w~le-understanding-of-how-news-appe
ars-in-their-social-media-feeds -remains-low/>

Booth, R et al., 'Russia used hundreds of fake accounts to tweet about Brexit, data shows', *The Guardian* (15 November 2017) <https://www.theguardian.com/world/2017/nov/14/how-400-russia-run-fake-accounts-posted-bogus-brexit-tweets>

Calvano, E et al, 'Artificial intelligence, algorithmic pricing, and collusion', *Vox* (3 February 2019) <https://voxeu.org/article/artificial-intelligence-algorithmic-pricing-and-collusion>

Chen, D, 'Judicial Analytics and the Great Transformation of American Law' (2019) 27(1) *Journal of Artificial Intelligence and the Law* 15

Chia, H, 'In Machines We Trust: Are Robo-Advisers More Trustworthy than Human Financial Advisers?' (2019) 1(1) *Law, Technology and Humans* 129

Devlin, H, 'Discrimination by algorithm: scientists devise test to detect AI bias', *The Guardian* (19 December 2016) <https://www.theguardian.com/technology/2016/dec/19/discrimination-by-algorithm-scientists-devise-test-to-detect-ai-bias>

Diamantis, ME, 'The Problem of Algorithmic Corporate Misconduct' (16 September 2019) Compliance and Enforcement, Program on Corporate Compliance and Enforcement at NYU School of Law <https://wp.nyu.edu/compliance_enforcement/2019/09/16/the-problem-of-algorithmic-corporate-misconduct/>

Doffman, Z, 'Facebook Admits It Can't Control Facebook Live – Is This The End For Live Streaming?', *Forbes* (24 March 2019) <https://www.forbes.com/sites/zakdoffman/2019/03/24/could-this-really-be-the-beginning-of-the-end-for-facebook-live/?sh=2db94bc2ac8b>

Dopplick, R (ACM Director of Public Policy), 'New Statement on Algorithmic Transparency and Accountability by ACM U.S. Public Policy Council', United States Association for Computing Machinery (14 January 2017) <https://techpolicy.acm.org/2017/01/new-statement-on-algorithmic-transparency-and-accountability-by-acm-u-s-public-policy-council/>

The Economist, 'Fake news: you ain't seen nothing yet', *The Economist* (1 July 2017) <https://www.economist.com/science-and-technology/2017/07/01/fake-news-you-aint-seen-nothing-yet>

The Economist, 'Fake news is fooling more conservatives than liberals. Why?', *The Economist* (6 June 2020) <https://www.economist.com/international/2020/06/03/fake-news-is-fooling-more-conservatives-than-liberals-why>

The Economist, 'Censorious governments are abusing 'fake news' laws', *The Economist* (11 February 2021) <https://www.economist.com/international/2021/02/11/censorious-governments-are-abusing-fake-news-laws>

Facebook, 'Election Integrity', *Facebook* (25 January 2021)

Facebook, 'Facebook Business Help', *Facebook* (Retrieved 14 March 2021) <https://www.facebook.com/business/help/626637251511853>

Ferlie, E, *The Oxford Handbook of Public Management* (Oxford University Press, 2005)

Gaudiano, P, 'Inclusion is invisible: How to measure it', *Forbes.com* (23 April 2019) <https://www.forbes.com/sites/paologaudiano/2019/04/23/inclusion-is-invisible-how-to-measure-it/?sh=7e1c4411a3d2>

Goldenziel, JI and M Cheema, 'The New Fighting Words?: How U.S. Law Hampers the Fight against Information Warfare' (2019) 22(1) *University of Pennsylvania Journal of Constitutional Law* 81

Google AI, *Artificial Intelligence at Google: Our Principles* (February 2021) <https://ai.google/principles/?>

Green, M. 'Why I'm worried about Google', *Slate* (3 October 2018) <https://slate.com/technology/2018/10/google-is-losing-users-trust.html>

Guszcza, J et al, 'Why We Need to Audit Algorithms', *Harvard Business Review* (28 November 2018) <https://hbr.org/2018/11/why-we-need-to-audit-algorithms>

Hoffmann, AL, 'Science Will Not Save Us: Medicine, Research Ethics, and My Transgender Body', *Autostraddle* (16 July 2014) <http://www.autostraddle.com/science-will-not-save-us-medicine-research-ethics-and-my-transgender-body-240296/>

Horton, BJ, 'Malign Manipulations: Can Google's Shareholders Save Democracy' (2019) 54(3) *Wake Forest Law Review* 707

Hurley, M and J Adebayo, 'Credit Scoring in the Era of Big Data' (2016) 18 *Yale JL & Tech* 148

Huxley, P et al, *Development of a social inclusion index to capture subjective and objective life domains (Phase II): Psychometric development study. Health technology assessment* (Winchester, England, 2018)

Knight, W, 'Canada and France plan an international panel to assess AI's dangers', *MIT Technology Review* (7 December 2018) <https://www.technologyreview.com/s/612555/canada-and-france-propose-an-international-panel-to-assess-ais-dangers/>

Lee, RM, 'Beta-Testing the Particular Machine: The Machine-or-Transformation Test in Peril and Its Impact on Cloud Computing' (2013) 11(2) *Duke Law & Technology Review* 175

Leicht-Deobald, U et al, 'The Challenges of Algorithm-Based HR Decision-Making for Personal Integrity' (2019) 160 *J Bus Ethics* 377

Levinson-Waldman, R, 'Government Access to and Manipulation of Social Media: Legal and Policy Challenges' (2018) 61(3) *Howard Law Journal* 523

Licsandru, TC and CC Cui, 'Subjective social inclusion: A conceptual critique for socially inclusive marketing' (2018) 82 *Journal of Business Research* 330

Livingstone, S, 'Audiences in an Age of Datafication: Critical Questions for Media Research' (2019) 20(2) *Television & New Media* 170

Lowrie, I, 'Algorithms and Automation: An introduction' (2018) 33(3) *Cultural Anthropology* 349 <https://doi.org/10.14506/ca33.3.01>

Miller, CC, 'When Algorithms Discriminate', *The New York Times* (9 June 2015) <https://www.nytimes.com/2015/07/10/upshot/when-algorithms-discriminate.html>

Miller, CC, 'Can an algorithm hire better than a human?', *The New York Times* (25 June 2015)

NY Attorney General, 'Attorney General James Leads Multistate Lawsuit Seeking to End Facebook's Illegal Monopoly' (Press Release, 9 December 2020) <https://ag.ny.gov/press-release/2020/attorney-general-james-leads-multistate-lawsuit-seeking-end-facebooks-illegal>

NYC, 'Mayor de Blasio Announces First-In-Nation Task Force To Examine Automated Decision Systems Used By The City', NYC.gov (Press Release, 16 May 2018) <https://www1.nyc.gov/office-of-the-mayor/news/251-18/mayor-de-blasio-first-in-nation-task-force-examine-automated-decision-systems-used-by>

Pichai, S, *AI at Google: Our Principles* (Blog, 7 June 2018) <https://www.blog.google/technology/ai/ai-principles/>

Polyakova, A and D Fried, 'Democratic Defense Against Disinformation 2.0' (June 2019) *Atlantic Council* 2

Radavoi, CN, 'The Impact of Artificial Intelligence on Freedom, Rationality, Rule of Law and Democracy: Should We Not Be Debating It?' (2020) 25(2) *Texas Journal on Civil Liberties & Civil Rights* 107

Ritchin, F, 'In the live-streaming era, the trauma is widespread', *Time* (11 July 2016) <https://time.com/4400930/philando-castile/>

Roberts, T and G Marchais, 'Assessing the Role of Social Media and Digital Technology in Violence Reporting' (2018) 10(2) *Contemporary Readings in Law and Social Justice* 9

Ryan, PA, *Trust and Distrust in Digital Economies* (Routledge, 2019)

Scaife, L, 'Learning from the Laws of the Sea, Foucault and Regulatory Theory: Proposing a Regulatory Harbour Model for the Regulation of Social Media that Serves Rather than Rules the Waves' (2018) 69(4) *Northern Ireland Legal Quarterly* 433

Shattock, E, 'Rights Based Principles: Protecting Free Elections and Free Expression in Irish Policy Responses to Fake News Online' (2020) 1(1) *Dublin Law and Politics Review* 1

Sims, R (Conference Chair), 'Can Robots Collude?', *ACCC Conference* (16 November 2017) <https://www.accc.gov.au/speech/the-accc%E2%80%99s-approach-to-colluding-robots>

Statista Research Department, 'Social network advertising revenue in the United States in 2019, by company', *Statista.com* (14 January 2021) <https://www.statista.com/statistics/1103339/social-media-ad-revenue-platform/>

Stucke, ME and A Ezrachi, 'How Digital Assistants Can Harm Our Economy, Privacy, and Democracy' (2017) 32 *Berkeley Tech LJ* 1239

Surman, M, 'How to keep AI from turning into the Terminator', *CNN.com* (15 January 2019) <https://www.google.com.au/amp/s/amp.cnn.com/cnn/2019/01/15/opinions/artificial-intelligence-ethical-responsible-programming-surman/index.html>

USACM, 'Statement on Algorithmic Transparency and Accountability', *Association for Computing Machinery US Public Policy Council* (12 January 2017) <https://www.acm.org/binaries/content/assets/public-policy/2017usacmstatementalgorithms.pdf>

Wadhwa, V, 'Laws and Ethics Can't Keep Pace with Technology', *MIT Technology Review* (15 April 2014) <https://www.technologyreview.com/s/526401/laws-and-ethics-cant-keep-pace-with-technology/>

Watson, A, 'U.S. magazine industry – statistics & facts', *Statista.com* (18 February 2021) <https://www.statista.com/topics/1265/magazines>

Wayne, T, 'The trauma of violent news on the Internet', *The New York Times* (10 September 2016) <https://www.nytimes.com/2016/09/11/fashion/the-trauma-of-violent-news-on-the-internet.html>

World Bank, *Credit Reporting Knowledge Guide 2019* (2019) <http://documents.worldbank.org/curated/en/262691559115855583/pdf/Credit-Reporting-Knowledge-Guide-zo19.pdf>

World Bank, *Credit Reporting Knowledge Guide 2019* (Financial Sector Study, 6 June 2019) <https://openknowledge.worldbank.org/handle/10986/2185>

Zichermann, G, 'I've worked in tech for 22 years – and it's clear we're living in an "addiction economy"', *Business Insider Australia* (15 December 2017) <https://www.businessinsider.com.au/tech-addiction-product-of-an-addiction-economy-2017-12#oZgDezzCOLBLr8yM.99>

Legislation

Australia (Commonwealth and States)
Age Discrimination Act 2004 (Cth)
Anti-Discrimination Act 1977 (NSW)
Anti-Discrimination Act 1996 (NT)
Anti-Discrimination Act 1991 (Qld)
Anti-Discrimination Act 1998 (Tas)
Australian Human Rights Commission Act 1986 (Cth)
Disability Discrimination Act 1992 (Cth)
Discrimination Act 1991 (ACT)
Equal Opportunity Act 1984 (SA)
Equal Opportunity Act 1984 (WA)
Equal Opportunity Act 2010 (Vic)
Racial Discrimination Act 1975 (Cth)
Sex Discrimination Act 1984 (Cth)

United Kingdom
Equality Act 2010 (UK)

United States
Digital Millennium Copyright Act 1998 (U.S.)

15. Models and data trade regulation and the road to an agreement

Henry Gao[1]

1. INTRODUCTION

'Data is the new oil'. Just like oil, which powered the economy in the last century, data are what moves the world today. This is especially true for international trade. The crucial role played by data can be observed at every step of the process, from the conception of a new product and the sourcing of raw materials and parts, to the manufacturing process and the transportation of products across borders, until they finally reach the hands of consumers from every corner of the world.

To be sure, the process of international trade has always been accompanied by the exchange of data, be it about the product, the seller or the buyer. What is unprecedented, though, is the ubiquity of data in the modern economy. This is a manifestation of the many important changes that emerged in the first two decades of the new century. For trade in goods, these include the following factors: the emergence of regional and even global supply chains, which involves the sharing and exchange of data among many parts manufacturers during the various stages leading to the final products; the invention of 3D printing, which makes it easy to customize products based on the needs of customers and blurs the boundary between the manufacturer and the consumer; and the Internet of Things, which turns traditional products into conduits for the collection, analysis and utilization of data. Similar changes can also be observed in the realm of services trade, where the advent of the internet has not only removed the natural barrier of physical distance and made many hereto

[1] The author is grateful for the helpful comments of Mark Findlay. All errors are the author's own. This research is supported by the National Research Foundation, Singapore under its Emerging Areas Research Projects (EARP) Funding Initiative. Any opinions, findings and conclusions or recommendations expressed in this material are those of the author(s) and do not reflect the views of the National Research Foundation, Singapore.

non-tradable services tradable, but also, through the servicification of goods,[2] rendered the movements of physical goods unnecessary and turned them into new categories of services trade.

More importantly, rather than acquiring the goods or services for their sole use, consumers nowadays often find that all they get is the temporary right to access and deploy data. At the same time, as the access to data is democratized, the amount of data generated by users also grows exponentially. A report by McKinsey, for example, estimated that global data flow has grown 45 times in the decade from 2005 to 2014.[3] Such phenomenal growth also led to break-throughs in artificial intelligence, where powerful machine-learning helped to unleash the full potential of big data to generate refreshing insights into everything it touches. In the area of trade, for example, big data not only helps us to gain more comprehensive and accurate information about the shifts in demand and supply so that manufacturers may better adjust their productions, but also churns out more refined granular analysis about the crucial differences between different segments in the market so as to better tailor the same product into many variations to cater to the individual needs of consumers.

With the deepening of the globalization process, despite the recent reverse energies of protectionism, trade in data is increasingly recognized not only as a commercial reality but also as a necessary global trading frame. In view of developments in the commodification of a contestable market 'product' that is data, data regulation also increasingly becomes an important issue on the regulatory agenda. Here, the instinctive reaction of many national regulators is to deal with the issue as a purely domestic matter, arguing in terms of data sovereignty. Yet, the very nature of data as an omnipresent component of the global economy makes it inappropriate to be regulated solely on a national basis. Instead, the growing consensus among the leading players in global trade regulation is that data permeates national borders and should be regulated on a cross-border basis, making trade agreements the ideal instrument in data regulation. This chapter will examine the divergent regulatory approaches on data trade emerging from the various trade agreements concluded by the major

---

[2]   R Lanz and Maurer, 'Services and global value chains: Some evidence on servicification of manufacturing and services networks' (Working Paper, WTO, 2 March 2015) <https://ideas.repec.org/p/zbw/wtowps/ersd201503.html>; World Trade Organization (WTO), *World Trade Report* (World Trade Organization, 2018) 111–116, 157.

[3]   J Manyika et al, 'Digital Globalization: The New Era of Global Flows', *McKinsey Global Institute* (March 2016) <https://www.mckinsey.com/~/media/ McKinsey/Business%20Functions/McKinsey%20Digital/Our%20Insights/Digital %20globalization%20The%20new%20era%20of%20global%20flows/MGI-Digital -globalization-Full-report.ashx>.

jurisdictions, and offer some practical suggestions on how to pave the way for a global deal on data regulation.

2.   NATIONAL REGULATIONS

Given the growing importance of data in business and trade, more and more firms are trying to gather as much data as possible in this new gold rush. Due to the network effects,[4] the electronic commerce industry is, more often than not, a winner-takes-all game. This means that data is increasingly being concentrated into the hands of a few e-commerce giants such as Amazon, Facebook and Google. Such concentration of power leads to concerns over potential abuse, which in turn heightens the need to regulate the flow and transfer of data, both within and across national borders.

Any framework for data regulation would involve three groups of players: the individual, who provides the raw data, and uses the processed data; the firm, which processes the raw inputs from the consumer, and usually controls such data; and the state, which monitors and regulates the data used by the first two groups. Their different interests often result in conflicting priorities, with the individual advocating privacy protection, the firm promoting unhindered data flow, and the state focusing on the security implications.

While all regulators would agree on the need to strike a balance between the clashing interests of different stakeholders, their approaches often differ in practice. Some jurisdictions prioritize the need to safeguard the privacy of users. A good example in this regard is the General Data Protection Regulation (GDPR) of the European Union, which recognizes '[t]he protection of natural persons in relation to the processing of personal data' as 'a fundamental right'.[5] On the other hand, some jurisdictions put the commercial interests of firms first. In the United States, this is reflected in the 1996 Telecommunication Act, which notes that it is 'the policy of the United States ... to preserve ... free market ...unfettered by Federal or State regulation'.[6] In contrast, national security concerns are often cited to justify restrictions on cross-border data flows, albeit in varying degrees in different countries. A recent example is China's

---

[4]   Organisation for Economic Co-operation and Development (OECD), 'Key Issues for Digital Transformation in the G20' (12 January 2017) 135 <https://www.oecd.org/g20/key-issues-for-digital-transformation-in-the-g20.pdf>.

[5]   Regulation (EU) 2016/679 of the European Parliament and of the Council of 27 April 2016 on the protection of natural persons with regard to the processing of personal data and on the free movement of such data, and repealing Directive 95/46/EC (General Data Protection Regulation), OJ L 119, 04.05.2016; cor. OJ L 127, 23.5.2018, Recital 1.

[6]   Telecommunication Act of 1996, 47 USC 230(b)(2).

2017 Cybersecurity Law, which imposes several restrictions aiming to 'safeguard cyber security, protect cyberspace sovereignty and national security'.[7]

Traditionally, restrictions on cross-border data flow were the most common type of digital protectionism.[8] More recently, however, data localization requirements have also become popular, with the following as main variations:[9]

(1)   Local commercial presence or residency requirements: The origin for such requirements can be traced back to the General Agreement on Trade in Services (GATS), where service providers are often required to have a local commercial presence before they can provide a service. While such requirements could potentially affect all service sectors, e-commerce is especially vulnerable as it is often detached from traditional brick-and-mortar establishments.

(2)   Local infrastructure requirements: These include both hardware requirements for service providers to use computing facilities located in the host territory and software requirements to use computer processing and/or storage services located in such territory.

(3)   Local content requirements. Depending on the *modus operandi* of the local content requirements, this obligation can be further divided into two categories. One is granting preferences or advantages to goods or electronically transmitted contents produced in a territory, or to local computing facilities, computer processing or storage services supplied locally. The other is requiring foreign service suppliers to purchase or use local goods or electronically transmitted contents.

(4)   Local technology requirements. This can also be broken down into two types of obligations. The first is the requirement for foreign service suppliers to transfer technologies as a condition of providing a service. This is often tied to the requirement to have a local partner. The other is the requirement for foreign service suppliers to purchase or use local technologies.

---

[7]   *Cybersecurity Law of the People's Republic of China* [Zhonghua Renmin Gongheguo Wangluo Anquan Fa], as adopted at the 24th Session of the Standing Committee of the Twelfth National People's Congress of the People's Republic of China on 7 November 2016, Art 1.

[8]   M Wu, 'Digital Trade-Related Provisions in Regional Trade Agreements: Existing Models and Lessons for the Multilateral Trade System' (Overview Paper, ICTSD, November 2017) 22–23 <http://e15initiative.org/publications/digital-trade-related-provisions-in-regional-trade-agreements-existing-models-and-lessons-for-the-multilateral-trade-system/>.

[9]   H Gao, 'Digital or Trade? The Contrasting Approaches of China and US to Digital Trade' (2018) 21(2) *International Economic Law* 297, 303–304.

While data flow restrictions and data localization requirements are both barriers to e-commerce, it is important to note the differences between the two. Data flow restrictions curb the cross-border transfer of data. This normally targets the outflow, but can also affect the inflow, such as banning certain websites. As such restrictions uniformly affect both domestic and foreign firms alike, they are more akin to a most-favoured nation (MFN) treatment type of restriction. While such constraints make it more difficult for firms to move data around, they could reduce data breach risks for individuals and regulatory costs for states. On the other hand, data localization requirements tend to affect mostly foreign firms so they can be viewed more as a National Treatment issue. Such requirements obviously would increase costs for foreign firms, but they could also increase risks of personal data breach and even regulatory costs for states due to the duplication of data on both local and offshore servers. Given the different ways MFN and National Treatment obligations under trade agreements are structured, a proper understanding of the differences between the two restrictions can help inform regulatory approaches and negotiations in trade agreements.

At the same time, notwithstanding their differences, it is also important to keep in mind that both types of restrictions could have major implications for international trade, especially given the growing importance of data to trade in general. Moreover, due to their binding nature, trade agreements have also become the forum of choice for regulating data issues at the international level. The next section reviews the attempts to regulate data issues both in the WTO and in various regional trade agreements, and discusses the emergence of divergent approaches by the leading players.

3.   EMERGING APPROACHES

E-commerce has been featured in the World Trade Organization (WTO) negotiating agenda since 1998, when the members adopted the Declaration on Global Electronic Commerce,[10] which also established a temporary moratorium on customs duties on digital transmission. Pursuant to the Declaration, the General Council adopted the Work Programme on Electronic Commerce,[11] which divided up the work among several WTO bodies such as the Council for Trade in Services, the Council for Trade in Goods, the Council for

---

[10]   WTO, *Declaration on Global Electronic Commerce*, adopted on 20 May 1998 at the Second WTO Ministerial Conference in Geneva, WT/MIN(98)/DEC/2, 25 May 1998.

[11]   WTO, *Work Programme on Electronic Commerce: Ministerial Decision of 13 December 2017*, Ministerial Conference, Eleventh Session, Buenos Aires, 10–13 December 2017, WT/MIN(17)/65, WT/L/1032, 18 December 2017.

Trade-Related Aspects of Intellectual Property Rights and the Committee on Trade and Development. However, notwithstanding its ambitious agenda, the Work Programme has so far languished along with the rest of the Doha Round. This changed only very recently, when renewed interests among the membership led to the launch of the Joint Statement Initiative on E-commerce on 25 January 2019.[12]

Even absent new rules, however, some of the existing rules in the WTO can still be expanded to cover e-commerce. To the extent that e-commerce affects trade in goods, such rules could include the existing MFN and National Treatment rules in the General Agreement on Tariffs and Trade 1994 (GATT 1994), as well as the prohibition of local content requirements under the Agreement on Trade-Related Investment Measures (TRIMs). As most e-commerce activities do not involve tangible products, however, it seems that the GATS is more promising. For example, as mentioned earlier, data flow restrictions and data localization requirements could potentially be subject to GATS MFN and National Treatment obligations. Moreover, to the extent that data regulations are part of the specific commitments undertaken by a WTO member, they would be subject to the domestic regulation obligations under Article VI of the GATS, such as the requirements for the rules to be based on objective and transparent criteria, not more burdensome than necessary, and administered in a reasonable, objective and impartial manner. Given the close relationship between the internet and telecommunication, one may also argue for the application of the existing GATS disciplines on the telecom sector,[13] such as the GATS Telecom Annex and the Telcom Reference Paper.

In contrast to the slow progress in the WTO, many regional trade agreements (RTAs) have been able to include new rules on data regulations.[14] The three main players in this regard are the United States, the European Union and China, with each having its own model.

3.1 The US Model

As the world leader in digital trade, the United States has included rules on data regulation in many of its free trade agreements (FTAs), with the now-defunct Trans-Pacific Partnership (TPP) Agreement and the recently concluded United States-Mexico-Canada Agreement (USMCA) as leading

---

[12] WTO, *Joint Statement on Electronic Commerce*, WT/L/1056, 25 January 2019.

[13] H Gao, 'Google's China Problem: A Case Study on Trade, Technology and Human Rights Under the GATS' (2011) 6 *Asian Journal of WTO & International Health Law and Policy* 347.

[14] Wu (n 8).

examples.[15] The obligations in the two agreements can be divided into the following categories:

The first are passive obligations, which prohibit the members from adopting various protectionist policies such as customs duties on electronic transmission, discrimination against foreign digital products, restrictions on cross-border transfer of information, forced localization requirements and forced transfer of source codes. The provisions are designed to minimize the distortions created by government interventions and leave the development of the e-commerce market in the hands of the e-commerce players.

The second type are enabling provisions, which require member governments to introduce or maintain regulatory frameworks that facilitate the development of e-commerce. These include, for example, the requirements for the members to adopt domestic laws in line with the principles of the United Nations Commission on International Trade Law (UNCITRAL) Model Law on Electronic Commerce 1996 and the United Nations Convention on the Use of Electronic Communications in International Contracts, the recognition of the legal validity of electronic signatures or electronic authentication methods, and the acceptance of electronic documents as the legal equivalent of their paper versions. These provisions all deal with one key issue facing the e-commerce sector, i.e. the recognition of e-commerce transactions as equivalents of the traditional pre-internet ones.

In addition, recognizing the huge market power of the big digital players, the two agreements also include rules to check corporate power. First, market players that own or control key infrastructures could abuse their power by unreasonably denying their business users access to their infrastructures, making it impossible for these users to conduct e-commerce activities. To address this problem, the agreements provide consumers (including business users) with the freedom of access to and use of the internet for e-commerce, subject only to network management and network safety restrictions. Second, to deal with potential misuse of consumer information, the agreements also include provisions on online consumer protection, personal information protection and unsolicited commercial electronic messages.

Recognizing the special needs of governments, both agreements have excluded government procurement and information held or processed by the government from the coverage of the digital trade chapters. Both also carved out the financial services sector, except that the USMCA provides that the prohibition on data localization requirements would continue to apply to

---

[15]   For an analysis of the US approach, see H Gao, 'Regulation of Digital Trade in US Free Trade Agreements: From Trade Regulation to Digital Regulation' (2018) 45(1) *Legal Issues of Economic Integration* 47.

the sector so long as a financial regulator has access to the relevant data for regulatory purposes. Both agreements also include language to cooperate on cybersecurity matters, with the USMCA going one step further by calling for risk-based regulations.

As the main proponent of the plurilateral Trade in Services Agreement (TISA) negotiations, the United States also proposed similar provisions in the draft TISA. Most of these can be found in the e-commerce chapter, where the United States called for provisions that guarantee service suppliers the freedom to transfer information across countries for the conduct of their business; freedom for network users to access and use services and applications of their choice online, and to connect their choice of devices; prohibition of data local-ization requirements as a condition of supplying a service or investing; and prohibition of discrimination against electronic authentication and electronic signatures. In addition, the horizontal provisions also include prohibitions on a host of localization requirements as mentioned earlier. While they apply to all service sectors, they would be of particular relevance to e-commerce due to the nature of the sector.

3.2   The EU Model

The main concern of the European Union, when it comes to e-commerce, is privacy protection. This is demonstrated by the GDPR, which recognizes privacy as not only a consumer right, but also a fundamental human right. The GDPR provides that prior authorization is required before personal data can be transferred to a third country, unless that country is recognized by the European Union as providing an equivalent level of data protection.

However, in its RTAs, the European Union has not been able to include substantive language on such issues. This is due to the internal differences between the two Directors-General (DGs) with overlapping jurisdictions on the issue, i.e. DG-Trade, which favours free trade for the sector, and DG-Justice, which has concerns over personal information protection.[16] Thus, notwithstanding its strong interest in privacy protection, the EU positions in its existing FTAs have been rather modest, which usually requires parties to adopt their own laws for personal data protection to help maintain consumer trust and confidence in electronic commerce. In February 2018, however, the two DGs were finally able to reach a compromise position, which includes, on the one hand, horizontal clauses on the free flow of all data and a ban on localization

---

[16]   SA Aaronson and P Leblond, 'Another Digital Divide: The Rise of Data Realms and its Implications for the WTO' (2018) 21(2) *Journal of International Economic Law* 245, 261–262.

requirements, while, on the other hand, affirming the EU's right to regulate in the sector by making clear that it shall not be subject to investor-state arbitration.[17] Given the potentially intrusive rules in the GDPR, we might start to see a more aggressive push for stronger language on personal data protection in the EU's RTAs in the future.

3.3   The China Model

In contrast with the European Union and the United States, China has traditionally taken a cautious approach to data regulation in trade agreements. Until very recently, it has not even included e-commerce chapters in its RTAs.[18] This only changed with its FTAs with Australia and Korea, which were both signed in 2015. Moreover, the provisions in these two FTAs are rather modest, as they mainly address trade facilitation-related issues, such as a moratorium on customs duties on electronic transmission, recognition of electronic authentication and electronic signature, protection of personal information in e-commerce, paperless trading, domestic legal frameworks governing electronic transactions, and the need to provide consumers using electronic commerce a level of protection equivalent to that in traditional forms of commerce.

3.4   Reasons for the Differences?

The diverging approaches among the three major players are not randomly chosen. Instead, they reflect deeper differences in their respective commercial interests and regulatory approaches within each jurisdiction. Further, it could be said that they represent distinctly different attitudes to data rights, data sovereignty, and the importance of globalization in world trading.

First, the global e-commerce market is mostly dominated by China and the United States. Among the ten biggest digital trade firms in the world, six are American and four are Chinese.[19] Of course, this does not necessarily mean that they must share the same position. Upon closer examination, one can see that the US firms on the list tend to be pure digital service firms. Firms like

---

[17]   Horizontal provisions on cross-border data flows and personal data protection, 18 May 2018 <https://ec.europa.eu/newsroom/just/document.cfm?action=display&doc_id=52384>.

[18]   For an overview of the evolution of digital trade related provisions in China's FTAs, see H Gao, 'E-Commerce in ChAFTA: New Wine in Old Wineskins?' in C Piker, H Wang and W Zhou (eds), *The China-Australia Free Trade Agreement: A 21st-Century Model* (Hart Publishing, 2018) 283.

[19]   Wikipedia, 'List of Largest Internet Companies' <https://en.wikipedia.org/wiki/List_of_largest_Internet_companies>.

Facebook, Google and Netflix do not sell physical products, but only provide digitalized services such as online search, social network and content services. In contrast, two of the top three Chinese firms – Alibaba and JD.com – sell mainly physical goods. This is why the United States focuses on digital services while China focuses on traditional trade in goods enabled by the internet.

One may argue that China also has giant pure digital firms like Baidu and Tencent, which are often referred to, respectively, as the Google and the Facebook of China. However, because they serve almost exclusively the domestic Chinese market and most of their facilities and operations are based in China, they do not share the demands for free cross-border data flow like their US counterparts, which have data centres in strategic locations around the world.

As for the European Union, with no major players in the game, their restrictive privacy rules could be viewed as a form of digital protectionism[20] to fend off the invasions of American and Chinese firms into Europe, as well as representing data-subject concessions.

The second influence is their different domestic regulatory approaches. In the United States, the development of the sector has long benefited from its 'permissive legal framework', which aims to minimize government regulation on the internet and relies heavily on self-regulation in the sector. Such policy is even codified in the law, with the Telecommunication Act of 1996 explicitly stating that it is 'the policy of the United States ... to preserve the vibrant and competitive free market that presently exists for the Internet and other interactive computer services, unfettered by Federal or State regulation'. Therefore, it is no surprise that the United States wishes to push for deregulation and the free flow of information at the international level. At the same time, the United States does not have a comprehensive privacy protection framework. Instead, it relies on a patchwork of sector-specific laws which provide privacy protection for consumers of a variety of sectors such as credit reports and video rental. This is further complemented by case-by-case enforcement actions by the Federal Trade Commission (FTC), and self-regulation by firms themselves. This explains why, in its RTAs, the United States does not mandate uniform rules on personal information protection but allows members to adopt their own domestic laws.

On the other hand, in China, the internet has always been subject to heavy government regulations, which not only dictate the hardware one must use to connect to international networks, but also the content that may be transmitted

---

[20]   SA Aaronson, 'What Are We Talking about When We Talk about Digital Protectionism?' (2019) 18 *World Trade Review* 541.

online.[21] Many foreign websites are either filtered or blocked in China, which confirms China's cautious position on free flow of data. Moreover, in 2017, China also adopted the Cybersecurity Law, which requires the operators of critical information infrastructure to store locally personal information they collected or that is generated in China. This is at odds with the US demand to prohibit data localization requirements. Privacy protection is also weak in China, as it was only incorporated into the Chinese legal system in 2009, along with extensive exemptions for the government.

The European Union, in contrast, has a long tradition of human rights protection, partly in response to the atrocities of the Second World War. Coupled with the absence of major digital players wielding significant market power and the lack of a strong central government with overriding security concerns, this translates into a strong emphasis on privacy in the digital sphere. Moreover, the European Union is also able to transcend the narrow mercantilist confines of the United States, and recognize privacy as not only a consumer right, but also a fundamental human right. Such a refreshing perspective is probably the biggest contribution made by the European Union to digital trade issues.

4.   ELEMENTS FOR THE WAY FORWARD

With the revival of e-commerce discussions in the WTO in 2016, many members have made new submissions. Most of these largely reiterate their existing positions in RTAs and other plurilateral agreements. For example, in its July 2016 'non-paper', the United States called for the dismantling of both cross-border and domestic barriers to digital trade such as restrictions on cross-border data flow and government regulations requiring localization or forced transfer of technology or source code, and urged e-commerce firms to be given more autonomy including the freedom to use the technology, authentication methods, encryption methods, and facilities and services of their own choice. The Chinese submission in November 2016, on the other hand, focused more on trade facilitation measures such as simplified border measures and customs clearance, paperless trade and single window, and the establishment of platforms for cross-border e-commerce transactions such as the electronic World Trade Platform (eWTP), an idea first proposed by Alibaba Chairman Jack Ma. These positions have largely been carried over in their submissions in the Joint Statement Initiatives, which as of 10 February 2020 have received

---

[21]   For an overview of Chinese data regulation, see H Gao, 'Data Regulation with Chinese Characteristics' in M Burri (ed), *Big Data and Global Trade Law* (Cambridge University Press, 2021) 245.

52 submissions from the 77 participants.[22] We can gather the following from these submissions:

First, most developed countries and some developing countries seem to agree on the need to ensure free cross-border data flow in principle. At the same time, such freedom is often reserved for provision of covered services or investment only, and has been subject to exceptions on grounds ranging from personal information protection to the special needs of specific sectors like financial services. Some developing countries are more hesitant on the issue, due to either security or revenue concerns.

Second, almost all countries agree with the goal of privacy or personal information protection, but they differ on how to get there. While many countries are content with each country adopting its own domestic laws that meet certain minimum standards, privacy regimes with strong extraterritorial elements like the GDPR could create pressure for affected trade partners to adopt similar or even uniform rules. This tension is a good example not just of how different approaches to privacy protection play out, but also where some countries clearly value commercial maximization over personal data integrity. While the talk is about balancing interests, the practicalities are determined by what each country deems to be a more important national interest.

Third, prohibition on data localization requirements is also widely accepted among more advanced economies, subject to carve-outs for government data, government procurement, financial services, privacy protection and security measures. While some countries are considering data localization requirements in the false hope that such measures could create more local jobs or nurture local digital champions, more and more countries are coming to the realization that such measures would be more likely to harm rather than help the development of their digital sectors.

Given the uneven development of the sector in different countries, the most promising way forward would be to adopt a negotiation structure similar to the Trade Facilitation Agreement (TFA), with tiered obligations corresponding to the individual level of development of different members. At the core, there should be a set of commonly accepted minimum standards or basic principles, probably along the lines of the highly successful example of the Telecom Reference Paper. To enhance the participation of developing countries, there should also be technical assistance provisions to help developing countries progressively undertake more and more obligations. A major part of the technical assistance activities would undoubtedly be devoted to building the technological capacities by equipping them with the necessary hardware and

---

[22]   The submissions can be found on the WTO website starting with INF/ECOM document symbol.

software, but there should also be regulatory assistance projects since many developing countries lack the necessary regulatory experience with the sector.

In terms of the substantive content, such an agreement shall include the following elements: freedom of data flow for the provision of covered services, investments and intellectual property rights; prohibition of data localization requirements relating to the hardware, software or location of data storage, with narrowly defined exceptions for measures to protect data security or personal information; and commitment for each party to introduce or maintain its own domestic laws on privacy protection that meets certain minimum standards.

Like any negotiation in the WTO, getting WTO members to agree on data regulation would not be easy. Adding to the difficulty is the divergent views on the nature of data by WTO Members. As outlined earlier, while countries like the US view data more as a tradable commodity, other countries could take a different approach by focusing on the security issues raised by data, or on the potential of data as a social good or facilitator of development. If the latter approaches are taken, then the individualistic ownership-model of data rights would have to give way to the collective public-interest model of data rights, making data trade impossible or at least more difficult. Moreover, such view would be hard to square with the existing modus operandi of international trade, which requires clearly delineated property rights. This could also affect global trade regulation as the power to regulate is no longer confined to national boundaries but must be shared among countries.

That said, the problem with the 'data rights' approach is that it requires the designation of data as 'property'. This designation is far from legally settled. If an alternative view is entertained, such as has been argued concerning internet access and the information it offers being considered a universal human right (rather than a limited property right) then the emphasis shifts from trade for profit to trading for more generalized social advantage. There is a case to put that the focus of data trading should be opportunities to access and use data rather than a restrictive 'property rights for value' regime.

In this regard, the recently concluded Regional Comprehensive Economic Partnership (RCEP) provided an interesting experiment on how a compromise might be struck. With its diverse membership, which includes developed countries like Japan and Australia, major developing countries like China, and even less developed countries like Myanmar, the RCEP has provided a perfect example of how data regulation in a trade agreement can be concluded even with a heterogeneous membership. More importantly, with inclusion of provisions on free flow of data across border and prohibitions on data localization requirements coupled with extensive security and privacy exceptions, the RCEP also demonstrates how a compromise might be struck among countries with conflicting positions. This is the best rebuttal against sceptics who argue that a multilateral deal like the joint statement initiative is impossible.

To garner support among the membership, it would be useful to conduct a stock-taking exercise of existing issues regarding data flow and localization requirements, followed by discussion and identification of best practices, so that the members can better understand the potential of data trade. Most importantly, data regulation should be negotiated as part of a broader deal on digital trade, because trade, rather than the underlying data, is the raison d'être of the WTO.

BIBLIOGRAPHY

Articles/Books/Reports

Aaronson, SA, 'What Are We Talking about When We Talk about Digital Protectionism?' (2019) 18 *World Trade Review* 541

Aaronson, SA and P Leblond, 'Another Digital Divide: The Rise of Data Realms and its Implications for the WTO' (2018) 21(2) *Journal of International Economic Law* 245

Gao, H, 'Google's China Problem: A Case Study on Trade, Technology and Human Rights Under the GATS' (2011) 6 *Asian Journal of WTO & International Health Law and Policy* 347

Gao, H, 'Digital or Trade? The Contrasting Approaches of China and US to Digital Trade' (2018) 21(2) *International Economic Law* 297

Gao, H, 'Regulation of Digital Trade in US Free Trade Agreements: From Trade Regulation to Digital Regulation' (2018) 45(1) *Legal Issues of Economic Integration* 47

Gao, H, 'E-Commerce in ChAFTA: New Wine in Old Wineskins?' in C Piker, H Wang and W Zhou (eds), *The China-Australia Free Trade Agreement: A 21st-Century Model* (Hart Publishing, 2018) 283

Gao, H, 'Data Regulation with Chinese Characteristics' in M Burri (ed), *Big Data and Global Trade Law* (Cambridge University Press, 2021) 245

Lanz, R and Maurer, 'Services and global value chains: Some evidence on servicification of manufacturing and services networks' (Working Paper, WTO, 2 March 2015) <https://www.wto.org/english/res_e/reser_e/ersd201503_e.pdf >

Manyika, J et al, 'Digital Globalization: The New Era of Global Flows', McKinsey Global Institute (March 2016) <https://www.mckinsey.com/~/media/McKinsey/Business%20Functions/McKinsey%20Digital/Our%20Insights/Digital%20globalization%20The%20new%20era%20of%20global%20flows/MGI-Digital-globalization-Full-report.ashx>

Organisation for Economic Co-operation and Development (OECD), 'Key Issues for Digital Transformation in the G20' (12 January 2017) <https://www.oecd.org/g20/key-issues-for-digital-transformation-in-the-g20.pdf>

World Trade Organization (WTO), *World Trade Report* (World Trade Organisation, 2018)

Wu, M, 'Digital Trade-Related Provisions in Regional Trade Agreements: Existing Models and Lessons for the Multilateral Trade System' (Overview Paper, ICTSD, November 2017) <http://e15initiative.org/publications/digital-trade-related

-provisions-in-regional-trade-agreements-existing-models-and-lessons-for-the
-multilateral-trade-system/>

Legislation

Cybersecurity Law of the People's Republic of China [Zhonghua Renmin Gongheguo Wangluo Anquan Fa], as adopted at the 24th Session of the Standing Committee of the Twelfth National People's Congress of the People's Republic of China on 7 November 2016
Telecommunication Act of 1996, 47 USC 230(b)(2)

International Materials

Regulation (EU) 2016/679 of the European Parliament and of the Council of 27 April 2016 on the protection of natural persons with regard to the processing of personal data and on the free movement of such data, and repealing Directive 95/46/EC (General Data Protection Regulation), OJ L 119, 04.05.2016; cor. OJ L 127, 23.5.2018
WTO, *Declaration on Global Electronic Commerce*, adopted on 20 May 1998 at the Second WTO Ministerial Conference in Geneva, WT/MIN(98)/DEC/2, 25 May 1998
WTO, *Work Programme on Electronic Commerce: Ministerial Decision of 13 December 2017*, Ministerial Conference, Eleventh Session, Buenos Aires, 10–13 December 2017, WT/MIN(17)/65, WT/L/1032, 18 December 2017
WTO, *Joint Statement on Electronic Commerce*, WT/L/1056, 25 January 2019

Index

3D printing 262

abdication
    of governmental responsibility 213
    of regulatory power 225
accessibility 191, 200–202, 204–6, 209,
    212
access to code 178
accountability 2, 4, 10, 11, 14, 112–13,
    115, 117, 120, 124, 201, 202, 211
    of algorithms 240–57
    non-accountability 225
administration of contracts 134
ad preferences 40
advertisers 40
aged-care institutions 104
agency law 151
aggregated data deviations and distortion
    102, 127
Agreement on Trade-Related Investment
    Measures (TRIMs) 267
AI see artificial intelligence (AI)
Alexander, Nadja 129
algorithmic bias 246
algorithmic conditions 164
algorithmic decision-making 242
algorithmic decision-systems 133, 140
algorithmic design 134
algorithmic insights 243
algorithmic law 140, 147
algorithmic misconduct 245–6, 250
algorithmic obscurity 65
algorithmic parameters 246
algorithmic systems 134, 141, 142, 143,
    145, 147
algorithms 5, 7, 10, 14, 157–60, 215,
    219, 223, 240–57
    audits 107
Alibaba 271, 272
alienation/disaggregation 61
Amadio principle 158, 159

Amazon 47, 49, 55, 56, 216, 264
    Web Services 49
Amnesty International 80
Amsterdam 158
anti-discrimination 111, 112, 144, 251
anxiety reduction 113–14
appellate judges 136
Apple 72, 75, 98
arbitrariness 147
arbitration 108, 123, 127, 157, 158, 165,
    167, 175, 182, 188–90, 193, 195,
    197, 198
arms length bargaining 174
artificial intelligence (AI) 1–14, 16, 17,
    18, 19–42, 47, 48, 50–53, 56, 58,
    59, 61, 63, 66, 71, 76, 80, 84–6,
    88, 91, 93, 96, 100, 133–5, 141,
    142, 151–60, 188–213, 215,
    219–38, 242, 244, 245, 247, 248,
    250, 254, 255, 256, 263
    assisted decision-making 52
    assisted information technologies
        17, 50, 53, 63, 66
    assisted public services 17
    assisted solutions 10
    ecosystems 61
    enabled systems 222
    exposure 91
    governance 218, 219, 223, 225, 227,
        229, 232, 234
    hub 100
    human intersection 12
    machine learning 219, 220, 222, 225
    for profit 51
    strategies 242
    summit 234
    technologies 2, 5, 6, 37, 42, 151,
        153, 154–8, 197, 219, 221,
        223, 224, 228–31, 248
ASIC v Kobelt 160
Asset Divider 196
assisted-decision outcomes 10

audio-visual platforms for mediation 191
Australia 104, 106, 107, 118, 119, 152–6,
　　158–60, 219–24, 227, 228, 230,
　　232, 233, 234–7
Australian Competition and Consumer
　　Commission (ACCC) 155, 160
Australian Consumer Law 152, 155
Australian Securities and Investments
　　Commission (ASIC) 155
Australian Securities and Investments
　　Commission Act 2001 (ASIC Act)
　　155
authoritarian regimes 254
automated decision-making 3, 9, 244
automation 48, 54, 60, 63, 133, 134, 140,
　　141, 143, 144, 145
　　automated decision systems 137,
　　　140, 144
　　automated negotiation 193, 194
　　automated planning 135, 144
　　automated service delivery 4
　　automated systems 245
avatars 250

Baidu 271
balanced reporting 113, 114
bargain principle 152
Bateman, Will 129
Beijing 221, 222
Beijing Academy of AI 15 principles
　　on AI development, use and
　　governance 221
Best Alternatives to Negotiated
　　Agreements (BATNAs) 196
best-practice reputation 110
beyond ethics regulatory proposal 233
bias 5, 6, 9
big data 2, 3, 4, 5, 8, 9, 10, 11, 13, 14,
　　48, 55, 59–61, 64, 68, 218, 245,
　　254
big tech 1, 6, 121, 233, 234
big tech firms 1, 6, 234
binary code 134
biometric data 23, 25, 32, 34, 36
Biometric Information Privacy Act of
　　2008 (BIPA) 23, 30
black boxes 18
blind bidding 191, 193, 194
blockchain 7, 163–5, 168, 173, 178–82

blockchain technology 164, 165, 178,
　　180
Braithwaite, John 52, 137, 138
Brexit referendum 249
Brussels 225, 237
bullying 157
business partners 165, 175

calculability 136
California Consumer Privacy Act 2018
　　(CCPA) 21, 30, 31
California Data Safeguard Law 31
California Privacy Rights Act (2020) 20,
　　21, 32
Cambridge Analytica 31, 35, 40, 252
　　scandal 31, 40
Canada 28, 29, 256
capitalism 49, 55, 56, 60, 61, 64
Castile, Philando 248
celebrity Twitter account-holders 243
centralised data storage 106
chain of transmission 72
Charter of Fundamental Rights 26
Children's Online Privacy Protection Act
　　of 1998 (COPPA) 29
China 116, 264, 265, 267, 270–72, 274
　　Cybersecurity Law (2017) 265
Christchurch 248
citizen-engagement/participatory
　　methods 16
civil rights 248, 250, 251
civil society 17
　　Civil Society Empowerment
　　　Initiatives 109, 127
　　monitoring 112
clickbait 244
CNN 250, 257
Codelfa 153
Cogito 56
collaborative service systems 174
collective bargaining power 50
commercial contracts 175, 177
commercial practice 151, 155
Committee on Trade and Development
　　267
common law 152, 155
　　jurisdictions 166
communication history 82, 86, 89, 90, 91
community internet radio 212
computational interface 48

computer scientists 137, 147
computing experience 91, 93
computing power 219
conditionality 163, 167
    of contract 163
confidentiality 191, 199–200, 204, 211
confirmation bias 247
conscience 154–7
conspiracy theories 244, 254
constitutional rights of privacy 106
consumer contracts 144
consumer credit 160
consumer preferences 31, 37
consumer satisfaction 59
contact tracing 71–99
    applications 16
    technology 71–99
contract as code 163, 165, 167, 169, 178
contract construction 153
contract law 152, 153, 158
contracts 163–7, 169–75, 177–82
    expressed as text 170
contractual ambiguity 153
contractual mistake 153
contractual relationship 154, 156, 157, 158
Copyright law 256
corruption 250
cost reductions 191
cost saving 211
Council for Trade in Goods 266
Council for Trade in Services 266
Council for Trade-Related Aspects of
    Intellectual Property Rights 267
Council of Europe 20, 21, 22, 23, 26, 39
Council of Europe Convention 108 (CoE
    108) 21
COVID-19 pandemic 46–8, 51, 71–4,
    76, 77, 79, 80–83, 96, 98, 102–26,
    110, 112, 189, 190, 192, 193, 197,
    200, 206
    control regulation 17
    control technologies 102
    mediation protocols 190
    Personal Data Commissioner
        (CPDC) 108–9
    restrictions due to 131
        online mediation 131
        social distancing 131
    surveillance infrastructures 17

virus 71
credit card information 82, 85, 89, 90, 91
CREK 198
criminal investigations 74, 100
cross-border matters 190
cross-border transfer of information 268
cryptocurrencies 165
customs duties 266, 268, 270
cyber-attack 250
cybersecurity 118, 124–5, 265, 269

data 262–75
    aggregation 122–3
    collection 16
    collectors 117
    colonialism 60
    commodification 60, 61
    firewalls 102, 127
    flow restrictions 266, 267
    integrity 114, 115, 124
    management 7, 8, 14
    protection 16, 107, 109
data-driven technologies 52
datafication 55, 60
data-harvesters 109, 110, 115
data-processing standards 125
data protection
    administration 109
    commissions 107
    regulation 19, 20, 24, 27, 38, 41
data regulations 263, 264, 267, 270, 272,
    274, 275
    European Union's and China's
        models of 217
data security concerns 73, 97
data-sharing 123
data subjects 103, 106, 115, 117, 118,
    121, 122, 124–6
data surveillance 54
    technologies for 120
data trade 217
data trusts 66
de Blasio, Bill 255, 256
deception 159
declaration on Global Electronic
    Commerce 266
decompliers 182
deep learning 13
democracy 244, 248, 249

demographic information 82, 86, 89, 90, 91
depersonalisation of welfare and consumer protection 4
de-personalising social media content 257
desiderata 136
desirability bias 247
determinate legal norms 138, 139, 141
deterministic algorithms 141, 242
deterministic decision-making 241, 242, 244, 250, 252, 254
digital economy 55, 59–65
digital finance 129
digital mediation 131
Digital Millennium Copyright Act (1998) 256
digital readiness 188, 189, 192, 205, 206, 207, 211, 213
digital revolution 191
Digital Service Standard 254, 255
digital technology 190
Directive 95/46/EC 20, 23, 24, 26
disaggregation 61
discrimination 102, 111–13
    against foreign digital products 268
discriminatory practices 111
dispute resolution 188–201, 203–7, 211, 212
distortion of social media data 244, 250, 252
distrust 113
divorce proceedings 195
Doha Round 267
DoorDash 61

eBay's Dispute Resolution Centre 193
echo chambers of public opinion 241
e-commerce 264–70, 272
    market 268, 270
    players 268
economic duress 153
economic growth 2, 6, 9
economic recession 51
Economist, The 225
Edelman Trust Barometer 2020 (Singapore Report) 79, 80
educational qualification 91–3
e-government 133

services 129
electronic authentication methods 268–70
electronic commerce industry 264
electronic documents, acceptance of 268
Electronic World Trade Platform (eWTP) 272
employment displacement 4
end-game norms (EGNs) 167, 176
Endicott, Timothy 138
Enforced Self-regulation Units (ESU) 109, 127
enforcement by public bodies 227
England 153, 158
entire agreement clause 172, 177
entrenchment of historical unfairness 244
environmental compliance 165
equality legislation 251
equitable doctrines 152
equity 152, 153, 155
e-rooms 193
Esser, John 174, 176
estoppel 153
ethical AI 219–38
Ethical Artificial Intelligence Framework 219
ethical frameworks 1, 220–23, 224, 226, 227, 234, 235, 236
ethics-based frameworks 220
ethics-based principles 223
ethics-led strategies 232
Europe 106
European Commission 23, 24, 107, 113, 115, 219–21, 230, 231, 233
    AI White Paper 219–21, 230, 231, 233
European Data Protection Board Guidance for COVID-19 119
European Group on Ethics in Science and New Technologies 225
European Union (EU) 264, 267, 269–72
    Directors-General 269
    General Data Protection Regulation 2016 (GDPR) 20
    member states 236
expiration of the use of data 125–6
explainability 2, 7, 10, 120–21, 221, 223
exploitation 154, 157, 158–60
exponential death tolls 110

Facebook 32, 35, 36, 40, 41, 48, 55, 79, 80, 216, 240, 243, 244, 245, 246, 248, 250, 252–4, 264, 271
Facebook Live 248
facial recognition 215
facilitated negotiation 190, 193
fairness 220, 221, 223, 224, 238
fake news 113–14, 241, 246, 249–50, 254, 257
family mediator 196
family winner 195, 196
Federal Trade Commission (FTC) 30, 271
Federal Trade Commission Act (FTCA) 30
fiduciaries 117, 118
fiduciary duties 118
fiduciary rules 117
financial disadvantage 160
financial industry 165
financial information of borrowers 251
financial markets 245
    misconduct 138
financial Modernization Act of 1999 (Gramm-Leach-Bliley Act) 30
financial services sector 268
force majeure clauses 178
Ford, Jolyon 215
France 256
free expression 249, 254
freelancers 62
freelancing 49
free trade agreements (FTAs) 267, 268, 270
fulfilment centers 56

G20 221
gamification of work 157
Gao, Henry 215
GATS Telecom Annex 267
General Agreement on Tariffs and Trade 1994 (GATT 1994) 267
General Agreement on Trade in Services (GATS) 265
General Data Protection Regulation (GDPR) 264
Generation X 86, 87, 98
genetic data 23, 25, 33
Genetic Information Nondiscrimination Act of 2008 (GINA) 29

Germany 77, 79, 81
gig economy 157, 159
gigging 49
gig platforms 131
gig workers 46, 47, 50, 52–6, 58, 62
    re-categorisation of 17
Github 181
global data flow 263
globalization process 263
Global South 212, 246
global supply chains 262
González Cabañas, José 40
Google 72, 75, 76, 80, 98, 221, 242, 244, 250, 253, 264, 267, 271
    maps 121
    ousting 216
governance principles for responsible AI 221
government identification 82, 86, 89, 90, 91
government-mandated measures 77, 99
GPS location data 82
grass-roots transparency 112–13
guidance capacity 145, 146
Guidelines of the Art 29 Working Party 38, 39

harm alleviation 18, 21, 39, 40, 42
hashtags 178
health history 76, 77, 82, 83, 86, 89–96
Health Insurance Portability and Accountability Act of 1998 (HIPPA) 29
heterogenous membership 274
HIV-AIDS medication 116
Hobbesian choice 160
human agency 48, 63
human bias 244, 254
human capital 48, 52
humane isolation 111
human errors 180
human language 134, 141, 142
human mediator 193, 196
human rights 165
    norms 227
    protection 272
humbugging 160

IBM guidance on 5 principles 222

identity verification 215
if-then 163–82
IMODRE 196
impartial dispute resolution professionals
          204
impressions 241
inaccessibility of online mediation 205
incorrect execution 180
independent contracting 49, 56
independent contractors 49, 56
Independent Mediators (UK) 192, 203,
          205
independent recurrent evaluation 107
India 20, 28, 29, 107
Indigenous customers 160
individual agency 170
individualised data storage 106
industrialisation 170
industry level arbitration 182
industry regulation 138
infection rates 110, 114
inferred data 16
influential bloggers 243
information asymmetry 154, 157, 158
Information Commissioner's Office
          (ICO) 38–41
information fiduciaries 117
information fiduciary rules 117
information platform alliances 107
inherent biases 247
Instagram 48, 216, 240, 250
institutional complexity 136, 137
institutional decision-making 242
institutional service providers of
          mediation 188
intellectual property 151
International Competition Network 255
International Council for Online Dispute
          Resolution Conference (ICODR)
          200
international dispute resolution 188–90,
          197, 198, 199, 203–5
International Standards Organisation 221
international trade 262, 266, 268, 274
international trading agreements 116
internet service providers (ISPs) 78
IP 151
iPhone 73
ISIS 257

James, Letitia 253
Japan 274
JD.com 271
Joint Pledge on AI Industry
          Self-Discipline 222
joint product development 174
Joint Statement Initiative on
          E-Commerce on 25 January 2019
          267
judicial analytics 254
Justice Edelman 152, 160
just-in-time (JIT) 54, 57

Korea 270

labour-force 53, 63, 68
labour markets 48, 50, 59, 61
labour revaluation 47
labour value 49, 60, 62, 63
law and artificial intelligence 135
Law as Project Management 130, 134,
          137–40
law as rules 130, 135–7
law-backed mechanisms 226
law-based mechanisms 219, 223, 226,
          235
law expressed as code 168
Law in Action 130, 166, 167, 173–7,
          182, 183
lawmakers 147
law of contracts 152, 153, 156, 160
law of rules 136
Law's regulatory engagement with AI
          and big data 4
legal governance 146
legal norms 133–7
          codification of 131
legal risk 134
legal vagueness 134
legislators 137, 138
LinkedIn 240, 251
litigation 190
live-streamed violence 248
live-streamers 248
live-streaming 246, 248
local content requirements 265, 267
local infrastructure requirements 265
localization requirements 265–9, 272,
          273, 274

local technology requirements 265
location 74, 76, 77, 82, 84, 86, 89–96
Louth v Diprose 154, 159

Macaulay, Stewart 166, 173
machine code 140–43
machine learning (ML) 16, 19, 20, 39,
    48, 134, 141, 142, 215, 219, 263
    inferred data 16
    technologies 134, 141
machine-readable code 180
machine rules 143–7
Ma, Jack 272
Malgieri, Gianclaudio 41
managerial law 135, 139, 140, 142, 144,
    146, 147
managerial legal regimes 134, 139, 140,
    143, 144
manipulation 157, 159
    of social perspectives 244
manipulative algorithms 250
manual supervision systems 143
market-centred self-regulation 50
market stimulus 52–3
market sustainability 47, 48, 63
mass digitalised surveillance 54
mathematisation of language and social
    practices 141–2
McKinsey 263
mechanistic codification 134
mediation
    mediation-relevant technology 192,
        197
    as pandemic-proof process 189
    services 188, 190, 192, 195, 200,
        202, 204, 205
    as user-centric process 189
    values 192, 199–206
Member States 22–6
mental health patients 104
mentions 241
merger clause 172
message-based online mediation systems
    191
meta-posture 219
Microsoft 6 Principles 221
Microsoft Teams 193
migrant workers 104, 111, 112
military robotics 4
Millennial 86, 87, 98

Ministry of Health 97
misinformation 247–50, 253, 256
misleading or deceptive purposes 241
misrepresentation 153
missing governance piece 219–38
misuse of personal information 246,
    250–53
Mittelstadt, Brent 41
mobile application 72, 73
mobile networks 82
mobile telephony 212
modern slavery 165
Modria 193, 196
moral obloquy 160
most-favoured nation (MFN) 266
multivariable resolution optimisation
    programs (MROP) 195
mutualized resolution process 189
Myanmar 274

national identification systems 24
National Registration Identity Card
    (NRIC) 107
National Treatment 266, 267
negotiated commercial contracts 133
negotiation support systems 191, 194,
    197
neoliberal pushback 47
Netflix 271
New Zealand 28, 29
NHS Apps Library 125
non-accountability 225
non-discrimination 2, 224
non-sensitive data 20
normative tools 147
North World states 104

objective commercial bystander 153
OECD 27, 28, 221, 222
    Competition Committee 255
    Guidelines on the Protection of
        Privacy and Transborder
        Flows of Personal Data
        (1980) 27
Ohm, Paul 20, 30, 33, 34, 36
online marketers 245
online mediation practice 188, 205, 206
open access 53, 66, 67
openness 254

Oracles 164
oral contracts 170

Pakistan 20, 28, 29
Palka, P 7, 8
pandemic 46, 47, 52, 58, 77, 79, 81, 96,
        97, 102, 103, 105, 106, 108, 109,
        110, 112, 113, 116, 118, 124, 125
Parliament of Australia 152
parol evidence rule 172, 174
party autonomy 189, 199, 200, 202, 203,
        207, 211
paternalist state 113
peculiar attributes of AI technologies 231
pernicious reporting 113
personal contact information 82, 85, 89,
        90, 91
personal data 50, 54, 58, 59, 62, 66,
        67, 74–8, 80, 81–6, 88, 89, 91,
        96–100
    collection of 84, 99
    protection conventions 112
personal identity cards 107
personal information 78, 79, 82, 85,
        90–92
Personal Information Protection and
        Electronic Documents Act 2000
        (PIPEDA) 28
Pettit, Philip 136
philosophical values 24, 25, 27, 32, 33,
        34, 38, 41
physical safety and professional
        indemnity 4
Pichai, Sundar 242
piecemeal regulatory schemes 235
Pinterest 240
platform containment 65
platform ecosystem 54
platform facilitation 48
platform technologies 48, 58, 65
platform workers 54
pluralistic ethical AI governance 229
policymaking 6, 9, 12
policy-oriented scholarship 232
political views 40, 41
predatory capitalism 49
predictable legal norms 135
predictive analytics 245
predictive/pattern logics 7
pre-emptive regulation 8

press councils 114
pre-trial mediation 195
principles-based regulation 228, 232,
        235, 236
prisoners 104, 111
privacy 102–6, 117–20, 122–4
    by design 123, 124
    rights 3, 5, 8
Privacy Act (1974) 29
Privacy Act 1988 (Cth) 21, 27
private law 151
probabilistic algorithmic systems 141
probabilistic behaviour 243
probabilistic decision-making 242, 243
procedural flexibility 199, 200, 202, 203,
        208
proceduralised jurisprudential theories
        136
profit motivation 60
programming experience 84, 86, 88,
        91–3
programming language 179–81
progressive re-integration protocols 111
propaganda 248, 249
protectionism 52
protection of personal data 26, 34, 106,
        110
public law 226, 232, 235
public opinion 17
Public Policy Council 242, 244, 255
public/private provider data sharing 102,
        127
public safety 103, 106, 110
public sector
    fiscal constraints 140
    service delivery 133
purchase history 82, 86, 89, 90, 91
python 163, 180

QR code 107, 114
qualtrics LLC 88
quarantining control Measures 111
Quinn, Paul 20, 41, 42

race profile 86
ransomware attacks 124
rapid digitisation of mediation 189–91
rating systems 58, 59
recession 51

recognition of the legal validity of electronic signatures 268
Regional Comprehensive Economic Partnership (RCEP) 274
regional supply chains 262
regional trade agreements (RTAs) 265–7
regulating ethical AI governance frameworks 226–36
regulation of self-regulation 230
regulatory
    agenda 106, 263
    approaches 263, 266, 270, 271
    arbitrage 138, 145
    attribution 106, 109, 115, 120, 121
    chasm 5–7
    choice 103
    design 6, 9, 12
    elitism 68
    enhancement 9–13
    frameworks 108, 127
    insights 1–14
    multiplicity 229
    policy 2, 7
    polycentricity 229
    rationales 233
    reversion 3–5
    techniques 104, 108
    terrain 5
relationship preserving norms (RPNs) 167, 176
reliability 200–202, 204–6, 208, 212
religious beliefs 27, 34, 40, 41
remedy 2
remote hearings 190
republicanism 136
research-driven regulation 8–9
responsible corporate behaviour 222
responsible governance 103
rights-based approach 3
robodebt payments scandal 153
rule-based legal norms 134, 136, 145
rule-like norms 138
rule of law 2, 134, 136, 137, 224, 225, 227, 229, 237
Ryan, Philippa 215

safe explorations 217
safe harbour protection 256
salesforce 234, 236
sandboxes 217

search engines 78, 79
secondary data 46–68
Second World War (WWII) 272
security vulnerability 180
self-help remedies 178
self-regulation 50–53, 65–8
    self-regulatory approach to AI technologies 233, 234
    technologies 109
sensitive data 16, 20, 21, 23–30, 32–42
    harms hierarchy 36
sensitive inferences 16, 19–42
service delivery 47, 48, 54, 55
servicification of goods 263
sexuality 30, 34
SIDRA Survey Report on International Dispute Resolution 2020 199
Singapore 16, 17, 28, 29, 102, 104, 105, 106, 107, 112, 114, 118, 119, 124, 153, 158, 221
    citizens 86, 98
    government 71, 72, 76, 77, 78, 79, 80, 81, 82, 85, 86, 88, 89, 91, 96, 97, 100
    residents 71–99
Skype 193
smart contracts 133, 140, 163–5, 167, 172, 173, 178, 179–82
smartphone locator 121
Smartsettle 193, 194, 196
smoke screen algorithms 246
Snapchat 240
social behaviour 133, 142
social benefit 2
social distancing 104, 111, 113, 121, 131, 206
social harms 2, 16
sociality 173, 179, 182
social justice 116
social media 105, 114, 131
    companies 156
    data 244, 250, 252
    forums 246
    giants 240
    news platform providers 114
    platforms 240–57
social network friends' information 82, 83, 86, 89, 90–96
socio-demographic characteristics 87, 88, 91

software engineers 137
solidity 163
source of infection 72
South Korea 79
Spearman correlations 92
special data 16, 19, 24, 25, 27, 42
special exemption status 46
speech 169, 170
spread of rumours and disinformation 241
standard terms 166, 174, 182
state-centred protectionism 52
state intervention 165
state sector surveillance 118–19
state sponsorship 109
stationarity 142, 143, 145
sub-contractors 165
supply chain 48
Supreme Court of Canada 157
surplus data 60
surveillance capitalism 49, 60
surveillance technologies 107, 109, 118, 120, 127
survey 75–9, 81, 82, 84, 85–8, 98
surveying 17
syntactical rules 178
syntax 179, 180, 181

taxation legislation 143
tax evasion 138
technologisation of human interaction 243
technologised oligopolies 51
technology giants 240
Telcom Reference Paper 267
Tencent 271
text-based contract terms 168
text-based procedure 191
Thampapillai, Dilan 129–31
theory of change 233
Total Quality Control (TQC) 57
TraceTogether app 71–6, 82, 83, 85, 96, 97
TraceTogether technology 72, 75, 82, 83, 85, 97, 99, 100
TraceTogether token 72–4, 96, 97
tracking 102, 107, 109, 119–21, 123, 127
trade agreements 263, 265, 266–8, 270, 274
Trade Facilitation Agreement (TFA) 273

Trade in Services Agreement (TISA) 269
traditional news services 246
transactional imbalance 153, 154, 157, 158, 159
Trans-Pacific Partnership Agreement (TPP) 267
transparency 2, 10, 11, 14, 220, 221, 223
troll farm 249
True North concept 235–6
trust beneficiaries 117
trust concerns 77
trust indicators 253
Trust Project 253
trusts 117
trustworthiness 175
Trustworthy AI Framework 221
Twitter 216, 240, 243, 246, 250
typeface 170

Uber 157
ubiquity of data 262
UK Anti-terrorism, Crime and Security Act 126
UK Prevention of Terrorism Act 126
unbiased news coverage 113
UNCITRAL Model Law on Electronic Commerce 1996 268
unconscionability principle 151–60
unconscionable conduct 152, 153, 155, 157–60
undue influence 153, 155
United Kingdom (UK) 104, 107
    Prevention of Terrorism Act (2005) 126
United Nations (UN)
    Commission on International Trade Law (UNCITRAL) 268
    Convention on the Use of Electronic Communications in International Contracts 268
    Guiding Principles on Business and Human Rights 227
    Secretary-General 51
United States (US) 21, 27, 29–31, 33, 81, 264, 267, 269, 270, 271, 272
    Association for Computing Machinery 244, 255
    Patriot Act (2001) 126
    Presidential election (2016) 249

Telecommunication Act (1996) 264, 271
United States-Mexico-Canada Agreement (USMCA) 267
universal rights 110
University 12
unwritten law 153
urban and community reconfiguration 4
urbanised environments 46
usability 200, 201–2, 205, 206, 207, 211
user attention 241

vaccination 116
vague legal norms 134, 139, 140, 142–4, 147
Video Privacy Protection Act of 1988 (VPPA) 29
virtual collaborative workspaces 193
Vismann, Cornelia 19
voluntarism 221, 225, 233
voluntaristic codes of ethics 225
voluntaristic corporate-internal or national normative frameworks 5
voluntaristic ethics-based principles 233
voluntary compliance 138

voluntary ethical frameworks 236

Wachter, Sandra 39, 41
Walmart 56
Weaponisation of AI systems 248
web-surfing history 82, 86, 89–91
Western liberalism 136
WhatsApp 246
Wheeler, Sally 129
Wifi 203
Wilcoxon matched pairs 89, 90
Willingness to share personal data 79
Wing, Leah 201
work contact information 82, 85, 89, 90, 91
worker engagement 54, 57, 58, 60, 65
Work Programme on Electronic Commerce 266
World Trade Organization (WTO) 263, 266
World Values Survey Wave 2014 79

Zoom 192, 193, 197
Zoom mediation 197